Machine Learning with R Cookbook

Second Edition

Analyze data and build predictive models

AshishSingh Bhatia

Yu-Wei, Chiu (David Chiu)

BIRMINGHAM - MUMBAI

Machine Learning with R Cookbook

Second Edition

First published: March 2015

Second edition: October 2017

Production reference: 1171017

Published by Packt Publishing Ltd.
Livery Place
35 Livery Street
Birmingham
B3 2PB, UK.

ISBN 978-1-78728-439-5

www.packtpub.com

Credits

Authors
AshishSingh Bhatia
Yu-Wei, Chiu (David Chiu)

Copy Editor
Safis Editing

Reviewers
Ratanlal Mahanta
Saibal Dutta

Project Coordinator
Kinjal Bari

Commissioning Editor
Veena Pagare

Proofreader
Safis Editing

Acquisition Editor
Divya Poojari

Indexer
Francy Puthiry

Content Development Editor
Trusha Shriyan

Graphics
Kirk D'Penha

Technical Editor
Akash Patel

Production Coordinator
Aparna Bhagat

About the Authors

AshishSingh Bhatia is a reader and learner at his core. He has more than 11 years of rich experience in different IT sectors, encompassing training, development, and management. He has worked in many domains, such as software development, ERP, banking, and training. He is passionate about Python and Java, and recently he has been exploring R. He is mostly involved in web and mobile developments in various capacity. He always likes to explore new technologies and share his views and thoughts through various online medium and magazines. He believes in sharing his experience with new generation and do take active part in training and teaching also.

First and foremost, I would like to thank God almighty. I would like to thank my father, mother, brother and friends. I am also thankful to whole team at PacktPub especially Divya and Trusha. My special thanks go to my mother Smt. Ravindrakaur Bhatia for guiding and motivating me when its required most. I also want to take this opportunity to show my gratitude for Mitesh Soni, he is the one who introduced me to Packt and started the ball rolling.

Thanks to all who are directly or indirectly involved in this endeavor.

Yu-Wei, Chiu (David Chiu) is the founder of LargitData Company. He has previously worked for Trend Micro as a software engineer, with the responsibility of building up big data platforms for business intelligence and customer relationship management systems. In addition to being a startup entrepreneur and data scientist, he specializes in using Spark and Hadoop to process big data and apply data mining techniques to data analysis. Yu-Wei is also a professional lecturer, and has delivered talks on Python, R, Hadoop, and tech talks at a variety of conferences.

In 2013, Yu-Wei reviewed *Bioinformatics with R Cookbook,* a book compiled for Packt Publishing.

He feels immense gratitude to his family and friends for supporting and encouraging him to complete this book. Here, he sincerely says thanks to his mother, Ming-Yang Huang (Miranda Huang); his mentor, Man-Kwan Shan; proofreader of this book, Brendan Fisher; Taiwan R User Group; Data Science Program (DSP); and more friends who have offered their support.

About the Reviewers

Ratanlal Mahanta has several years of experience in the modeling and simulation of quantitative trading. He works as a senior quantitative analyst at GPSK Investment Group, Kolkata. Ratanlal holds a master's degree of science in computational finance, and his research areas include quant trading, optimal Execution, Machine Learning and high-frequency trading.

He has also reviewed *Mastering R for Quantitative Finance, Mastering Scientific Computing with R, Machine Learning with R Cookbook,* and *Mastering Python for Data Science and Building a Recommendation System with R* all by Packt Publishing.

Saibal Dutta has been working as analytical consultant in SAS Research and Development. He is also pursuing PhD in data mining and machine learning from Indian Institute of Technology, Kharagpur. He holds Master of Technology in electronics and communication from National Institute of Technology, Rourkela. He has worked at TATA communications, Pune and HCL Technologies Limited, Noida, as a consultant. In his 7 years of consulting experience, he has been associated with global players such as IKEA (in Sweden), Pearson (in the U.S.), and so on. His passion for entrepreneurship has led him to start his own start-up in the field of data analytics, which is in the bootstrapping stage. His areas of expertise include data mining, machine learning, image processing, and business consultation.

I would like to thank my advisor, Prof. Sujoy Bhattacharya, all my colleagues specially, Ashwin Deokar, Lokesh Nagar, Savita Angadi, Swarup De and my family and friends specially, Madhuparna Bit for their encouragement, support, and inspiration.

www.PacktPub.com

For support files and downloads related to your book, please visit www.PacktPub.com. Did you know that Packt offers eBook versions of every book published, with PDF and ePub files available? You can upgrade to the eBook version at www.PacktPub.com and as a print book customer, you are entitled to a discount on the eBook copy. Get in touch with us at service@packtpub.com for more details. At www.PacktPub.com, you can also read a collection of free technical articles, sign up for a range of free newsletters and receive exclusive discounts and offers on Packt books and eBooks.

https://www.packtpub.com/mapt

Get the most in-demand software skills with Mapt. Mapt gives you full access to all Packt books and video courses, as well as industry-leading tools to help you plan your personal development and advance your career.

Why subscribe?

- Fully searchable across every book published by Packt
- Copy and paste, print, and bookmark content
- On demand and accessible via a web browser

Customer Feedback

Thanks for purchasing this Packt book. At Packt, quality is at the heart of our editorial process. To help us improve, please leave us an honest review on this book's Amazon page at https://www.amazon.com/dp/1787284395.

If you'd like to join our team of regular reviewers, you can email us at customerreviews@packtpub.com. We award our regular reviewers with free eBooks and videos in exchange for their valuable feedback. Help us be relentless in improving our products!

Table of Contents

Preface

Big data has become a popular buzzword across many industries. An increasing number of people have been exposed to the term and are looking at how to leverage big data in their own businesses, to improve sales and profitability. However, collecting, aggregating, and visualizing data is just one part of the equation. Being able to extract useful information from data is another task, and much more challenging.

Traditionally, most researchers perform statistical analysis using historical samples of data. The main downside of this process is that conclusions drawn from statistical analysis are limited. In fact, researchers usually struggle to uncover hidden patterns and unknown correlations from target data. Aside from applying statistical analysis, machine learning has emerged as an alternative. This process yields a more accurate predictive model with the data inserted into a learning algorithm. Through machine learning, the analysis of business operations and processes is not limited to human-scale thinking. Machine-scale analysis enables businesses to discover hidden value in big data.

The most widely used tool for machine learning and data analysis is the R language. In addition to being the most popular language used by data scientists, R is open source and is free for use for all users. The R programming language offers a variety of learning packages and visualization functions, which enable users to analyze data on the fly. Any user can easily perform machine learning with R on their dataset without knowing every detail of the mathematical models behind the analysis.

Machine Learning with R Cookbook takes a practical approach to teaching you how to perform machine learning with R. Each of the 14 chapters are introduced to you by dividing this topic into several simple recipes. Through the step-by-step instructions provided in each recipe, the reader can construct a predictive model by using a variety of machine learning packages.

What this book covers

Chapter 1, *Practical Machine Learning with R*, shows how to install and setup R environment, it covers package installation basic syntax and data types followed by reading and writing data from various sources. It also covers basic statistics and visualization using R.

Chapter 2, *Data Exploration with Air Quality Datasets*, shows how actual data looks in R. It covers loading of data, exploring and visualizing the data.

Chapter 3, *Analyzing Time Series Data,* shows a totally different type of data which consist of time factor. It covers how to handle time series in R.

Chapter 4, *R and Statistics,* covers data sampling, probability distribution, univariate descriptive statistics, correlation, multivariate analysis, linear regression. Exact binomial test, student – t test, Kolmogorov-Smirnov test, Wilcoxon Rank Sum and Signed Rank test, Pearson's Chi-squared Test, One-way ANOVA, and Two-way ANOVA.

Chapter 5, *Understanding Regression Analysis,* introduces to the supervised learning, to analyze the relationship between dependent and independent variable. It covers different type of distribution model followed by generalized additive model.

Chapter 6, *Survival Analysis,* shows how to analyze the data where the outcome variable is time for occurrence of an event, widely used in clinical trials.

Chapter 7, *Classification 1 – Tree, Lazy and Probabilistic,* Tree, Lazy and Probabilistic, deals with classification model built from the training dataset, of which the categories are already known.

Chapter 8, *Classification 2 – Neural Network and SVM,* shows how to train a support vector machine and neural network, how to visualize and tune the both.

Chapter 9, *Model Evaluation,* shows to evaluate the performance of a fitted model.

Chapter 10, *Ensemble Learning,* shows bagging and boosting to classify the data, perform the cross validation to estimate the error rate. It also covers the random forest.

Chapter 11, *Clustering,* means grouping similar objects widely used in business applications. It covers four clustering techniques, validating clusters internally.

Chapter 12, *Association Analysis and Sequence Mining,* covers finding the hidden relationships within a transaction data set. It shows how to create and inspect the transaction data set, performing association analysis with an Aprori algorithm, visualizing associations in various graphs formats, using Eclat algorithm finding frequent itemset.

Chapter 13, *Dimension Reduction,* shows how to deal with redundant data and removing irrelevant data. It shows how to perform feature ranking and selection, extraction and dimension reduction using linear and nonlinear methods.

Chapter 14, *Big Data Analysis (R and Hadoop),* shows how R can be used with big data. It covers preparing of Hadoop environment, performing MapReduce from R, operate a HDFS, performing common data operation.

What you need for this book

All the examples cover in this book have been tested on R version 3.4.1 and R studio version 1.0.153. chapter 1, *Practical Machine Learning with R,* covers how to download and install them.

Who this book is for

This book is for data science professionals, data analysts, or anyone who has used R for data analysis and machine learning, and now wishes to become the go-to person for machine learning with R. Those who wish to improve the efficiency of their machine learning models and need to work with different kids of datasets will find this book quite insightful.

Sections

In this book, you will find several headings that appear frequently (Getting ready, How to do it..., How it works..., There's more..., and See also).

To give clear instructions on how to complete a recipe, we use these sections as follows:

Getting ready

This section tells you what to expect in the recipe, and describes how to set up any software or any preliminary settings required for the recipe.

How to do it...

This section contains the steps required to follow the recipe.

How it works...

This section usually consists of a detailed explanation of what happened in the previous section.

There's more...

This section consists of additional information about the recipe in order to make the reader more knowledgeable about the recipe.

See also

This section provides helpful links to other useful information for the recipe.

Conventions

In this book, you will find a number of styles of text that distinguish between different kinds of information. Here are some examples of these styles, and an explanation of their meaning.

Code words in text, database table names, folder names, filenames, file extensions, pathnames, dummy URLs, user input, and Twitter handles are shown as follows:

"The acf function will plot the correlation between all pairs of data points with lagged values."

A block of code is set as follows:

```
> install.packages("forecast")
> require(forecast)
> forecast(my_series, 4)
```

New terms and **important words** are shown in bold. Words that you see on the screen, in menus or dialog boxes for example, appear in the text like this: "Click on **Download R for Windows**, as shown in the following screenshot."

Warnings or important notes appear in a box like this.

Tips and tricks appear like this.

Reader feedback

Feedback from our readers is always welcome. Let us know what you think about this book-what you liked or disliked. Reader feedback is important for us as it helps us develop titles that you will really get the most out of. To send us general feedback, simply e-mail feedback@packtpub.com, and mention the book's title in the subject of your message. If there is a topic that you have expertise in and you are interested in either writing or contributing to a book, see our author guide at www.packtpub.com/authors.

Customer support

Now that you are the proud owner of a Packt book, we have a number of things to help you to get the most from your purchase.

Downloading the example code

You can download the example code files for this book from your account at http://www.packtpub.com. If you purchased this book elsewhere, you can visit http://www.packtpub.com/support and register to have the files e-mailed directly to you.

You can download the code files by following these steps:

1. Log in or register to our website using your e-mail address and password.
2. Hover the mouse pointer on the **SUPPORT** tab at the top.
3. Click on **Code Downloads & Errata**.
4. Enter the name of the book in the **Search** box.
5. Select the book for which you're looking to download the code files.
6. Choose from the drop-down menu where you purchased this book from.
7. Click on **Code Download**.

Once the file is downloaded, please make sure that you unzip or extract the folder using the latest version of:

- WinRAR / 7-Zip for Windows
- Zipeg / iZip / UnRarX for Mac
- 7-Zip / PeaZip for Linux

The code bundle for the book is also hosted on GitHub at `https://github.com/PacktPublishing/Machine-Learning-with-R-Cookbook-Second-Edition`. We also have other code bundles from our rich catalog of books and videos available at`https://github.com/PacktPublishing/`. Check them out!

Errata

Although we have taken every care to ensure the accuracy of our content, mistakes do happen. If you find a mistake in one of our books-maybe a mistake in the text or the code-we would be grateful if you could report this to us. By doing so, you can save other readers from frustration and help us improve subsequent versions of this book. If you find any errata, please report them by visiting `http://www.packtpub.com/submit-errata`, selecting your book, clicking on the **Errata Submission Form** link, and entering the details of your errata. Once your errata are verified, your submission will be accepted and the errata will be uploaded to our website or added to any list of existing errata under the Errata section of that title.

To view the previously submitted errata, go to `https://www.packtpub.com/books/content/support` and enter the name of the book in the search field. The required information will appear under the **Errata** section.

Piracy

Piracy of copyrighted material on the Internet is an ongoing problem across all media. At Packt, we take the protection of our copyright and licenses very seriously. If you come across any illegal copies of our works in any form on the Internet, please provide us with the location address or website name immediately so that we can pursue a remedy.

Please contact us at `copyright@packtpub.com` with a link to the suspected pirated material.

We appreciate your help in protecting our authors and our ability to bring you valuable content.

Questions

If you have a problem with any aspect of this book, you can contact us at `questions@packtpub.com`, and we will do our best to address the problem.

1
Practical Machine Learning with R

In this chapter, we will cover the following topics:

- Downloading and installing R
- Downloading and installing RStudio
- Installing and loading packages
- Understanding basic data structures
- Basic commands for subsetting
- Reading and writing data
- Manipulating data
- Applying basic statistics
- Visualizing data
- Getting a dataset for machine learning

Introduction

The aim of machine learning is to uncover hidden patterns and unknown correlations, and to find useful information from data. In addition to this, through incorporation with data analysis, machine learning can be used to perform predictive analysis. With machine learning, the analysis of business operations and processes is not limited to human scale thinking; machine scale analysis enables businesses to capture hidden values in big data.

Machine learning has similarities to the human reasoning process. Unlike traditional analysis, the generated model cannot evolve as data is accumulated. Machine learning can learn from the data that is processed and analyzed. In other words, the more data that is processed, the more it can learn.

R, as a dialect of GNU-S, is a powerful statistical language that can be used to manipulate and analyze data. Additionally, R provides many machine learning packages and visualization functions, which enable users to analyze data on the fly. Most importantly, R is open source and free.

Using R greatly simplifies machine learning. All you need to know is how each algorithm can solve your problem and then you can simply use a written package to quickly generate prediction models on data with a few command lines. For example, you can perform Naïve Bayes for spam mail filtering, conduct k-means clustering for customer segmentation, use linear regression to forecast house prices, or implement a hidden Markov model to predict the stock market, as shown in the following screenshot:

Stock market prediction using R

Moreover, you can perform nonlinear dimension reduction to calculate the dissimilarity of image data and visualize the clustered graph, as shown in the following screenshot. All you need to do is follow the recipes provided in this book:

A clustered graph of face image data

This chapter serves as an overall introduction to machine learning and R; the first few recipes introduce how to set up the R environment and the integrated development environment, RStudio. After setting up the environment, the following recipe introduces package installation and loading. In order to understand how data analysis is practiced using R, the next four recipes cover data read/write, data manipulation, basic statistics, and data visualization using R. The last recipe in the chapter lists useful data sources and resources.

Downloading and installing R

To use R, you must first install it on your computer. This recipe gives detailed instructions on how to download and install R.

Getting ready

If you are new to the R language, you can find a detailed introduction, language history, and functionality on the official website (http://www.r-project.org/). When you are ready to download and install R, please access the following link: http://cran.r-project.org/.

How to do it...

Please perform the following steps to download and install R for Windows and macOS:

1. Go to the R CRAN website, http://www.r-project.org/, and click on the **download R** link, that is, http://cran.r-project.org/mirrors.html):

[Home]

Download

CRAN

R Project

About R
Logo
Contributors
What's New?
Reporting Bugs
Development Site
Conferences
Search

R Foundation

Foundation
Board
Members
Donors
Donate

Help With R

Getting Help

Documentation

The R Project for Statistical Computing

Getting Started

R is a free software environment for statistical computing and graphics. It compiles and runs on a wide variety of UNIX platforms, Windows and MacOS. To download R, please choose your preferred CRAN mirror.

If you have questions about R like how to download and install the software, or what the license terms are, please read our answers to frequently asked questions before you send an email.

News

- **The R Journal Volume 9/1** is available.

- **R version 3.4.1 (Single Candle)** has been released on Friday 2017-06-30.

- **R version 3.3.3 (Another Canoe)** has been released on Monday 2017-03-06.

- **The R Journal Volume 8/2** is available.

- **useR! 2017** (July 4 - 7 in Brussels) has opened registration and more at http://user2017.brussels/

- Tomas Kalibera has joined the R core team.

- The R Foundation welcomes five new ordinary members: Jennifer Bryan, Dianne Cook, Julie Josse, Tomas Kalibera, and Balasubramanian Narasimhan.

- **The R Journal Volume 8/1** is available.

- The **useR! 2017** conference will take place in Brussels, July 4 - 7, 2017.

- **R version 3.2.5 (Very, Very Secure Dishes)** has been released on 2016-04-14. This is a rebadging of the quick-fix release 3.2.4-revised.

R Project home page

2. You may select the mirror location closest to you:

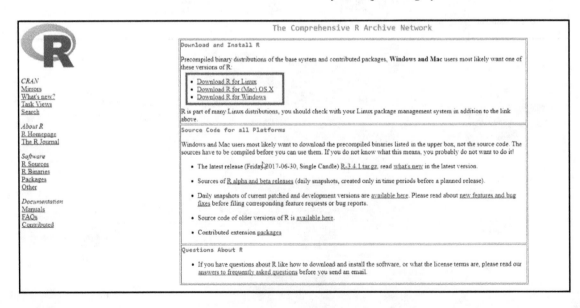

CRAN mirrors

3. Select the correct download link based on your operating system:

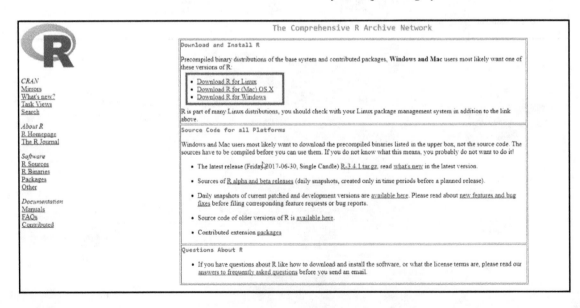

Click on the download link based on your OS

As the installation of R differs for Windows and macOS, the steps required to install R for each OS are provided here.

For Windows:

1. Click on **Download R for Windows,** as shown in the following screenshot, and then click on **base:**

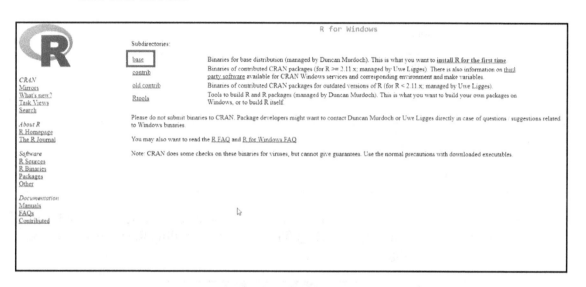

2. Click on **Download R 3.x.x for Windows**:

3. The installation file should be downloaded. Once the download is finished, you can double-click on the installation file and begin installing R, It will ask for you selecting setup language:

Installation step - Selecting Language

4. The next screen will be an installation screen; click on **Next** on all screens to complete the installation. Once installed, you can see the shortcut icon on the desktop:

R icon for 32 bit and 64 bit on desktop

5. Double-click on the icon and it will open the R Console:

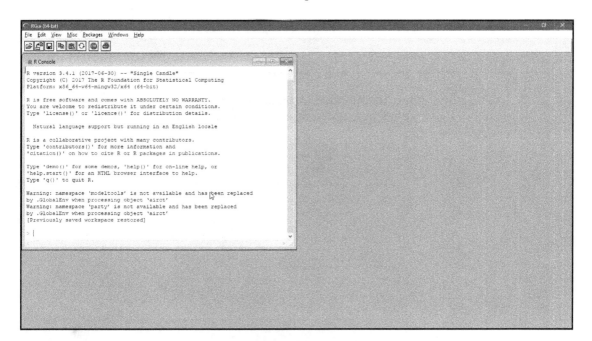

The Windows R Console

For macOS X:

1. Go to **Download R for (Mac) OS X,** as shown in the following screenshot.

2. Click on the latest version (R-3.4.1.pkg file extension) according to your macOS version:

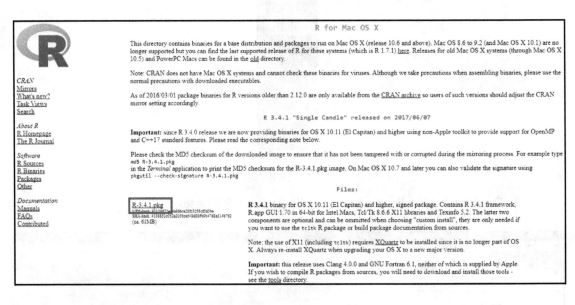

3. Double-click on the downloaded installation file (.pkg extension) and begin to install R. Leave all the installation options as the default settings if you do not want to make any changes:

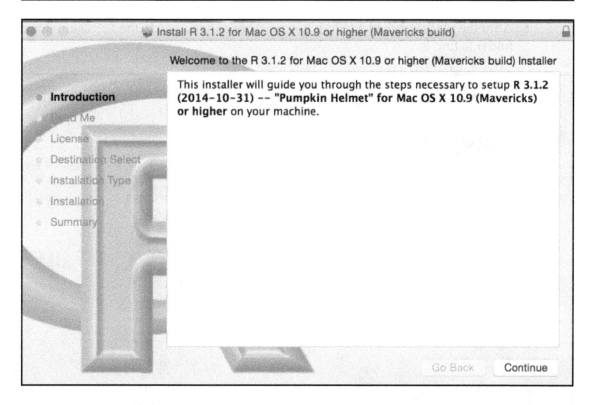

4. Follow the onscreen instructions through **Introduction**, **Read Me**, **License**, **Destination Select**, **Installation Type**, **Installation**, and **Summary**, and click on **Continue** to complete the installation.

5. After the file is installed, you can use spotlight search or go to the `Applications` folder to find R:

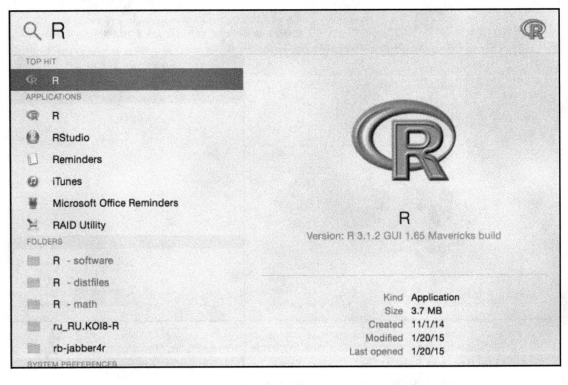

Use spotlight search to find R

6. Click on R to open **R Console**:

As an alternative to downloading a Mac `.pkg` file to install R, Mac users can also install R using Homebrew:

1. Download `XQuartz-2.X.X.dmg` from
   `https://xquartz.macosforge.org/landing/`.
2. Double-click on the `.dmg` file to mount it.
3. Update brew with the following command line:

```
$ brew update
```

4. Clone the repository and `symlink` all its formulae to `homebrew/science`:

```
$ brew tap homebrew/science
```

5. Install `gfortran`:

```
$ brew install gfortran
```

6. Install R:

```
$ brew install R
```

For Linux users, there are precompiled binaries for Debian, RedHat, SUSE, and Ubuntu. Alternatively, you can install R from a source code. Besides downloading precompiled binaries, you can install R for Linux through a package manager. Here are the installation steps for CentOS and Ubuntu.

Downloading and installing R on Ubuntu:

1. Add the entry to the `/etc/apt/sources.list` file replace <> with appropriate value:

```
$ sudo sh -c "echo 'deb http:// <cran mirros site
url>/bin/linux/ubuntu <ubuntu version>/' >> /etc/apt/sources.list"
```

2. Then, update the repository:

```
$ sudo apt-get update
```

3. Install R with the following command:

```
$ sudo apt-get install r-base
```

4. Start R in the command line:

```
$ R
```

Downloading and installing R on CentOS 5:

1. Get the rpm CentOS 5 RHEL EPEL repository of CentOS 5:

```
$ wget
http://dl.fedoraproject.org/pub/epel/5/x86_64/epel-release-5-
4.noarch.rpm
```

2. Install the CentOS 5 RHEL EPEL repository:

```
$ sudo rpm -Uvh epel-release-5-4.noarch.rpm
```

3. Update the installed packages:

```
$ sudo yum update
```

4. Install R through the repository:

```
$ sudo yum install R
```

5. Start R in the command line:

```
$ R
```

Downloading and installing R on CentOS 6:

1. Get the rpm CentOS 5 RHEL EPEL repository of CentOS 6:

```
$ wget
http://dl.fedoraproject.org/pub/epel/6/x86_64/epel-release-6-
8.noarch.rpm
```

2. Install the CentOS 5 RHEL EPEL repository:

```
$ sudo rpm -Uvh epel-release-6-8.noarch.rpm
```

3. Update the installed packages:

```
$ sudo yum update
```

4. Install R through the repository:

```
$ sudo yum install R
```

5. Start R in the command line:

```
$ R
```

Downloading and installing R on Fedora [Latest Version]:

```
$ dnf install R
```

This will install R and all its dependencies.

How it works...

CRAN provides precompiled binaries for Linux, macOS X, and Windows. For macOS and Windows users, the installation procedures are straightforward. You can generally follow onscreen instructions to complete the installation. For Linux users, you can use the package manager provided for each platform to install R or build R from the source code.

See also

- For those planning to build R from the source code, refer to **R Installation and Administration** (http://cran.r-project.org/doc/manuals/R-admin.html), which illustrates how to install R on a variety of platforms

Downloading and installing RStudio

To write an R script, one can use R Console, R commander, or any text editor (such as EMACS, VIM, or sublime). However, the assistance of RStudio, an **integrated development environment** (**IDE**) for R, can make development a lot easier.

RStudio provides comprehensive facilities for software development. Built-in features, such as syntax highlighting, code completion, and smart indentation, help maximize productivity. To make R programming more manageable, RStudio also integrates the main interface into a four-panel layout. It includes an interactive R Console, a tabbed source code editor, a panel for the currently active objects/history, and a tabbed panel for the file browser/plot window/package install window/R help window. Moreover, RStudio is open source and is available for many platforms, such as Windows, macOS X, and Linux. This recipe shows how to download and install RStudio.

Getting ready

RStudio requires a working R installation; when RStudio loads, it must be able to locate a version of R. You must therefore have completed the previous recipe with R installed on your OS before proceeding to install RStudio.

How to do it...

Perform the following steps to download and install RStudio for Windows and macOS users:

1. Access RStudio's official site by using the following URL:
   `http://www.rstudio.com/products/RStudio/`

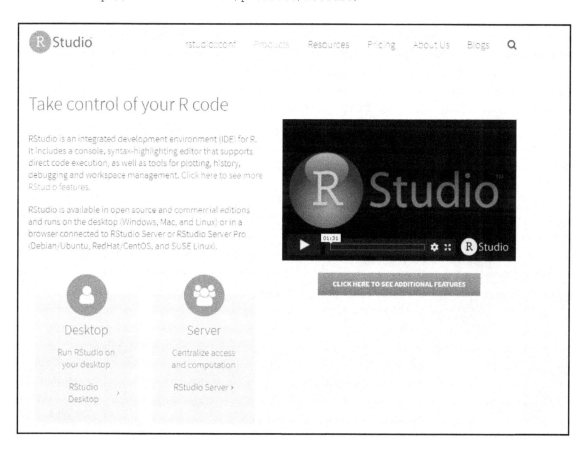

RStudio home page

2. For the desktop version installation, click on **RStudio Desktop** under the **Desktop** section. It will redirect you to the bottom of the home page:

3. Click on the **DOWNLOAD RSTUDIO DESKTOP** button (`http://www.rstudio.com/products/rstudio/download/`), it will display download page, with the option of open source license and commercial license. Scroll down to **RStudio Desktop Open Source License** and click on **DOWNLOAD** button:

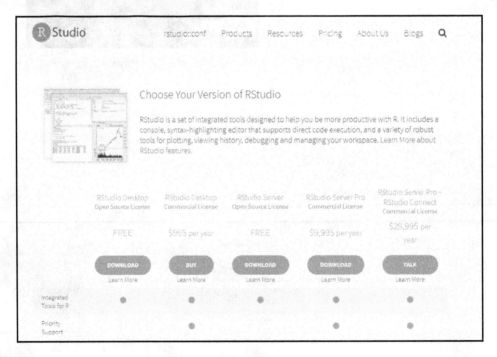

RStudio Download page

4. It will display different installers for different OS types. Select the appropriate option and download the RStudio:

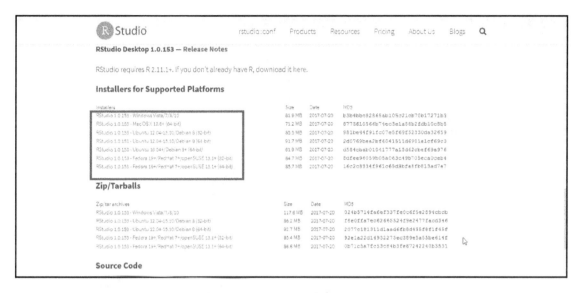

RStudio Download page

5. Install RStudio by double-clicking on the downloaded packages. For Windows users, follow the onscreen instructions to install the application:

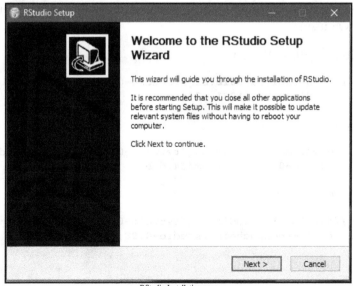

RStudio Installation page

6. For Mac users, simply drag the RStudio icon to the `Applications` folder.
7. Start RStudio:

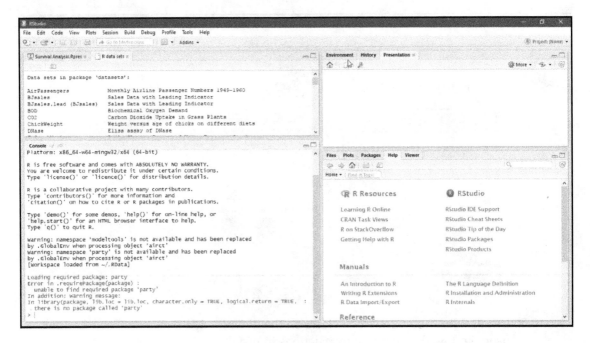

The RStudio console

Perform the following steps for downloading and installing RStudio for Ubuntu/Debian and RedHat/CentOS users:

For Debian(6+)/Ubuntu(10.04+) 32 bit:

```
$ wget http://download1.rstudio.org/rstudio-0.98.1091-i386.deb
$ sudo gdebi rstudio-0.98. 1091-i386.deb
```

For Debian(6+)/Ubuntu(10.04+) 64 bit:

```
$ wget http://download1.rstudio.org/rstudio-0.98. 1091-amd64.deb
$ sudo gdebi rstudio-0.98. 1091-amd64.deb
```

For RedHat/CentOS(5,4+) 32 bit:

```
$ wget http://download1.rstudio.org/rstudio-0.98. 1091-i686.rpm
$ sudo yum install --nogpgcheck rstudio-0.98. 1091-i686.rpm
```

For RedHat/CentOS(5,4+) 64 bit:

```
$ wget http://download1.rstudio.org/rstudio-0.98. 1091-x86_64.rpm
$ sudo yum install --nogpgcheck rstudio-0.98. 1091-x86_64.rpm
```

How it works...

The RStudio program can be run on the desktop or through a web browser. The desktop version is available for the Windows, macOS X, and Linux platforms with similar operations across all platforms. For Windows and macOS users, after downloading the precompiled package of RStudio, follow the onscreen instructions, shown in the preceding steps, to complete the installation. Linux users may use the package management system provided for installation.

See also

- In addition to the desktop version, users may install a server version to provide access to multiple users. The server version provides a URL that users can access to use the RStudio resources. To install RStudio, please refer to the following link: http://www.rstudio.com/ide/download/server.html. This page provides installation instructions for the following Linux distributions: Debian (6+), Ubuntu (10.04+), RedHat, and CentOS (5.4+).
- For other Linux distributions, you can build RStudio from the source code.

Installing and loading packages

After successfully installing R, users can download, install, and update packages from the repositories. As R allows users to create their own packages, official and non-official repositories are provided to manage these user-created packages. **CRAN** is the official R package repository. Currently, the CRAN package repository features 11,589 available packages (as of 10/11/2017). Through the use of the packages provided on CRAN, users may extend the functionality of R to machine learning, statistics, and related purposes. CRAN is a network of FTP and web servers around the world that store identical, up-to-date versions of code and documentation for R. You may select the closest CRAN mirror to your location to download packages.

Getting ready

Start an R session on your host computer.

How to do it...

Perform the following steps to install and load R packages:

1. Load a list of installed packages:

   ```
   > library()
   ```

2. Set the default CRAN mirror:

   ```
   > chooseCRANmirror()
   ```

R will return a list of CRAN mirrors, and then ask the user to either type a mirror ID to select it, or enter zero to exit:

1. Install a package from CRAN; take package e1071 as an example:

   ```
   > install.packages("e1071")
   ```

2. Update a package from CRAN; take package e1071 as an example:

   ```
   > update.packages("e1071")
   ```

3. Load the package:

   ```
   > library(e1071)
   ```

4. If you would like to view the documentation of the package, you can use the help function:

   ```
   > help(package ="e1071")
   ```

5. If you would like to view the documentation of the function, you can use the help function:

   ```
   > help(svm, e1071)
   ```

6. Alternatively, you can use the help shortcut, ?, to view the help document for this function:

```
> ?e1071::svm
```

7. If the function does not provide any documentation, you may want to search the supplied documentation for a given keyword. For example, if you wish to search for documentation related to svm:

```
> help.search("svm")
```

8. Alternatively, you can use ?? as the shortcut for help.search:

```
> ??svm
```

9. To view the argument taken for the function, simply use the args function. For example, if you would like to know the argument taken for the lm function:

```
> args(lm)
```

10. Some packages will provide examples and demos; you can use example or demo to view an example or demo. For example, one can view an example of the lm package and a demo of the graphics package by typing the following commands:

```
> example(lm)
> demo(graphics)
```

11. To view all the available demos, you may use the demo function to list all of them:

```
> demo()
```

How it works...

This recipe first introduces how to view loaded packages, install packages from CRAN, and load new packages. Before installing packages, those of you who are interested in the listing of the CRAN package can refer to
http://cran.r-project.org/web/packages/available_packages_by_name.html.

When a package is installed, documentation related to the package is also provided. You are, therefore, able to view the documentation or the related help pages of installed packages and functions. Additionally, demos and examples are provided by packages that can help users understand the capability of the installed package.

See also

- Besides installing packages from CRAN, there are other R package repositories, including Crantastic, a community site for rating and reviewing CRAN packages, and R-Forge, a central platform for the collaborative development of R packages. In addition to this, Bioconductor provides R packages for the analysis of genomic data.
- If you would like to find relevant functions and packages, please visit the list of task views at http://cran.r-project.org/web/views/, or search for keywords at http://rseek.org.

Understanding of basic data structures

Ensure you have completed the previous recipes by installing R on your operating system.

Data types

You need to have brief idea about basic data types and structures in R in order to grasp all the recipies in book. This section will give you an overview for the same and make you ready for using R. R supports all the basic data types supported by any other programming and scripting language. In simple words, data can be of numeric, character, date, and logical type. As the name suggests, numeric means all type of numbers, while logical allows only true and false. To check the type of data, the class function, which will display the class of the data, is used.

Perform following task on R Console or RStudio:

```
> x=123
> class(x)
Output:
[1] "numeric"
> x="ABC"
> class(x)
Output:
[1] "character"
```

Data structures

R supports different types of data structures to store and process data. The following is a list of basic and commonly used data structures used in R:

- Vectors
- List
- Array
- Matrix
- DataFrames

Vectors

A vector is a container that stores data of same type. It can be thought of as a traditional array in programming language. It is not to be confused with mathematical vector which have rows and columns. To create a vector the `c()` function, which will combine the arguments, is used. One of the beautiful features of vectors is that any operation performed on vector is performed on each element of the vector. If a vector consists of three elements, adding two will increases every element by two.

How to do it...

Perform the following steps to create and see vector in R:

```
> x=c(1,2,3,4)  # c(1:4)
> x
Output:
[1] 1 2 3 4
> x=c(1,2,3,4,"ABC")
> x
Output:
[1] "1" "2" "3" "4" "ABC"
> x * 2
Output:
[1] 2 4 6 8
> sqrt(x)
Output:
[1] 1.000000 1.414214 1.732051 2.000000
> y = x==2
> y
Output:
[1] FALSE TRUE FALSE FALSE
```

```
> class(y)
Output:
[1] "logical"
> t = c(1:10)
> t
Output:
[1] 1 2 3 4 5 6 7 8 9 10
```

How it works...

Printing a vector will starts with index [1] which shows the elements are indexed in vector and it starts from 1, not from 0 like other languages. Any operation done on a vector is applied on individual elements of the vector, so the multiplication operation is applied on individual elements of the vector. If vector is passed as an argument to any inbuilt function, it will be applied on individual elements. You can see how powerful it is and it removes the need to write the loops for doing the operation. The vector changes the type on basis of data it holds and operation we apply on it. Using x==2 will check each element of vector for equality with two and returns the vector with logical value, that is, TRUE or FALSE. There are many other ways of creating a vector; one such way is shown in creating vector t.

Lists

Unlike a vector, a list can store any type of data. A list is, again, a container that can store arbitrary data. A list can contain another list, a vector, or any other data structure. To create a list, the list function is used.

How to do it...

Perform the following steps to create and see a list in R:

```
> y = list(1,2,3,"ABC")
> y
Output:
[[1]]
[1]1
[[2]]
[1]2
[[3]]
[1]3
[[4]]
[1] "ABC"
> y = list(c(1,2,3),c("A","B","C"))
```

```
> y
Output:
[[1]]
[1] 1 2 3
[[2]]
[1] "A" "B" "C"
```

How it works...

A list, as said, can contain anything; we start with a simple example to store some elements in a list using the list function. In the next step, we create a list with a vector as element of the list. So, y is a list with its first element as vector of 1, 2, 3 and its second element as vector of A, B, and C.

Array

An array is nothing but a multidimensional vector, and can store only the same type of data. The way to create a multidimensional vector dimension is specified using dim.

How to do it...

Perform the following steps to create and see an array in R:

```
> t = array(c(1,2,3,4), dim=c(2,2)) # Create two dimensional array
> t
Output:
      [,1]          [,2]
[1,] 1             3
[2,] 2             4
> arr = array(c(1:24), dim=c(3,4,2)) # Creating three dimensional array
> arr
Output:
, , 1

      [,1] [,2] [,3] [,4]
[1,]   1    4    7   10
[2,]   2    5    8   11
[3,]   3    6    9   12
, , 2
      [,1] [,2] [,3] [,4]
[1,]   13   16   19   22
[2,]   14   17   20   23
[3,]   15   18   21   24
```

How it works...

Creating an array is straightforward. Use the `array` function and provide the value for n[th] row; it will create a two-dimensional array with appropriate columns.

Matrix

A matrix is like a DataFrame, with the constraint that every element must be of the same type.

How to do it...

Perform the following steps to create and see a matrix in R:

```
> m = matrix(c(1,2,3,4,5,6), nrow=3)
> m
Output:
     [,1]        [,2]
[1,]  1           4
[2,]  2           5
[3,]  3           6
```

DataFrame

DataFrame can be seen as an Excel spreadsheet, with rows and columns where every column can have different data types. In R, each column of a DataFrame is a vector.

How to do it...

Perform the following steps:

```
> p = c(1,2,3)
> q = c("A","B","C")
> r = c(TRUE, FALSE, FALSE)
> d = data.frame(No=p, Name=q, Attendance=r)
> d
Output:
        No      Name    Attendance
1       1       A       TRUE
2       2       B       FALSE
3       3       C       FALSE
```

Basic commands for subsetting

R allows data to be sliced or to get the subset using various methods.

How to do it...

Perform the following steps to see subsetting. It is assumed that the DataFrame d and matrix m exist from the previous exercise:

```
> d$No     # Slice the column
Output:
[1] 1 2 3
> d$Name   # Slice the column
Output:
[1] A B C
> d$Name[1]
Output:
[1] A
> d[2,]    # get Row
Output:
        No        Name     Attendance
2       2          B           FALSE
> temp = c(1:100) # Creates a vector of 100 elements from 1 to 100
> temp[14:16]   # Part from vector
Output:
[1] 14 15 16
> m[,2]     # To access second column from matrix m
Output:
[1] 4 5 6
> m[3,]   # To access third row from matrix m
Output:
[1] 3 6
> m[2,1]   # To access single element from matrix m
Output:
[1] 2
> m[c(1,3), c(2)] # Access [1,2] and [3,2]
Output:
[1] 4 6
```

Data input

R provides various ways to read data for processing. It supports reading data from CSV files, Excel files, databases, other statistical tools, binary files, and websites. Apart from this, there are many datasets that come bundled with the R. Just execute the `data()` command on RStudio or R prompt it will list the datasets available. If you want to create quick dataset you can create a blank DataFrame and use `edit` command as shown here:

```
> temp = data.frame()
> edit(temp)
```

This will open an Excel like screen for data manipulation as shown in the following screenshot:

	var1	var2	var3	var4	var5	var6
1						
2						
3						
4						
5						
6						
7						
8						
9						
10						
11						
12						
13						
14						
15						
16						
17						
18						
19						

Reading and writing data

Before starting to explore data, you must load the data into the R session. This recipe will introduce methods to load data from a file into the memory, use the predefined data within R, using the data from database.

Getting ready

First, start an R session on your machine. As this recipe involves steps toward the file I/O, if the user does not specify the full path, read and write activity will take place in the current working directory. For working with databases, it is assumed you have working PostgreSQL on your system with some data.

You can simply type `getwd()` in the R session to obtain the current working directory location. However, if you would like to change the current working directory, you can use `setwd("<path>")`, where `<path>` can be replaced with your desired path, to specify the working directory.

How to do it...

Perform the following steps to read and write data with R:

1. To view the built-in datasets of R, type the following command:

   ```
   > data()
   ```

2. R will return a list of datasets in a `dataset` package, and the list comprises the name and description of each dataset.

3. To load the dataset `iris` into an R session, type the following command:

   ```
   > data(iris)
   ```

4. The dataset `iris` is now loaded into the DataFrame format, which is a common data structure in R to store a data table.

5. To view the data type of iris, simply use the `class` function:

```
> class(iris)
[1] "data.frame"
```

6. The `data.frame` console print shows that the `iris` dataset is in the structure of DataFrame.

7. Use the `save` function to store an object in a file. For example, to save the loaded `iris` data into `myData.RData`, use the following command:

```
> save(iris, file="myData.RData")
```

8. Use the `load` function to read a saved object into an R session. For example, to load `iris` data from `myData.RData`, use the following command:

```
> load("myData.RData")
```

9. In addition to using built-in datasets, R also provides a function to import data from text into a DataFrame. For example, the `read.table` function can format a given text into a DataFrame:

```
> test.data = read.table(header = TRUE, text = "
+ a b
+ 1 2
+ 3 4
+ ")
```

10. You can also use `row.names` and `col.names` to specify the names of columns and rows:

```
> test.data = read.table(text = "
+ 1 2
+ 3 4",
+ col.names=c("a","b"),
+ row.names = c("first","second"))
```

11. View the class of the `test.data` variable:

```
> class(test.data)
[1] "data.frame"
```

12. The `class` function shows that the `test.data` variable contains a DataFrame.

13. In addition to importing data by using the `read.table` function, you can use the `write.table` function to export data to a text file:

```
> write.table(test.data, file = "test.txt" , sep = " ")
```

14. The `write.table` function will write the content of `test.data` into `test.txt` (the written path can be found by typing `getwd()`), with a separation delimiter as white space.

15. Similar to `write.table`, `write.csv` can also export data to a file. However, `write.csv` uses a comma as the default delimiter:

```
> write.csv(test.data, file = "test.csv")
```

16. With the `read.csv` function, the `csv` file can be imported as a DataFrame. However, the last example writes column and row names of the DataFrame to the `test.csv` file. Therefore, specifying header to `TRUE` and row names as the first column within the function can ensure the read DataFrame will not treat the header and the first column as values:

```
> csv.data = read.csv("test.csv", header = TRUE, row.names=1)
> head(csv.data)
  a b
1 1 2
2 3 4
```

This section will cover how to work with the database. To connect with PostgreSQL, the RPostgreSQL package is required which can be installed using this command:

```
> install.packages("RPostgreSQL")
```

 It will install package in your system. You need to have active internet connection for this command to complete. Once installed you can use the package for accessing database. You need to have username, password, database name for accessing the PostgreSQL. Replace the value with your values for parameter in `dbconnect` function.

```
> require("RPostgreSQL")
> driver = dbDriver("PostgreSQL")
> connection = dbConnect(driver, dbname="restapp", host="localhost",
        port=5432, user="postgres", password="postgres")
> dbExistsTable(connection, "country")
[1] TRUE
```

TRUE shows that table exists in the database. To query the table use.

```
> data = dbGetQuery(connection, "select * from country")
> class(data)
Output:
[1] "data.frame"
> data
Output:
      id        code      name
1     1         US        USA
2     43        AS        Austria
3     55        BR        Brazil
```

Reading table data will result in to DataFrame in R.

How it works...

Generally, data for collection may be in multiple files and different formats. To exchange data between files and RData, R provides many built-in functions, such as save, load, read.csv, read.table, write.csv, and write.table.

This example first demonstrates how to load the built-in dataset iris into an R session. The iris dataset is the most famous and commonly used dataset in the field of machine learning. Here, we use the iris dataset as an example. The recipe shows how to save RData and load it with the save and load functions. Furthermore, the example explains how to use read.table, write.table, read.csv, and write.csv to exchange data from files to a DataFrame. The use of the R I/O function to read and write data is very important as most of the data sources are external. Therefore, you have to use these functions to load data into an R session.

You need to install the package for reading from the database. For all database, you can find the package, after installing the steps mostly remains the same for reading the data from the database.

There's more...

For the load, read.table, and read.csv functions, the file to be read can also be a complete URL (for supported URLs, use ?url for more information).

On some occasions, data may be in an Excel file instead of a flat text file. The `WriteXLS` package allows writing an object into an Excel file with a given variable in the first argument and the file to be written in the second argument:

1. Install the `WriteXLS` package:

   ```
   > install.packages("WriteXLS")
   ```

2. Load the `WriteXLS` package:

   ```
   > library("WriteXLS")
   ```

3. Use the `WriteXLS` function to write the DataFrame `iris` into a file named `iris.xls`:

   ```
   > WriteXLS("iris", ExcelFileName="iris.xls")
   ```

Manipulating data

This recipe will discuss how to use the built-in R functions to manipulate data. As data manipulation is the most time-consuming part of most analysis procedures, you should gain knowledge of how to apply these functions on data.

Getting ready

Ensure you have completed the previous recipes by installing R on your operating system.

How to do it...

Perform the following steps to manipulate the data with R.

Subset the data using the bracelet notation:

1. Load the dataset `iris` into the R session:

   ```
   > data(iris)
   ```

2. To select values, you may use a bracket notation that designates the indices of the dataset. The first index is for the rows and the second for the columns:

```
> iris[1,"Sepal.Length"]
Output:
[1] 5.1
```

3. You can also select multiple columns using `c()`:

```
> Sepal.iris = iris[, c("Sepal.Length", "Sepal.Width")]
```

4. You can then use `str()` to summarize and display the internal structure of `Sepal.iris`:

```
> str(Sepal.iris)
Output:
'data.frame':  150 obs. of  2 variables:
$ Sepal.Length: num   5.1 4.9 4.7 4.6 5 5.4 4.6 5 4.4 4.9 ...
$ Sepal.Width : num   3.5 3 3.2 3.1 3.6 3.9 3.4 3.4 2.9 3.1 ..
```

5. To subset data with the rows of given indices, you can specify the indices at the first index with the bracket notation. In this example, we show you how to subset data with the top five records with the `Sepal.Length` column and the `Sepal.Width` selected:

```
> Five.Sepal.iris = iris[1:5, c("Sepal.Length", "Sepal.Width")]
> str(Five.Sepal.iris)
Output:
'data.frame':   5 obs. of  2 variables:
$ Sepal.Length: num   5.1 4.9 4.7 4.6 5
$ Sepal.Width : num   3.5 3 3.2 3.1 3.6
```

6. It is also possible to set conditions to filter the data. For example, to filter returned records containing the `setosa` data with all five variables. In the following example, the first index specifies the returning criteria, and the second index specifies the range of indices of the variable returned:

```
> setosa.data = iris[iris$Species=="setosa",1:5]
> str(setosa.data)
Output:
'data.frame':   50 obs. of  5 variables:
$ Sepal.Length: num   5.1 4.9 4.7 4.6 5 5.4 4.6 5 4.4 4.9 ...
$ Sepal.Width : num   3.5 3 3.2 3.1 3.6 3.9 3.4 3.4 2.9 3.1 ...
$ Petal.Length: num   1.4 1.4 1.3 1.5 1.4 1.7 1.4 1.5 1.4 1.5 ...
$ Petal.Width : num   0.2 0.2 0.2 0.2 0.2 0.4 0.3 0.2 0.2 0.1 ...
$ Species     : Factor w/ 3 levels "setosa","versicolor",..: 1 1 1
```

```
1 1 1 1 1 1 1 ...
```

7. Alternatively, the `which` function returns the indexes of satisfied data. The following example returns the indices of the `iris` data containing species equal to `setosa`:

```
> which(iris$Species=="setosa")
Output:
 [1]  1  2  3  4  5  6  7  8  9 10 11 12 13 14 15 16 17 18
[19] 19 20 21 22 23 24 25 26 27 28 29 30 31 32 33 34 35 36
[37] 37 38 39 40 41 42 43 44 45 46 47 48 49 50
```

8. The indices returned by the operation can then be applied as the index to select the `iris` containing the `setosa` species. The following example returns the `setosa` with all five variables:

```
> setosa.data = iris[which(iris$Species=="setosa"),1:5]
> str(setosa.data)
Output:
'data.frame':    50 obs. of  5 variables:
 $ Sepal.Length: num  5.1 4.9 4.7 4.6 5 5.4 4.6 5 4.4 4.9 ...
 $ Sepal.Width : num  3.5 3 3.2 3.1 3.6 3.9 3.4 3.4 2.9 3.1 ...
 $ Petal.Length: num  1.4 1.4 1.3 1.5 1.4 1.7 1.4 1.5 1.4 1.5 ...
 $ Petal.Width : num  0.2 0.2 0.2 0.2 0.2 0.4 0.3 0.2 0.2 0.1 ...
 $ Species     : Factor w/ 3 levels "setosa","versicolor",..: 1 1 1
1 1 1 1 1 1 1 ...
```

Subset data using the `subset` function:

1. Besides using the bracket notation, R provides a `subset` function that enables users to subset the DataFrame by observations with a logical statement.

2. First, subset species, sepal length, and sepal width out of the `iris` data. To select the sepal length and width out of the `iris` data, one should specify the column to be subset in the `select` argument:

```
> Sepal.data = subset(iris, select=c("Sepal.Length", "Se-
pal.Width"))
> str(Sepal.data)
Output:
'data.frame': 150 obs. of  2 variables:
 $ Sepal.Length: num  5.1 4.9 4.7 4.6 5 5.4 4.6 5 4.4 4.9 ...
 $ Sepal.Width : num  3.5 3 3.2 3.1 3.6 3.9 3.4 3.4 2.9 3.1 ...
```

This reveals that `Sepal.data` contains 150 objects with the `Sepal.Length` variable and `Sepal.Width`.

1. On the other hand, you can use a subset argument to get subset data containing `setosa` only. In the second argument of the subset function, you can specify the subset criteria:

```
> setosa.data = subset(iris, Species =="setosa")
> str(setosa.data)
Output:
'data.frame': 50 obs. of  5 variables:
 $ Sepal.Length: num  5.1 4.9 4.7 4.6 5 5.4 4.6 5 4.4 4.9 ...
 $ Sepal.Width : num  3.5 3 3.2 3.1 3.6 3.9 3.4 3.4 2.9 3.1 ...
 $ Petal.Length: num  1.4 1.4 1.3 1.5 1.4 1.7 1.4 1.5 1.4 1.5 ...
 $ Petal.Width : num  0.2 0.2 0.2 0.2 0.2 0.4 0.3 0.2 0.2 0.1 ...
 $ Species     : Factor w/ 3 levels "setosa","versicolor",..: 1 1 1
 1 1 1 1 1 1 1 ...
```

2. Most of the time, you may want to apply a union or intersect a condition while subsetting data. The OR and AND operations can be further employed for this purpose. For example, if you would like to retrieve data with `Petal.Width` >=0.2 and `Petal.Length` < = 1.4:

```
> example.data= subset(iris, Petal.Length <=1.4 & Petal.Width >=
0.2, select=Species )
> str(example.data)
Output:
'data.frame': 21 obs. of  1 variable:
 $ Species: Factor w/ 3 levels "setosa","versicolor",..: 1 1 1 1 1 1
 1 1 1 ...
```

- **Merging data**: Merging data involves joining two DataFrames into a merged DataFrame by a common column or row name. The following example shows how to merge the `flower.type` DataFrame and the first three rows of the iris with a common row name within the `Species` column:

```
> flower.type = data.frame(Species = "setosa", Flower = "iris")
> merge(flower.type, iris[1:3,], by ="Species")
Output:
  Species Flower Sepal.Length Sepal.Width Petal.Length Petal.Width
1  setosa   iris          5.1         3.5          1.4         0.2
2  setosa   iris          4.9         3.0          1.4         0.2
3  setosa   iris          4.7         3.2          1.3         0.2
```

- **Ordering data**: The `order` function will return the index of a sorted DataFrame with a specified column. The following example shows the results from the first six records with the sepal length ordered (from big to small) iris data:

```
> head(iris[order(iris$Sepal.Length, decreasing = TRUE),])
Output:
    Sepal.Length Sepal.Width Petal.Length Petal.Width   Species
132          7.9         3.8          6.4         2.0 virginica
118          7.7         3.8          6.7         2.2 virginica
119          7.7         2.6          6.9         2.3 virginica
123          7.7         2.8          6.7         2.0 virginica
136          7.7         3.0          6.1         2.3 virginica
106          7.6         3.0          6.6         2.1 virginica
```

How it works...

Before conducting data analysis, it is important to organize collected data into a structured format. Therefore, we can simply use the R DataFrame to subset, merge, and order a dataset. This recipe first introduces two methods to subset data: one uses the bracket notation, while the other uses the `subset` function. You can use both methods to generate the subset data by selecting columns and filtering data with the given criteria. The recipe then introduces the `merge` function to merge DataFrames. Last, the recipe introduces how to use `order` to sort the data.

There's more...

The `sub` and `gsub` functions allow using regular expression to substitute a string. The `sub` and `gsub` functions perform the replacement of the first and all the other matches, respectively:

```
> sub("e", "q", names(iris))
Output:
[1] "Sqpal.Length" "Sqpal.Width"  "Pqtal.Length" "Pqtal.Width"  "Spqcies"
> gsub("e", "q", names(iris))
Output:
[1] "Sqpal.Lqngth" "Sqpal.Width"  "Pqtal.Lqngth" "Pqtal.Width"  "Spqciqs"
```

Applying basic statistics

R provides a wide range of statistical functions, allowing users to obtain the summary statistics of data, generate frequency and contingency tables, produce correlations, and conduct statistical inferences. This recipe covers basic statistics that can be applied to a dataset.

Getting ready

Ensure you have completed the previous recipes by installing R on your operating system.

How to do it...

Perform the following steps to apply statistics to a dataset:

1. Load the `iris` data into an R session:

   ```
   > data(iris)
   ```

2. Observe the format of the data:

   ```
   > class(iris)
   [1] "data.frame"
   ```

3. The `iris` dataset is a DataFrame containing four numeric attributes: `petal length`, `petal width`, `sepal width`, and `sepal length`. For numeric values, you can perform descriptive statistics, such as `mean`, `sd`, `var`, `min`, `max`, `median`, `range`, and `quantile`. These can be applied to any of the four attributes in the dataset:

   ```
   > mean(iris$Sepal.Length)
   Output:
   [1] 5.843333
   > sd(iris$Sepal.Length)
   Output:
   [1] 0.8280661
   > var(iris$Sepal.Length)
   Output:
   [1] 0.6856935
   > min(iris$Sepal.Length)
   Output:
   [1] 4.3
   ```

```
> max(iris$Sepal.Length)
Output:
[1] 7.9
> median(iris$Sepal.Length)
Output:
[1] 5.8
> range(iris$Sepal.Length)
Output:
[1] 4.3 7.9
> quantile(iris$Sepal.Length)
Output:
0%   25%   50%   75% 100%
4.3   5.1   5.8   6.4   7.9
```

4. The preceding example demonstrates how to apply descriptive statistics to a single variable. In order to obtain summary statistics on every `numeric` attribute of the DataFrame, one may use `sapply`. For example, to apply the mean on the first four attributes in the `iris` DataFrame, ignore the `na` value by setting `na.rm` as TRUE:

```
> sapply(iris[1:4], mean, na.rm=TRUE)
Output:
Sepal.Length  Sepal.Width Petal.Length   Petal.Width
    5.843333     3.057333     3.758000      1.199333
```

5. As an alternative to using `sapply` to apply descriptive statistics on given attributes, R offers the `summary` function that provides a full range of descriptive statistics. In the following example, the `summary` function provides the mean, median, 25th and 75th quartiles, min, and max of every `iris` dataset `numeric` attribute:

```
> summary(iris)
Output:
Sepal.Length  Sepal.Width   Petal.Length    Petal.Width    Species
Min.  4.300 Min.   :2.000 Min.   :1.000 Min.   :0.100 setosa    :50
1st Qu.:5.100 1st Qu.:2.800 1st Qu.:1.600 1st Qu.:0.300
versicolor:50
Median :5.800 Median :3.000 Median :4.350 Median :1.300
virginica :50
Mean :5.843 Mean   :3.057 Mean   :3.758 Mean   :1.199
3rd Qu.:6.400 3rd Qu.:3.300 3rd Qu.:5.100 3rd Qu.:1.800
Max. :7.900 Max.   :4.400 Max.   :6.900 Max.   :2.500
```

6. The preceding example shows how to output the descriptive statistics of a single variable. R also provides the correlation for users to investigate the relationship between variables. The following example generates a 4x4 matrix by computing the correlation of each attribute pair within the iris:

```
> cor(iris[,1:4])
Output:
             Sepal.Length Sepal.Width Petal.Length Petal.Width
Sepal.Length    1.0000000  -0.1175698    0.8717538    0.8179411
Sepal.Width    -0.1175698   1.0000000   -0.4284401   -0.3661259
Petal.Length    0.8717538  -0.4284401    1.0000000    0.9628654
Petal.Width     0.8179411  -0.3661259    0.9628654    1.0000000
```

7. R also provides a function to compute the covariance of each attribute pair within the iris dataset:

```
> cov(iris[,1:4])
Output:
             Sepal.Length Sepal.Width Petal.Length Petal.Width
Sepal.Length    0.6856935  -0.0424340    1.2743154    0.5162707
Sepal.Width    -0.0424340   0.1899794   -0.3296564   -0.1216394
Petal.Length    1.2743154  -0.3296564    3.1162779    1.2956094
Petal.Width     0.5162707  -0.1216394    1.2956094    0.5810063
```

8. Statistical tests are performed to access the significance of the results; here we demonstrate how to use a t-test to determine the statistical differences between two samples. In this example, we perform a t.test on the petal width an of an iris in either the setosa or versicolor species. If we obtain a p-value less than 0.5, we can be certain that the petal width between the setosa and versicolor will vary significantly:

```
> t.test(iris$Petal.Width[iris$Species=="setosa"],
+         iris$Petal.Width[iris$Species=="versicolor"])
Output:
Welch Two Sample t-test
data:  iris$Petal.Width[iris$Species == "setosa"] and
iris$Petal.Width[iris$Species == "versicolor"]
t = -34.0803, df = 74.755, p-value < 2.2e-16
alternative hypothesis: true difference in means is not equal to 0
95 percent confidence interval:
-1.143133 -1.016867
sample estimates:
mean of x mean of y
0.246     1.326
```

9. Alternatively, you can perform a correlation test on the sepal length to the sepal width of an iris, and then retrieve a correlation score between the two variables. The stronger the positive correlation, the closer the value is to 1. The stronger the negative correlation, the closer the value is to −1:

```
> cor.test(iris$Sepal.Length, iris$Sepal.Width)
Output:
Pearson's product-moment correlation
data:  iris$Sepal.Length and iris$Sepal.Width
t = -1.4403, df = 148, p-value = 0.1519
alternative hypothesis: true correlation is not equal to 0
95 percent confidence interval:
-0.27269325  0.04351158
sample estimates:
     cor
-0.1175698
```

How it works...

R has a built-in statistics function, which enables the user to perform descriptive statistics on a single variable. The recipe first introduces how to apply mean, sd, var, min, max, median, range, and quantile on a single variable. Moreover, in order to apply the statistics on all four numeric variables, one can use the sapply function. In order to determine the relationships between multiple variables, one can conduct correlation and covariance. Finally, the recipe shows how to determine the statistical differences of two given samples by performing a statistical test.

There's more...

If you need to compute an aggregated summary of statistics against data in different groups, you can use the aggregate and reshape functions to compute the summary statistics of data subsets:

1. Use aggregate to calculate the mean of each iris attribute group by the species:

```
> aggregate(x=iris[,1:4],by=list(iris$Species),FUN=mean)
```

2. Use `reshape` to calculate the mean of each `iris` attribute group by the species:

```
>  library(reshape)
>  iris.melt <- melt(iris,id='Species')
>  cast(Species~variable,data=iris.melt,mean,
      subset=Species %in% c('setosa','versicolor'),
      margins='grand_row')
```

For information on `reshape` and `aggregate`, refer to the help documents by using `?reshape` or `?aggregate`.

Visualizing data

Visualization is a powerful way to communicate information through graphical means. Visual presentations make data easier to comprehend. This recipe presents some basic functions to plot charts, and demonstrates how visualizations are helpful in data exploration.

Getting ready

Ensure that you have completed the previous recipes by installing R on your operating system.

How to do it...

Perform the following steps to visualize a dataset:

1. Load the iris data into the R session:

```
> data(iris)
```

2. Calculate the frequency of species within the iris using the `table` command:

```
> table.iris = table(iris$Species)
> table.iris
Output:

setosa versicolor  virginica
   50          50         50
```

3. As the frequency in the table shows, each species represents 1/3 of the `iris` data. We can draw a simple pie chart to represent the distribution of species within the iris:

```
> pie(table.iris)
Output:
```

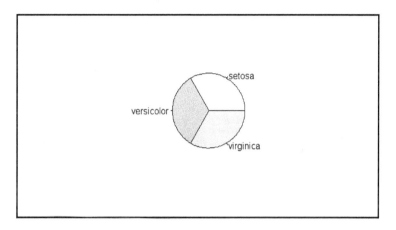

The pie chart of species distribution

4. The histogram creates a frequency plot of sorts along the *x*-axis. The following example produces a histogram of the sepal length:

```
> hist(iris$Sepal.Length)
```

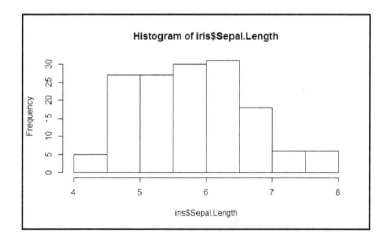

The histogram of the sepal length

5. In the histogram, the x-axis presents the sepal length and the *y*-axis presents the count for different sepal lengths. The histogram shows that for most irises, sepal lengths range from **4** cm to **8** cm.

6. Boxplots, also named box and whisker graphs, allow you to convey a lot of information in one simple plot. In such a graph, the line represents the median of the sample. The box itself shows the upper and lower quartiles. The whiskers show the range:

```
> boxplot(Petal.Width ~ Species, data = iris)
```

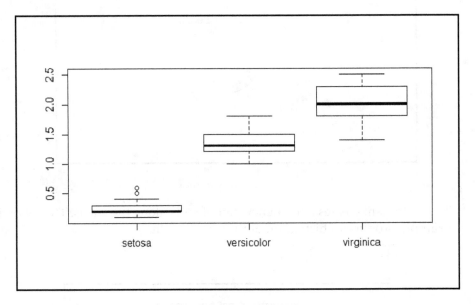

The boxplot of the petal width

7. The preceding screenshot clearly shows the median and upper range of the petal width of the `setosa` is much shorter than `versicolor` and `virginica`. Therefore, the petal width can be used as a substantial attribute to distinguish iris species.

8. A scatter plot is used when there are two variables to plot against one another. This example plots the petal length against the petal width and color dots in accordance to the species it belongs to:

```
> plot(x=iris$Petal.Length, y=iris$Petal.Width, col=iris$Species)
```

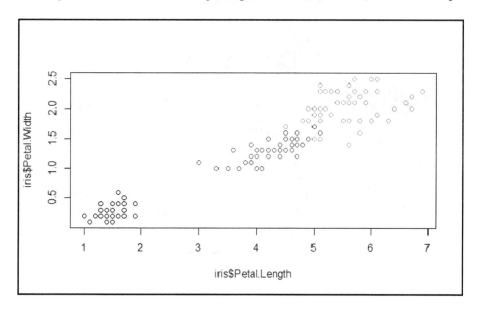

The scatter plot of the sepal length

9. The preceding screenshot is a scatter plot of the petal length against the petal width. As there are four attributes within the `iris` dataset, it takes six operations to plot all combinations. However, R provides a function named `pairs`, which can generate each subplot in one figure:

```
> pairs(iris[1:4], main = "Edgar Anderson's Iris Data", pch = 21,
  bg = c("red", "green3", "blue")[unclass(iris$Species)])
```

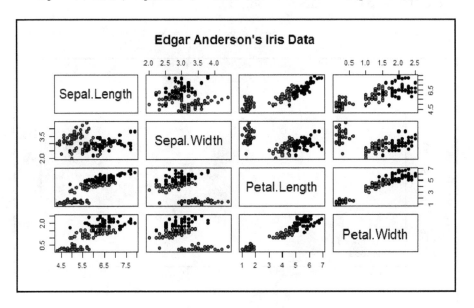

Pairs scatterplot of iris data

How it works...

R provides many built-in plot functions, which enable users to visualize data with different kinds of plots. This recipe demonstrates the use of pie charts that can present category distribution. A pie chart of an equal size shows that the number of each species is equal. A histogram plots the frequency of different sepal lengths. A box plot can convey a great deal of descriptive statistics, and shows that the petal width can be used to distinguish an iris species. Lastly, we introduced scatter plots, which plot variables on a single plot. In order to quickly generate a scatter plot containing all the pairs of `iris` dataset, one may use the `pairs` command.

See also

- ggplot2 is another plotting system for R, based on the implementation of Leland Wilkinson's grammar of graphics. It allows users to add, remove, or alter components in a plot with a higher abstraction. However, the level of abstraction results is slow compared to lattice graphics. For those of you interested in the topic of ggplot, you can refer to this site: http://ggplot2.org/.

Getting a dataset for machine learning

While R has a built-in dataset, the sample size and field of application is limited. Apart from generating data within a simulation, another approach is to obtain data from external data repositories. A famous data repository is the UCI machine learning repository, which contains both artificial and real datasets. This recipe introduces how to get a sample dataset from the UCI machine learning repository.

Getting ready

Ensure that you have completed the previous recipes by installing R on your operating system.

How to do it...

Perform the following steps to retrieve data for machine learning:

1. Access the UCI machine learning repository: http://archive.ics.uci.edu/ml/.
2. Click on **view all data sets**. Here you will find a list of datasets containing field names, such as **Name**, **Data Types**, **Default Task**, **Attribute Types**, **#Instances**, **#Attributes**, and **Year**:
3. Use *Ctrl + F* to search for **Iris**:
4. Click on **Iris**. This will display the data folder and the dataset description:
5. Click on **Data Folder**, which will display a directory containing the iris dataset:

6. You can then either download `iris.data` or use the `read.csv` function to read the dataset:

```
> iris.data = read.csv(url("http://archive.ics.uci.edu/ml/machine-
learning-databases/iris/iris.data"), header = FALSE,  col.names =
c("Sepal.Length", "Sepal.Width", "Petal.Length", "Petal.Width",
"Species"))
> head(iris.data)
Output:
Sepal.Length Sepal.Width Petal.Length Petal.Width    Species
1            5.1         3.5          1.4         0.2 Iris-setosa
2            4.9         3.0          1.4         0.2 Iris-setosa
3            4.7         3.2          1.3         0.2 Iris-setosa
4            4.6         3.1          1.5         0.2 Iris-setosa
5            5.0         3.6          1.4         0.2 Iris-setosa
6            5.4         3.9          1.7         0.4 Iris-setosa
```

How it works...

Before conducting data analysis, it is important to collect your dataset. However, to collect an appropriate dataset for further exploration and analysis is not easy. We can, therefore, use the prepared dataset with the UCI repository as our data source. Here, we first access the UCI dataset repository and then use the iris dataset as an example. We can find the iris dataset by using the browser's find function *(Ctrl + F)*, and then enter the file directory. Last, we can download the dataset and use the R I/O function, `read.csv`, to load the `iris` dataset into an R session.

See also

- KDnuggets (`http://www.kdnuggets.com/datasets/index.html`) offers a resourceful list of datasets for data mining and data science. You can explore the list to find the data that satisfies your requirements.

2

Data Exploration with Air Quality Datasets

In this chapter, we will cover the following recipes:

- Accessing air quality datasets in R
- Converting attributes to factors
- Detecting missing values
- Imputing missing values
- Exploring and visualizing data
- Predicting temperature using available data

Introduction

As a data consumer, the focus is always on searching for right information to form a true analysis from the information gathered over time. Data Exploration is a term used for finding insightful information from data. To find insights from data various steps such as data munging, data analysis, data modeling, and model evaluation are taken.

In any real data exploration project, commonly six steps are involved in the exploration process. They are as follows:

- **Asking the right questions**: Asking the right questions will help in understanding the objective and target information sought from the data. Questions can be asked such as *What are my expected findings after the exploration is finished?*, or *What kind of information can I extract through the exploration?*.

- **Data collection**: Once the right questions have been asked the target of exploration is cleared. Data collected from various sources is in unorganized and diverse format. Data may come from various sources such as files, databases, internet, and so on. Data collected in this way is raw data and needs to be processed to extract meaningful information. Most of the analysis and visualizing tools or applications expect data to be in a certain format to generate results and hence the raw data is of no use for them.

- **Data munging**: Raw data collected needs to be converted into the desired format of the tools to be used. In this phase, raw data is passed through various processes such as parsing the data, sorting, merging, filtering, dealing with missing values, and so on. The main aim is to transform raw data in the format that the analyzing and visualizing tools understand. Once the data is compatible with the tools, analysis and visualizing tools are used to generate the different results.

- **Basic exploratory data analysis**: Once the data munging is done and data is formating for the tools, it can be used to perform data exploration and analysis. Tools provide various methods and techniques to do the same. Most analyzing tools allow statistical functions to be performed on the data. Visualizing tools help in visualizing the data in different ways. Using basic statistical operations and visualizing the same data can be understood in better way.

- **Advanced exploratory data analysis**: Once the basic analysis is done it's time to look at an advanced stage of analysis. In this stage, various prediction models are formed on basis of requirement. Machine learning algorithms are utilized to train the model and generate the inferences. Various tuning on the model is also done to ensure correctness and effectiveness of the model.

- **Model assessment**: When the models are mare, they are evaluated to find the best model from the given different models. The major factor to decide the best model is to see how perfect or closely it can predict the values. Models are tuned here also for increasing the accuracy and effectiveness. Various plots and graphs are used to see the models prediction.

In this chapter, we will be performing a sample data exploration based on the dataset of air quality for different months. We will study the data, clean data through data munging; perform basic exploratory data analysis to discover important attributes that might give a prediction of the temperature, and generate a prediction model.

Using air quality dataset

Air quality datasets come bundled with R. They contain data about the New York Air Quality Measurements of 1973 for five months from May to September recorded daily. To view all the available datasets use the data() function, it will display all the datasets available with R installation.

Getting ready

In this recipe, we will use air quality datasets, which are available with R.

How to do it...

Perform the following step to see all the datasets in R and using airquality:

```
> data()
> str(airquality)
Output
'data.frame': 153 obs. of 6 variables:
 $ Ozone : int 41 36 12 18 NA 28 23 19 8 NA ...
 $ Solar.R: int 190 118 149 313 NA NA 299 99 19 194 ...
 $ Wind : num 7.4 8 12.6 11.5 14.3 14.9 8.6 13.8 20.1 8.6 ...
 $ Temp : int 67 72 74 62 56 66 65 59 61 69 ...
 $ Month : int 5 5 5 5 5 5 5 5 5 5 ...
 $ Day : int 1 2 3 4 5 6 7 8 9 10 ...
> head(airquality)
Output
Ozone Solar.R Wind Temp Month Day
1 41 190 7.4 67 5 1
2 36 118 8.0 72 5 2
3 12 149 12.6 74 5 3
4 18 313 11.5 62 5 4
5 NA NA 14.3 56 5 5
6 28 NA 14.9 66 5 6
```

How it works...

The `str` command is used to display the structure of the dataset, as you can see it contains the information about the observation of `ozone`, `solar`, `wind`, and `temp` attributes recorded each day for five months. Using the `head` function, you can see the first few lines of actual data. The dataset is very basic and is enough to start processing and analyzing data at a very basic level.

There's more...

Datasets provided with R are great, but to find the real-time datasets you can visit the Kaggle website, which has various diverse kinds of datasets. Apart from datasets it also holds many competitions in data science fields to solve real-world problems.

You can find the competitions, datasets, kernels, and jobs at `https://www.kaggle.com/`. Many competitions are organized by large corporate bodies, government agencies, or from academia. Many of the competitions have prize money associated with them. The following screenshot shows competitions and prize money:

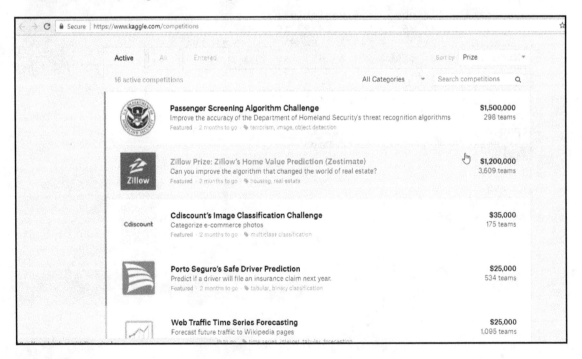

You can simply create an account and start participating in competitions by submitting code and the output and the same will be assessed. Assessment or evaluation criteria is available on the detail page of each competition. By participating and using `https://www.kaggle.com/` one gains experience in solving real-world problems. It gives you a taste of what data scientist do.

On the jobs page various jobs for data scientists and analysis is listed and you can apply is the profile is suitable or matches with your interests.

Converting attributes to factor

In R, since nominal, ordinal, interval, and ratio variable are treated differently in statistical modeling, we have to convert a nominal variable from a character or int into a factor.

Getting ready

You need to have completed the previous recipe, that is, viewing the airquality dataset using the `str` and `head` commands, to get an idea about what it contains.

How to do it...

Perform the following steps to convert the types of character variables:

1. Assign the airquality dataset to mydata:

   ```
   > mydata <- airquality
   ```

2. To transform the variable from the `int` numeric type to the `factor` categorical type, you can cast `factor`:

   ```
   > mydata$Month = factor(mydata$Month)
   ```

3. Print out the variable with the `str` function and again, you can see that Month is now transformed into the factor as follows:

   ```
   > str(mydata)
   Output
   'data.frame': 153 obs. of 6 variables:$ Ozone :
   int 41 36 12 18 NA 28 23 19 8 NA ...
    $ Solar.R: int 190 118 149 313 NA NA 299
   ```

```
99 19 194 ...
 $ Wind : num 7.4 8 12.6 11.5 14.3 14.9 8.6 13.8
20.1 8.6 ...
 $ Temp : int 67 72 74 62 56 66 65 59 61 69 ...
 $ Month : Factor w/ 5 levels "5","6","7","8",..:
1 1 1 1 1 1 1 1 1 1 ...
 $ Day : int 1 2 3 4 5 6 7 8 9 10 ...
```

How it works...

In statistics, observations or data can be treated as nominal, ordinal, interval, and ratio variables or values. Label variables such as gender and name are known as nominal variables. Non-numeric concepts such as happiness, sadness, and so on qualify for ordinal variables. Interval variables show numeric scales, such as the wind in the previous example. Ratio variables shows the ratio of magnitude such as the height and weight dataset.

In this recipe, we first display the structure of the airquality data using the `str` function. From the structure of data, you can find the attribute month is a categorical type. As a result, we transform the data from an integer type to a factor type using the `factor` function.

There's more...

Besides factors, there are many other functions that help in conversion. For numeric types, there are `is.numeric()` and `as.numeric()`; for character, there are: `is.character()` and `as.character()`. For vector, there are: `is.vector()` and `as.vector()`; for matrix, there are: `is.matrix()` and `as.matrix()`. Finally, for data frame, there are: `is.data.frame()` and `as.data.frame()`.

Detecting missing values

Missing values reduce the representativeness of the sample, and furthermore, might distort inferences about the population. This recipe will focus on detecting missing values within the airquality dataset.

Getting ready

You need to have completed the previous recipes, which involve converting Month into a factor type.

In R, a missing value is noted with the symbol **NA** (**not available**), and an impossible value is **NaN** (**not a number**).

How to do it...

Perform the following steps to detect the missing value:

1. The is.na function is used to denote which index of the attribute contains the NA value. Here, we apply it to the Ozone attribute first:

```
> is.na(mydata$Ozone)
Output

 [1] FALSE FALSE FALSE FALSE TRUE FALSE FALSE FALSE FALSE TRUE
 FALSE FALSE FALSE
[14] FALSE FALSE FALSE FALSE FALSE FALSE FALSE FALSE FALSE FALSE
 FALSE TRUE TRUE
[27] TRUE FALSE FALSE FALSE FALSE TRUE TRUE TRUE TRUE TRUE TRUE
FALSE TRUE
[40] FALSE FALSE TRUE TRUE FALSE TRUE TRUE FALSE FALSE FALSE
FALSE FALSE TRUE
[53] TRUE TRUE TRUE TRUE TRUE TRUE TRUE TRUE TRUE FALSE FALSE
FALSE TRUE
[66] FALSE FALSE FALSE FALSE FALSE FALSE TRUE FALSE FALSE TRUE
FALSE FALSE FALSE
[79] FALSE FALSE FALSE FALSE TRUE TRUE FALSE FALSE FALSE FALSE
FALSE FALSE FALSE
[92] FALSE FALSE FALSE FALSE FALSE FALSE FALSE FALSE FALSE FALSE
TRUE TRUE FALSE
[105] FALSE FALSE TRUE FALSE FALSE FALSE FALSE FALSE FALSE FALSE
TRUE FALSE FALSE
[118] FALSE TRUE FALSE FALSE FALSE FALSE FALSE FALSE FALSE FALSE
FALSE FALSE FALSE
[131] FALSE FALSE FALSE FALSE FALSE FALSE FALSE FALSE FALSE FALSE
FALSE FALSE FALSE
[144] FALSE FALSE FALSE FALSE FALSE FALSE TRUE FALSE FALSE FALSE
```

2. The `is.na` function indicates the missing value of the `Ozone` attribute. `TRUE` means value is `NA` and `FALSE` means the attribute has a value. This can be used with all the other attributes to find the missing value. Before doing that let's get a general number of how many missing values there are, you can perform a `sum` to calculate this:

```
> sum(is.na(mydata$Ozone)==TRUE)
 Output
[1] 37
```

3. To calculate the percentage of missing values, one method adopted is to count the number of missing values against non-missing values and multiply by 100:

```
> sum(is.na(mydata$Ozone)==TRUE) / length(mydata$Ozone) * 100
Output
[1] 24.18301
```

4. So in the `Ozone` attribute 24% of values are missing. To get a percentage of the missing values of all the attributes, you can use `sapply` to calculate the percentage of all the attributes:

```
> sapply(mydata, function(df){
+ sum(is.na(df)==TRUE)/length(df) *100
+ })
Output
Ozone     Solar.R      Wind       Temp       Month        Day
24.183007  4.575163  0.000000   0.000000   0.000000   0.000000
```

5. You can see attributes `Wind`, `Temp`, `Month`, and `Day` have no missing value. Besides simply viewing the percentage of missing data, one may also use the `Amelia` package to visualize the missing values. Here, we use `install.packages` and `require` to install `Amelia` and load the package. The `Amelia` package requires `Rcpp`, which will get installed automatically, by using the following commands:

```
> install.packages("Amelia")
> require(Amelia)
```

6. Then, use the `missmap` function to plot the missing value map:

```
> missmap(mydata, main="Missing Map")
```

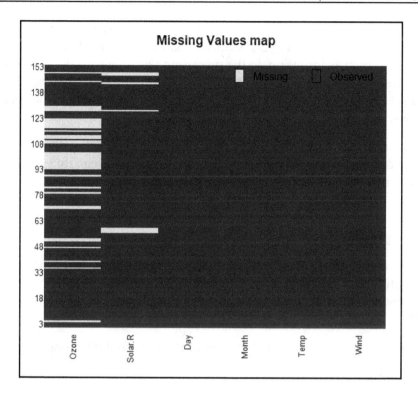

Missing map of the airquality dataset

How it works...

In any dataset there is always a chance that some values are missing. In R, a missing value is often noted with the NA symbol, which stands for not available. Almost all the functions in R have some way to deal with missing values, for example, the mean or sum function will not work with NA. Consider the following simple example where a vector with missing value NA is created. When we try to find the mean it gives NA as an answer due to NA values in a set. The mean function also supports a parameter na.rm that removes NA from the set and computes the mean:

```
> t = c(1,2,3,NA,4,5) # Created a vector with missing value
> mean(t) # finding mean will give NA
[1] NA
> mean(t, na.rm = TRUE) # using na.rm = TRUE will work
[1] 3
```

This approach works as most of the functions provide the workaround to deal with the NA value. It is always better to remove such values or observations from the set. Removing the NA values is also known as imputing. In the preceding recipe, we used `an.na` function to find the NA values in observation. In the next step we compute the percentage of missing values in the set. Using the `sapply` function, we compute the missing values percentage for all observations.

To visualize the missing values, the `Amelia` package is used, which will plot the missing value map for each observations on one chart. From the plot it is clearly visible that `Ozone` observation or attribute has maximum missing values followed by `Solar.R`.

There's more...

To handle the missing values, we introduced `Amelia` to visualize them. Apart from typing console commands, you can also use the interactive GUI of `Amelia` and `AmeliaView`, which allows users to load datasets, manage options, and run `Amelia` from a windowed environment.

To start running `AmeliaView`, simply type `AmeliaView()` in the R Console:

```
> AmeliaView()
```

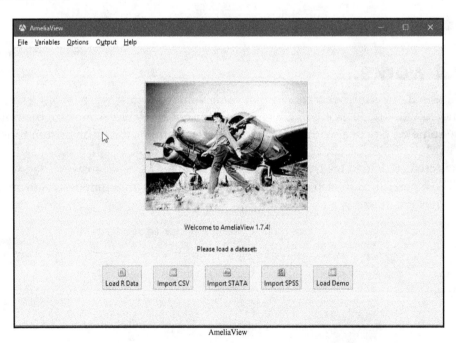

AmeliaView

Imputing missing values

After detecting the number of missing values within each attribute, we have to impute them since they might have a significant effect on the conclusions that can be drawn from the data.

Getting ready

This recipe will require `mydata` to be loaded in the R session and have the previous recipe completed.

How to do it...

Perform the following steps to impute the missing values:

1. List the `Ozone` attribute:

```
> mydata$Ozone
Output
  [1]  41  36  12  18  NA  28  23  19   8  NA   7  16  11  14  18  14  34   6  30  11
 [21]   1  11   4  32  NA  NA  NA  23  45 115  37  NA  NA  NA  NA  NA  NA  29  NA  71
 [41]  39  NA  NA  23  NA  NA  21  37  20  12  13  NA  NA  NA  NA  NA  NA  NA  NA  NA
 [61]  NA 135  49  32  NA  64  40  77  97  97  85  NA  10  27  NA   7  48  35  61  79
 [81]  63  16  NA  NA  80 108  20  52  82  50  64  59  39   9  16  78  35  66 122  89
[101] 110  NA  NA  44  28  65  NA  22  59  23  31  44  21   9  NA  45 168  73  NA  76
[121] 118  84  85  96  78  73  91  47  32  20  23  21  24  44  21  28   9  13  46  18
[141]  13  24  16  13  23  36   7  14  30  NA  14  18  20
```

2. We want to replace the `NA` values with the most repeated observation. Use the `table` command to find the frequency of the observations:

```
> max(table((factor(mydata$Ozone)),useNA="always"))
Output
 1  4  6  7  8  9 10 11 12 13 14 16 18 19 20 21 22
 1  1  1  3  1  3  1  3  2  4  4  4  4  1  4  4  1
23 24 27 28 29 30 31 32 34 35 36 37 39 40 41 44 45
 6  2  1  3  1  2  1  3  1  2  2  2  2  1  1  3  2
46 47 48 49 50 52 59 61 63 64 65 66 71 73 76 77 78
 1  1  1  1  1  1  2  1  1  2  1  1  1  2  1  1  2
79 80 82 84 85 89 91 96 97 108 110 115 118 122 135 168 <NA>
 1  1  1  1  2  1  1  1  2   1   1   1   1   1   1   1   37
```

You can see that last <NA> holds value 37, which means NA is repeated 37 times in the Ozone attribute. To find the max number use max:

```
> max(table((factor(mydata$Ozone))))
Output
[1] 6
```

You can see 6 is the highest number and it stands for 23, which means 23 is repeated six times, which is the maximum repeated value in the Ozone attribute observation. Now it's time to replace NA with 23. Remember: This is not the correct way as it will replace 37 NA values with 23, finding the average and replacing may be a better way:

```
> mydata$Ozone[which(is.na(mydata$Ozone))]=23
> table((factor(mydata$Ozone)),useNA="always")
Output


  1  4  6  7  8  9 10 11 12 13 14 16 18 19 20 21 22
  1  1  1  3  1  3  1  3  2  4  4  4  4  1  4  4  1
 23 24 27 28 29 30 31 32 34 35 36 37 39 40 41 44 45
 43  2  1  3  1  2  1  3  1  2  2  2  2  1  1  3  2
 46 47 48 49 50 52 59 61 63 64 65 66 71 73 76 77 78
  1  1  1  1  1  1  2  1  1  2  1  1  1  2  1  1  2
 79 80 82 84 85 89 91 96 97 108 110 115 118 122 135 168 <NA>
  1  1  1  1  2  1  1  1  2  1   1   1   1   1   1   1   0
```

1. Use the same steps for the Solar.R attribute:

```
> table((factor(mydata$Solar.R)),useNA="always")
Output


  7  8 13 14 19 20 24 25 27 31 36 37 44 47 48 49 51
  1  1  1  1  1  1  2  1  1  1  1  1  1  1  1  1  1
 59 64 65 66 71 77 78 81 82 83 91 92 95 98 99 101 112
  1  1  1  1  1  1  1  1  1  1  1  2  1  1  1  1   1
115 118 120 127 131 135 137 138 139 145 148 149 150 153 157 167
175
  1   1   2   1   1   2   1   2   1   1   1   1   1   1   1   3
183 186 187 188 189 190 191 192 193 194 197 201 203 207 212 213
215
  1   1   1   1   1   2   2   1   1   1   1   1   1   1   1   1
220 222 223 224 225 229 230 236 237 238 242 244 248 250 252 253
254
  3   1   3   1   1   1   1   2   2   4   1   1   1   2   2   1   1
255 256 258 259 260 264 266 267 269 272 273 274 275 276 279 284
285
  2   1   1   4   1   2   1   1   1   1   2   2   1   1   1   1
```

```
     286 287 290 291 294 295 299 307 313 314 320 322 323 332 334 <NA>
       1   1   2   1   1   1   1   1   1   1   2   1   1   1   1   7
> max(table((factor(mydata$Solar.R))))
Output
[1] 4
> mydata$Solar.R[which(is.na(mydata$Solar.R))]=259
> table((factor(mydata$Solar.R)),useNA="always")
Output

       7   8  13  14  19  20  24  25  27  31  36  37  44  47  48  49  51
       1   1   1   1   1   1   2   1   1   1   1   1   1   1   1   1   1
      59  64  65  66  71  77  78  81  82  83  91  92  95  98  99 101 112
       1   1   1   1   1   1   1   1   1   1   1   2   1   1   1   1   1
     115 118 120 127 131 135 137 138 139 145 148 149 150 153 157 167
     175
       1   1   2   1   1   2   1   2   1   1   1   1   1   1   1   3
     183 186 187 188 189 190 191 192 193 194 197 201 203 207 212 213
     215
       1   1   1   1   1   2   2   1   1   1   1   1   1   1   1   1   1
     220 222 223 224 225 229 230 236 237 238 242 244 248 250 252 253
     254
       3   1   3   1   1   1   1   2   4   1   1   1   2   2   1   1
     255 256 258 259 260 264 266 267 269 272 273 274 275 276 279 284
     285
       2   1   1  11   1   2   1   1   1   1   2   2   1   1   1   1   1
     286 287 290 291 294 295 299 307 313 314 320 322 323 332 334 <NA>
       1   1   2   1   1   1   1   1   1   1   2   1   1   1   0
```

The Solar.R attribute now contains no NA values.

How it works...

To impute the missing value of the Ozone attribute, we first produce the statistics of the Ozone with the table function. The table function counts 37 NA values in mydata. Using the max function on the table we find the highest count excluding the NA, which is 6, and we can see that 23 is repeated six times. Since we do not have any knowledge about the exact value for NA we assume it can be 23 or near to 23 in most cases. We replace NA with 23. This approach can be changed to find the average or some other ways to find the appropriate value. We repeat the same procedure for the Solar.R attribute.

In some cases, if attributes have so many missing values we can decide that it cannot be used for further analysis.

Exploring and visualizing data

After imputing the missing values, one should perform an exploratory analysis, which involves using a visualization plot and an aggregation method to summarize the data characteristics. The result helps the user gain a better understanding of the data in use. The following recipe will introduce how to use basic plotting techniques with a view to help the user with exploratory analysis.

Getting ready

This recipe needs the previous recipe to be completed by imputing the missing value in the Ozone and Solar.R attribute.

How to do it...

Perform the following steps to explore and visualize data:

1. First, you can use a bar plot and histogram to generate descriptive statistics for each attribute, starting with Ozone. The following code gives us a bar plot for Ozone Observations:

```
> barplot(table(mydata$Ozone), main="Ozone Observations",
xlab="O bservations", ylab="Frequency")
```

Ozone observation

2. We can generate the bar plot of `Temp` using the following code:

```
> barplot(table(mydata$Temp), main="Temperature Observations",
xlab="Temprature", ylab="Frequency")
```

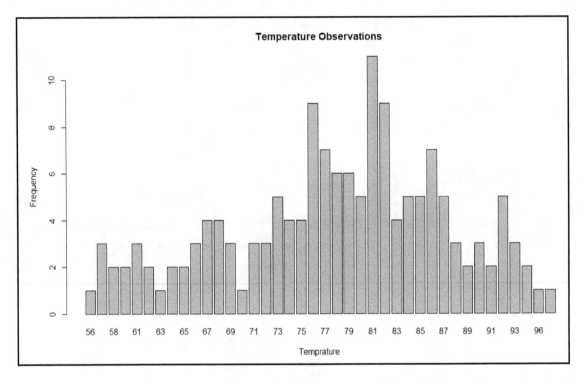

Temperature observation

3. In the same way you can generate bar plots for other attributes.

4. We then plot the histogram of the different `Temp` with the `hist` function:

```
> hist(mydata$Temp,  main="Temperature", xlab = " Temperature ")
```

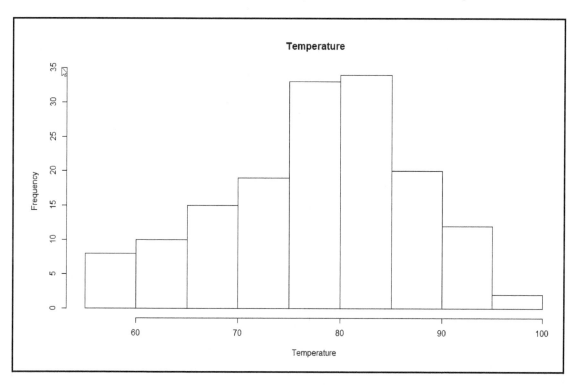

Temperature observation

5. The histogram will select appropriate bins, but it can be changed using the `breaks` arguments:

```
> hist(mydata$Temp,  main="Temperature", xlab = " Temperature ",
breaks= 5)
```

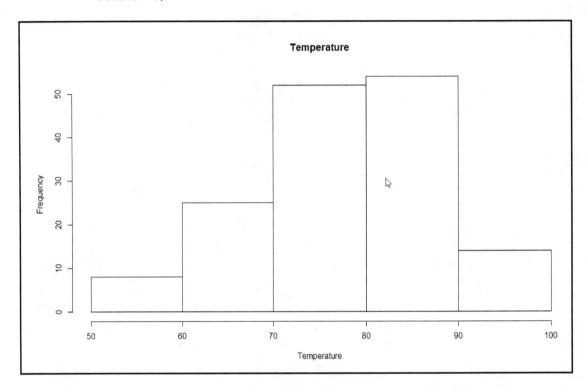

Temperature observation using breaks

6. Instead of printing using density, you can also use relative frequency using the `prob` argument:

```
> hist(mydata$Temp,  main="Temperature", xlab = " Temperature ",
prob=TRUE)
```

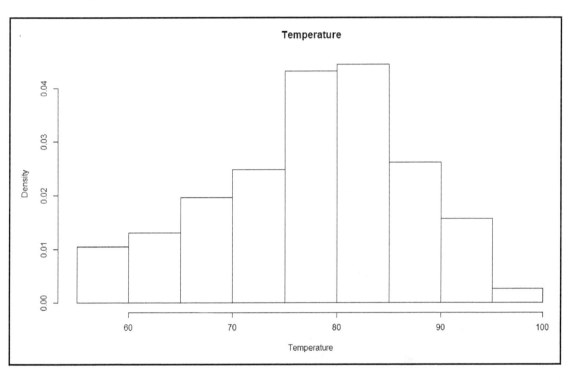

Temperature observation using breaks

7. Use the `summary` function, on the `Temp` attribute:

```
> summary(mydata)
Output
 Ozone Solar.R Wind Temp Month
 Min. : 1.00 Min. : 7.0 Min. : 1.700 Min. :56.00 Min. :5.000
 1st Qu.: 21.00 1st Qu.:120.0 1st Qu.: 7.400 1st Qu.:72.00 1st
Qu.:6.000
 Median : 23.00 Median :215.0 Median : 9.700 Median :79.00 Median
:7.000
 Mean : 47.65 Mean :189.3 Mean : 9.958 Mean :77.88 Mean :6.993
 3rd Qu.: 52.00 3rd Qu.:259.0 3rd Qu.:11.500 3rd Qu.:85.00 3rd
Qu.:8.000
 Max. :259.00 Max. :334.0 Max. :20.700 Max. :97.00 Max. :9.000
```

```
Day
Min.  : 1.0
1st Qu.: 8.0
Median :16.0
Mean  :15.8
3rd Qu.:23.0
Max.  :31.0

> boxplot(mydata)
```

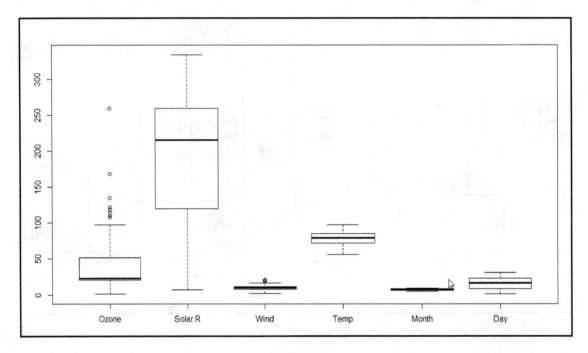

Boxplot for mydata

8. A box plot can also be generated for only one attribute:

```
> summary(mydata$Temp)
 Min. 1st Qu. Median Mean 3rd Qu. Max.
 56.00 72.00 79.00 77.88 85.00 97.00
> boxplot(mydata$Temp)
```

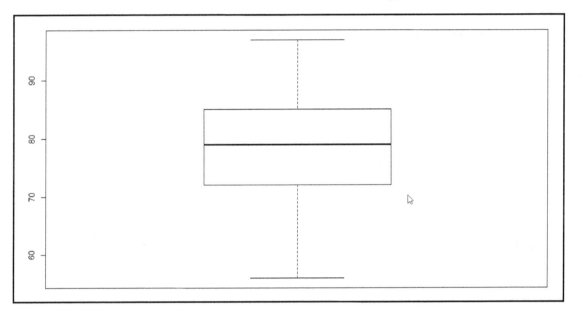

Box plot for temperature

9. To print the box plot for every month and temperature, use the following:

```
> boxplot(mydata$Temp ~ mydata$Month, main="Month Wise
Temperature",
xlab="Month", ylab="Temperature")
```

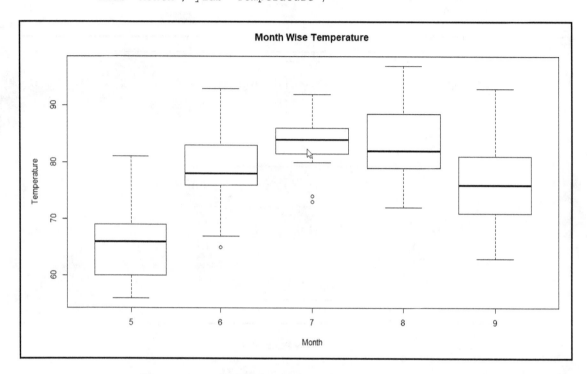

Box plot of temperature and months

Before we start predicting the values we need to find the relationship between attributes. Perform the following command to plot the `Temp` versus all other attributes and it will display different scatter plots one by one. A total of four plots will be generated:

```
> plot(mydata$Temp ~ mydata$Day + mydata$Solar.R + mydata$Wind +
mydata$Ozone, col="blue")
```

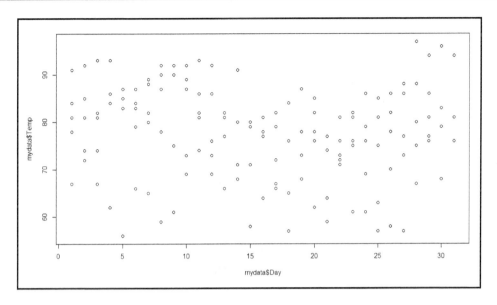

Scatter plot of temperature and Day

On the console it will display the following:

```
Hit <Return> to see next plot:
Press enter and second plot will be displayed
```

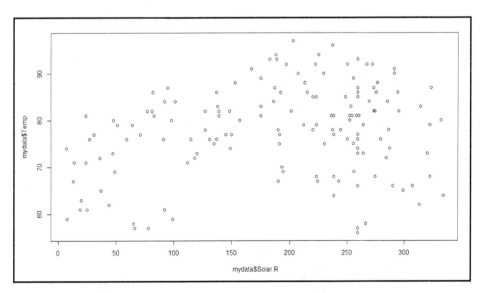

Scatter plot of temperature and Solar.R

On the console it will display the following:

```
Hit <Return> to see next plot:
Press enter and third plot will be displayed
```

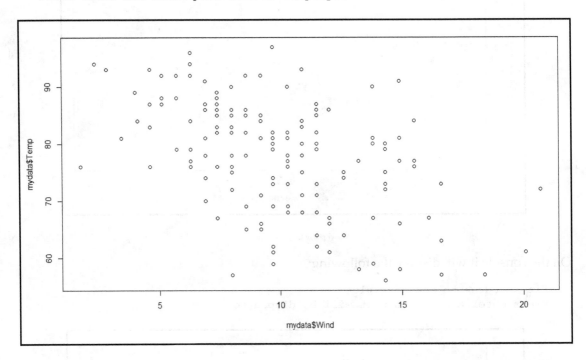

Scatter plot of temperature and Wind

On the console it will display the following:

```
Hit <Return> to see next plot:
Press enter and fourth plot will be displayed
```

Scatter plot of temperature and Ozone

From the scatter plot we can see that there is a linear relationship between temperature and all other attributes except wind. Wind holds a negative relationship with temperature.

Predicting values from datasets

The exploratory analysis helps users gain insights into single or multiple variables. However, it does not determine what combinations may generate a prediction model, so as to predict the temperature. On the other hand, machine learning can generate a prediction model from a training dataset, so that the user can apply the model to predict the possible labels from the given attributes. In this recipe, we will introduce how to predict the temperature and find the correlation between attributes.

Getting ready

We will use the data, `mydata`, which we have already used in previous recipes.

How to do it...

Before predicting we need to see how variables are related and what is the confidence level. We need a `corrplot` package to see this. Perform the following steps to find the correlation matrix and confidence interval:

```
> install.packages("corrplot")
> require(corrplot)
> mydata$Month = airquality$Month # Removing factors, using original data
Following command will generate the correlation plot of mydata
> corrplot(cor(mydata),method="number")
```

Correlation plot

`corrplot` will produce a correlation matrix and we can easily see how variables or attributes are related to each other. We can now start predicting, perform the following steps to predict; the temperature for the given Ozone concentration:

```
> attach(mydata)
> reg <- lm(Temp~Ozone)
> summary(reg)
Output
Call:
lm(formula = Temp ~ Ozone)
Residuals:
     Min        1Q    Median        3Q       Max
-29.2983   -5.4734    0.9827    5.9827   18.1230
Coefficients:
              Estimate Std. Error t value Pr(>|t|)
(Intercept)  76.21024    0.99623  76.499   <2e-16 ***
Ozone         0.03509    0.01372   2.557   0.0115 *
---
Signif. codes:  0 '***' 0.001 '**' 0.01 '*' 0.05 '.' 0.1 ' ' 1
Residual standard error: 9.297 on 151 degrees of freedom
Multiple R-squared:  0.04151, Adjusted R-squared:  0.03517
F-statistic:  6.54 on 1 and 151 DF,  p-value: 0.01153
> predict(reg, data.frame(Ozone=c(80)))
Output
       1
79.01735
```

1. Let's create a model and predict the temperature:

```
> Solar.R = 190
> Wind = 10
> Ozone = 45
> Month = 9
> new_data = data.frame(Solar.R,Wind,Ozone,Month)
> new_data
Output
  Solar.R Wind Ozone Month
1     190   10    45     9
> reg<-lm(Temp~Ozone+Solar.R+Month,mydata)
> predict(reg,newdata = new_data)
Output
       1
83.76764
```

How it works...

This recipe introduces how to create a correlation matrix using `corrplot`, it displays coefficients in different colors. Before using `corrplot` we need to remove the factors from the month, we simply replace month in `mydata` with `airquality` month. We can generate different visualizations in `corrplot` by changing method argument to `circle`, `pie`, `color`, `shade`, `ellipse` and so on:

```
> corrplot(cor(mydata),method="color")
```

Using `method` as `color` will generate the following figure:

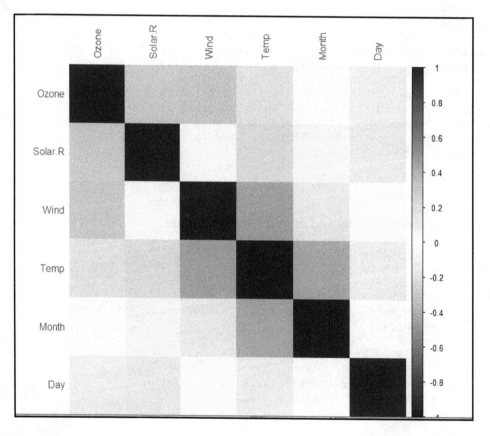

Using method = color

```
> corrplot(cor(mydata),method="circle")
```

Using method as circle will generate the following figure:

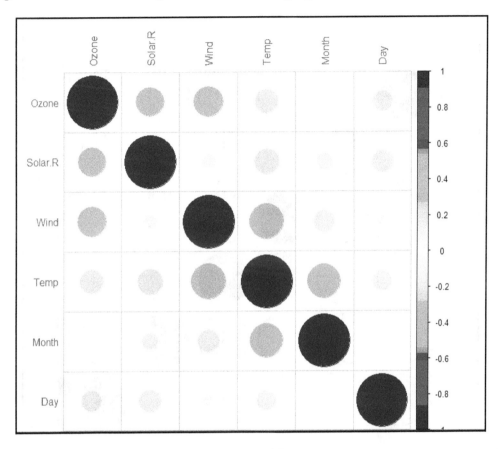

Using method = circle

```
> corrplot(cor(mydata),method="pie")
```

Using `method` as `pie` will generate the following figure:

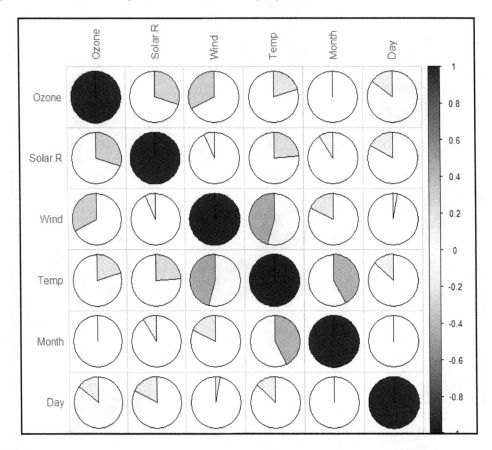

Using method = pie

In the next step we have used the `lm` function to form a linear regression model. Before that using the `attach` function we attached our `mydata` dataset to the search path, hence we can now write `Month` instead of `mydata$Month`. We stored the model in `reg` and printed the summary for `reg`. It will give us all required values for regression such as residuals, coefficients, errors, and so on. Using the `predict` function we pass our model and value of ozone concentration to predict the temperature from the dataset.

We create a regression using all the attributes and predict the temperature for given Ozone, `Solar.R`, and Wind in a given Month.

3
Analyzing Time Series Data

In this chapter, we will cover the following topics:

- Introduction to time series
- Looking at time series data
- Plotting and forecasting time series data
- Learning extracting, subnetting, merging, filling, and padding
- Successive differences and moving averages
- Exponential smoothing
- Plotting the autocorrelation function

Introduction

When we think about time, we think about years, days, months, hours, minutes, and seconds. Think of any datasets and you will find some attributes which will be in the form of time, especially data related to stock, sales, purchase, profit, and loss. All these have time associated with them. For example, the price of stock in the stock exchange at different points on a given day or month or year. Think of any industry domain, and sales are an important factor; you can see time series in sales, discounts, customers, and so on. Other domains include but are not limited to statistics, economics and budgets, processes and quality control, finance, weather forecasting, or any kind of forecasting, transport, logistics, astronomy, patient study, census analysis, and the list goes on. In simple words, it contains data or observations in time order, spaced at equal intervals.

Time series analysis means finding the meaning in the time-related data to predict what will happen next or forecast trends on the basis of observed values. There are many methods to fit the time series, smooth the random variation, and get some insights from the dataset.

When you look at time series data you can see the following:

- **Trend**: Long term increase or decrease in the observations or data.
- **Pattern**: Sudden spike in sales due to christmas or some other festivals, drug consumption increases due to some condition; this type of data has a fixed time duration and can be predicted for future time also.
- **Cycle**: Can be thought of as a pattern that is not fixed; it rises and falls without any pattern. Such time series involve a great fluctuation in data.

Looking at time series data

We will start with looking at some already existing time series datasets. We will move on to creating or defining our own time series on the basis of some hypothetical case. We will see how to work with time series. We will also use some packages specifically created for handling time series.

Getting ready

There are many datasets available with R that are of the time series types. Using the command class, one can know if the dataset is time series or not. We will look into the AirPassengers dataset that shows monthly air passengers in thousands from 1949 to 1960. We will also create new time series to represent the data.

How to do it...

Perform the following commands in RStudio or R Console:

```
> class(AirPassengers)
Output:
[1] "ts"
> start(AirPassengers)
Output:
[1] 1949 1
> end(AirPassengers)
Output:
[1] 1960 12
> summary(AirPassengers)
Output:
   Min.  1st Qu.  Median    Mean 3rd Qu.    Max.
  104.0   180.0   265.5   280.3   360.5   622.0
```

In the next recipe, we will create the time series and print it out.

Let's think of the share price of some company in the range of 2,500 to 4,000 from 2011 to be recorded monthly. Perform the following codeing in R:

```
> my_vector = sample(2500:4000, 72, replace=T)
> my_series = ts(my_vector, start=c(2011,1), end=c(2016,12), frequency =
12)
> my_series
Output:
      Jan  Feb  Mar  Apr  May  Jun  Jul  Aug  Sep  Oct  Nov  Dec
2011 2888 3894 3675 3113 3421 3870 2644 2677 3392 2847 2543 3147
2012 2973 3538 3632 2695 3475 3971 2695 2963 3217 2836 3525 2895
2013 3984 3811 2902 3602 3812 3631 2625 3887 3601 2581 3645 3324
2014 3830 2821 3794 3942 3504 3526 3932 3246 3787 2894 2800 2732
2015 3326 3659 2993 2765 3881 3983 3813 3172 2667 3517 3445 2805
2016 3668 3948 2779 2881 3285 2733 3203 3329 3854 3285 3800 2563
```

How it works...

In the first recipe, we used the `AirPassengers` dataset, using the `class` function. We saw that it is `ts` (`ts` stands for time series). The `start` and `end` functions will give the starting year and ending year of the dataset with the values. The `frequency` function tells us the interval of observations; 1 means annually, 4 means quarterly, 12 means yearly, and so on.

In the next recipe, we want to generate samples between 2,500 to 40,000 to represent the price of a share. Using a sample function, we can create a sample; it takes the range as the first argument, and the number of samples required as the second argument. The last argument decides whether duplication is to be allowed in the sample or not. We stored the sample in the `my_vector`. Now we create a time series using the `ts` function. The `ts` function takes the vector as an argument followed by the `start` and `end` to show the period for which the time series is being constructed. The `frequency` specifies the number of observations in the `start` and `end` to be recorded. 12. In the next step we print the `my_series` and can see the time series created for 2001 to 2016 for every month.

See also

- Apart from `AirPassengers`, many datasets are of type `ts`; that is, time series. Use `data ()` to list all the datasets and use the `class` function on datasets to see whether it is time series or not

Plotting and forecasting time series data

Once we have a time series dataset, we want to plot the time series to see the trend. We can also forecast from the given time series.

Getting ready

You have completed the previous recipe and have `my_series` time series ready. You also need to install a forecast package.

How to do it...

Perform the following steps in R:

```
> plot(my_series)
```

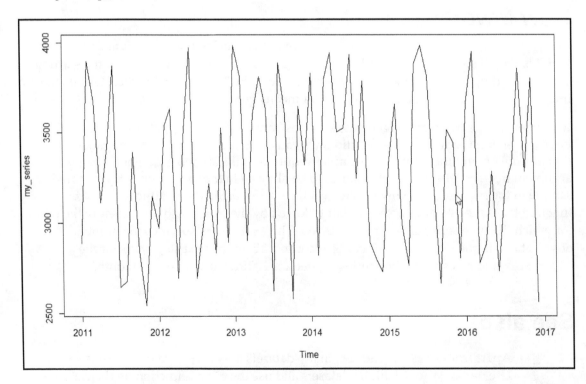

Plot of m y_series

```
> plot(AirPassengers)
```

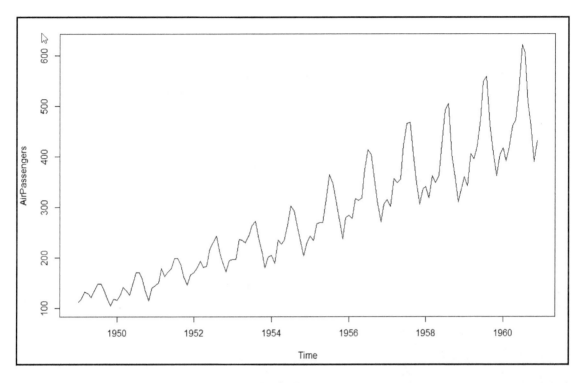

Plot of AirPassengers

```
> cycle(AirPassengers)
Output:
     Jan Feb Mar Apr May Jun Jul Aug Sep Oct Nov Dec
1949  1   2   3   4   5   6   7   8   9  10  11  12
1950  1   2   3   4   5   6   7   8   9  10  11  12
1951  1   2   3   4   5   6   7   8   9  10  11  12
1952  1   2   3   4   5   6   7   8   9  10  11  12
1953  1   2   3   4   5   6   7   8   9  10  11  12
1954  1   2   3   4   5   6   7   8   9  10  11  12
1955  1   2   3   4   5   6   7   8   9  10  11  12
1956  1   2   3   4   5   6   7   8   9  10  11  12
1957  1   2   3   4   5   6   7   8   9  10  11  12
1958  1   2   3   4   5   6   7   8   9  10  11  12
1959  1   2   3   4   5   6   7   8   9  10  11  12
1960  1   2   3   4   5   6   7   8   9  10  11  12
> aggregate(AirPassengers)
Output:
Time Series:
```

```
Start = 1949
End = 1960
Frequency = 1
  [1] 1520 1676 2042 2364 2700 2867 3408 3939 4421 4572 5140 5714

> plot(aggregate(AirPassengers))
```

Plot of AirPassengers using aggregate

```
> boxplot(AirPassengers~cycle(AirPassengers))
```

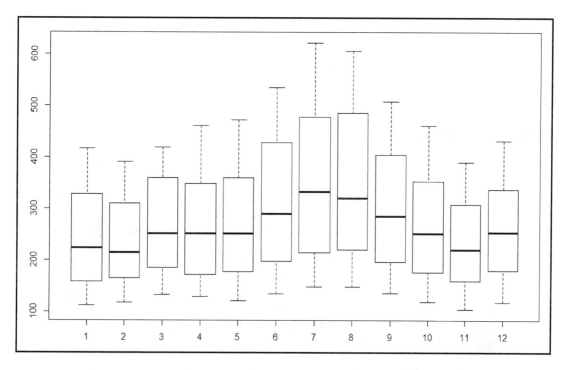

Box plot to see month wise pattern

```
> install.packages("forecast")
> require(forecast)
> forecast(my_series, 4)
Output:
         Point Forecast    Lo 80     Hi 80     Lo 95     Hi 95
Jan 2017        3306.796 2722.674 3890.918 2413.459 4200.133
Feb 2017        3306.796 2722.674 3890.918 2413.459 4200.133
Mar 2017        3306.796 2722.674 3890.918 2413.459 4200.133
Apr 2017        3306.796 2722.674 3890.918 2413.459 4200.133

> f = HoltWinters(my_series)
> forecast(f,4)
Output:
         Point Forecast    Lo 80     Hi 80     Lo 95     Hi 95
Jan 2017        3597.549 2944.407 4250.691 2598.655 4596.444
Feb 2017        3701.691 3048.549 4354.833 2702.797 4700.585
Mar 2017        3172.856 2519.714 3825.997 2173.961 4171.750
Apr 2017        3106.034 2452.892 3759.176 2107.140 4104.928
```

```
> forecast(AirPassengers, 4)
Output:
          Point Forecast    Lo 80     Hi 80     Lo 95     Hi 95
Jan 1961        441.7479  420.9284  462.5675  409.9071  473.5887
Feb 1961        433.0931  407.5924  458.5938  394.0931  472.0931
Mar 1961        496.6067  462.3205  530.8930  444.1705  549.0430
Apr 1961        483.5263  445.6985  521.3541  425.6737  541.3790
```

How it works...

The `plot` function will plot the time series with the time intervals on the *x* axis and observations on the *y* values. From the plot, one can see the where things are heading. In the air passenger plot, the number of passengers are steadily increasing. With `my_series`, the prices go up and down in the given graph. In the year 2014, the prices are at an all-time high. From the plotting, one can make out the trends and get some vital insight.

The `cycle` function gives the position of the observation in a cycle. The `aggregate` function splits the data and gives the summary of the subset. In our case, it splits the data into years and presents the total of number of passengers traveling in a year. Plotting the aggregate gives a clearer picture of the time series. We create a box plot the cycle to see how the months taken together for years affects the number of passengers. We can try to see if any seasonal pattern is there or not.

Based on the dataset of the past, one can predict or forecast for the coming time using the `forecast` package. The `forecast` package can be made directly from the time series or using some methods to remove the randomness and smooth the curve to forecast. We used a forecast on pure time series and in the next step we used the forecast on the fitted model using a Holt-Winters filtering using the Holt-Winters function and forecast the value for the next four months. Holt-Winters is used for exponential smoothing, which is covered later in this chapter.

See also

Instead of using the forecast directly on the time series, we can create a model using exponential smoothing, Holts exponential smoothing, and Holt-Winter smoothing, and perform the forecast. Apart from this, the ARIMA model can also be used. Refer to the CRAN website for more details.

Extracting, subsetting, merging, filling, and padding

Time series may contain large observations spanning many years. You may want to work on a specific portion of time series; for example, finding the sales for first 3 months, or sales for the last 3 months, or sales between 2007 to 2009, and so on. This section will explore various ways to get the required or desired data or subset from the time series.

Getting ready

You have completed the preceding recipes and should be familiar with the time series data now. You have `my_series` time series ready from the previous recipe.

How to do it...

Perform the following steps in R:

```
> head(my_series)
Output:

      Jan  Feb  Mar  Apr  May  Jun
2011 2888 3894 3675 3113 3421 3870
> tail(my_series)
Output:

      Jul  Aug  Sep  Oct  Nov  Dec
2016 3203 3329 3854 3285 3800 2563
> tail(my_series, 20)
Output:

      Jan  Feb  Mar  Apr  May  Jun  Jul  Aug  Sep  Oct  Nov  Dec
2015                     3881 3983 3813 3172 2667 3517 3445 2805
2016 3668 3948 2779 2881 3285 2733 3203 3329 3854 3285 3800 2563
> head(my_series,5)
Output:

      Jan  Feb  Mar  Apr  May
2011 2888 3894 3675 3113 3421

> require(xts)
> first(my_series)
Output:
```

```
[1] 2888

> last(my_series)
Output:

[1] 2563

> first(my_series, "3 months")
Output:

[1] 2888 3894 3675

> first(my_series, "3 years")
Output:

 [1] 2888 3894 3675 3113 3421 3870 2644 2677 3392 2847 2543 3147 2973 3538
3632 2695
[17] 3475 3971 2695 2963 3217 2836 3525 2895 3984 3811 2902 3602 3812 3631
2625 3887
[33] 3601 2581 3645 3324

> last(my_series, "3 months")
Output:

[1] 3285 3800 2563

> last(my_series, "3 years")
Output:

 [1] 3830 2821 3794 3942 3504 3526 3932 3246 3787 2894 2800 2732 3326 3659
2993 2765
[17] 3881 3983 3813 3172 2667 3517 3445 2805 3668 3948 2779 2881 3285 2733
3203 3329
[33] 3854 3285 3800 2563

> window(my_series, start=c(2009,1), end=c(2013,12))
Output:

      Jan  Feb  Mar  Apr  May  Jun  Jul  Aug  Sep  Oct  Nov  Dec
2011 2888 3894 3675 3113 3421 3870 2644 2677 3392 2847 2543 3147
2012 2973 3538 3632 2695 3475 3971 2695 2963 3217 2836 3525 2895
2013 3984 3811 2902 3602 3812 3631 2625 3887 3601 2581 3645 3324

> my_series1 = ts(my_vector1, start=c(2011,1), end=c(2013,12), frequency =
4)
> my_series1[c(2,5,10,13)]=NA
> my_series1
Output:
```

```
     Qtr1 Qtr2 Qtr3 Qtr4
2011  866   NA  497  650
2012   NA  601  740  576
2013  852   NA  569  864
2014   NA  434  686  845
2015 1000  725  789  613
> mean(my_series1, na.rm = TRUE)
Output:

[1] 706.6875
> my_series1[is.na(my_series1)]=706
> my_series1
Output:

     Qtr1 Qtr2 Qtr3 Qtr4
2011  866  706  497  650
2012  706  601  740  576
2013  852  706  569  864
2014  706  434  686  845
2015 1000  725  789  613
```

How it works...

The head and tail functions lets you extract data from the start and end part from the datasets. The head and tail serve a purpose only if you know the numbers of the data points to be extracted. For example, get 10 data at the start or at the end of the dataset. But this will be not always be the case. In time series, you may want to extract data in a form such as extracting the last 3 months of data or 3 weeks of data, and so on. It will be tedious with head and tail functions to find the exact number. The zoo and xts package provides the first and last functions that can be used to extract data from the time series in the required fashion. Using this function, you can clearly extract data for 3 months, 3 years, and so on. To get the subset in the form of a range, the window function is used; for example; extract data from the starting year 2011 to the ending year 2014.

See also

- Look in to the xts and zoo package; they provide a great way to create, convert, and handle the time series in R

Successive differences and moving averages

A successive difference means the difference between the successive observations. For time series y, the successive difference will be *(y2-y1), (y3-y2), (y4-y3)*.

The moving average is used to understand the direction of the current trend.

The moving average will smooth the data if there is a variation in consecutive points. It will smoothen the curve on the base of the average.

R does not have any direct implementation of the moving average, but `zoo` and the `forecast` package provides the various functions to find the moving average.

Getting ready

You have completed the preceding recipes and have `my_series` and `my_series1` in R available.

How to do it...

Perform the following steps with R:

```
> ma(my_series, order=10)
Output:

          Jan      Feb      Mar      Apr      May      Jun      Jul      Aug      Sep
2011       NA       NA       NA       NA       NA  3224.85  3170.25  3097.80
3083.95
2012  3156.60  3186.45  3157.40  3196.90  3215.05  3227.10  3222.55  3208.00
3281.40
2013  3388.10  3391.90  3414.85  3471.20  3459.30  3426.65  3385.35  3407.40
3414.75
2014  3474.85  3473.35  3523.15  3563.50  3549.10  3476.10  3420.15  3392.30
3354.75
2015  3245.15  3283.30  3298.50  3305.75  3338.35  3383.55  3346.80  3337.85
3430.75
2016  3194.75  3199.60  3217.00  3228.05  3272.50  3303.10  3240.45       NA
NA
          Oct      Nov      Dec
2011  3115.75  3067.55  3050.35
2012  3308.55  3261.45  3298.85
```

```
2013 3374.80 3389.45 3448.95
2014 3315.05 3251.45 3210.85
2015 3434.80 3324.60 3243.10
2016      NA      NA      NA


> plot(ma(my_series, order=10))
```

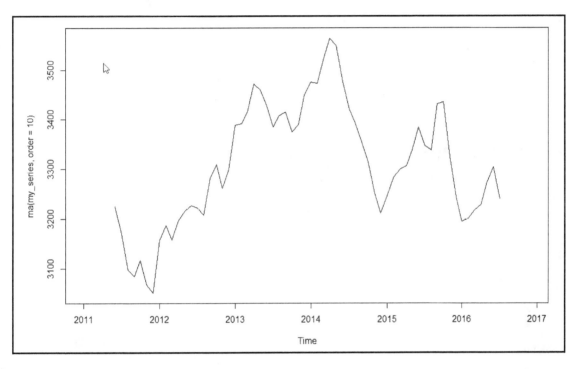

Plot of my_series after using moving average

How it works...

The ma function will compute the moving average; in the process, it may eliminate some data to avoid randomness in the data. It will smother averages to the nearest order period of each observation.

See also

Look into the `zoo` package; it has many methods for computing rolling mean, median, max, and many more functions related to time series.

Exponential smoothing

In moving averages, all observations are weighted equally, whereas in exponential smoothing, the weights are assigned in exponentially decreasing order as the observation gets older. This ensures that the recent or latest observations are given more weightage as compared to older observations and thus can forecast on the basis of recent observations.

Getting ready

You have completed the preceding recipes and the `AirPassengers` dataset is available or loaded in R.

How to do it...

Perform the following steps with R:

```
> library(forecast)
> t = ets(AirPassengers)
> t
Output:

ETS(M,Ad,M)

Call:
 ets(y = AirPassengers)

  Smoothing parameters:
    alpha = 0.7322
    beta  = 0.0188
    gamma = 1e-04
    phi   = 0.98

  Initial states:
    l = 120.9759
    b = 1.8015
    s=0.8929 0.7984 0.9211 1.0604 1.2228 1.2324
```

```
      1.1107 0.9807 0.9807 1.0106 0.8843 0.9051

  sigma:   0.0368

      AIC       AICc       BIC
  1395.092 1400.564 1448.548


> plot(t)
```

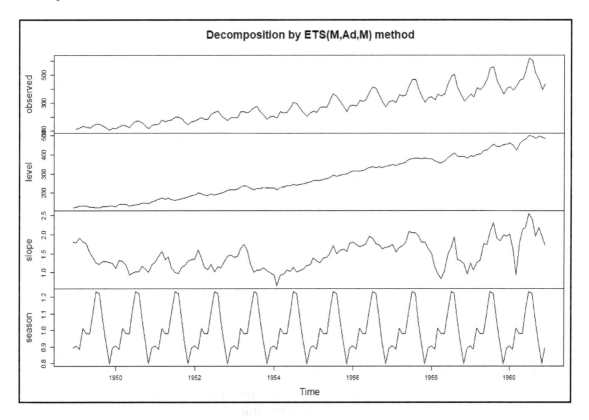

Plot of ets showing all different plot

```
> val = forecast(t)
> plot(val)
```

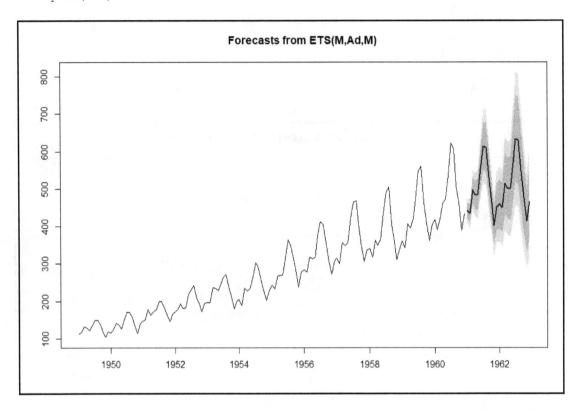

Forecast from exponential smoothing

How it works...

The `ets` function is an exponential smoothing state space model, which created the `ets` model from the time series. It estimates the initial value and smoothing parameters by optimizing the likelihood function.

See also

Look into Holt-Winters function discussed in the previous topic; it is also used for exponential smoothing.

Plotting the autocorrelation function

The autocorrelation function, is very important if you want to find the interrelationship between time series using the lagged values. The `acf` function will plot the correlation between all pairs of data points with lagged values. The plot will have two horizontal blue dashed lines at -0.2 and 0.2, representing the upper and lower bounds. If auto-correlation coefficients are close to zero, this means that there is no relationship, so time series are also known as white noise.

Getting ready

You have already completed the previous recipes and familiar with time series.

How to do it...

Perform the following steps with R:

```
> sales = sample(400:10000, 72, replace= TRUE)
> sales
Output:

 [1] 3304 7697 6715 3906 8963 9240 1423 5330 8298 7747 1686 2917 2004 4591
2213 1977
[17] 1101 7624 2814 4002 8284 6016 5875 6936 1336 6090 4190 7437 1968 3070
4013 5186
[33] 6560 7981 5496 8818 1991 3531 4624  895 5720 8481  826  435 6940 1723
9797 8261
[49] 8811 4933 6746 3978  913 5003 2372 3530 4724 7202 2765 4096 9258 8650
2719 7634
[65] 5129 5096 5449 7352 2729 5035 6370 9327
> my_newseries = ts(sales, start=c(2011,1), end=c(2016,12), frequency = 12)
> my_newseries
Output:

       Jan  Feb  Mar  Apr  May  Jun  Jul  Aug  Sep  Oct  Nov  Dec
2011  3304 7697 6715 3906 8963 9240 1423 5330 8298 7747 1686 2917
```

```
2012 2004 4591 2213 1977 1101 7624 2814 4002 8284 6016 5875 6936
2013 1336 6090 4190 7437 1968 3070 4013 5186 6560 7981 5496 8818
2014 1991 3531 4624  895 5720 8481  826  435 6940 1723 9797 8261
2015 8811 4933 6746 3978  913 5003 2372 3530 4724 7202 2765 4096
2016 9258 8650 2719 7634 5129 5096 5449 7352 2729 5035 6370 9327
>lag.plot(AirPassengers, lags=10)
```

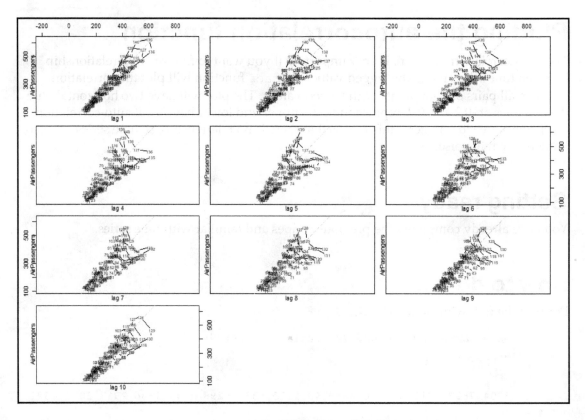

Plot for lags 1 to 10

```
>lag.plot(newseries, lags=10)
```

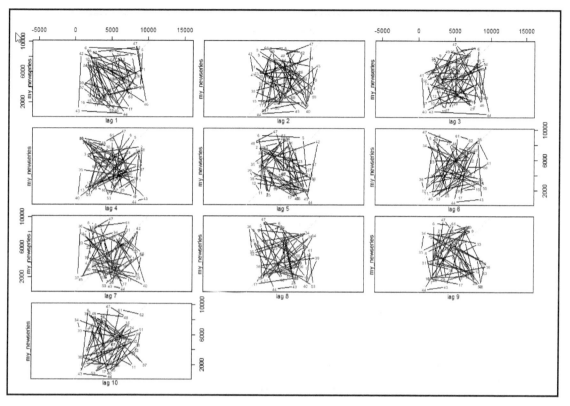

Plot for lags 1 to 10

```
> acf(AirPassengers)
```

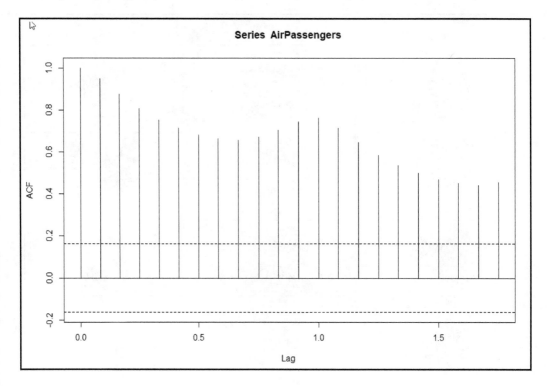

Autocorrelation for AirPassengers

```
> acf(my_newseries)
```

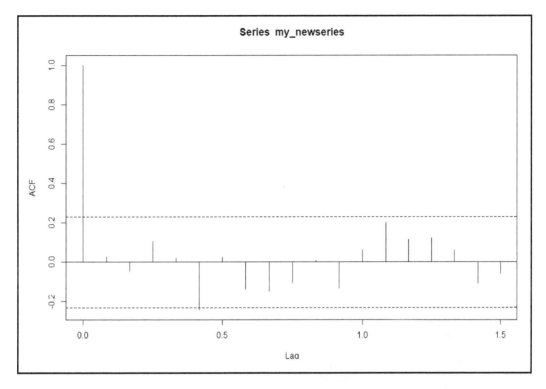

Autocorrelation for my_newseries

How it works...

We have two time series and we try to find the autocorrelation between them. Using
`lag.plot`, we compute the lag time series with lags from 1 to 10 for both time series. From
the plot, it is clear that in `AirPassengers`, there is some autocorrelation, whereas
`my_newseries` has no such relation. Use `acf`, which will graph the autocorrelation
coefficient versus the lag. From it we can see `AirPassegners`; autocorrelation coefficients
are not close to 0, where in `my_newseries` they are close to 0.

See also

Apart from `acf`, you can also look at `pacf`, the partial autocorrelation function.

4
R and Statistics

In this chapter, we will cover the following topics:

- Understanding data sampling in R
- Operating a probability distribution in R
- Working with univariate descriptive statistics in R
- Performing correlations and multivariate analysis
- Conducting an exact binomial test
- Performing student's t-test
- Performing the Kolmogorov-Smirnov test
- Understanding the Wilcoxon Rank Sum and Signed Rank test
- Working with Pearson's Chi-squared test
- Conducting a One-way ANOVA
- Performing a Two-way ANOVA

Introduction

The R language, as the descendent of the statistics language, S, has become the preferred computing language in the field of statistics. Moreover, due to its status as an active contributor in the field, if a new statistical method is discovered, it is very likely that this method will first be implemented in the R language. As such, a large quantity of statistical methods can be fulfilled by applying the R language.

To apply statistical methods in R, the user can categorize the method of implementation into descriptive statistics and inferential statistics:

- **Descriptive statistics**: These are used to summarize the characteristics of the data. The user can use mean and standard deviation to describe numerical data, and use frequency and percentages to describe categorical data.
- **Inferential statistics**: Based on the pattern within a sample data, the user can infer the characteristics of the population. The methods related to inferential statistics are for hypothesis testing, data estimation, data correlation, and relationship modeling. Inference can be further extended to forecasting, prediction, and estimation of unobserved values either in or associated with the population being studied.

In the following recipes, we will discuss examples of data sampling, probability distribution, univariate descriptive statistics, correlations and multivariate analysis, linear regression and multivariate analysis, Exact Binomial Test, student's t-test, **Kolmogorov-Smirnov** test, **Wilcoxon Rank Sum** and **Signed Rank** test, **Pearson's Chi-squared** Test, **One-way ANOVA**, and **Two-way ANOVA**.

Understanding data sampling in R

Sampling is a method to select a subset of data from a statistical population, which can use the characteristics of the population to estimate the whole population. The following recipe will demonstrate how to generate samples in R.

Getting ready

Make sure that you have an R working environment for the following recipe.

How to do it...

Perform the following steps to understand data sampling in R:

1. To generate random samples of a given population, the user can simply use the `sample` function:

```
> sample(1:10)
```

2. To specify the number of items returned, the user can set the assigned value to the `size` argument:

```
> sample(1:10, size = 5)
```

3. Moreover, the sample can also generate Bernoulli trials by specifying `replace = TRUE` (default is `FALSE`):

```
> sample(c(0,1), 10, replace = TRUE)
```

4. If we want to do a coin flipping trail, where the outcome is `Head` or `Tail`, we can use:

```
> outcome <- c("Head","Tail")
> sample(outcome, size=1)
```

5. To generate result for `100` times, we can use:

```
> sample(outcome, size=100, replace=TRUE)
```

6. The sample can be useful when we want to select random data from datasets, selecting `10` observations from `AirPassengers`:

```
> sample(AirPassengers, size=10)
```

How it works...

As we saw in the preceding demonstration, the `sample` function can generate random samples from a specified population. The returned number from records can be designated by the user simply by specifying the argument of `size`. By assigning the `replace` argument as `TRUE`, you can generate Bernoulli trials (a population with 0 and 1 only).

See also

- In R, the default package provides another sample method, `sample.int`, where both n and `size` must be supplied as integers:

```
> sample.int(20, 12)
```

Operating a probability distribution in R

Probability distribution and statistics analysis are closely related to each other. For statistics analysis, analysts make predictions based on a certain population, which is mostly under a probability distribution. Therefore, if you find that the data selected for a prediction does not follow the exact assumed probability distribution in the experiment design, the upcoming results can be refuted. In other words, probability provides the justification for statistics. The following examples will demonstrate how to generate probability distribution in R.

Getting ready

Since most distribution functions originate from the stats package, make sure the library stats are loaded.

How to do it...

Perform the following steps:

1. For a normal distribution, the user can use dnorm, which will return the height of a normal curve at 0:

    ```
    > dnorm(0)
    Output:
    [1] 0.3989423
    ```

2. Then, the user can change the mean and the standard deviation in the argument:

    ```
    > dnorm(0,mean=3,sd=5)
    Output:
    [1] 0.06664492
    ```

3. Next, plot the graph of a normal distribution with the `curve` function:

```
> curve(dnorm,-3,3)
```

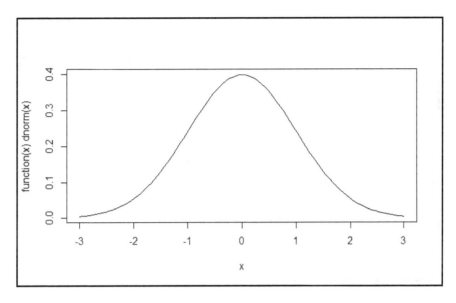

Standard normal distribution

4. In contrast to `dnorm`, which returns the height of a normal curve, the `pnorm` function can return the area under a given value:

```
> pnorm(1.5)
Output:
[1] 0.9331928
```

5. Alternatively, to get the area over a certain value, you can specify the option, `lower.tail`, as `FALSE`:

```
> pnorm(1.5, lower.tail=FALSE)
Output:
[1] 0.0668072
```

6. To plot the graph of `pnorm`, the user can employ a `curve` function:

```
> curve(pnorm(x), -3,3)
```

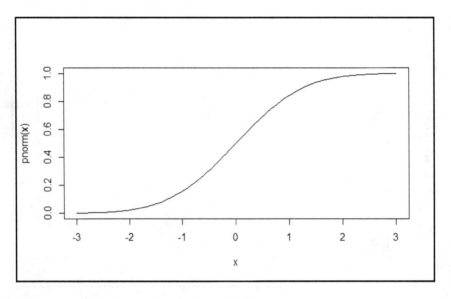

Cumulative density function (pnorm)

7. To calculate the quantiles for a specific distribution, you can use `qnorm`. The function, `qnorm`, can be treated as the inverse of `pnorm`, which returns the Z-score of a given probability:

```
> qnorm(0.5)
Output:
[1] 0
> qnorm(pnorm(0))
Output:
[1] 0
```

8. To generate random numbers from a normal distribution, one can use the `rnorm` function and specify the number of generated numbers. Also, one can define optional arguments, such as the mean and standard deviation:

```
> set.seed(50)
> x = rnorm(100,mean=3,sd=5)
> hist(x)
```

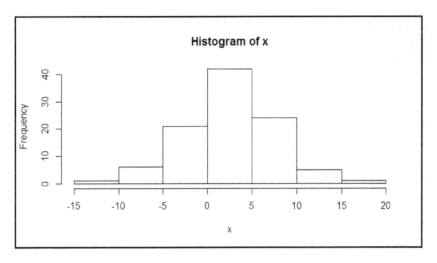

Histogram of a normal distribution

9. To calculate the uniform distribution, the `runif` function generates random numbers from a uniform distribution. The user can specify the range of the generated numbers by specifying variables, such as the minimum and maximum. For the following example, the user generates `100` random variables from 0 to 5:

```
> set.seed(50)
> y = runif(100,0,5)
> hist(y)
```

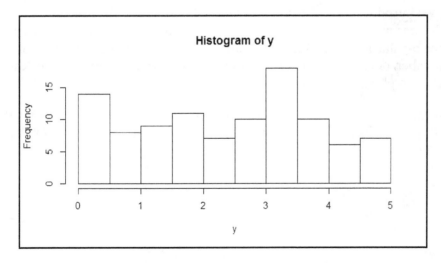

Histogram of a uniform distribution

10. Lastly, if you would like to test the normality of the data, the most widely used test for this is the Shapiro-Wilks test. Here, we demonstrate how to perform a test of normality on samples from both the normal and uniform distributions, respectively:

```
> shapiro.test(x)
Output:
   Shapiro-Wilk normality test

data: x
W = 0.9938, p-value = 0.9319
> shapiro.test(y)

   Shapiro-Wilk normality test
data: y
W = 0.9563, p-value = 0.002221
```

How it works...

In this recipe, we first introduce `dnorm`, a probability density function, which returns the height of a normal curve. With a single input specified, the input value is called a standard score or a z-score. Without any other arguments specified, it is assumed that the normal distribution is in use with a mean of zero and a standard deviation of 1. We then introduce three ways to draw standard and normal distributions.

After this, we introduce `pnorm`, a cumulative density function. The function, `pnorm`, can generate the area under a given value. In addition to this, `pnorm` can be also used to calculate the p-value from a normal distribution. One can get the p-value by subtracting 1 from the number, or assigning True to the option, `lower.tail`. Similarly, one can use the `plot` function to plot the cumulative density.

In contrast to `pnorm`, `qnorm` returns the z-score of a given probability. Therefore, the example shows that the application of a `qnorm` function to a `pnorm` function will produce the exact input value.

Next, we show you how to use the `rnrom` function to generate random samples from a normal distribution, and the `runif` function to generate random samples from the uniform distribution. In the function, `rnorm`, one has to specify the number of generated numbers and we may also add optional augments, such as the mean and standard deviation. Then, by using the `hist` function, one should be able to find a bell-curve in figure 3. On the other hand, for the `runif` function, with the minimum and maximum specifications, one can get a list of sample numbers between the two. However, we can still use the `hist` function to plot the samples. The output figure (shown in the preceding figure) is not in a bell shape, which indicates that the sample does not come from the normal distribution.

Finally, we demonstrate how to test data normality with the Shapiro-Wilks test. Here, we conduct the normality test on both the normal and uniform distribution samples, respectively. In both outputs, one can find the p-value in each test result. The p-value shows the changes, which show that the sample comes from a normal distribution. If the p-value is higher than 0.05, we can conclude that the sample comes from a normal distribution. On the other hand, if the value is lower than 0.05, we conclude that the sample does not come from a normal distribution.

There's more...

Besides the normal distribution, you can obtain a *t* distribution, binomial distribution, and Chi-squared distribution by using the built-in functions of R. You can use the `help` function to access further information about this:

- For a t distribution:

```
> help(TDist)
```

- For a binomial distribution:

```
> help(Binomial)
```

- For the Chi-squared distribution:

```
> help(Chisquare)
```

To learn more about the distributions in the package, the user can access the `help` function with the keyword `distributions` to find all related documentation on this:

```
> help(distributions)
```

Working with univariate descriptive statistics in R

Uni means *one* and dealing with one variable for looking into data in univariate descriptive statistics, describes a single variable for unit analysis, which is also the simplest form of quantitative analysis. To find the pattern or find the meaning in data in cases of univariate analysis use central tendencies such as mean, median, mode, range, variance, maximum, minimum, and standard deviation. Bar charts, histograms, pie charts, and frequency polygons are the best option for representing the univariate data. In this recipe, we introduce some basic functions used to describe a single variable.

Getting ready

We need to apply descriptive statistics to a sample data. Here, we use the built-in `mtcars` data as our example.

How to do it...

Perform the following steps:

1. First, load the `mtcars` data into a DataFrame with a variable named `mtcars`:

   ```
   > data(mtcars)
   ```

2. To obtain the vector range, the `range` function will return the lower and upper bound of the vector:

   ```
   > range(mtcars$mpg)
   Output:
   [1] 10.4 33.9
   ```

3. Compute the length of the variable:

   ```
   > length(mtcars$mpg)
   Output:
   [1] 32
   ```

4. To obtain the mean of mpg:

```
> mean(mtcars$mpg)
Output:
[1] 20.09062
```

5. To obtain the median of the input vector:

```
> median(mtcars$mpg)
Output:
[1] 19.2
```

6. To obtain the standard deviation of the input vector:

```
> sd(mtcars$mpg)
Output:
[1] 6.026948
```

7. To obtain the variance of the input vector:

```
> var(mtcars$mpg)
Output:
[1] 36.3241
```

8. The variance can also be computed with the square of the standard deviation:

```
> sd(mtcars$mpg) ^ 2
Output:
[1] 36.3241
```

9. To obtain the **Interquartile Range (IQR)**:

```
> IQR(mtcars$mpg)
Output:
[1] 7.375
```

10. To obtain the quantile:

```
> quantile(mtcars$mpg,0.67)
Output:
67%
21.4
```

11. To obtain the maximum of the input vector:

```
> max(mtcars$mpg)
Output:
[1] 33.9
```

12. To obtain the minima of the input vector:

```
> min(mtcars$mpg)
Output:
[1] 10.4
```

13. To obtain a vector with elements that are the cumulative maxima:

```
> cummax(mtcars$mpg)
Output:
[1] 21.0 21.0 22.8 22.8 22.8 22.8 22.8 24.4 24.4 24.4 24.4 24.4
24.4 24.4 24.4 24.4
[17] 24.4 32.4 32.4 33.9 33.9 33.9 33.9 33.9 33.9 33.9 33.9 33.9
33.9 33.9 33.9 33.9
```

14. To obtain a vector with elements that are the cumulative minima:

```
> cummin(mtcars$mpg)
Output:
[1] 21.0 21.0 21.0 21.0 18.7 18.1 14.3 14.3 14.3 14.3 14.3 14.3
14.3 14.3 10.4 10.4
[17] 10.4 10.4 10.4 10.4 10.4 10.4 10.4 10.4 10.4 10.4 10.4 10.4
10.4 10.4 10.4 10.4
```

15. To summarize the dataset, you can apply the summary function:

```
> summary(mtcars)
```

```
> summary(mtcars)
      mpg             cyl             disp             hp             drat             wt             qsec
 Min.   :10.40   Min.   :4.000   Min.   : 71.1   Min.   : 52.0   Min.   :2.760   Min.   :1.513   Min.   :14.50
 1st Qu.:15.43   1st Qu.:4.000   1st Qu.:120.8   1st Qu.: 96.5   1st Qu.:3.080   1st Qu.:2.581   1st Qu.:16.89
 Median :19.20   Median :6.000   Median :196.3   Median :123.0   Median :3.695   Median :3.325   Median :17.71
 Mean   :20.09   Mean   :6.188   Mean   :230.7   Mean   :146.7   Mean   :3.597   Mean   :3.217   Mean   :17.85
 3rd Qu.:22.80   3rd Qu.:8.000   3rd Qu.:326.0   3rd Qu.:180.0   3rd Qu.:3.920   3rd Qu.:3.610   3rd Qu.:18.90
 Max.   :33.90   Max.   :8.000   Max.   :472.0   Max.   :335.0   Max.   :4.930   Max.   :5.424   Max.   :22.90
       vs              am             gear            carb
 Min.   :0.0000   Min.   :0.0000   Min.   :3.000   Min.   :1.000
 1st Qu.:0.0000   1st Qu.:0.0000   1st Qu.:3.000   1st Qu.:2.000
 Median :0.0000   Median :0.0000   Median :4.000   Median :2.000
 Mean   :0.4375   Mean   :0.4062   Mean   :3.688   Mean   :2.812
 3rd Qu.:1.0000   3rd Qu.:1.0000   3rd Qu.:4.000   3rd Qu.:4.000
 Max.   :1.0000   Max.   :1.0000   Max.   :5.000   Max.   :8.000
```

16. To obtain a frequency count of the categorical data, take `cyl` of `mtcars` as an example:

```
> table(mtcars$cyl)
Output:
 4  6  8
11  7 14
```

17. To obtain a frequency count of numerical data, you can use a stem plot to outline the data shape; `stem` produces a stem-and-leaf plot of the given values:

```
> stem(mtcars$mpg)
Output:
  The decimal point is at the |

  10 | 44
  12 | 3
  14 | 3702258
  16 | 438
  18 | 17227
  20 | 00445
  22 | 88
  24 | 4
  26 | 03
  28 |
  30 | 44
  32 | 49
```

18. You can use a histogram of `ggplot` to plot the same stem-and-leaf figure:

```
> library(ggplot2)
> qplot(mtcars$mpg, binwidth=2)
```

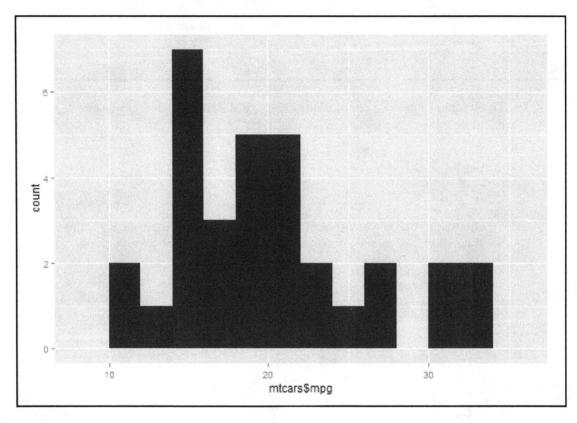

Histogram of mpg of mtcars

```
> pie(table(mtcars$cyl), main="Number of Cylinders")
```

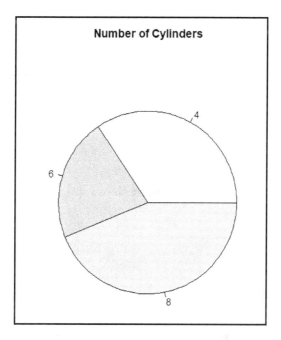

Pie chart of number of cylinders in cars

How it works...

Univariate descriptive statistics generate the frequency distribution of datasets. Moreover, they can be used to identify the obvious patterns in the data, and the characteristics of the variates, to provide a better understanding of the data from a holistic viewpoint. Additionally, they can provide information about the central tendency and descriptors of the skewness of individual cases. Therefore, it is common to see that univariate analysis is conducted at the beginning of the data exploration process.

To begin the exploration of data, we first load the dataset, `mtcars`, to an R session. From the data, we apply `range`, `length`, `mean`, `median`, `sd`, `var`, `IQR`, `quantile`, `min`, `max`, `cumin`, and `cumax` to obtain the descriptive statistic of the attribute, `mpg`. Then, we use the `summary` function to obtain summary information about `mtcars`.

Next, we obtain a frequency count of the categorical data (`cyl`). To obtain a frequency count of the numerical data, we use a `stem` plot to outline the data shape. Lastly, we use a histogram with the `binwidth` argument in 2 to generate a plot similar to the stem-and-leaf plot.

There's more...

One common scenario in univariate descriptive statistics is to find the mode of a vector. In R, there is no built-in function to help the user obtain the mode of the data. However, one can implement the mode function by using the following code:

```
> mode = function(x) {
+ temp = table(x)
+ names(temp)[temp == max(temp)]
+ }
```

By applying the mode function on the vector, mtcars$mpg, you can find the most frequently occurring numeric value or category of a given vector:

```
> x = c(1,2,3,3,3,4,4,5,5,5,6)
> mode(x)
Output:
[1] "3" "5"
```

Performing correlations and multivariate analysis

To analyze the relationship of more than two variables, you would need to conduct multivariate descriptive statistics, which allows the comparison of factors. Additionally, it prevents the effect of a single variable from distorting the analysis. In this recipe, we will discuss how to conduct multivariate descriptive statistics using a correlation and covariance matrix.

Getting ready

Ensure that mtcars has already been loaded into a DataFrame within an R session.

How to do it...

Perform the following steps:

1. Here, you can get the covariance matrix by inputting the first three variables in mtcars to the cov function:

   ```
   > cov(mtcars[1:3])
   ```

```
Output:
            mpg          cyldisp
mpg   36.324103      -9.172379   -633.0972
cyl   -9.172379       3.189516    199.6603
disp -633.097208  199.660282  15360.7998
```

2. To obtain a correlation matrix of the dataset, we input the first three variables of `mtcars`to the `cor` function:

```
> cor(mtcars[1:3])
Output:
            mpg          cyldisp
mpg    1.0000000   -0.8521620   -0.8475514
cyl   -0.8521620    1.0000000    0.9020329
disp  -0.8475514    0.9020329    1.0000000
```

How it works...

In this recipe, we have demonstrated how to apply correlation and covariance to discover the relationship between multiple variables.

First, we compute a covariance matrix of the first three `mtcars` variables. Covariance can measure how variables are linearly related. Thus, a positive covariance (for example, `cyl` versus `mpg`) indicates that the two variables are positively linearly related. On the other hand, a negative covariance (for example, `mpg` versus `disp`) indicates the two variables are negatively linearly related. However, due to the variance of different datasets, the covariance scores of these datasets are not comparable. As a result, if you would like to compare the strength of the linear relation between two variables in a different dataset, you should use the normalized score - that is, the correlation coefficient instead of covariance.

Next, we apply a `cor` function to obtain a correlation coefficient matrix of three variables within the `mtcars` dataset. In the correlation coefficient matrix, the numeric element of the matrix indicates the strength of the relationship between the two variables. If the correlation coefficient of a variable against itself scores 1, the variable has a positive relationship against itself. The `cyl` and `mpg` variables have a correlation coefficient of -0.85, which means they have a strong, negative relationship. On the other hand, the `disp` and `cyl` variables score 0.90, which may indicate that they have a strong, positive relationship.

See also

- You can use `ggplot` to plot the heatmap of the correlation coefficient matrix:

```
> library(reshape2)
> qplot(x=Var1, y=Var2, data=melt(cor(mtcars[1:3])), fill=value,
  geom="tile")
```

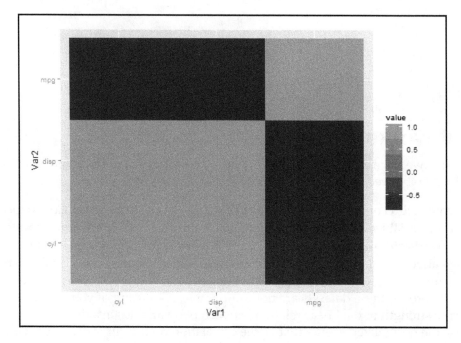

The correlation coefficient matrix heatmap

Conducting an exact binomial test

While making decisions, it is important to know whether the decision error can be controlled or measured. In other words, we would like to prove that the hypothesis formed is unlikely to have occurred by chance, and is statistically significant. In hypothesis testing, there are two kinds of hypotheses: the null hypothesis and the alternative hypothesis (or research hypothesis). The purpose of hypothesis testing is to validate whether the experiment results are significant. However, to validate whether the alternative hypothesis is acceptable, it is deemed to be true if the null hypothesis is rejected.

In the following recipes, we will discuss some common statistical testing methods. First, we will cover how to conduct an exact binomial test in R.

Getting ready

Since the `binom.test`function originates from the `stats` package, make sure the `stats` library is loaded.

How to do it...

Perform the following steps:

1. Assume there is a game where a gambler can win by rolling the number-six-on a dice. As part of the rules, gamblers can bring their own dice. If a gambler tried to cheat in a game, he would use a loaded dice to increase his chance of winning. Therefore, if we observe that the gambler won 92 out of 315 games, we could determine whether the dice was fair by conducting an exact binomial test:

```
> binom.test(x=92, n=315, p=1/6)
Output:
          Exact binomial test
data: 92 and 315
number of successes = 92, number of trials = 315, p-value =
3.458e-08
alternative hypothesis: true probability of success is not equal to
0.1666667
95 percent confidence interval:
0.2424273 0.3456598
sample estimates:
probability of success
          0.2920635
```

How it works...

A binomial test uses the binomial distribution to find out whether the true success rate is likely to be P for n trials with the binary outcome. The formula of the probability, P, can be defined in following equation:

$$P(X = k) = \binom{n}{k} p^k q^{n-k}$$

Here, X denotes the random variables, counting the number of outcomes of the interest; n denotes the number of trials; k indicates the number of successes; p indicates the probability of success; and q denotes the probability of failure.

After we have computed the probability, P, we can then perform a sign test to determine whether the success probability is as we expected. If the probability is not equal to what we expected, we can reject the null hypothesis.

The null hypothesis is a skeptical perspective or a statement about the population parameter that will be tested. The null hypothesis is denoted by H0. An alternative hypothesis is represented by a range of population values, which are not included in the null hypothesis. The alternative hypothesis is denoted by H1. In this case, the null and alternative hypothesis, respectively, are illustrated as:

- **H0 (null hypothesis)**: The true probability of success is equal to what we expected
- **H1 (alternative hypothesis)**: The true probability of success is not equal to what we expected

In this example, we demonstrate how to use a binomial test to determine the number of times the dice is rolled, the frequency of rolling the number six, and the probability of rolling a six from an unbiased dice. The result of the t-test shows that the p-value = 3.458e-08 (lower than 0.05). For significance, at the 5 percent level, the null hypothesis (the dice is unbiased) is rejected as too many sixes were rolled (the probability of success = 0.2920635).

See also

- To read more about the usage of the exact binomial test, please use the `help` function to view related documentation on this:

    ```
    > ?binom.test
    ```

Performing a student's t-test

A one sample t-test enables us to test whether two means are significantly different; a two sample t-test allows us to test whether the means of two independent groups are different. Using t-tests, we can find how significant the difference is and if the difference has happened by chance. In this recipe, we will discuss how to conduct one sample t-test and two sample t-tests using R.

Getting ready

Ensure that mtcars has already been loaded into a DataFrame within an R session. As the t.test function originates from the stats package, make sure the library, stats, is loaded.

How to do it...

Perform the following steps:

1. First, we visualize the attribute, mpg, against am using a boxplot:

    ```
    > boxplot(mtcars$mpg, mtcars$mpg[mtcars$am==0], ylab = "mpg",
    names=c("overall","automobile"))
    > abline(h=mean(mtcars$mpg),lwd=2, col="red")
    > abline(h=mean(mtcars$mpg[mtcars$am==0]),lwd=2, col="blue")
    ```

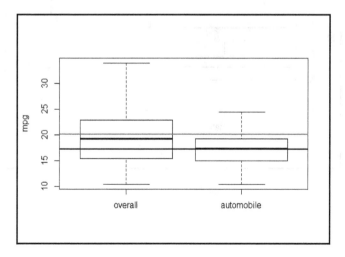

The boxplot of mpg of the overall population and automobiles

2. We then perform a statistical procedure to validate whether the average mpg of automobiles is lower than the average of the overall mpg:

```
> mpg.mu = mean(mtcars$mpg)
> mpg_am = mtcars$mpg[mtcars$am == 0]
> t.test(mpg_am, mu = mpg.mu)
```

```
            One Sample t-test

data:  mpg_am
t = -3.3462, df = 18, p-value = 0.003595
alternative hypothesis: true mean is not equal to 20.09062
95 percent confidence interval:
 15.29946 18.99528
sample estimates:
mean of x
 17.14737
```

3. We begin visualizing the data by plotting a boxplot:

```
> boxplot
(mtcars$mpg~mtcars$am,ylab='mpg',names=c('automatic','manual'))
> abline(h=mean(mtcars$mpg[mtcars$am==0]),lwd=2, col="blue")
> abline(h=mean(mtcars$mpg[mtcars$am==1]),lwd=2, col="red")
```

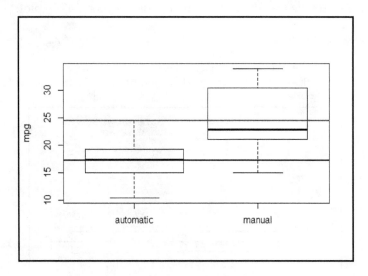

The boxplot of mpg of automatic and manual transmission cars

4. The preceding figure reveals that the mean mpg of automatic transmission cars is lower than the average mpg of manual transmission vehicles:

```
> t.test(mtcars$mpg~mtcars$am)
Output:
        Welch Two Sample t-test

data: mtcars$mpg by mtcars$am
t = -3.7671, df = 18.332, p-value = 0.001374
alternative hypothesis: true difference in means is not equal
to 0
95 percent confidence interval:
 -11 .280194 -3.209684
sample estimates:
mean in group 0 mean in group 1
        17.14737 24.39231
```

The next recipe will let you create your own data and perform the t-test. Think of 60 students divided into two equal divisions: A and B of 30 each. Perform the following steps in R:

```
> data = data.frame(marks=sample(40:100, 60, replace-TRUE),division=c(re
p('A',30), rep('B',30)))
> head(data)
> boxplot(data$marks, data$marks[data$division=='A'], ylab="Marks", names
=c("All Marks", "Div A"))
> abline(h=mean(data$marks), lwd=2, col="red")
> abline(h=mean(data$marks[data$division=='A']), lwd=2, col="blue")
```

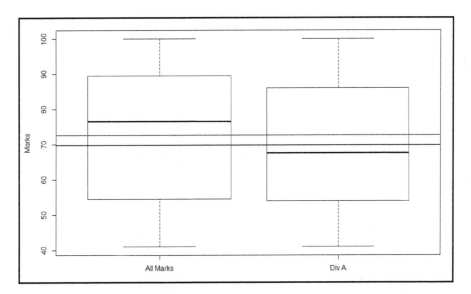

```
>meanmarks = mean(data$marks)
>marksA = data$marks[data$division=='A']
>t.test(marksA, mu = meanmarks)
Output:
 One Sample t-test
data: marksA
t = -0.80284, df = 29, p-value = 0.4286
alternative hypothesis: true mean is not equal to 72.5
95 percent confidence interval:
 62.68524 76.78143
sample estimates:
mean of x
 69.73333

>boxplot(data$marks~data$division, ylab="Marks", names=c("A", "B"))
>abline(h=mean(data$marks[data$division=="A"]), lwd=2, col="red")
>abline(h=mean(data$marks[data$division=="B"]), lwd=2, col="blue")
```

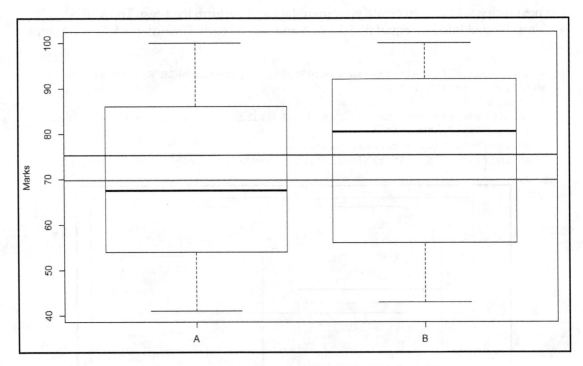

Boxplot for division A and B

```
> t.test(data$marks~data$division)
Output:
 Welch Two Sample t-test
data: data$marks by data$division
```

```
t = -1.1407, df = 57.995, p-value = 0.2587
alternative hypothesis: true difference in means is not equal to 0
95 percent confidence interval:
 -15.243379 4.176712
sample estimates:
mean in group A mean in group B
   69.73333 75.26667
```

How it works...

A student's t-test is where the test statistic follows a normal distribution (the student's t distribution) if the null hypothesis is true. It can be used to determine whether there is a difference between two independent datasets. A student's t-test is best used with the problems associated with an inference based on small samples.

In this recipe, we discuss one sample student's t-test and two sample student's t-tests. In the one sample student's t-test, a research question often asked is, *Is the mean of the population different from the null hypothesis?* Thus, in order to test whether the average mpg of automobiles is lower than the overall average mpg, we first use a boxplot to view the differences between populations without making any assumptions. From the preceding figure, the mean of mpg of automobiles (the blue line) is lower than the average mpg (red line) of the overall population. Then, we apply the one sample t-test; the low p-value of 0.003595 (< 0.05) suggests that we should reject the null hypothesis that the mean mpg for automobiles is less than the average mpg of the overall population.

As a one sample t-test enables us to test whether two means are significantly different, a two-sample t-test allows us to test whether the means of two independent groups are different. Like in a one sample t-test, we first use a boxplot to see the differences between populations and then apply a two-sample t-test. The test results show the p-value = 0.01374 ($p < 0.05$). In other words, the test provides evidence that rejects the null hypothesis, which shows the mean mpg of cars with automatic transmission differs from the cars with manual transmission.

To elaborate on this, the next recipe creates the dummy student marks data and performs the same test.

See also

- To read more about the usage of student's t-test, please use the `help` function to view the related documents:

  ```
  > ?t.test
  ```

Performing the Kolmogorov-Smirnov test

A one-sample Kolmogorov-Smirnov test is used to compare a sample with a reference probability. A two-sample Kolmogorov-Smirnov test compares the cumulative distributions of two datasets. In this recipe, we will demonstrate how to perform the Kolmogorov-Smirnov test with R.

Getting ready

Ensure that `mtcars` has already been loaded into a DataFrame within an R session. As the `ks.test` function is originated from the `stats` package, make sure the `stats` library is loaded.

How to do it...

Perform the following steps:

1. Validate whether the dataset, x (generated with the `rnorm` function), is distributed normally with a one-sample Kolmogorov-Smirnov test:

   ```
   > x = rnorm(50)
   > ks.test(x,"pnorm")
   Output:
    One-sample Kolmogorov-Smirnov test
   data: x
   D = 0.1698, p-value = 0.0994
   alternative hypothesis: two-sided
   ```

2. Next, you can generate uniformly distributed sample data:

```
> set.seed(3)
> x = runif(n=20, min=0, max=20)
> y = runif(n=20, min=0, max=20)
```

3. We first plot the `ecdf` of two generated data samples:

```
> plot(ecdf(x), do.points = FALSE, verticals=T, xlim=c(0, 20))
> lines(ecdf(y), lty=3, do.points = FALSE, verticals=T)
```

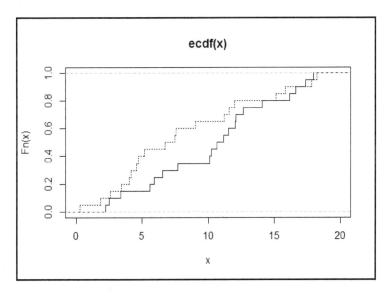

The ecdf plot of two generated data samples

4. Finally, we apply a two-sample Kolmogorov-Smirnov test on two groups of data:

```
> ks.test(x,y)
Output:
 Two-sample Kolmogorov-Smirnov test
data: x and y
D = 0.3, p-value = 0.3356
alternative hypothesis: two-sided
```

This recipe will create a sample data and perform the Kolmogorov-Smirnov test. Perform the following in R:

```
> g1 = sample(50:100, 30, replace=TRUE)
> g2 = sample(50:100, 30, replace=TRUE)
> plot.ecdf(g1, verticals=TRUE, do.points=FALSE, col="red")
> lines(ecdf(g2), verticals=TRUE, do.points=FALSE, col="blue")
```

ECDF plot of g1 and g2

```
> ks.test(g1,g2)
Output:
  Two-sample Kolmogorov-Smirnov test
data: g1 and g2
D = 0.2, p-value = 0.586
alternative hypothesis: two-sided
```

How it works...

The **Kolmogorov-Smirnov test (K-S test)** is a nonparametric and statistical test, used for the equality of continuous probability distributions. It can be used to compare a sample with a reference probability distribution (a one sample K-S test), or it can directly compare two samples (a two sample K-S test). The test is based on the **Empirical Distribution Function (ECDF)**. Let it be a random sample of size, n; the empirical distribution function is defined as:

$$F_n(x) = \frac{1}{n} \sum_{i=1}^{n} I\{x_i \leq x\}$$

Here, is the indicator function. If, the function equals to 1. Otherwise, the function equals to 0.

The Kolmogorov-Smirnov statistic (D) is based on the greatest (where `supx` denotes the supremum) vertical difference between $F(x)$ and $Fn(x)$. It is defined as:

$$D_n = \sup_x \left| F_n(x) - F(x) \right|$$

H_0 in the sample follows the specified distribution. H_1 in the sample does not follow the specified distribution.

If D_n is greater than the critical value obtained from a table, then we reject H_0 at the level of significance α.

We first test whether a random number generated from a normal distribution is normally distributed. At the 5 percent significance level, the p-value of 0.0994 indicates that the input is normally distributed.

Then, we plot an empirical cumulative distribution function (`ecdf`) plot to show how a two-sample test calculates the maximum distance D (showing 0.3), and apply the two-sample Kolmogorov-Smirnov test to discover whether the two input datasets possibly come from the same distribution.

The p-value is above 0.05, which does not reject the null hypothesis. In other words, it means the two datasets are possibly from the same distribution.

See also

- To read more about the usage of the Kolmogorov-Smirnov test, please use the `help` function to view the related documents:

  ```
  > ?ks.test
  ```

- As for the definition of an empirical cumulative distribution function, please refer to the help page of `ecdf`:

  ```
  > ?ecdf
  ```

Understanding the Wilcoxon Rank Sum and Signed Rank test

The Wilcoxon Rank Sum and Signed Rank test (or Mann-Whitney-Wilcoxon) is a nonparametric test of the null hypothesis, which shows that the population distribution of two different groups are identical without assuming that the two groups are normally distributed. This recipe will show how to conduct the Wilcoxon Rank Sum and Signed Rank test in R.

Getting ready

Ensure that `mtcars` has already been loaded into a DataFrame within an R session. As the `wilcox.test` function is originated from the `stats` package, make sure the library, `stats`, is loaded.

How to do it...

Perform the following steps:

1. We first plot the data of `mtcars` with the `boxplot` function:

   ```
   > boxplot
   (mtcars$mpg~mtcars$am,ylab='mpg',names=c('automatic','manual'))
   ```

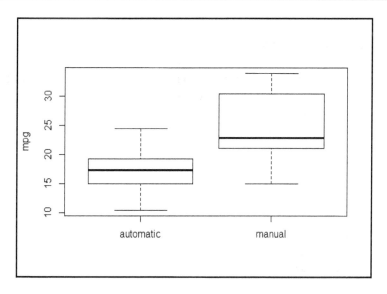

The boxplot of mpg of automatic cars and manual transmission cars

2. Next, we still perform a Wilcoxon Rank Sum test to validate whether the distribution of **automatic** transmission cars is identical to that of **manual** transmission cars:

```
> wilcox.test(mpg ~ am, data=mtcars)
Output:
 Wilcoxon rank sum test with continuity correction
data: mpg by am
W = 42, p-value = 0.001871
alternative hypothesis: true location shift is not equal to 0
Warning message:
In wilcox.test.default(x = c(21.4, 18.7, 18.1, 14.3, 24.4, 22.8, :
 cannot compute exact p-value with ties
```

How it works...

In this recipe, we discuss a nonparametric test method, the Wilcoxon Rank Sum test (also known as the Mann-Whitney U-test). For a student's t-test, it is assumed that the differences between the two samples are normally distributed (and it also works best when the two samples are normally distributed). However, when the normality assumption is uncertain, one can adopt the Wilcoxon Rank Sum Test to test a hypothesis.

Here, we used a Wilcoxon Rank Sum test to determine whether the mpg of automatic and manual transmission cars in the dataset, `mtcars`, is distributed identically. From the test result, we see that the p-value = 0.001871 (< 0.05) rejects the null hypothesis, and also reveals that the distribution of mpg in automatic and manual transmission cars is not identical. When performing this test, you may receive the warning message, *cannot compute exact p-value with ties*, which indicates that there are duplicate values within the dataset. The warning message will be cleared once the duplicate values are removed.

See also

- To read more about the usage of the Wilcoxon Rank Sum and Signed Rank Test, please use the `help` function to view the related documents:

  ```
  > ?wilcox.test
  ```

Working with Pearson's Chi-squared test

In this recipe, we introduce Pearson's Chi-squared test, which is used to examine whether the distributions of categorical variables of two groups differ. We will discuss how to conduct Pearson's Chi-squared Test in R.

Getting ready

Ensure that `mtcars` has already been loaded into a DataFrame within an R session. Since the `chisq.test` function is originated from the `stats?` package, and make sure the library, `stats`, is loaded.

How to do it...

Perform the following steps:

1. To make the counting table, we first use the contingency table built with the inputs of the transmission type and number of forward gears:

   ```
   > ftable = table(mtcars$am, mtcars$gear)
   > ftable
    Output:
   ```

```
    3  4  5
0  15  4  0
1   0  8  5
```

2. We then plot the mosaic plot of the contingency table:

```
> mosaicplot(ftable, main="Number of Forward Gears Within Automatic
and Manual Cars", color = TRUE)
```

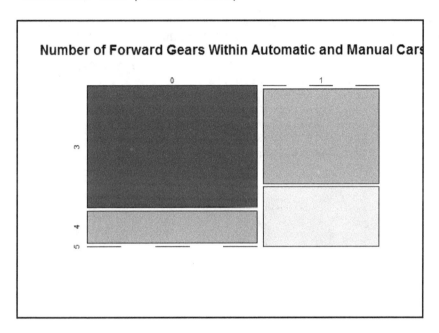

Number of forward gears in automatic and manual cars

3. Next, we perform the Pearson's Chi-squared test on the contingency table to test whether the numbers of gears in automatic and manual transmission cars is the same:

```
> chisq.test(ftable)
Output:

 Pearson's Chi-squared test
data: ftable
X-squared = 20.9447, df = 2, p-value = 2.831e-05

Warning message:
In chisq.test(ftable) : Chi-squared approximation may be incorrect
```

Take another example. Perform the following steps:

```
> library(MASS)
> str(survey)
Output:
'data.frame': 237 obs. of 12 variables:
 $ Sex : Factor w/ 2 levels "Female","Male": 1 2 2 2 2 1 2 1 2 2 ...
 $ Wr.Hnd: num 18.5 19.5 18 18.8 20 18 17.7 17 20 18.5 ...
 $ NW.Hnd: num 18 20.5 13.3 18.9 20 17.7 17.7 17.3 19.5 18.5 ...
 $ W.Hnd : Factor w/ 2 levels "Left","Right": 2 1 2 2 2 2 2 2 2 2 ...
 $ Fold : Factor w/ 3 levels "L on R","Neither",..: 3 3 1 3 2 1 1 3 3 3 ...
 $ Pulse :int 92 104 87 NA 35 64 83 74 72 90 ...
 $ Clap : Factor w/ 3 levels "Left","Neither",..: 1 1 2 2 3 3 3 3 3 3 ...
 $ Exer : Factor w/ 3 levels "Freq","None",..: 3 2 2 2 3 3 1 1 3 3 ...
 $ Smoke : Factor w/ 4 levels "Heavy","Never",..: 2 4 3 2 2 2 2 2 2 2 ...
 $ Height: num 173 178 NA 160 165 ...
 $ M.I : Factor w/ 2 levels "Imperial","Metric": 2 1 NA 2 2 1 1 2 2 2 ...
 $ Age :num 18.2 17.6 16.9 20.3 23.7 ...
> tbl = table(survey$Smoke, survey$Exer)
> tbl
Output:
      Freq None Some
Heavy 7    1    3
Never 87   18   84
Occas 12   3    4
Regul 9    1    7
>chisq.test(tbl)

Pearson's Chi-squared test

data: tbl
X-squared = 5.4885, df = 6, p-value = 0.4828
```

How it works...

Pearson's Chi-squared test is a statistical test used to discover whether there is a relationship between two categorical variables. It is best used for unpaired data from large samples. If you would like to conduct Pearson's Chi-squared test, you need to make sure that the input samples satisfy two assumptions: firstly, the two input variables should be categorical. Secondly, the variable should include two or more independent groups.

In Pearson's Chi-squared test, the assumption is that we have two variables, A and B; we can illustrate the null and alternative hypothesis in the following statements:

- H_0: Variable A and variable B are independent
- H_1: Variable A and variable B are not independent

To test whether the null hypothesis is correct or incorrect, the Chi-squared test takes these steps.

It calculates the Chi-squared test statistic x^2:

$$X^2 = \sum_{i=1}^{r}\sum_{j=1}^{c}\frac{\left(O_{i,j} - E_{i,j}\right)^2}{E_{i,j}}$$

Here, r is the number of rows in the contingency table, c is the number of columns in the contingency table, $O_{i,j}$ is the observed frequency count, and $E_{i,j}$ is the expected frequency count.

It determines the degrees of freedom, df, of that statistic. The degree of freedom is equal to:

$$df = (r-1) \times (c-1)$$

Here, r is the number of levels for one variable, and c is the number of levels for another variable.

It compares to the critical value from the Chi-squared distribution with the degrees of freedom.

In this recipe, we use a contingency table and mosaic plot to illustrate the differences in count numbers. It is obvious that the number of forward gears is less in automatic transmission cars than in manual transmission cars.

Then, we perform the Pearson's Chi-squared test on the contingency table to determine whether the gears in automatic and manual transmission cars are the same. The output, p-value = 2.831e-05 (< 0.05), refutes the null hypothesis and shows the number of forward gears is different in automatic and manual transmission cars. However, the output message contains a warning message that the Chi-squared approximation may be incorrect, which is because the number of samples in the contingency table is less than five.

There's more...

To read more about the usage of Pearson's Chi-squared test, please use the `help` function to view the related documents:

```
> ? chisq.test
```

Besides some common hypothesis testing methods mentioned in previous examples, there are other hypothesis methods provided by R:

- The Proportional test (`prop.test`): This is used to test whether the proportions in different groups are the same
- The Z-test (`simple.z.test` in the `UsingR` package): This compares the sample mean with the population mean and standard deviation
- The Bartlett Test (`bartlett.test`): This is used to test whether the variance of different groups is the same
- The Kruskal-Wallis Rank Sum Test (`kruskal.test`): This is used to test whether the distribution of different groups is identical without assuming that they are normally distributed
- The Shapiro-Wilk test (`shapiro.test`): This is used to test for normality

Conducting a one-way ANOVA

Analysis of variance (ANOVA) investigates the relationship between categorical independent variables and continuous dependent variables. It can be used to test whether the means of several groups are equal. If there is only one categorical variable as an independent variable, you can perform a one-way ANOVA. On the other hand, if there are more than two categorical variables, you should perform a two-way ANOVA. In this recipe, we discuss how to conduct a one-way ANOVA with R.

Getting ready

Ensure that `mtcars` has already been loaded into a DataFrame within an R session. Since the `oneway.test` and `TukeyHSD` functions originated from the `stats` package, make sure the library, `stats`, is loaded.

How to do it...

Perform the following steps:

1. We begin exploring by visualizing the data with a boxplot:

```
> boxplot(mtcars$mpg~factor(mtcars$gear),xlab='gear',ylab='mpg')
```

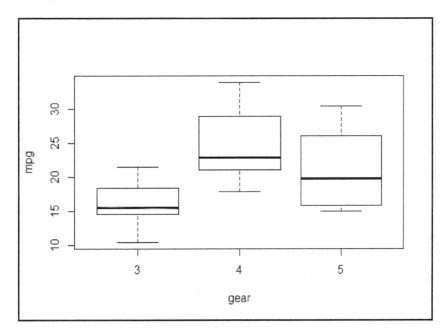

Comparison of mpg of different numbers of forward gears

2. To visualize how `gear` and `mpg` is related, a dot plot is created using the following steps:

```
> library(ggplot2)
> ggplot(mtcars,aes(mtcars$mpg,mtcars$gear, color
  =mtcars$gear))+geom_point()
```

Graph for mpg vs gears

3. Next, we conduct a one-way ANOVA to examine whether the mean of `mpg` changes with different numbers of forward gears. We use the function, `oneway.test`:

```
> oneway.test(mtcars$mpg~factor(mtcars$gear))
Output:
 One-way analysis of means (not assuming equal variances)
data: mtcars$mpg and factor(mtcars$gear)
F = 11.2848, numdf = 2.000, denomdf = 9.508, p-value = 0.003085
```

4. In addition to `oneway.test`, a standard function, `aov`, is used for the ANOVA analysis:

```
> mtcars.aov = aov(mtcars$mpg ~ as.factor(mtcars$gear))
> summary(mtcars.aov)
Output:
Df Sum Sq Mean Sq F value Pr(>F)
as.factor(mtcars$gear) 2 483.2 241.62 10.9 0.000295 ***
Residuals 29 642.8 22.17
---
Signif. codes: 0 '***' 0.001 '**' 0.01 '*' 0.05 '.' 0.1 ' ' 1
```

5. The model generated by the `aov` function can also generate a summary as a fitted table:

```
> model.tables(mtcars.aov, "means")
Output:
Tables of means
Grand mean
20.09062
as.factor(mtcars$gear)
      3    4    5
  16.11 24.53 21.38
rep 15.00 12.00 5.00
```

6. For the `aov` model, one can use `TukeyHSD` for a post hoc comparison test:

```
> mtcars_posthoc =TukeyHSD(mtcars.aov)
> mtcars_posthoc
Output:
  Tukey multiple comparisons of means
    95% family-wise confidence level

Fit: aov(formula = mtcars$mpg ~ as.factor(mtcars$gear))

$`as.factor(mtcars$gear)`
Output:
        diff       lwrupr         p         adj
4-3  8.426667  3.9234704 12.929863 0.0002088
5-3  5.273333 -0.7309284 11.277595 0.0937176
5-4 -3.153333 -9.3423846  3.035718 0.4295874
```

7. Further, we can visualize the differences in the mean level with a `plot` function:

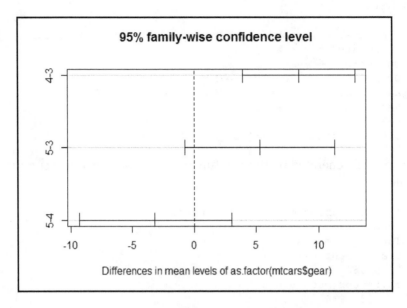

The Tukey mean-difference plot of groups with different numbers of gears

How it works...

In order to understand whether cars with a different number of forward gears have different means in mpg, we first plot the boxplot of mpg by the number of forward gears. This offers a simple indication of if cars with a different number of forward gears have different means of mpg. We then perform the most basic form of ANOVA, a one-way ANOVA, to test whether the populations have different means.

In R, there are two functions to perform the ANOVA test: `oneway.test` and `aov`. The advantage of `oneway.test` is that the function applies a Welch correction to address the non-homogeneity of a variance. However, it does not provide as much information as `aov`, and it does not offer a post hoc test. Next, we perform `oneway.test` and `aov` on the independent variable, `gear`, with regard to the dependent variable, `mpg`. Both test results show a small p-value, which rejects the null hypothesis that the mean between cars with a different number of forward gears have the same `mpg` mean.

As the results of ANOVA only suggest that there is a significant difference in the means within overall populations, you may not know which two populations differ in terms of their mean. Therefore, we apply the `TukeyHSD` post hoc comparison test on our ANOVA model. The result shows that cars with four forward gears and cars with three gears have the largest difference, as their confidence interval is the furthest to the right within the plot.

There's more...

ANOVA relies on an F-distribution as the basis of all probability distribution. An F score is obtained by dividing the between-group variance by the in-group variance. If the overall F test was significant, you can conduct a post hoc test (or multiple comparison tests) to measure the differences between groups. The most commonly used post hoc tests are Scheffé's method, the Tukey-Kramer method, and the Bonferroni correction.

In order to interpret the output of ANOVA, you need to have a basic understanding of certain terms, including the degrees of freedom, the sum of square total, the sum of square groups, the sum of square errors, the mean square errors, and the F statistic. If you require more information about these terms, you may refer to *Using Multivariate Statistics* (Fidell, L. S., and Tabachnick, B. G. (2006) *Boston: Allyn & Bacon.*), or refer to the Wikipedia entry of Analysis of Variance (`http://en.wikipedia.org/wiki/Analysis_of_variance#cite_ref-31`).

Performing a two-way ANOVA

A two-way ANOVA can be viewed as the extension of a one-way ANOVA, for the analysis covers more than two categorical variables rather than one. In this recipe, we will discuss how to conduct a two-way ANOVA in R.

Getting ready

Ensure that `mtcars` has already been loaded into a DataFrame within an R session. Since the `twoway.test`, `TukeyHSD`, and `interaction.plot` functions are originated from the `stats` package, make sure the library, `stats`, is loaded.

How to do it...

Perform the following steps:

1. First we plot the two boxplots of factor gears regarding mpg, with the plot separated from the transmission type:

```
> par(mfrow=c(1,2))
> boxplot
  (mtcars$mpg~mtcars$gear,subset=(mtcars$am==0),xlab='gear'
  , ylab = "mpg",main='automatic')
> boxplot
  (mtcars$mpg~mtcars$gear,subset=(mtcars$am==1),xlab='gear',
  ylab = "mpg", main='manual')
```

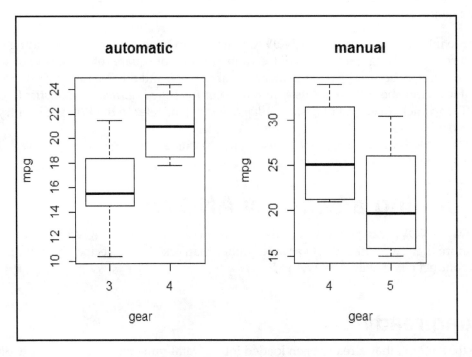

The boxplots of mpg by the gear group and the transmission type

2. Also, you may produce a boxplot of mpg by the number of forward gears *
   transmission type, with the use of the * operation in the `boxplot` function:

```
> boxplot(mtcars$mpg~factor(mtcars$gear)*
factor(mtcars$am),xlab='gear * transmission', ylab =
"mpg",main='Boxplot of mpg by gear * transmission')
```

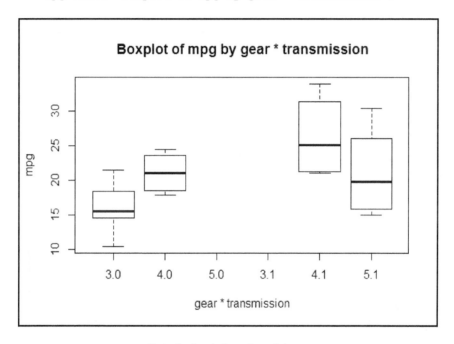

The boxplot of mpg by the gear * transmission type

3. Next, we use an interaction plot to characterize the relationship between variables:

```
> interaction.plot(mtcars$gear, mtcars$am, mtcars$mpg, type="b",
col=c(1:3),leg.bty="o", leg.bg="beige", lwd=2, pch=c(18,24,22),
xlab="Number of Gears", ylab="Mean Miles Per Gallon",
main="Interaction Plot")
```

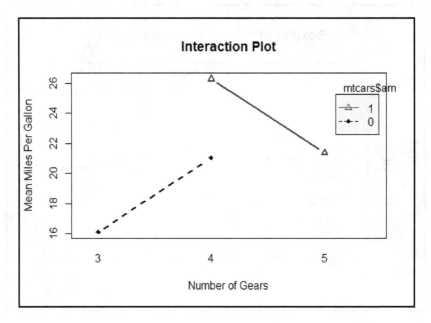

Interaction between the transmission type and the number of gears with the main effects, mpg

4. We then perform a two-way ANOVA on mpg with a combination of the gear and transmission-type factors:

```
> mpg_anova2 =
 aov(mtcars$mpg~factor(mtcars$gear)*factor(mtcars$am))
> summary(mpg_anova2)
Output:
Df Sum Sq Mean Sq F value Pr(>F)
factor(mtcars$gear) 2 483.2 241.62 11.869 0.000185 ***
factor(mtcars$am) 1 72.8 72.80 3.576 0.069001 .
Residuals 28 570.0 20.36
---
Signif. codes: 0 '***' 0.001 '**' 0.01 '*' 0.05 '.' 0.1 ' ' 1
```

5. Similar to a one-way ANOVA, we can perform a post hoc comparison test to see the results of the two-way ANOVA model:

```
> TukeyHSD(mpg_anova2)
Output:
  Tukey multiple comparisons of means
    95% family-wise confidence level
Fit: aov(formula = mtcars$mpg ~ factor(mtcars$gear) *
factor(mtcars$am))
$`factor(mtcars$gear)`
Output:
        diff       lwrupr        p         adj
4-3  8.426667  4.1028616 12.750472 0.0001301
5-3  5.273333 -0.4917401 11.038407 0.0779791
5-4 -3.153333 -9.0958350  2.789168 0.3999532
$`factor(mtcars$am)`
Output:
        diff       lwrupr       p        adj
1-0 1.805128 -1.521483 5.13174 0.2757926
```

6. We then visualize the differences in mean levels with the `plot` function:

```
par(mfrow=c(1,2))
> plot(TukeyHSD(mpg_anova2))
```

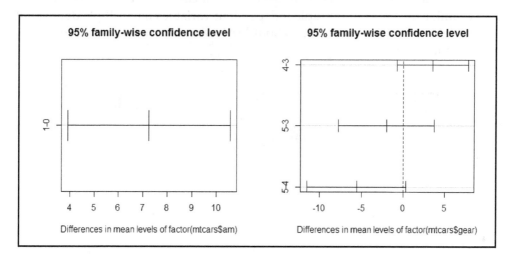

The comparison plot of differences in mean levels by the transmission type and the number of gears

How it works...

In this recipe, we perform a two-way ANOVA to examine the influences of the independent variables, gear and am, on the dependent variable, mpg. In the first step, we use a boxplot to examine the mean of mpg by the number of gears and the transmission type. Secondly, we apply an interaction plot to visualize the change in mpg through the different numbers of gears, with lines separated by the transmission type.

The resulting plot shows that the number of gears does have an effect on the mean of mpg, but does not show a positive relationship either. Thirdly, we perform a two-way ANOVA with the aov function. The output shows that the p-value of the gear factor rejects the null hypothesis, while the factor, transmission type, does not reject the null hypothesis. In other words, cars with different numbers of gears are more likely to have different means of mpg. Finally, in order to examine which two populations have the largest differences, we perform a post hoc analysis, which reveals that cars with four gears and three gears, respectively, have the largest difference in terms of the mean mpg.

See also

- For multivariate analysis of variances, the function, manova, can be used to examine the effect of multiple independent variables on multiple dependent variables. Further information about MANOVA is included within the help function in R:

```
> ?MANOVA
```

5
Understanding Regression Analysis

In this chapter, we will cover the following recipes:

- Different types of regression
- Fitting a linear regression model with `lm`
- Summarizing linear model fits
- Using linear regression to predict unknown values
- Generating a diagnostic plot of a fitted model
- Fitting multiple regression
- Summarizing multiple regression
- Using multiple regression to predict the values
- Fitting a polynomial regression model with `lm`
- Fitting a robust linear regression model with `rlm`
- Studying a case of linear regression on SLID data
- Applying the Gaussian model for generalized linear regression
- Applying the Poisson model for generalized linear regression
- Applying the Binomial model for generalized linear regression
- Fitting a generalized additive model to data
- Visualizing a generalized additive model
- Diagnosing a generalized additive model

Introduction

Regression is a supervised learning method, which is employed to model and analyze the relationship between a dependent (response) variable and one or more independent (predictor) variables. One can use regression to build a prediction model, which can first be used to find the best fitted model with minimum squared errors of the fitted values. The fitted model can then be further applied to data for continuous value predictions.

There are many types of regression. If there is only one predictor variable, and the relationship between the response variable and independent variable is linear, we can apply a linear model. However, if there is more than one predictor variable, a multiple linear regression method should be used. When the relationship is nonlinear, one can use a nonlinear model to model the relationship between the predictor and response variables.

In this chapter, we will introduce how to fit a linear model into data with the `lm` function. Next, for distribution in other than the normal Gaussian model (for example, Poisson or Binomial), we use the `glm` function with an appropriate `link` function correspondent to the data distribution. Finally, we will cover how to fit a generalized additive model into data using the `gam` function.

Different types of regression

This section will cover different types of regression:

- **Linear regression**: This is the oldest type and most widely known type of regression. In this the dependent variable is continuous and the independent variable can be discrete or continuous and the regression line is linear. Linear regression is very sensitive to outliers and cross-correlations.
- **Logistic regression**: This is used when the dependent variable is binary in nature (0 or 1, success or failure, survived or died, yes or no, true or false). It is widely used in clinical trials, fraud detection, and so on. It does not require there to be a linear relationship between dependent and independent variables.
- **Polynomial regression**: This implies of polynomial equation here the power of the independent variable is more than one. In this case the regression line is not a straight line, but a curved line.

- **Ridge regression**: This is a more robust version of linear regression and is used when data variables are highly correlated. Using some constraints on regression coefficients, it is made some more natural, closer to real estimates.
- **Lasso regression**: This is like ridge regression by penalizing the absolute size of regression coefficients. It also automatically performs the variable reduction.
- **Ecologic regression**: This is used when data is divided in different group or strata, performing regression per group or strata. One should be cautious when using this kind of regression as best regression may get over shadowed by noisy ones.
- **Logic regression**: This is same as Logistic regression, but it is used in scoring algorithms where all variables are of binary nature.
- **Bayesian regression**: This uses Bayesian interface of conditional probability. It uses the same approach as ridge regression, which involved penalizing estimator, making it more flexible and stable. It assumes some prior knowledge about regression coefficient and error terms and the error information is loaded with approximated probability distribution.
- **Quantile regression**: This is used when the area of interest is to study extreme limits, for example pollution level to study interest in death due to pollution. In this conditional quantile function of independent variable is used. It tries to estimate the value with conditional quantiles.
- **Jackknife regression**: This uses a resampling algorithm to remove the bias and variance.

Fitting a linear regression model with lm

The simplest model in regression is linear regression, which is best used when there is only one predictor variable, and the relationship between the response variable and the independent variable is linear. In R, we can fit a linear model to data with the lm function.

Getting ready

We need to prepare data with one predictor and response variable, and with a linear relationship between the two variables.

How to do it...

Perform the following steps to perform linear regression with `lm`:

1. You should install the `car` package and load its library:

   ```
   > install.packages("car")
   > library(car)
   ```

2. From the package, you can load the `Quartet` dataset:

   ```
   > data(Quartet)
   ```

3. You can use the `str` function to display the structure of the `Quartet` dataset:

   ```
   > str(Quartet)
   Output:
   'data.frame':    11 obs. of  6 variables:
   $ x : int   10 8 13 9 11 14 6 4 12 7 ...
   $ y1: num   8.04 6.95 7.58 8.81 8.33 ...
   $ y2: num   9.14 8.14 8.74 8.77 9.26 8.1 6.13 3.1 9.13 7.26 ...
   $ y3: num   7.46 6.77 12.74 7.11 7.81 ...
   $ x4: int   8 8 8 8 8 8 8 19 8 8 ...
   $ y4: num   6.58 5.76 7.71 8.84 8.47 7.04 5.25 12.5 5.56 7.91 ...
   ```

4. Draw a scatter plot of the x and y variables with `plot`, and append a fitted line through the `lm` and `abline` functions:

   ```
   > plot(Quartet$x, Quartet$y1)
   > lmfit = lm(y1~x, Quartet)
   > abline(lmfit, col="red")
   ```

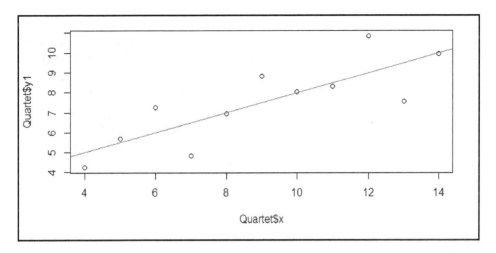

A simple regression plot fitted by lm

5. To view the fit model, execute the following:

```
> lmfit
Output:
  Call:
  lm(formula = y1 ~ x, data = Quartet)
  Coefficients:
  (Intercept)              x
  3.0001          0.5001
```

How it works...

The regression model has the `response ~ terms` form, where `response` is the response vector, and `terms` is a series of terms that specifies a predictor. We can illustrate a simple regression model with the formula $y=\alpha+\beta x$, where α is the intercept while the slope, β, describes the change in y when x changes. By using the least squares method, we can estimate and (where indicates the mean value of y and denotes the mean value of x).

To perform linear regression, we first prepare the data that has a linear relationship between the predictor variable and response variable. In this example, we load Anscombe's quartet dataset from the package car. Within the dataset, the x and y1 variables have a linear relationship, and we prepare a scatter plot of these variables. To generate the regression line, we use the lm function to generate a model of the two variables. Furthermore, we use abline to plot a regression line on the plot. As per the previous screenshot, the regression line illustrates the linear relationship of x and y1 variables. We can see that the coefficient of the fitted model shows the intercept equals *3.0001* and coefficient equals *0.5001*. As a result, we can use the intercept and coefficient to infer the response value. For example, we can infer the response value when x at 3 is equal to *4.5103* (*3 * 0.5001 + 3.0001*).

There's more...

Besides the lm function, you can also use the lsfit function to perform simple linear regression. For example:

```
> plot(Quartet$x, Quartet$y1)
> lmfit2 = lsfit(Quartet$x,Quartet$y1)
> abline(lmfit2, col="red")
```

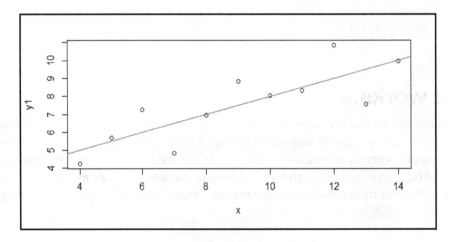

A simple regression fitted by the lsfit function.

Summarizing linear model fits

The `summary` function can be used to obtain the formatted coefficient, standard errors, degree of freedom, and other summarized information of a fitted model. This recipe introduces how to obtain overall information on a model through the use of the `summary` function.

Getting ready

You need to have completed the previous recipe by computing the linear model of the `x` and `y1` variables from the quartet, and have the fitted model assigned to the `lmfit` variable.

How to do it...

Perform the following step to summarize linear model fits:

1. Compute a detailed summary of the fitted model:

```
> summary(lmfit)
Output:
Call:
lm(formula = y1 ~ x)

Residuals:
    Min 1Q Median 3Q Max
-1.92127 -0.45577 -0.04136 0.70941 1.83882

Coefficients:
            Estimate Std. Error t value Pr(>|t|)
(Intercept) 3.0001 1.1247 2.667 0.02573 *
Quartet$x 0.5001 0.1179 4.241 0.00217 **
---
Signif. codes: 0 '***' 0.001 '**' 0.01 '*' 0.05 '.' 0.1 ' ' 1

Residual standard error: 1.237 on 9 degrees of freedom
Multiple R-squared: 0.6665, Adjusted R-squared: 0.6295
F-statistic: 17.99 on 1 and 9 DF, p-value: 0.00217
```

How it works...

The summary function is a generic function used to produce summary statistics. In this case, it computes and returns a list of the summary statistics of the fitted linear model. Here, it will output information such as residuals, coefficient standard error R-squared, f-statistic, and a degree of freedom. In the Call section, the function called to generate the fitted model is displayed. In the Residuals section, it provides a quick summary (Min, 1Q, Median, 3Q, Max) of the distribution.

In the Coefficients section, each coefficient is a Gaussian random variable. Within this section, Estimate represents the mean distribution of the variable; Std.Error displays the standard error of the variable; the t value is Estimate divided by Std.Error and the p value indicates the probability of getting a value larger than the t value. In this sample, the p value of both intercepts (0.002573) and x (0.00217) have a 95 percent level of confidence.

Residual standard error outputs the standard deviation of residuals, while the degree of freedom indicates the differences between the observation in training samples and the number used in the model. Multiple R-squared is obtained by dividing the sum of squares. One can use R-squared to measure how close the data is to fitting into the regression line. Mostly, the higher the R-squared, the better the model fits your data. However, it does not necessarily indicate whether the regression model is adequate. This means you might get a good model with a low R-squared or you can have a bad model with a high R-squared. Since multiple R-squared ignores a degree of freedom, the calculated score is biased. To make the calculation fair, an adjusted R-squared (0.6295) uses an unbiased estimate, and will be slightly less than multiple R-squared (0.6665). F-statistic is retrieved by performing an f-test on the model. A p value equal to 0.00217 (< 0.05) rejects the null hypothesis (no linear correlation between variables) and indicates that the observed F is greater than the critical F value. In other words, the result shows that there is a significant positive linear correlation between the variables.

See also

- For more information on the parameters used for obtaining a summary of the fitted model, you can use the `help` function or `?` to view the help page:

    ```
    > ?summary.lm
    ```

- Alternatively, you can use the following functions to display the properties of the model:

    ```
    > coefficients(lmfit) # Extract model coefficients
    > confint(lmfit, level=0.95)   # Computes confidence intervals for
      model parameters.
    > fitted(lmfit) # Extract model fitted values
    > residuals(lmfit) # Extract model residuals
    > anova(lmfit) # Compute analysis of variance tables for fitted
      model object
    > vcov(lmfit) # Calculate variance-covariance matrix for a fitted
      model object
    > influence(lmfit) # Diagnose quality of regression fits
    ```

Using linear regression to predict unknown values

With a fitted regression model, we can apply the model to predict unknown values. For regression models, we can express the precision of prediction with a prediction interval and a confidence interval. In the following recipe, we will introduce how to predict unknown values under these two measurements.

Getting ready

You need to have completed the previous recipe by computing the linear model of the x and $y1$ variables from the `quartet` dataset.

How to do it...

Perform the following steps to predict values with linear regression:

1. Fit a linear model with the x and y1 variables:

   ```
   > lmfit = lm(y1~x, Quartet)
   ```

2. Assign values to be predicted into `newdata`:

   ```
   > newdata = data.frame(x = c(3,6,15))
   ```

3. Compute the prediction result using the confidence interval with `level` set as 0.95:

   ```
   > predict(lmfit, newdata, interval="confidence", level=0.95)
   Output:
        fit lwr upr
   1 4.500364 2.691375 6.309352
   2 6.000636 4.838027 7.163245
   3 10.501455 8.692466 12.310443
   ```

4. Compute the prediction result using this prediction interval:

   ```
   > predict(lmfit, newdata, interval="predict")
   Output:
        fit lwr upr
   1 4.500364 1.169022 7.831705
   2 6.000636 2.971271 9.030002
   3 10.501455 7.170113 13.832796
   ```

How it works...

We first build a linear fitted model with x and y1 variables. Next, we assign values to be predicted into a DataFrame, `newdata`. It is important to note that the generated model is in the form of y1 ~ x.

Next, we compute the prediction result using a confidence interval by specifying `confidence` in the argument interval. From the output of row 1, we get fitted `y1` of the `x=3` input, which equals to `4.500364`, and a 95 percent confidence interval (set `0.95` in the `level` argument) of the `y1` mean for `x=3` is between `2.691375` and `6.309352`. In addition to this, row 2 and 3 give the prediction result of `y1` with an input of `x=6` and `x=15`.

Next, we compute the prediction result using a prediction interval by specifying `prediction` in the argument interval. From the output of row 1, we can see fitted `y1` of the `x=3` input is equal to `4.500364`, and a 95 percent prediction interval of `y1` for `x=3` is between `1.169022` and `7.831705`. Row 2 and 3 output the prediction result of `y1` with an input of `x=6` and `x=15`.

See also

- For those who are interested in the differences between prediction intervals and confidence intervals, you can refer to the wikipedia entry *contrast with confidence intervals* at
  `http://en.wikipedia.org/wiki/Prediction_interval#Contrast_with_confidence_intervals`.

Generating a diagnostic plot of a fitted model

Diagnostics are methods to evaluate assumptions of the regression, which can be used to determine whether a fitted model adequately represents the data. In the following recipe, we will introduce how to diagnose a regression model through the use of a diagnostic plot.

Getting ready

You need to have completed the previous recipe by computing a linear model of the `x` and `y1` variables from the quartet, and have the model assigned to the `lmfit` variable.

How to do it...

Perform the following step to generate a diagnostic plot of the fitted model:

1. Plot the diagnostic plot of the regression model:

```
> par(mfrow=c(2,2))
> plot(lmfit)
```

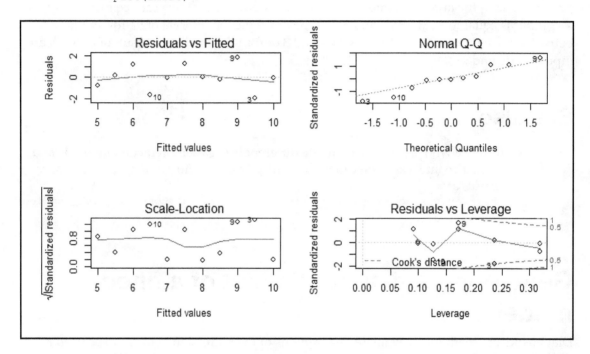

Diagnostic plots of the regression model

How it works...

The `plot` function generates four diagnostic plots of a regression model:

- The upper-left plot shows residuals versus fitted values. Within the plot, residuals represent the vertical distance from a point to the regression line. If all points fall exactly on the regression line, all residuals will fall exactly on the dotted gray line. The red line within the plot is a smooth curve with regard to residuals, and if all the dots fall exactly on the regression line, the position of the red line should exactly match the dotted gray line.
- The upper-right shows the normal for the residuals. This plot verifies the assumption that residuals were normally distributed. Thus, if the residuals were normally distributed, they should lie exactly on the gray dotted line.
- The **Scale-Location** plot on the bottom-left is used to measure the square root of the standardized residuals against the fitted value. Therefore, if all dots lie on the regression line, the value of y should be close to zero. Since it is assumed that the variance of residuals does not change the distribution substantially, if the assumption is correct, the red line should be relatively flat.
- The bottom-right plot shows standardized residuals versus leverage. The leverage is a measurement of how each data point influences the regression. It is a measurement of the distance from the centroid of regression and level of isolation (measured by whether it has neighbors). Also, you can find the contour of Cook's distance, which is affected by high leverage and large residuals. You can use this to measure how regression would change if a single point is deleted. The red line is smooth with regard to standardized residuals. For a perfect fit regression, the red line should be close to the dashed line with no points over 0.5 in Cook's distance.

There's more...

To see more of the diagnostic plot function, you can use the `help` function to access further information:

```
> ?plot.lm
```

In order to discover whether there are points with large Cook's distance, one can use the `cooks.distance` function to compute the Cook's distance of each point, and analyze the distribution of distance through visualization:

```
> plot(cooks.distance(lmfit))
```

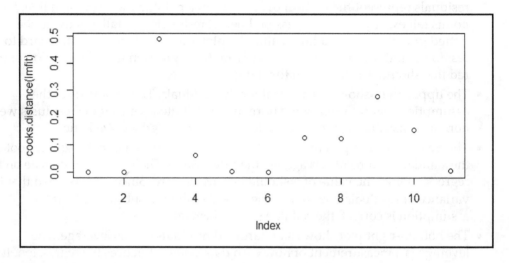

A plot of Cook's distance

In this case, where the point on index 3 shows greater Cook's distance than other points, one can investigate whether this point might be an outlier.

Fitting multiple regression

Multiple regression includes multiple predictors and using the same `lm` function we can create a model.

Getting ready

You have completed the previous recipes and have installed the `car` package. You are also aware of using the `lm` function. In this recipe, we will use the `Prestige` dataset from the `car` package.

How to do it...

Perform the following step to perform multiple regression with `lm`:

```
> head(Prestige)
Output:
 education income women prestige census type
gov.administrators 13.11 12351 11.16 68.8 1113 prof
general.managers 12.26 25879 4.02 69.1 1130 prof
accountants 12.77 9271 15.70 63.4 1171 prof
purchasing.officers 11.42 8865 9.11 56.8 1175 prof
chemists 14.62 8403 11.68 73.5 2111 prof
physicists 15.64 11030 5.13 77.6 2113 prof
> str(Prestige)
Output
'data.frame': 102 obs. of 6 variables:
 $ education: num 13.1 12.3 12.8 11.4 14.6 ...
 $ income : int 12351 25879 9271 8865 8403 11030 8258 14163 11377 11023 ...
 $ women : num 11.16 4.02 15.7 9.11 11.68 ...
 $ prestige : num 68.8 69.1 63.4 56.8 73.5 77.6 72.6 78.1 73.1 68.8 ...
 $ census : int 1113 1130 1171 1175 2111 2113 2133 2141 2143 2153 ...
 $ type : Factor w/ 3 levels "bc","prof","wc": 2 2 2 2 2 2 2 2 2 2 ...
> attach(Prestige)
> model = lm(income~prestige+women)
> scatter3d(income~prestige+women, Prestige)
```

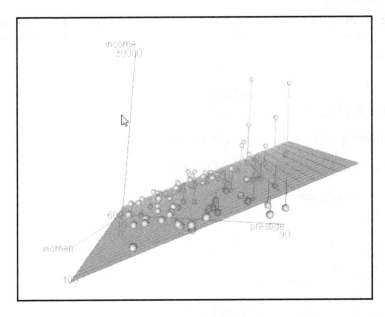

3d scatterplot

How it works...

The regression model has the `income ~ prestige + women` form, where `income` is the response vector, and `prestige and women` specifies a predictor. We can illustrate a simple regression model in the formula $y = \alpha + \beta_1 x_1 + \beta_2 x_2$, where α is the intercept while the slope, β_1 and β_2, describes the change in y when x changes. By using the least squares method, we can estimate and (where indicates the mean value of y and denotes the mean value of x_1 and x_2).

In this example, we load the `Prestige` dataset from the `car` package. To generate the regression line, we use the `lm` function to generate a model of the three variables. Further, we use `scatter3d` to plot a regression line in a 3d plot.

Summarizing multiple regression

The `summary` function can be used to obtain the formatted coefficient, standard errors, degree of freedom, and other summarized information of a fitted model. This recipe introduces how to obtain overall information on a model using the `summary` function.

Getting ready

You need to have completed the previous recipe by computing the linear model of the `income`, `prestige` and `women` variables from the `Prestige` dataset, and have the fitted model assigned to the `model` variable.

How to do it...

Perform the following step to summarize linear model fits:

1. Compute a detailed summary of the fitted model:

    ```
    > summary(model)
    Output:
    Call:
    lm(formula = income ~ prestige + women)
    Residuals:
    Min 1Q Median 3Q Max
    -7620.9 -1008.7 -240.4 873.1 14180.0
    Coefficients:
     Estimate Std. Error t value Pr(>|t|)
    ```

```
(Intercept) 431.574 807.630 0.534 0.594
prestige 165.875 14.988 11.067 < 2e-16 ***
women -48.385 8.128 -5.953 4.02e-08 ***
---
Signif. codes: 0 '***' 0.001 '**' 0.01 '*' 0.05 '.' 0.1 ' ' 1
Residual standard error: 2573 on 99 degrees of freedom
Multiple R-squared: 0.64, Adjusted R-squared: 0.6327
F-statistic: 87.98 on 2 and 99 DF, p-value: < 2.2e-16
```

How it works...

The `summary` function is a generic function used to produce summary statistics. In this case, it computes and returns a list of the summary statistics of the fitted linear model. Here, it will output information such as residuals, coefficient standard error R-squared, f-statistic, and a degree of freedom. In the `Call` section, the function called to generate the fitted model is displayed. In the `Residuals` section, it provides a quick summary (min, 1Q, median, 3Q, max) of the distribution.

In the `Coefficients` section, each coefficient is a Gaussian random variable. Within this section, `Estimate` represents the mean distribution of the variable; `Std.Error` displays the standard error of the variable; the `t` value is `Estimate` divided by `Std.Error` and the p-value indicates the probability of getting a value larger than the `t` value.

Residual standard error outputs the standard deviation of residuals, while the degree of freedom indicates the differences between the observation in training samples and the number used in the model. Multiple R-squared is obtained by dividing the sum of squares. One can use R-squared to measure how close the data is to fit into the regression line. Mostly, the higher the R-squared, the better the model fits your data. However, it does not necessarily indicate whether the regression model is adequate. This means you might get a good model with a low R-squared or you can have a bad model with a high R-squared. Since multiple R-squared ignores a degree of freedom, the calculated score is biased. To make the calculation fair, an adjusted R-squared (0.6327) uses an unbiased estimate, and will be slightly less than multiple R-squared (0.64).

See also

- For more information on the parameters used for obtaining a summary of the fitted model, you can use the `help` function or `?` to view the help page:

  ```
  > ?summary.lm
  ```

- Alternatively, you can use the following functions to display the properties of the model:

  ```
  > coefficients(model) # Extract model coefficients
  > confint(model, level=0.95)  # Computes confidence intervals for
    model parameters.
  > fitted(modelmodel) # Extract model fitted values
  > residuals(lmfit) # Extract model residuals
  > anova(model) # Compute analysis of variance tables for fitted
    model object
  > vcov(model) # Calculate variance-covariance matrix for a fitted
    model object
  > influence(model) # Diagnose quality of regression fits
  ```

Using multiple regression to predict unknown values

With a fitted regression model, we can apply the model to predict unknown values. For regression models, we can express the precision of prediction with a prediction interval and a confidence interval. In the following recipe, we will introduce how to predict unknown values under these two measurements.

Getting ready

You need to have completed the previous recipe by computing the linear model of the `income`, `prestige`, and `women` variables from the `Prestige` dataset.

How to do it...

Perform the following steps to predict values with multiple regression:

1. Fit a linear model with the `income`, `prestige`, and `women` variables:

   ```
   > model = lm(income ~ prestige + women, Prestige)
   ```

2. Assign values to be predicted into `newdata`:

   ```
   > newdat = data.frame(prestige = c(75,80), women=c(14,13))
   ```

3. Compute the prediction result using the confidence interval with `level` set as 0.95:

   ```
   > predict(model, newdata = newdat)
   Output:
          1        2
   12194.80 13072.56
   ```

Compute the prediction result using this prediction interval:

```
> predict(model, newdata = newdat, interval="predict")
Output:
     fit      lwr      upr
1 12194.80 6994.903 17394.69
2 13072.56 7847.050 18298.06
```

How it works...

We first build a multiple regression model with `income`, `prestige` and `women` variables. Next, we assign values to be predicted into a DataFrame, `newdat`. It is important to note that the generated model is in the form of `income ~ prestige + women`.

Next, we compute the prediction result using a confidence interval by specifying `confidence` in the argument interval.

See also

For those who are interested in the differences between prediction intervals and confidence intervals, you can refer to the wikipedia entry *contrast with confidence intervals* at `http://en.wikipedia.org/wiki/Prediction_interval#Contrast_with_confidence_inter vals`.

Fitting a polynomial regression model with lm

Some predictor variables and response variables may have a non-linear relationship, and their relationship can be modeled as an nth order polynomial. In this recipe, we will introduce how to deal with polynomial regression using the lm and poly functions.

Getting ready

Prepare the dataset that includes a relationship between the predictor and response variable that can be modeled as an nth order polynomial. In this recipe, we will continue to use the Quartet dataset from the car package.

How to do it...

Perform the following steps to fit the polynomial regression model with lm:

1. First, we make a scatter plot of the x and y2 variables:

```
> plot(Quartet$x, Quartet$y2)
```

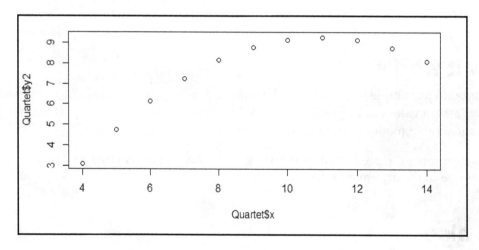

Scatter plot of variables x and y2

2. You can apply the `poly` function by specifying 2 in the argument:

```
> lmfit = lm(Quartet$y2~poly(Quartet$x,2))
> lines(sort(Quartet$x), lmfit$fit[order(Quartet$x)], col = "red")
```

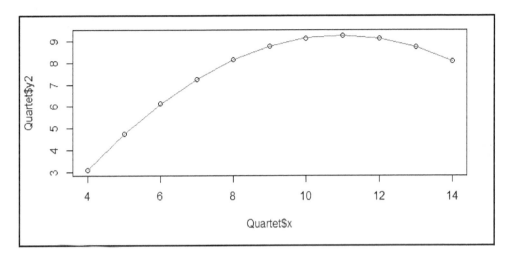

A quardratic fit example of the regression plot of variables x and y2

How it works...

We can illustrate the second order polynomial regression model in the formula, where α is the intercept, while β illustrates regression coefficients.

In the preceding screenshot (step 1), the scatter plot of the x and y2 variables does not fit in a linear relationship, but shows a concave downward curve (or convex upward) with the turning point at *x=11*. In order to model the nonlinear relationship, we apply the `poly` function with an argument of 2 to fit the independent x variable and the dependent y2 variable. The red line in the screenshot shows that the model perfectly fits the data.

There's more...

You can also fit a second order polynomial model with an independent variable equal to the formula of the combined first order x variable and the second order x variable:

```
> plot(Quartet$x, Quartet$y2)
> lmfit = lm(Quartet$y2~ I(Quartet$x)+I(Quartet$x^2))
```

Fitting a robust linear regression model with rlm

An outlier in the dataset will move the regression line away from the mainstream. Apart from removing it, we can apply a robust linear regression to fit datasets containing outliers. In this recipe, we will introduce how to apply `rlm` to perform robust linear regression to datasets containing outliers.

Getting ready

Prepare the dataset that contains an outlier that may move the regression line away from the mainstream. Here, we use the `Quartet` dataset loaded from the previous recipe.

How to do it...

Perform the following steps to fit the robust linear regression model with `rlm`:

1. Generate a scatter plot of the x variable against y3:

```
> plot(Quartet$x, Quartet$y3)
```

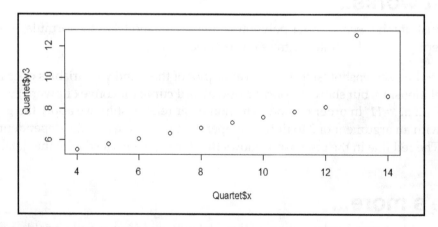

Scatter plot of variables x and y3

2. Next, you should import the MASS library first. Then, you can apply the `rlm` function to fit the model, and visualize the fitted line with the `abline` function:

```
> library(MASS)
> lmfit = rlm(Quartet$y3~Quartet$x)
> abline(lmfit, col="red")
```

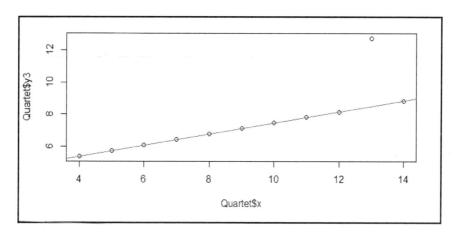

Robust linear regression to variables x and y3

How it works...

As per the preceding screenshot (step 1), you may encounter datasets that include outliers away from the mainstream. To remove the effect of an outlier, we demonstrate how to apply a robust linear regression (`rlm`) to fit the data. In the second screenshot (step 2), the robust regression line ignores the outlier and matches the mainstream.

There's more...

To see the effect of how an outlier can move the regression line away from the mainstream, you may replace the `rlm` function used in this recipe with `lm`, and replot the graph:

```
> plot(Quartet$x, Quartet$y3)
> lmfit = lm(Quartet$y3~Quartet$x)
> abline(lmfit, col="red")
```

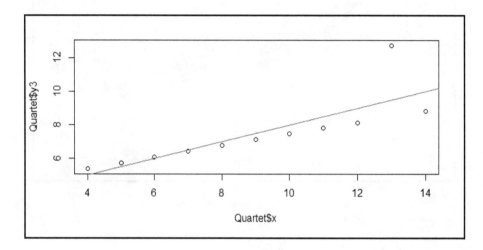

Linear regression on variables x and y3

It is obvious that outlier ($x=13$) moves the regression line away from the mainstream.

Studying a case of linear regression on SLID data

To summarize the contents of the previous section, we will explore more complex data with linear regression. In this recipe, we will demonstrate how to apply linear regression to analyze the **Survey of Labor and Income Dynamics (SLID)** dataset.

Getting ready

Check whether the `car` library is installed and loaded, as it is required to access the dataset SLID.

How to do it...

Follow these steps to perform linear regression on SLID data:

1. You can use the `str` function to get an overview of the data:

```
> str(SLID)
Output:
'data.frame': 7425 obs. of 5 variables:
 $ wages : num 10.6 11 NA 17.8 NA ...
 $ education: num 15 13.2 16 14 8 16 12 14.5 15 10 ...
 $ age : int 40 19 49 46 71 50 70 42 31 56 ...
 $ sex : Factor w/ 2 levels "Female","Male": 2 2 2 2 2 1 1
 1 2 1 ...
 $ language : Factor w/ 3 levels "English","French",..: 1 1 3 3
 1 1 1 1 1 1 ..
```

2. First, we visualize the variable wages against `language`, `age`, `education`, and `sex`:

```
> par(mfrow=c(2,2))
> plot(SLID$wages ~ SLID$language)
> plot(SLID$wages ~ SLID$age)
> plot(SLID$wages ~ SLID$education)
> plot(SLID$wages ~ SLID$sex)
```

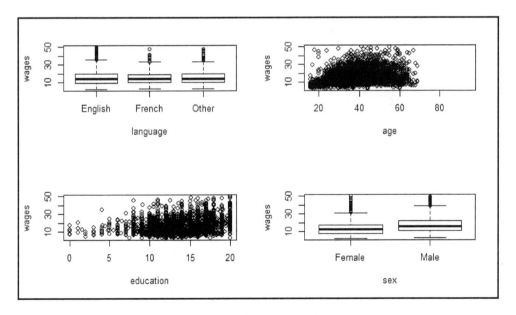

Plot of wages against multiple combinations

3. Then, we can use `lm` to fit the model:

```
> lmfit = lm(wages ~ ., data = SLID)
```

4. You can examine the summary of the fitted model through the `summary` function:

```
> summary(lmfit)
Output:
Call:
lm(formula = wages ~ ., data = SLID)

Residuals:
    Min 1Q Median 3Q Max
-26.062 -4.347 -0.797 3.237 35.908

Coefficients:
               Estimate Std. Error t value Pr(>|t|)
(Intercept) -7.888779 0.612263 -12.885 <2e-16 ***
education    0.916614 0.034762 26.368 <2e-16 ***
age          0.255137 0.008714 29.278 <2e-16 ***
sexMale      3.455411 0.209195 16.518 <2e-16 ***
languageFrench  -0.015223 0.426732 -0.036 0.972
languageOther   0.142605 0.325058 0.439 0.661
---
Signif. codes: 0 '***' 0.001 '**' 0.01 '*' 0.05 '.' 0.1 ' ' 1

Residual standard error: 6.6 on 3981 degrees of freedom
(3438 observations deleted due to missingness)
Multiple R-squared: 0.2973, Adjusted R-squared: 0.2964
F-statistic: 336.8 on 5 and 3981 DF, p-value: < 2.2e-16
```

5. Drop the `language` attribute, and refit the model with the `lm` function:

```
> lmfit = lm(wages ~ age + sex + education, data = SLID)
> summary(lmfit)
Output:
Call:
lm(formula = wages ~ age + sex + education, data = SLID)

Residuals:
    Min 1Q Median 3Q Max
-26.111 -4.328 -0.792 3.243 35.892

Coefficients:
               Estimate Std. Error t value Pr(>|t|)
(Intercept) -7.905243 0.607771 -13.01 <2e-16 ***
age          0.255101 0.008634 29.55 <2e-16 ***
sexMale      3.465251 0.208494 16.62 <2e-16 ***
```

```
education   0.918735 0.034514 26.62 <2e-16 ***
---
Signif. codes: 0 '***' 0.001 '**' 0.01 '*' 0.05 '.' 0.1 ' ' 1

Residual standard error: 6.602 on 4010 degrees of freedom
  (3411 observations deleted due to missingness)
 Multiple R-squared: 0.2972, Adjusted R-squared: 0.2967
F-statistic: 565.3 on 3 and 4010 DF, p-value: < 2.2e-16
```

6. We can then draw a diagnostic plot of `lmfit`:

```
> par(mfrow=c(2,2))
> plot(lmfit)
```

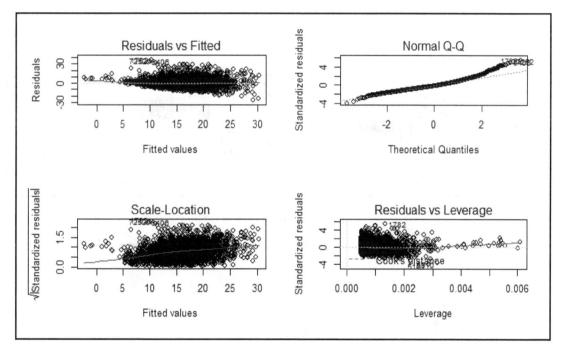

Diagnostic plot of fitted model

7. Next, we take the log of wages and replot the diagnostic plot:

```
> lmfit = lm(log(wages) ~ age + sex + education, data = SLID)
> plot(lmfit)
```

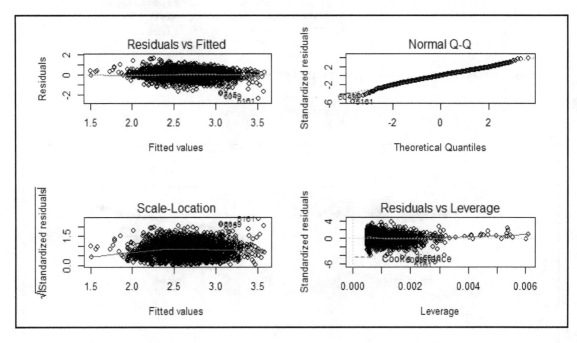

Diagnostic plot of adjusted fitted model

8. Next, you can diagnose the multi-colinearity of the regression model using the `vif` function:

```
> vif(lmfit)
Output:
      age sex education
 1.011613 1.000834 1.012179
> sqrt(vif(lmfit)) > 2
Output:
     age sex education
   FALSE FALSE FALSE
```

9. Then, you can install and load the `lmtest` package and diagnose the heteroscedasticity of the regression model with the `bptest` function:

```
> install.packages("lmtest")
> library(lmtest)
```

```
> bptest(lmfit)
Output:
    studentized Breusch-Pagan test

data: lmfit
BP = 29.0311, df = 3, p-value = 2.206e-06
```

10. Finally, you can install and load the `rms` package. Then, you can correct standard errors with `robcov`:

```
> install.packages("rms")
> library(rms)
> olsfit = ols(log(wages) ~ age + sex + education, data= SLID, x=
TRUE, y= TRUE)
> robcov(olsfit)
Output:

Linear Regression Model

ols(formula = log(wages) ~ age + sex + education, data = SLID,
    x = TRUE, y = TRUE)

Frequencies of Missing Values Due to Each Variable
log(wages)    age    sex    education
      3278      0      0          249


              Model Likelihood      Discrimination
                Ratio Test             Indexes
Obs      4014      LR chi2    1486.08    R2      0.309
sigma 0.4187      d.f.         3    R2 adj 0.309
d.f. 4010 Pr(> chi2) 0.0000 g 0.315


Residuals

  Min       1Q     Median    3Q     Max
-2.36252 -0.27716 0.01428 0.28625 1.56588


          Coef    S.E.    t    Pr(>|t|)
Intercept 1.1169 0.0387 28.90 <0.0001
age       0.0176 0.0006 30.15 <0.0001
sex=Male  0.2244 0.0132 16.96 <0.0001
education 0.0552 0.0022 24.82 <0.0001
```

How it works...

This recipe demonstrates how to conduct linear regression analysis on the SLID dataset. First, we load the SLID data and display its structure through the use of the `str` function. From the structure of the data, we know that there are four independent variables that will affect the wages of the dependent variable.

Next, we explore the relationship of each independent variable to the dependent variable, `wages`, through visualization; the visualization result is shown in the preceding screenshot (step 2). In the upper-left section of this screenshot, you can find the box plot of three different languages against wages; the correlation between the languages and wages is not obvious. The upper-right section of the screenshot shows that the age appears to have a positive relationship with the dependent variable, `wages`. In the bottom-left of the screenshot, it is shown that education also appears to have a positive relationship with wages. Finally, the box plot in the bottom-right section of the screenshot shows that the wages of males are slightly higher than females.

Next, we fit all the attributes except for `wages` to the model as predictor variables. By summarizing the model, it is shown that education, age, and sex show a significance (p-*value* < 0.05). As a result, we drop the insignificant `language` attribute (which has a p-value greater than 0.05) and fit the three independent variables (`education`, `sex`, and `age`) with regard to the dependent variable (`wages`) in the linear model. This accordingly raises the f-statistic from 336.8 to 565.3.

Next, we generate the diagnostic plot of the fitted model. Within the diagnostic plot, all the four plots indicate that the regression model follows the regression assumption. However, from residuals versus fitted and scale-location plot, residuals of smaller fitted values are biased toward the regression model. Since wages range over several orders of magnitude, to induce the symmetry, we apply a log transformation to wages and refit the data into a regression model. The red line of residuals versus fitted values plot and the Scale-Location plot are now closer to the gray dashed line.

Next, we would like to test whether multi-colinearity exists in the model. Multi-colinearity takes place when a predictor is highly correlated with others. If multi-colinearity exists in the model, you might see that some variables have a high R-squared value, but are shown as insignificant variables . To detect multi-colinearity, we can calculate the variance inflation and generalized variance inflation factors for linear and generalized linear models with the `vif` function. If multi-colinearity exists, we should find predictors with the square root of variance inflation factor above 2. Then, we may remove redundant predictors or use a principal component analysis to transform predictors to a smaller set of uncorrelated components.

Finally, we would like to test whether **heteroscedasticity** exists in the model. Before discussing the definition of heteroscedasticity, we first have to know that in classic assumptions, the ordinary regression model assumes that the variance of the error is constant or homogeneous across observations. On the contrary, heteroscedasticity means that the variance is unequal across observations. As a result, heteroscedasticity may be biased towards the standard errors of our estimates and, therefore, mislead the testing of the hypothes. To detect and test heteroscedasticity, we can perform the **Breusch-Pagan** test for heteroscedasticity with the `bptest` function within the `lmtest` package. In this case, the p-value shows 2.206e-06 (<0.5), which rejects the null hypothesis of homoscedasticity (not heteroscedasticity). Here, it implies that the standard errors of the parameter estimates are incorrect. However, we can use robust standard errors to correct the standard error (do not remove the heteroscedasticity) and increase the significance of truly significant parameters with `robcov` from the `rms` package. However, since it only takes the fitted model from the `rms` series as an input, we have to fit the ordinary least squares model beforehand.

See also

- For more information about the SLID dataset, you can use the `help` function to view the related documentation:

    ```
    >    ?SLID
    ```

Applying the Gaussian model for generalized linear regression

Generalized Linear Model (GLM) is a generalization of linear regression, which can include a `link` function to make a linear prediction. As a default setting, the family object for `glm` is Gaussian, which makes the `glm` function perform exactly the same as `lm`. In this recipe, we first demonstrate how to fit the model into the data using the `glm` function, and then show that `glm` with a Gaussian model performs exactly the same as `lm`.

Getting ready

Check whether the car library is installed and loaded as we require the SLID dataset from this package.

How to do it...

Perform the following steps to fit a generalized linear regression model with the Gaussian model:

1. Fit the independent variables, age, sex, and education, and dependent variable wages to glm:

```
> lmfit1 = glm(wages ~ age + sex + education, data = SLID, fami
ly=gaussian)
> summary(lmfit1)
Output:

Call:
glm(formula = wages ~ age + sex + education, family = gaussian,
    data = SLID)

Deviance Residuals:
    Min    1Q   Median    3Q     Max
-26.111 -4.328 -0.792 3.243 35.892

Coefficients:
      Estimate Std. Error t value Pr(>|t|)
(Intercept) -7.905243 0.607771 -13.01 <2e-16 ***
age          0.255101 0.008634 29.55 <2e-16 ***
sexMale      3.465251 0.208494 16.62 <2e-16 ***
education    0.918735 0.034514 26.62 <2e-16 ***
---
Signif. codes: 0 '***' 0.001 '**' 0.01 '*' 0.05 '.' 0.1 ' ' 1

(Dispersion parameter for Gaussian family taken to be 43.58492)

    Null deviance: 248686 on 4013 degrees of freedom
Residual deviance: 174776 on 4010 degrees of freedom
  (3411 observations deleted due to missingness)
  AIC: 26549

Number of Fisher Scoring iterations: 2
```

2. Fit the independent variables, age, sex, and education, and the dependent variable wages to lm:

```
> lmfit2 = lm(wages ~ age + sex + education, data = SLID)
> summary(lmfit2)
Output:
Call:
lm(formula = wages ~ age + sex + education, data = SLID)

Residuals:
    Min     1Q   Median   3Q    Max
-26.111 -4.328 -0.792 3.243 35.892
Coefficients:
      Estimate Std. Error t value Pr(>|t|)
(Intercept) -7.905243 0.607771 -13.01 <2e-16 ***
age          0.255101 0.008634  29.55 <2e-16 ***
sexMale      3.465251 0.208494  16.62 <2e-16 ***
education    0.918735 0.034514  26.62 <2e-16 ***
---
Signif. codes: 0 '***' 0.001 '**' 0.01 '*' 0.05 '.' 0.1 ' ' 1

Residual standard error: 6.602 on 4010 degrees of freedom
  (3411 observations deleted due to missingness)
Multiple R-squared: 0.2972, Adjusted R-squared: 0.2967
F-statistic: 565.3 on 3 and 4010 DF, p-value: < 2.2e-16
```

3. Use anova to compare the two fitted models:

```
> anova(lmfit1, lmfit2)
Output:
Analysis of Deviance Table

Model: gaussian, link: identity

Response: wages

Terms added sequentially (first to last)


        Df Deviance Resid. Df Resid. Dev
NULL                4013       248686
age    1    31953   4012       216733
sex    1    11074   4011       205659
education 1 30883 4010 174776
```

How it works...

The `glm` function fits a model to the data in a similar fashion to the `lm` function. The only difference is that you can specify a different `link` function in the parameter, `family` (you may use `?family` in the console to find different types of `link` functions). In this recipe, we first input the independent variables, `age`, `sex`, and `education`, and the dependent `wages` variable to the `glm` function, and assign the built model to `lmfit1`. You can use the built model for further prediction.

Next, to determine whether `glm` with a Gaussian model is exactly the same as `lm`, we fit the independent variables, `age`, `sex`, and `education`, and the dependent variable, `wages`, to the `lm` model. By applying the `summary` function to the two different models, it reveals that the residuals and coefficients of the two output summaries are exactly the same.

Finally, we further compare the two fitted models with the `anova` function. The result of the `anova` function shows that the two models are similar, with the same **residual degrees of freedom** (`Res.DF`) and **residual sum of squares** (`RSS Df`).

See also

- For a comparison of generalized linear models with linear models, you can refer to *Venables, W. N., & Ripley, B. D. (2002). Modern Applied Statistics with S. Springer.*

Applying the Poisson model for generalized linear regression

Generalized linear models allow response variables that have error distribution models other than a normal distribution (Gaussian). In this recipe, we will demonstrate how to apply Poisson as a family object within `glm` with regard to count data.

Getting ready

The prerequisite for this task is to prepare the count data, with all the input data values as integers.

How to do it...

Perform the following steps to fit the generalized linear regression model with the Poisson model:

1. Load the `warpbreaks` data, and use `head` to view the first few lines:

```
> data(warpbreaks)
> head(warpbreaks)
Output:
    breaks wool tension
1     26    A     L
2     30    A     L
3     54    A     L
4     25    A     L
5     70    A     L
6     52    A     L
```

2. We apply Poisson as a family object for the independent variable, `tension`, and the dependent variable, `breaks`:

```
> rs1 = glm(breaks ~ tension, data=warpbreaks, family="poisson")
> summary(rs1)
Output:

Call:
glm(formula = breaks ~ tension, family = "poisson", data =
warpbreaks)

Deviance Residuals:
    Min     1Q    Median     3Q      Max
-4.2464 -1.6031 -0.5872 1.2813 4.9366
Coefficients:
            Estimate Std. Error z value Pr(>|z|)
(Intercept) 3.59426  0.03907  91.988  < 2e-16 ***
tensionM   -0.32132  0.06027  -5.332 9.73e-08 ***
tensionH   -0.51849  0.06396  -8.107 5.21e-16 ***
---
Signif. codes: 0 '***' 0.001 '**' 0.01 '*' 0.05 '.' 0.1 ' ' 1
(Dispersion parameter for Poisson family taken to be 1)

    Null deviance: 297.37 on 53 degrees of freedom
Residual deviance: 226.43 on 51 degrees of freedom
AIC: 507.09
Number of Fisher Scoring iterations: 4
```

How it works...

Under the assumption of a Poisson distribution, the count data can be fitted to a log-linear model. In this recipe, we first loaded sample count data from the `warpbreaks` dataset, which contained data regarding the number of warp breaks per loom. Next, we applied the `glm` function with breaks as a dependent variable, `tension` as an independent variable, and Poisson as a family object. Finally, we viewed the fitted log-linear model with the `summary` function.

See also

- To understand more about how the Poisson model is related to count data, you can refer to *Cameron, A. C., & Trivedi, P. K. (2013). Regression Analysis of Count Data (No. 53). Cambridge University press.*

Applying the Binomial model for generalized linear regression

For a binary dependent variable, one may apply a binomial model as the family object in the `glm` function.

Getting ready

The prerequisite of this task is to prepare a binary dependent variable. Here, we use the `vs` variable (V engine or straight engine) as the dependent variable.

How to do it...

Perform the following steps to fit a generalized linear regression model with the Binomial model:

1. First, we examine the first six elements of vs within mtcars:

```
> head(mtcars$vs)
Output:
 [1] 0 0 1 1 0 1
```

2. We apply the glm function with binomial as the family object:

```
> lm1 = glm(vs ~ hp+mpg+gear,data=mtcars, family=binomial)
> summary(lm1)
Output:
Call:
glm(formula = vs ~ hp + mpg + gear, family = binomial, data =
mtcars)

Deviance Residuals:
    Min      1Q     Median    3Q      Max
 -1.68166 -0.23743 -0.00945 0.30884 1.55688

Coefficients:
            Estimate Std. Error z value Pr(>|z|)
(Intercept) 11.95183 8.00322 1.493 0.1353
hp -0.07322 0.03440 -2.129 0.0333 *
mpg 0.16051 0.27538 0.583 0.5600
gear -1.66526 1.76407 -0.944 0.3452
---
Signif. codes: 0 '***' 0.001 '**' 0.01 '*' 0.05 '.' 0.1 ' ' 1

(Dispersion parameter for binomial family taken to be 1)

    Null deviance: 43.860 on 31 degrees of freedom
Residual deviance: 15.651 on 28 degrees of freedom
AIC: 23.651

Number of Fisher Scoring iterations: 7
```

How it works...

Within the binary data, each observation of the response value is coded as either 0 or 1. Fitting into the regression model of the binary data requires a binomial distribution function. In this example, we first load the binary dependent variable, vs, from the mtcars dataset. The vs is suitable for the binomial model as it contains binary data. Next, we fit the model into the binary data using the glm function by specifying binomial as the family object. Last, by referring to the summary, we can obtain a description of the fitted model.

See also

- If you specify the family object in parameters only, you will use the default link to fit the model. However, to use an alternative link function, you can add a link argument. For example:

```
> lm1 = glm(vs ~ hp+mpg+gear,data=mtcars,
  family=binomial(link="probit"))
```

- If you would like to know how many alternative links you can use, please refer to the family document via the help function:

```
> ?family
```

Fitting a generalized additive model to data

Generalized Additive Model (GAM), which is used to fit generalized additive models, can be viewed as a semiparametric extension of GLM. While GLM holds the assumption that there is a linear relationship between dependent and independent variables, GAM fits the model on account of the local behavior of data. As a result, GAM has the ability to deal with highly nonlinear relationships between dependent and independent variables. In the following recipe, we will introduce how to fit regression using a generalized additive model.

Getting ready

We need to prepare a data frame containing variables, where one of the variables is a response variable and the others may be predictor variables.

How to do it...

Perform the following steps to fit a generalized additive model into data:

1. First, load the `mgcv` package, which contains the `gam` function:

```
> install.packages("mgcv")
> library(mgcv)
```

2. Then, install the `MASS` package and load the `Boston` dataset:

```
> install.packages("MASS")
> library(MASS)
> attach(Boston)
> str(Boston)
```

3. Fit the regression using `gam`:

```
> fit = gam(dis ~ s(nox))
```

4. Get the summary information of the fitted model:

```
> summary(fit)
Output:
Family: gaussian
Link function: identity

Formula:
dis ~ s(nox)

Parametric coefficients:
            Estimate Std. Error t value Pr(>|t|)
(Intercept) 3.79504 0.04507 84.21 <2e-16 ***
---
Signif. codes: 0 '***' 0.001 '**' 0.01 '*' 0.05 '.' 0.1 ' ' 1

Approximate significance of smooth terms:
        edf Ref.df F p-value
s(nox) 8.434 8.893 189 <2e-16 ***
---
Signif. codes: 0 '***' 0.001 '**' 0.01 '*' 0.05 '.' 0.1 ' ' 1

R-sq.(adj) = 0.768 Deviance explained = 77.2%
GCV = 1.0472 Scale est. = 1.0277 n = 506
```

How it works...

GAM is designed to maximize the prediction of a dependent variable, y, from various distributions by estimating the nonparametric functions of the predictors that link to the dependent variable through a `link` function. The notion of GAM is, where an exponential family, *E*, is specified for *y*, along with the `g` `link` function; `f` denotes the `link` function of predictors.

The `gam` function is contained in the `mgcv` package, so, install this package first and load it into an R session. Next, load the Boston dataset (*Housing Values in the Suburbs of Boston*) from the `MASS` package. From the dataset, we use `dis` (the weighted mean of the distance to five Boston employment centers) as the dependent variable, and `nox` (nitrogen oxide concentration) as the independent variable, and then input them into the `gam` function to generate a fitted model.

Similar to `glm`, `gam` allows users to summarize the `gam` fit. From the summary, one can find the parametric parameter, significance of smoothed terms, and other useful information.

See also

- Apart from `gam`, the `mgcv` package provides another generalized additive model, `bam`, for large datasets. The `bam` package is very similar to `gam`, but uses less memory and is relatively more efficient. Please use the `help` function for more information on this model:

    ```
    > ? bam
    ```

- For more information about generalized additive models in R, please refer to *Wood, S. (2006). Generalized Additive Models: An Introduction with R. CRC Press*.

Visualizing a generalized additive model

In this recipe, we demonstrate how to add a `gam` fitted regression line to a scatter plot. In addition, we visualize the `gam` fit using the `plot` function.

Getting ready

Complete the previous recipe by assigning a gam fitted model to the fit variable.

How to do it...

Perform the following steps to visualize the generalized additive model:

1. Generate a scatter plot using the nox and dis variables:

   ```
   > plot(nox, dis)
   ```

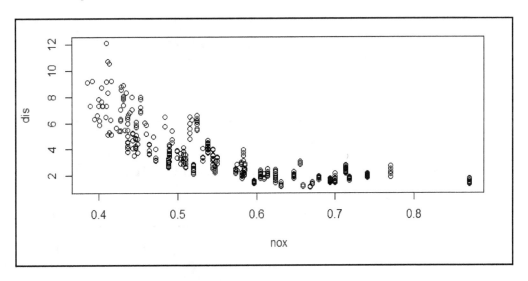

Scatter plot of variable nox against dis

2. Add the regression to the scatter plot:

```
> x = seq(0, 1, length = 500)
> y = predict(fit, data.frame(nox = x))
> lines(x, y, col = "red", lwd = 2)
```

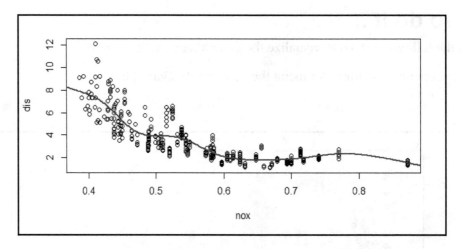

Fitted regression of gam on a scatter plot

3. Alternatively, you can plot the fitted model using the `plot` function:

```
> plot(fit)
```

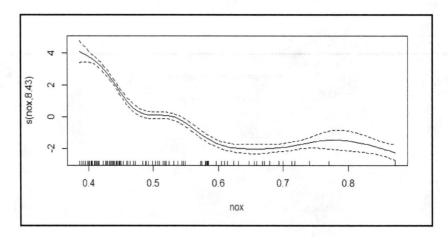

Plot of fitted gam

How it works...

To visualize the fitted regression, we first generate a scatter plot using the `dis` and `nox` variables. Then, we generate the sequence of *x*-axis, and respond *y* through the use of the `predict` function on the fitted model, `fit`. Finally, we use the `lines` function to add the regression line to the scatter plot.

Besides using the lines to add fitted regression lines on the scatter plot, `gam` has a `plot` function to visualize the fitted regression lines containing the confidence region. To shade the confidence region, we assign `shade = TRUE` within the function.

There's more...

The `vis.gam` function is used to produce perspective or contour plot views of the `gam` model predictions. It is helpful to observe how response variables interact with two predictor variables. The following is an example of a contour plot on the `Boston` dataset:

```
> fit2=gam(medv~crim+zn+crim:zn, data=Boston)
> vis.gam(fit2)
```

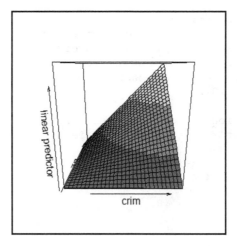

A sample contour plot produced by vis.gam

Diagnosing a generalized additive model

GAM also provides diagnostic information about the fitting procedure and results of the generalized additive model. In this recipe, we demonstrate how to plot diagnostic plots through the gam.check function.

Getting ready

Ensure that the previous recipe is completed with the gam fitted model assigned to the fit variable.

How to do it...

Perform the following step to diagnose the generalized additive model:

1. Generate the diagnostic plot using gam.check on the fitted model:

```
> gam.check(fit)
Output:
Method: GCV   Optimizer: magic
Smoothing parameter selection converged after 7 iterations.
The RMS GCV score gradient at convergence was 8.79622e-06 .
The Hessian was positive definite.
The estimated model rank was 10 (maximum possible: 10)
Model rank = 10 / 10

Basis dimension (k) checking results. Low p-value (k-index<1) may
indicate that k is too low, especially if edf is close to k'.

         k'  edf  k-index  p-value
s(nox) 9.000 8.434  0.397  0
```

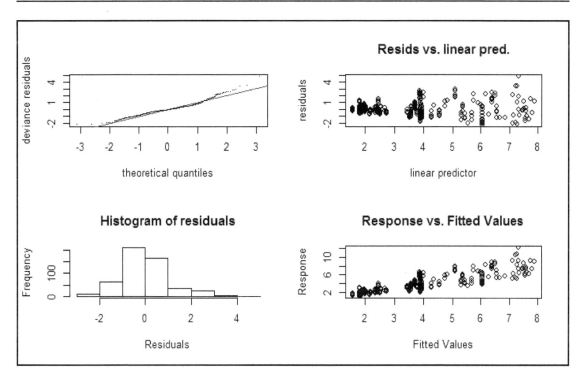

Diagnostic plot of fitted gam

How it works...

The `gam.check` function first produces the smoothing parameter estimation convergence information. In this example, the smoothing parameter, **Generalized Cross Validation/ Unbiased Risk Estimator (GCV/UBRE)**, score converges after seven iterations. The mean absolute gradient of the GCV/UBRE function at the minimum is 8.79622e-06 and the estimated rank is 10. The dimension check is to test whether the basis dimension for a smooth function is adequate. From this example, the low p-value indicates that the k is set too low. One may adjust the dimension choice for smooth by specifying the argument, k, by fitting `gam` to the data.

In addition to providing information regarding smoothing parameter estimation convergence, the function returns four diagnostic plots. The upper-left section of the plot in the screenshot shows a **quantile-comparison** plot. This plot is useful to identify outliers and heavy tails. The upper-right section of the plot shows residuals versus linear predictors, which are useful in finding nonconstant error variances. The bottom-left section of the plot shows a histogram of the residuals, which is helpful in detecting non-normality. The bottom-right section shows response versus the fitted value.

There's more...

You can access the `help` function for more information on `gam.check`. In particular, this includes a detailed illustration of smoothing parameter estimation convergence and four returned plots:

```
> ?gam.check
```

In addition, more information for `choose.k` can be accessed by using the following command:

```
> ?choose.k
```

6
Survival Analysis

In this chapter, we will cover the following recipes:

- Loading and observing data
- Viewing the summary of survival analysis
- Visualizing the survival curve
- Using the log-rank test
- Using the Cox proportional hazards model for survival analysis
- Nelson-Aalen estimator of cumulative hazard

Introduction

Survival analysis is also known as duration analysis, transition analysis, failure time analysis, and time-to-event analysis. In survival analysis, subjects are tracked until an event happens or we lose them from the sample. Events can be anything, such as death, marriage, divorce, and so on. Subjects are followed for a specific time and the focus is on the time the event occurs. The three terms used commonly while talking about survival analysis are birth event, death event, and censorship. A birth event is the time when the observation started, a death event is the time at the end of the event or study, and censorship means a death event will not always occur. Censoring occurs because the subject does not experience the event during the time, the subject is lost, or the subject withdraws from the study. Censoring can be thought of as a kind of missing data problem. Consider the study of a clinical trial being conducted for 2 years; if the person under observation does not show any symptoms during that period, it is said to be censored, or some patient leaves the trial before the said period then that case is also categorized as censored.

Censoring can be categorized as right censoring and left censoring. Right censoring means a subject leaves before the event occurs or the study ends before the event occurred. For example, in clinical trial for 2 years of disease A is conducted. Patients who do not have disease A in 2 years are censored. Left censoring means the event of interest has already occurred before the patient is taken in under observation. It is normally a rare case. Again, right censoring can be of two types: Type 1: Random dropout and Type 2: End of a study when the fixed or predetermined event has occurred. A response from the observations is normally referred as failure time, survival time, or event time. Survival analysis is widely used in medical or clinical trial fields to record the result and predict the outcome. Let's understand it with a few examples. Assume a medical or clinical trial is conducted to determine whether a particular treatment, say treatment A, is effective or not in, say, disease B. The study or trial is carried out with some patients under observation and records the patient response to treatment A. It studies whether the patient survives or not or leaves the study in between for some reason. Another example concerns a loan performance: if a borrower will repay the loan in time or will default. In terms of commerce or online shopping, the study time is between signup and the first order. It can also be used to study the market to determine how long it takes a person to replace his or her phone, the time until the machine part fails, Survival analysis is a type of regression model but the point of interest is to find the dropout, where the subjects under observation are not sure about the event.

The survival function *S(t)* is the probability that the subject survives longer than time *t*:

$$S(t) = Pr(\ T > t)$$

Here *t* is some time, *T* is a random variable denoting the time of death, *Pr* is the probability. *S(0) = 1*. The survival function approaches *0* as time increases. In theoretical terms, the survival function is smooth; that is, it is represented by the smooth curve. In practice, it may differ as the events are observed on a discrete time scale. One must also get accustomed to the hazard function and cumulative hazard function which are used to describe the rate at which an event occurs. For more details, visit
`https://en.wikipedia.org/wiki/Survival_analysis#Definitions_of_common_terms_in_`
`survival_analysis`.

Loading and observing data

In this recipe, we will see how to load and view survival data. We will create a response object to fit in the survival model.

Getting ready

This recipe requires survival package, as we will be using a dataset from it.

How to do it...

Perform the following steps to perform survival analysis:

1. You should install the `survival` package and load its library:

   ```
   > install.packages("survival")
   > library(survival)
   ```

2. From the package, you can load the `cancer` dataset:

   ```
   > data(cancer)
   ```

3. You can use the `str` function to display the structure of the `cancer` dataset:

   ```
   > str(cancer)
   Output
   'data.frame':     228 obs. of  10 variables:
    $ inst     : num  3 3 3 5 1 12 7 11 1 7 ...
    $ time     : num  306 455 1010 210 883 ...
    $ status   : num  2 2 1 2 2 1 2 2 2 2 ...
    $ age      : num  74 68 56 57 60 74 68 71 53 61 ...
    $ sex      : num  1 1 1 1 1 1 2 2 1 1 ...
    $ ph.ecog  : num  1 0 0 1 0 1 2 2 1 2 ...
    $ ph.karno : num  90 90 90 90 100 50 70 60 70 70 ...
    $ pat.karno: num  100 90 90 60 90 80 60 80 80 70 ...
    $ meal.cal : num  1175 1225 NA 1150 NA ...
    $ wt.loss  : num  NA 15 15 11 0 0 10 1 16 34 ...
   > View(cancer)
   ```

View of cancer dataset from R studio

4. The `cancer` dataset shows the survival of patient with advanced lung cancer. It shows the following:

inst	Institution code
time	Survival time in days
status	Censoring status 1=censored, 2=dead
age	Age in years
sex	Male=1, Female=2
ph.ecog	ECOG performance score (0=good 5=dead)
ph.karno	Karnofsky performance score (bad=0-good=100) rated by physician
pat.karno	Karnofsky performance score as rated by patient
meal.cal	Calories consumed at meals
wt.loss	Weight loss in last 6 months

5. Using the survfit function, we will create a survival curve:

```
> sfit <- survfit(Surv(time, status)~sex, data=cancer)
```

How it works...

The `surv` function will create a response variable on the basis of time and event. Using the response variable or `surv` function, the `survfit` function will create a survival curve in the form of stair steps. We divide the curve via gender; that is, male and female. It uses the Kaplan-Meier Estimate to compute the survival over time. It is a frequently used method.

There's more...

Explore other datasets in the `survival` package to see the data with the time and event.

Viewing the summary of survival analysis

Once we have the `survfit` object, we can see the summary of it to get some insights.

Getting ready

You need to have completed the previous recipe and have the sfit object from cancer dataset.

How to do it...

Perform the following steps to view the summary:

```
> sfit <- survfit(Surv(time, status)~sex, data=cancer)
> sfit
Output
Call: survfit(formula = Surv(time, status) ~ sex, data = cancer)

   n events median 0.95LCL 0.95UCL
sex=1 138 112 270 212 310
sex=2 90 53 426 348 550
```

```
> summary(sfit)
The following are a few lines from the output of the summary command:
Call: survfit(formula = s ~ sex, data = cancer)

 sex=1
 time n.risk n.event survival std.err lower 95% CI upper 95% CI
 11 138 3 0.9783 0.0124 0.9542 1.000
 12 135 1 0.9710 0.0143 0.9434 0.999
 13 134 2 0.9565 0.0174 0.9231 0.991
 15 132 1 0.9493 0.0187 0.9134 0.987
 26 131 1 0.9420 0.0199 0.9038 0.982
```

How it works...

The `surfit` function shows details for different genders. If we look at the first observation, where `sex=1` (Male), it states that a total of 138 males were in the `cancer` dataset, of which 112 people died; the median time is 270 days. It also points out that the 95% confidence interval for the median survival time for 212 is 310.

The summary of the `survfit` function displays the data in a tabular format for each time point in the dataset. At every step, it computes the total person at risk; that is, `n.risk`, the number of events at a given time point, and `n.point`: proportion who survived at a point of time with the standard error and confidence level. If we look at the first two lines of output:

```
 time n.risk n.event survival std.err lower 95% CI upper 95% CI
 11 138 3 0.9783 0.0124 0.9542 1.000
 12 135 1 0.9710 0.0143 0.9434 0.999
```

We can see that at time 11, in our case the time is in days, so on the 11th day, the total number of people at risk was 138, out of which an event occurred for 3; that is, three people died.

On the 12th day, the total number of people at risk was 138 - 3 = 135, of which one person died.

It also shows the standard error, and the upper and lower confidence of the curve.

Visualizing the Survival Curve

Once we have created a curve model, we want to plot and see it. When we plot the data, we can actually see the survival against the time for males and females in our case.

Getting ready

You need to have completed the previous recipe.

How to do it...

1. Perform the following step to generate a diagnostic plot of the fitted model:

```
> install.packages("survminer")
> library(survminer)
```

2. Generate `sfit` in case the previous recipe is not completed:

```
> hist(cancer$time, xlab="Survival Time", main="Histogram
of survival time")
```

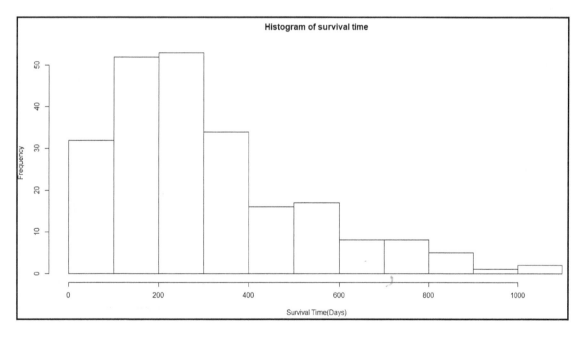

Histogram of survival times

3. We can see from the preceding diagram that as days increase, the survival chances are low. The survival rate is high for 100 to 300 days.

4. We want to see how gender plays a role in survival or we want to see the survival by gender. This can be achieved by the Kalpan-Meier Estimator plot. Perform the following step:

```
> s <- Surv(cancer$time, cancer$status)
> sfit <- survfit(Surv(time, status)~sex, data=cancer)
```

5. Lets plot the curve:

```
> plot(sfit)
```

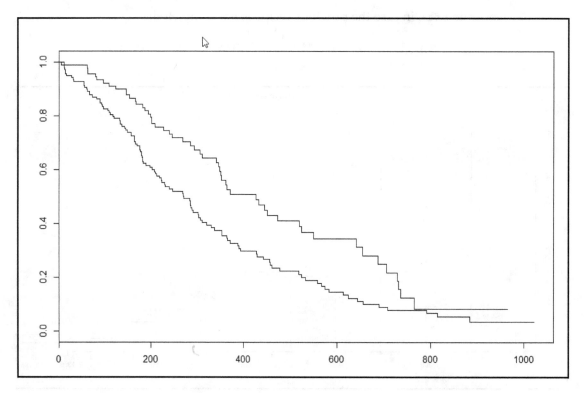

Plot of sfit (Kalpan-Meier Estimator)

6. Let's plot using `ggsurvplot`, which will beautify the plot:

```
> ggsurvplot(sfit)
```

7. Add the label for gender and the risk table:

```
> ggsurvplot(sfit, risk.table = TRUE, legend.labs=c("Male",
"Female"))
```

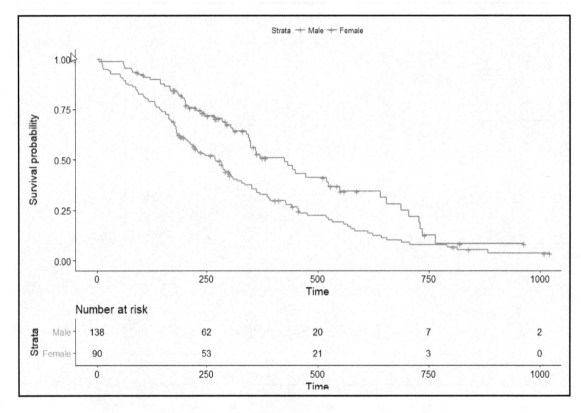

Survival plot with risk table.

8. In the same way, we can see the other options instead of gender. The following shows the survival rate by institute:

```
> ggsurvplot(survfit(Surv(time, status)~inst, data=cancer))
```

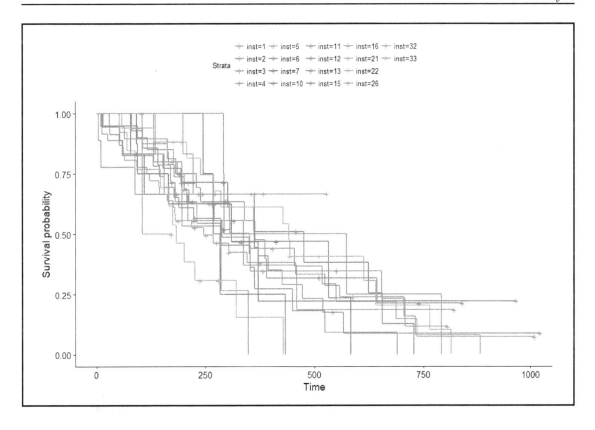

How it works...

The `plot` function will generate a plot of `suvfit` which displays two lines for male and female. But it is difficult to interpret. Using the `survminer` package, we can produce more interpretable results. The `ggsurvplot` function will automatically add colors to the lines and add the default label. We can change the label from sex *0* and *1* to male and female and print the risk table to understand more from the plot.

Using the log-rank test

The log-rank test is used to find the difference between two curves. It is a nonparametric test. It is also known as the Mantel-Cox test. It compares the estimates of hazard functions at each observed time. It will test two hypotheses: there is no difference in the survival function based on gender, and there is a difference in survival function based on gender.

Getting ready

You need to have performed the previous recipes.

How to do it...

Perform the following step:

```
> survdiff(Surv(cancer$time, cancer$status)~cancer$sex)
  Output
    Call:
    survdiff(formula = Surv(cancer$time, cancer$status) ~ cancer$sex)
    N Observed Expected (O-E)^2/E (O-E)^2/V
    cancer$sex=1 138 112 91.5817 4.55228 10.3267
    cancer$sex=2 90 53 73.4183 5.67850 10.3267
    Chisq= 10.3 on 1 degrees of freedom, p= 0.00131116
```

How it works...

The `survdiff` function displays the number of observations in a group; in our case, 138 males and 90 females. The observation shows the number of events that occurred in the group. We can see that testing the null hypothesis shows no difference in the survival function. The second argument is rho, which decides the log-rank test or the Peto and Peto test. The default is rho=0, which stands for log-rank test and rho=1 specifies Peto and Peto modification of the Gehman-Wilcoxon test.

Using the COX proportional hazard model

The survival function gives the probability that a subject will survive up to time t where t moves to infinity. The hazard function is a rate at which an event occurs or the potential that an event will occur, per time unit. The `survfit` function works on the basis of the Kaplan-Meier method which works best when we have to represent two categories such as gender (male or female), as shown previously. It fails when the categories are increased.

In a Cox proportional hazards regression model, the measure of effect is the **hazard rate**, which is the risk of failure (the risk or probability of suffering the event of interest), given that the participant has survived up to a specific time. A probability must lie in the range 0 to 1. However, the hazard represents the expected number of events per one unit of time. As a result, the hazard in a group can exceed 1. For example, if the hazard is 0.2 at time t and the time units are months, then on average, 0.2 events are expected per person at risk per month.

Getting ready

You need to have performed the previous recipes.

How to do it...

Perform the following steps to use the Cox proportional hazards regression model:

1. The Cox proportional hazard model is good for most cases and its syntax looks much like `lm` and `glm` functions.

    ```
    > coxph(formula=Surv(time, status)~sex, data=cancer)
    Output
    Call:
    coxph(formula = Surv(time, status) ~ sex, data = cancer)
    coef exp(coef) se(coef) z p
    sex -0.531 0.588 0.167 -3.18 0.0015
    Likelihood ratio test=10.6 on 1 df, p=0.00111
    n= 228, number of events= 165
    > coxph(formula=Surv(time, status)~sex + age, data=cancer)
    Output
    Call:
    coxph(formula = Surv(time, status) ~ sex + age, data = cancer)
    coef exp(coef) se(coef) z p
    sex -0.513219 0.598566 0.167458 -3.065 0.00218
    age 0.017045 1.017191 0.009223 1.848 0.06459
    Likelihood ratio test=14.12 on 2 df, p=0.000857443
    n= 228, number of events= 165
    ```

How it works...

The `coxph` function will fit the Cox proportional hazard model. The `exp(coef)` shows the hazard ratio. Hazard ratio 1 means no effect, >1 increased hazard, and <1 reduction in hazard. The preceding result can be exp(0.531) and will be 1.700, so the male result a 1.7 fold increase in hazard or males die 1.7 rate per unit as female. So it can be concluded that survival rate in females are better compared to male.

In the next step, we extend it by adding the age and test our hypothesis. Again by adding age in to the equation as a covariate, the results turned out to be same, as there is no difference in the survival function.

Nelson-Aalen Estimator of cumulative hazard

We have seen the Cox proportional hazard estimator in the previous recipe The Nelson-Aalen estimator is a non-parametric estimator that estimates the cumulative number of expected events. It gives an idea about the hazard rate shape.

Getting ready

You need to have performed the recipe dealing with the Cox proportional hazard.

How to do it...

Perform the following steps in R:

```
> sfitall = survfit(Surv(time, status)~1, data =cancer)
> c = coxph(formula=Surv(time, status)~1, data=cancer)
> n=basehaz(c)
```

Printing n will display all the hazard values with time. Plotting the same will be easy to understand:

```
> plot(n)
```

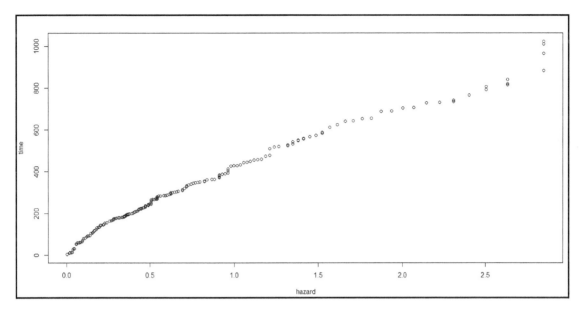

Plot of hazard and time

How it works...

Using the `basehaz` function will compute the hazard estimator for the Cox model using the Breslow estimator, which will be the same as the Nelson-Aalen estimator. It can also be computed using the `cumsum` function, which returns cumulative sums. The hazard function is simply an event divided by risk and can be computed using the following:

```
> nm = cumsum(ss$n.event/ss$n.risk)
```

If we compare the value of the `nm` variable with the `n` variable, they will be same.

See also

- For more information about the function, use the `help` function in R or refer to the documentation.

7
Classification 1 - Tree, Lazy, and Probabilistic

In this chapter, we will cover the following recipes:

- Preparing the training and testing datasets
- Building a classification model with recursive partitioning trees
- Visualizing a recursive partitioning tree
- Measuring the prediction performance of a recursive partitioning tree
- Pruning a recursive partitioning tree
- Handling missing data and split and surrogate variables
- Building a classification model with a conditional inference tree
- Conditional parameters in conditional inference trees
- Visualizing a conditional inference tree
- Measuring the prediction performance of a conditional inference tree
- Classifying data with a k-nearest neighbor classifier
- Classifying data with logistic regression
- Classifying data with the Naïve Bayes classifier

Introduction

Classification is used to identify a category of new observations (testing datasets) based on a classification model built from the training dataset of which the categories are already known. Similar to regression, classification is categorized as a supervised learning method as it employs known answers (label) of a training dataset to predict the answer (label) of the testing dataset. The main difference between regression and classification is that regression is used to predict continuous values.

In contrast to this, classification is used to identify the category of a given observation. For example, one may use regression to predict the future price of a given stock based on historical prices. However, one should use the classification method to predict whether the stock price will rise or fall.

In this chapter, we will illustrate how to use R to perform classification. We first build a training dataset and a testing dataset from the `churn` dataset, and then apply different classification methods to classify the `churn` dataset. In the following recipes, we will introduce the tree-based classification method using a traditional classification tree and a conditional inference tree, lazy-based algorithm, and a probabilistic-based method using the training dataset to build up a classification model, and then use the model to predict the category (class label) of the testing dataset. We will also use a confusion matrix to measure the performance.

Preparing the training and testing datasets

Building a classification model requires a training dataset to train the classification model, and testing data is needed to then validate the prediction performance. In the following recipe, we will demonstrate how to split the telecom `churn` dataset into training and testing datasets, respectively.

Getting ready

In this recipe, we will use the telecom `churn` dataset as the input data source, and split the data into training and testing datasets.

How to do it...

Perform the following steps to split the `churn` dataset into training and testing datasets:

1. You can retrieve the churn dataset from the `C50` package:

```
> install.packages("C50")
> library(C50)
> data(churn)
```

2. Use `str` to read the structure of the dataset:

```
> str(churnTrain)
```

3. We can remove the `state`, `area_code`, and `account_length` attributes, which are not appropriate for classification features:

```
> churnTrain = churnTrain[,! names(churnTrain) %in% c("state",
 "area_code", "account_length") ]
```

4. Then, split 70 percent of the data into the training dataset and 30 percent of the data into the testing dataset:

```
> set.seed(2)
> ind = sample(2, nrow(churnTrain), replace = TRUE,
prob=c(0.7, 0.3))
> trainset = churnTrain[ind == 1,]
> testset = churnTrain[ind == 2,]
```

5. Lastly, use `dim` to explore the dimensions of both the training and testing datasets:

```
> dim(trainset)
Output
   [1] 2315    17
> dim(testset)
Output
 [1] 1018    17
```

How it works...

In this recipe, we use the telecom churn dataset as our example data source. The dataset contains 20 variables with 3,333 observations. We would like to build a classification model to predict whether a customer will churn, which is very important to telecom company as the cost of acquiring a new customer is significantly more than retaining one.

Before building the classification model, we need to preprocess the data first. Thus, we load the churn data from the C50 package into the R session with the variable name churn. As we determined that attributes such as state, area_code, and account_length are not useful features for building the classification model, we remove these attributes.

After preprocessing the data, we split it into training and testing datasets, respectively. We then use a sample function to randomly generate a sequence containing 70 percent of the training dataset and 30 percent of the testing dataset with a size equal to the number of observations. Then, we use a generated sequence to split the churn dataset into the training dataset, trainset, and the testing dataset, testset. Lastly, by using the dim function, we find that 2,315 out of the 3,333 observations are categorized into the training dataset, trainset, while the other 1,018 are categorized into the testing dataset, testset.

There's more...

You can combine the split process of the training and testing datasets into the split.data function. Therefore you can easily split the data into the two datasets by calling this function and specifying the proportion and seed in the parameters:

```
> split.data = function(data, p = 0.7, s = 666){
+     set.seed(s)
+     index = sample(1:dim(data)[1])
+     train = data[index[1:floor(dim(data)[1] * p)], ]
+     test = data[index[((ceiling(dim(data)[1] * p)) + 1):dim(data)[1]], ]
+     return(list(train = train, test = test))
+ }
```

Building a classification model with recursive partitioning trees

A classification tree uses a split condition to predict class labels based on one or multiple input variables. The classification process starts from the root node of the tree; at each node, the process will check whether the input value should recursively continue to the right or left sub-branch according to the split condition, and stops when meeting any leaf (terminal) nodes of the decision tree. In this recipe, we will introduce how to apply a recursive partitioning tree on the customer `churn` dataset.

Getting ready

You need to have completed the previous recipe by splitting the churn dataset into the training dataset (`trainset`) and testing dataset (`testset`), and each dataset should contain exactly 17 variables.

How to do it...

Perform the following steps to split the churn dataset into training and testing datasets:

1. Load the `rpart` package:

```
> library(rpart)
```

2. Use the `rpart` function to build a classification tree model:

```
> churn.rp = rpart(churn ~ ., data=trainset)
```

3. Type `churn.rp` to retrieve the node detail of the classification tree:

```
> churn.rp
```

4. Next, use the `printcp` function to examine the complexity parameter:

```
> printcp(churn.rp)
Output

Classification tree:
rpart(formula = churn ~ ., data = trainset)

Variables actually used in tree construction:
```

```
[1] international_plan number_customer_service_calls
[3] total_day_minutes total_eve_minutes
[5] total_intl_calls total_intl_minutes
[7] voice_mail_plan

Root node error: 342/2315 = 0.14773

n= 2315

          CP nsplit rel error  xerror     xstd
1 0.076023  0 1.00000 1.00000 0.049920
2 0.074561  2 0.84795 0.99708 0.049860
3 0.055556  4 0.69883 0.76023 0.044421
4 0.026316  7 0.49415 0.52632 0.037673
5 0.023392  8 0.46784 0.52047 0.037481
6 0.020468 10 0.42105 0.50877 0.037092
7 0.017544 11 0.40058 0.47076 0.035788
8 0.010000 12 0.38304 0.47661 0.035993
```

5. Next, use the `plotcp` function to plot the cost complexity parameters:

```
> plotcp(churn.rp)
```

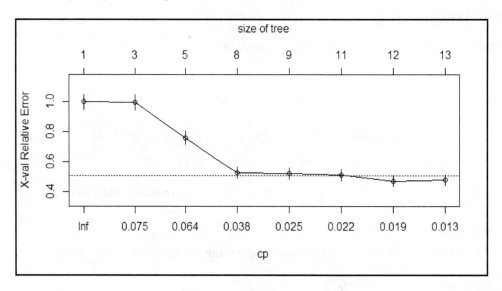

The cost complexity parameter plot

6. Lastly, use the `summary` function to examine the built model:

```
> summary(churn.rp)
```

How it works...

In this recipe, we use a recursive partitioning tree from the `rpart` package to build a tree-based classification model. The recursive portioning tree includes two processes: recursion and partitioning. During the process of decision induction, we have to consider a statistic evaluation question (or simply a yes/no question) to partition the data into different partitions in accordance with the assessment result. Then, as we have determined the child node, we can repeatedly perform the splitting until the stop criteria is satisfied.

For example, the data (shown in the following figure) in the root node can be partitioned into two groups with regard to the question whether **f1** is smaller than **X**. If so, the data is divided into the left-hand side. Otherwise, it is split into the right-hand side. Then, we can continue to partition the left-hand side data with the question whether **f2** is smaller than **Y**:

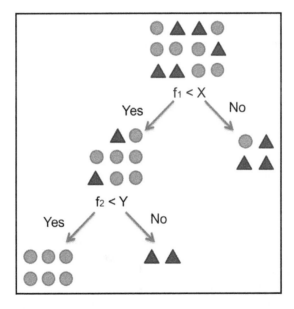

Recursive partioning tree

In the first step, we load the `rpart` package with the `library` function. Next, we build a classification model using the `churn` variable as a classification category (class label) and the remaining variables as input features.

After the model is built, you can type the variable name of the built model, `churn.rp`, to display the tree node details. In the printed node detail, `n` indicates the sample size, `loss` indicates the misclassification cost, `yval` stands for the classified membership (`no` or `yes`, in this case), and `yprob` stands for the probabilities of two classes (the left value refers to the probability reaching label `no`, and the right value refers to the probability reaching label, `yes`).

Then, we use the `printcp` function to print the complexity parameters of the built tree model. From the output of `printcp`, one should find the value of CP, a complexity parameter, which serves as a penalty to control the size of the tree. In short, the greater the CP value, the fewer the number of splits there are (`nsplit`). The output value (the `rel` error) represents the average deviance of the current tree divided by the average deviance of the null tree. An `xerror` value represents the relative error estimated by a 10-fold classification. `xstd` stands for the standard error of the relative error.

To make the cost **Complexity Parameter (CP)** table more readable, we use `plotcp` to generate an information graphic of the CP table. As per the screenshot (step 5), the x-axis at the bottom illustrates the `cp` value, the y-axis illustrates the relative error, and the upper x-axis displays the size of the tree. The dotted line indicates the upper limit of a standard deviation. From the screenshot, we can determine that minimum cross-validation error occurs when the tree is at a size of 12.

We can also use the `summary` function to display the function call, complexity parameter table for the fitted tree model, variable importance, which helps identify the most important variable for the tree classification (summing up to 100), and detailed information of each node.

The advantage of using the decision tree is that it is very flexible and easy to interpret. It works on both classification and regression problems, and more; it is nonparametric. Therefore, one does not have to worry about whether the data is linear separable. As for the disadvantage of using the decision tree, it is that it tends to be biased and over-fitted. However, you can conquer the bias problem through the use of a conditional inference tree, and solve the problem of over-fitting through a random forest method or tree pruning.

See also

- For more information about the `rpart`, `printcp`, and `summary` functions, please use the `help` function:

  ```
  > ?rpart
  > ?printcp
  > ?summary.rpart
  ```

- `C50` is another package that provides a decision tree and a rule-based model. If you are interested in the package, you may refer to the document at `http://cran.r-project.org/web/packages/C50/C50.pdf`.

Visualizing a recursive partitioning tree

From the last recipe, we learned how to print the classification tree in a text format. To make the tree more readable, we can use the `plot` function to obtain a graphical display of a built classification tree.

Getting ready

One needs to have the previous recipe completed by generating a classification model, and to assign the model into the `churn.rp` variable.

How to do it...

Perform the following steps to visualize the classification tree:

1. Use the `plot` function and the `text` function to plot the classification tree:

    ```
    > plot(churn.rp, margin= 0.1)
    > text(churn.rp, all=TRUE, use.n = TRUE)
    ```

The graphical display of a classification tree

2. You can also specify the `uniform`, `branch`, and `margin` parameter to adjust the layout:

    ```
    > plot(churn.rp, uniform=TRUE, branch=0.6, margin=0.1)
    > text(churn.rp, all=TRUE, use.n = TRUE)
    ```

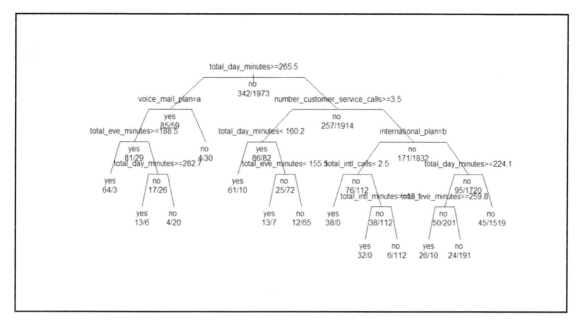

Adjust the layout of the classification tree

How it works...

Here, we demonstrate how to use the `plot` function to graphically display a classification tree. The `plot` function can simply visualize the classification tree, and you can then use the `text` function to add text to the plot.

In *The graphical display of a classification tree* figure, we assign margin = 0.1 as a parameter to add extra white space around the border to prevent the displayed text being truncated by the margin. It shows that the length of the branches displays the relative magnitude of the drop in deviance. We then use the text function to add labels for the nodes and branches. By default, the text function will add a split condition on each split, and add a category label in each terminal node. In order to add extra information on the tree plot, we set the parameter as all equal to TRUE to add a label to all the nodes. In addition to this, we add a parameter by specifying use.n = TRUE to add extra information, which shows that the actual number of observations falls into two different categories (no and yes).

In *Adjust the layout of the classification tree* figure, we set the option branch to 0.6 to add a shoulder to each plotted branch. In addition to this, in order to display branches of an equal length rather than relative magnitude of the drop in deviance, we set the option uniform to TRUE. As a result, *Adjust the layout of the classification tree* shows a classification tree with short shoulders and branches of equal length.

See also

- You may use `?plot.rpart` to read more about the plotting of the classification tree. This document also includes information on how to specify the parameters `uniform`, `branch`, `compress`, `nspace`, `margin`, and `minbranch` to adjust the layout of the classification tree.

Measuring the prediction performance of a recursive partitioning tree

Since we built a classification tree in the previous recipes, we can use it to predict the category (class label) of new observations. Before making a prediction, we first validate the prediction power of the classification tree, which can be done by generating a classification table on the testing dataset. In this recipe, we will introduce how to generate a predicted label versus a real label table with the `predict` function and the `table` function, and explain how to generate a confusion matrix to measure the performance.

Getting ready

You need to have the previous recipe completed by generating the classification model, `churn.rp`. In addition to this, you have to prepare the training dataset, `trainset`, and the testing dataset, `testset`, generated in the first recipe of this chapter.

How to do it...

Perform the following steps to validate the prediction performance of a classification tree:

1. You can use the `predict` function to generate a predicted label of testing the dataset:

   ```
   > predictions = predict(churn.rp, testset, type="class")
   ```

2. Use the `table` function to generate a classification table for the testing dataset:

   ```
   > table(testset$churn, predictions)
   Output
              predictions
                 yes   no
         yes 100   41
         no   18  859
   ```

3. One can further generate a confusion matrix using the `confusionMatrix` function provided in the `caret` package:

   ```
   > library(caret)
   > confusionMatrix(table(predictions, testset$churn))
   Output
   Confusion Matrix and Statistics

   predictions yes no
           yes 100 18
           no 41 859
                  Accuracy : 0.942
                    95% CI : (0.9259, 0.9556)
       No Information Rate : 0.8615
       P-Value [Acc > NIR] : < 2.2e-16

                     Kappa : 0.7393
    Mcnemar's Test P-Value : 0.004181

               Sensitivity : 0.70922
               Specificity : 0.97948
            Pos Pred Value : 0.84746
            Neg Pred Value : 0.95444
                Prevalence : 0.13851
            Detection Rate : 0.09823
      Detection Prevalence : 0.11591
         Balanced Accuracy : 0.84435
          'Positive' Class : yes
   ```

How it works...

In this recipe, we use a `predict` function and built up classification model, `churn.rp`, to predict the possible class labels of the testing dataset, `testset`. The predicted categories (class labels) are coded as either no or yes. Then, we use the `table` function to generate a classification table on the testing dataset. From the table, we discover that there are 859 correctly predicted as no, while 18 are misclassified as yes. 100 of the yes predictions are correctly predicted, but 41 observations are misclassified into no. Further, we use the `confusionMatrix` function from the `caret` package to produce a measurement of the classification model.

See also

- You may use `?confusionMatrix` to read more about the performance measurement using the confusion matrix
- For those who are interested in the definition output by the confusion matrix, please refer to the wikipedia entry, *Confusion matrix* (`http://en.wikipedia.org/wiki/Confusion_matrix`)

Pruning a recursive partitioning tree

In previous recipes, we built a complex decision tree for the `churn` dataset. However, sometimes we have to remove sections that are not powerful in classifying instances to avoid over-fitting and to improve prediction accuracy. Therefore, in this recipe, we introduce the cost complexity pruning method to prune the classification tree.

Getting ready

You need to have the previous recipe completed by generating a classification model, and to assign the model into the `churn.rp` variable.

How to do it...

Perform the following steps to prune the classification tree:

1. Find the minimum cross-validation error of the classification tree model:

    ```
    > min(churn.rp$cptable[,"xerror"])
    Output
    [1] 0.4707602
    ```

2. Locate the record with the minimum cross-validation errors:

    ```
    > which.min(churn.rp$cptable[,"xerror"])
    Output
    7
    ```

3. Get the cost complexity parameter of the record with the minimum cross-validation errors:

    ```
    > churn.cp = churn.rp$cptable[7,"CP"]
    > churn.cp
    Output
    [1] 0.01754386
    ```

4. Prune the tree by setting the `cp` parameter to the CP value of the record with minimum cross-validation errors:

    ```
    > prune.tree = prune(churn.rp, cp= churn.cp)
    ```

5. Visualize the classification tree by using the `plot` and `text` function:

```
> plot(prune.tree, margin= 0.1)
> text(prune.tree, all=TRUE , use.n=TRUE)
```

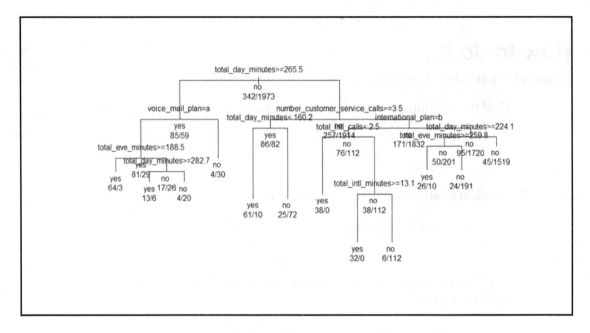

The pruned classification tree

6. Next, you can generate a classification table based on the pruned classification tree model:

```
> predictions = predict(prune.tree, testset, type="class")
> table(testset$churn, predictions)
Output
    predictions
      yes no
yes 95 46
no 14 863
```

7. Lastly, you can generate a confusion matrix based on the classification table:

```
> confusionMatrix(table(predictions, testset$churn))
```

```
Confusion Matrix and Statistics

predictions yes  no
        yes  95  14
        no   46 863

               Accuracy : 0.9411
                 95% CI : (0.9248, 0.9547)
    No Information Rate : 0.8615
    P-Value [Acc > NIR] : 2.786e-16

                  Kappa : 0.727
 Mcnemar's Test P-Value : 6.279e-05

            Sensitivity : 0.67376
            Specificity : 0.98404
         Pos Pred Value : 0.87156
         Neg Pred Value : 0.94939
             Prevalence : 0.13851
         Detection Rate : 0.09332
   Detection Prevalence : 0.10707
      Balanced Accuracy : 0.82890

       'Positive' Class : yes
```

How it works...

In this recipe, we discussed pruning a classification tree to avoid over-fitting and producing a more robust classification model. We first located the record with the minimum cross-validation errors within the cptable, and we then extracted the CP of the record and assigned the value to churn.cp. Next, we used the prune function to prune the classification tree with churn.cp as the parameter. Then, by using the plot function, we graphically displayed the pruned classification tree. From the preceding figure, it is clear that the split of the tree is less than the original classification tree (*The graphical display of a classification tree* figure). Lastly, we produced a classification table and used the confusion matrix to validate the performance of the pruned tree. The result shows that the accuracy (0.9411) is slightly lower than the original model (0.942), and also suggests that the pruned tree may not perform better than the original classification tree as we have pruned some split conditions (still, one should examine the change in sensitivity and specificity). However, the pruned tree model is more robust as it removes some split conditions that may lead to over-fitting.

See also

- For those who would like to know more about cost complexity pruning, please refer to the Wikipedia article for *Pruning (decision trees)*:
  `http://en.wikipedia.org/wiki/Pruning_(decision_trees)`

Handling missing data and split and surrogate variables

Missing data can be a curse for analysis and prediction. It leads to an inaccurate inference from data. One simple way to handle missing data is to refuse to take missing data in to account by simply ignoring it or removing it from the dataset. This approach seems good, but not in an efficient way. If the number of missing values is less than 5 percent of a total dataset then discarding such data will not affect the whole dataset.

Getting ready

This recipe will familiarize us with using `mice` packages for filling missing values.

How to do it...

Perform the following steps in R:

1. Find the minimum cross-validation error of the classification tree model:

```
> install.packages("mice")
> install.packages("randomForest")
> install.packages("VIM")
> t = data.frame(x=c(1:100), y=c(1:100))
> t$x[sample(1:100,10)]=NA
> t$y[sample(1:100,20)]=NA
> aggr(t)
```

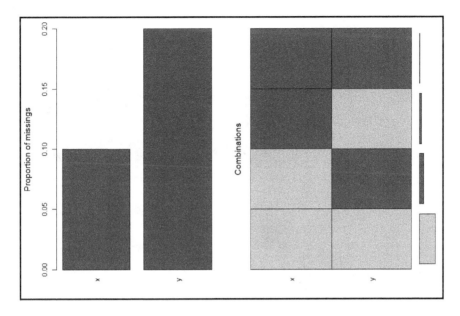

2. Tweaking the `aggr` function by adding prop and number will produce a slightly different output showing numbers for combinations also:

```
> aggr(t, prop=T, numbers=T)
```

```
> matrixplot(t)
```

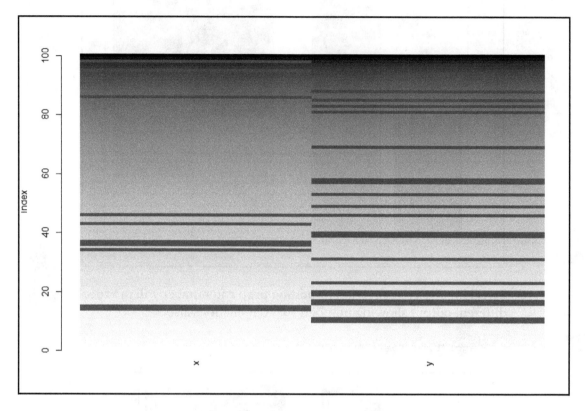

```
> md.pattern(t)
Output
     x y
71 1 1 0
 9 0 1 1
19 1 0 1
 1 0 0 2
10 20 30
> m <- mice(t, method="rf")
> m
Output
 iter imp variable
  1    1    x
> mc <- complete(m)
> anyNA(mc)
Output
[1] False
```

How it works...

In this recipe, we discussed handling missing data. We need the `mice`, `randomForest`, and `VIM` packages. We started by creating a DataFrame with two columns x and y with values 1 to 100. We can also generate random 100 numbers too, but for simplicity we generated a sequence. Using a sample we replaced 10 values in x and 20 values in y with NA [missing values]. The `VIM` package is used for Visualization and Imputation of Missing Values. Using the `aggr` function we can visualize missing values. We use `matrixplot` to see the missing values, where red shows missing values and darker shades are for higher values. Using the `mice` package, we find the missing values using `md.pattern`. To impute the missing values, we use the `mice` function with random forest as method. Finally, we complete the imputation using the complete function of the `mice` package.

See also

- For more information, read the mice manual:

    ```
    https://cran.r-project.org/web/packages/mice/mice.pdf
    ```

    ```
    https://cran.r-project.org/web/packages/VIMGUI/vignettes/VIM-Imput
    ation.pdf
    ```

There are many other R packages such as `Hmisc`, `mvnmle`, `cat`, `arrayimpute`, `arraymisspattern`, and `pan` which provide specialized methods for handling missing data.

Building a classification model with a conditional inference tree

In addition to traditional decision trees (`rpart`), conditional inference trees (`ctree`) are another popular tree-based classification method. Similar to traditional decision trees, conditional inference trees also recursively partition the data by performing a univariate split on the dependent variable. However, what makes conditional inference trees different from traditional decision trees is that conditional inference trees adapt the significance test procedures to select variables rather than selecting variables by maximizing information measures (`rpart` employs a Gini coefficient). In this recipe, we will introduce how to adapt a conditional inference tree to build a classification model.

Getting ready

You need to have the first recipe completed by generating the training dataset, `trainset`, and the testing dataset, `testset`.

How to do it...

Perform the following steps to build the conditional inference tree:

1. First, we use `ctree` from the `party` package to build the classification model:

```
> library(party)
> ctree.model = ctree(churn ~ . , data = trainset)
```

2. Then, we examine the built tree model:

```
> ctree.model
```

How it works...

In this recipe, we used a conditional inference tree to build a classification tree. The use of `ctree` is similar to `rpart`. Therefore, you can easily test the classification power using either a traditional decision tree or a conditional inference tree while confronting classification problems. Next, we obtain the node details of the classification tree by examining the built model. Within the model, we discover that `ctree` provides information similar to a split condition, criterion (1 - p-value), statistics (test statistics), and weight (the case weight corresponding to the node). However, it does not offer as much information as `rpart` does through the use of the `summary` function.

See also

- You may use the `help` function to refer to the definition of the binary tree class and read more about the properties of binary trees:

```
> help("BinaryTree-class")
```

Control parameters in conditional inference trees

In the preceding recipe, we saw how to use `ctree` for control inference trees. We can tweak the algorithm by specifying the control parameters.

Getting ready

You have completed the previous recipe and now understand the `ctree` function.

How to do it...

Perform the following steps in R:

```
> ctree.model = ctree(churn ~ . , data = trainset,
controls=ctree_control(testtype = "MonteCarlo", mincriterion =
0.90, minbucket = 15))
> ctree.model
```

How it works...

This recipe is a continuation of the previous recipe, providing some control parameters using a controls argument to the `ctree` function. We said we are going to use the MonteCarlo simulation with minimum weight on node at 15 and mincriterion at 0.90. We can also use Bonferroni, Univariate, and Teststatistic in place of MonteCarlo. There are many other parameters that can be changed.

See also

For more, execute the following command:

```
> help(ctree_control)
```

Or use the following command:

```
> ?ctree_control
```

Visualizing a conditional inference tree

Similar to `rpart`, the `party` package also provides a visualization method for users to plot conditional inference trees. In the following recipe, we will introduce how to use the `plot` function to visualize conditional inference trees.

Getting ready

You need to have the first recipe completed by generating the conditional inference tree model, `ctree.model`. In addition to this, you need to have both `trainset` and `testset` loaded in an R session.

How to do it...

Perform the following steps to visualize the conditional inference tree:

1. Use the `plot` function to plot `ctree.model` built in the last recipe:

   ```
   > plot(ctree.model)
   ```

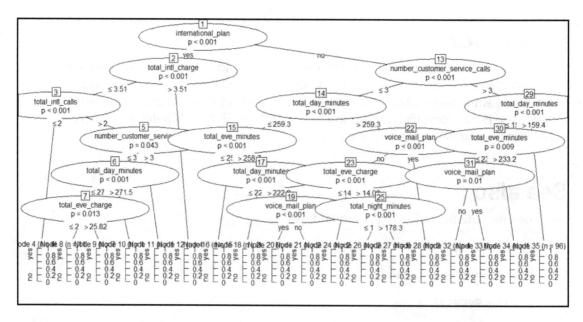

A conditional inference tree of churn data

2. To obtain a simple conditional inference tree, one can reduce the built model with less input features and redraw the classification tree:

```
> daycharge.model = ctree(churn ~ total_day_charge, data
 = trainset)
> plot(daycharge.model)
```

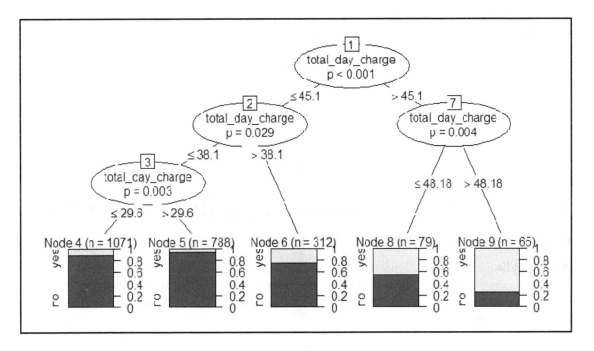

A conditional inference tree using the total_day_charge variable as only a split condition

How it works...

To visualize the node detail of the conditional inference tree, we can apply the plot function on a built classification model. The output figure reveals that every intermediate node shows the dependent variable name and the p-value. The split condition is displayed on the left and right branches. The terminal nodes show the number of categorized observations, *n*, and the probability of a class label of either *0* or *1*.

Taking the preceding as an example, we first build a classification model using `total_day_charge` as the only feature and `churn` as the class label. The built classification tree shows that when `total_day_charge` is above 48.18, the lighter gray area is greater than the darker gray in node 9, which indicates that the customer with a day charge of over 48.18 has a greater likelihood to churn (label = yes).

See also

- The visualization of the conditional inference tree comes from the `plot.BinaryTree` function. If you are interested in adjusting the layout of the classification tree, you may use the `help` function to read the following document:

  ```
  > ?plot.BinaryTree
  ```

Measuring the prediction performance of a conditional inference tree

After building a conditional inference tree as a classification model, we can use the `treeresponse` and `predict` functions to predict categories of the testing dataset, `testset`, and further validate the prediction power with a classification table and a confusion matrix.

Getting ready

You need to have the previous recipe completed by generating the conditional inference tree model, `ctree.model`. In addition to this, you need to have both `trainset` and `testset` loaded in an R session.

How to do it...

Perform the following steps to measure the prediction performance of a conditional inference tree:

1. You can use the `predict` function to predict the category of the testing dataset `testset`:

```
> ctree.predict = predict(ctree.model ,testset)
> table(ctree.predict, testset$churn)
Output
ctree.predict yes no
          yes 99 15
          no 42 862
```

2. Furthermore, you can use `confusionMatrix` from the `caret` package to generate the performance measurements of the prediction result:

```
> confusionMatrix(table(ctree.predict, testset$churn))
```

```
Confusion Matrix and Statistics

ctree.predict yes   no
          yes   99   15
          no    42  862

               Accuracy : 0.944
                 95% CI : (0.9281, 0.9573)
    No Information Rate : 0.8615
    P-Value [Acc > NIR] : < 2.2e-16

                  Kappa : 0.7449
 Mcnemar's Test P-Value : 0.0005736

            Sensitivity : 0.70213
            Specificity : 0.98290
         Pos Pred Value : 0.86842
         Neg Pred Value : 0.95354
             Prevalence : 0.13851
         Detection Rate : 0.09725
   Detection Prevalence : 0.11198
      Balanced Accuracy : 0.84251

       'Positive' Class : yes
```

3. You can also use the `treeresponse` function, which will tell you the list of class probabilities:

```
> tr = treeresponse(ctree.model, newdata = testset[1:5,])
> tr
Output
```

```
[[1]]
[1] 0.03497409 0.96502591

[[2]]
[1] 0.02586207 0.97413793

[[3]]
[1] 0.02586207 0.97413793

[[4]]
[1] 0.02586207 0.97413793

[[5]]
[1] 0.03497409 0.96502591
```

How it works...

In this recipe, we first demonstrate that one can use the prediction function to predict the category (class label) of the testing dataset testset, and then employ a table function to generate a classification table. Next, you can use the confusionMatrix function built into the caret package to determine the performance measurements.

In addition to the predict function, treeresponse is also capable of estimating the class probability, which will often classify labels with a higher probability. In this example, we demonstrated how to obtain the estimated class probability using the top five records of the testing dataset testset. The treeresponse function returns a list of five probabilities. You can use the list to determine the label of instance.

See also

- For the predict function, you can specify the type as response, prob, or node. If you specify the type as prob when using the predict function (for example, predict(... type="prob")), you will get exactly the same result as what treeresponse returns.

Classifying data with the k-nearest neighbor classifier

K-nearest neighbor (**knn**) is a nonparametric lazy learning method. From a nonparametric view, it does not make any assumptions about data distribution. In terms of lazy learning, it does not require an explicit learning phase for generalization. The following recipe will introduce how to apply the k-nearest neighbor algorithm on the churn dataset.

Getting ready

You need to have the previous recipe completed by generating the training and testing datasets.

How to do it...

Perform the following steps to classify the churn data with the k-nearest neighbor algorithm:

1. First, one has to install the `class` package and have it loaded in an R session:

   ```
   > install.packages("class")
   > library(class)
   ```

2. Replace yes and no of the `voice_mail_plan` and `international_plan` attributes in both the training dataset and testing dataset to 1 and 0:

   ```
   > levels(trainset$international_plan) = list("0"="no", "1"="yes")
   > levels(trainset$voice_mail_plan) = list("0"="no", "1"="yes")
   > levels(testset$international_plan) = list("0"="no", "1"="yes")
   > levels(testset$voice_mail_plan) = list("0"="no", "1"="yes")
   ```

2. Use the `knn` classification method on the training dataset and the testing dataset:

   ```
   > churn.knn  = knn(trainset[,! names(trainset) %in% c("churn")],
   testset[,! names(testset) %in% c("churn")], trainset$churn, k=3)
   ```

3. Then, you can use the `summary` function to retrieve the number of predicted labels:

```
> summary(churn.knn)
Output
  yes  no
  77 941
```

4. Next, you can generate the classification matrix using the `table` function:

```
> table(testset$churn, churn.knn)
Output
     churn.knn
      yes  no
yes   44  97
no    33 844
```

5. Lastly, you can generate a confusion matrix by using the `confusionMatrix` function:

```
> confusionMatrix(table(testset$churn, churn.knn))
Output
Confusion Matrix and Statistics

     churn.knn
      yes no
yes  44 97
no   33 844

             Accuracy : 0.8723
               95% CI : (0.8502, 0.8922)
  No Information Rate : 0.9244
  P-Value [Acc > NIR] : 1

                Kappa : 0.339
Mcnemar's Test P-Value : 3.286e-08

          Sensitivity : 0.57143
          Specificity : 0.89692
       Pos Pred Value : 0.31206
       Neg Pred Value : 0.96237
           Prevalence : 0.07564
       Detection Rate : 0.04322
 Detection Prevalence : 0.13851
    Balanced Accuracy : 0.73417

     'Positive' Class : yes
```

How it works...

knn trains all samples and classifies new instances based on a similarity (distance) measure. For example, the similarity measure can be formulated as follows:

- Euclidian Distance = $\sqrt{\sum_{i=1}^{k}(x_i - y_i)^2}$

- Manhattan Distance = $\sum_{i=1}^{k}\left|(x_i - y_i)\right|$

In knn, a new instance is classified to a label (class) that is common among the k-nearest neighbors. If $k = 1$, then the new instance is assigned to the class where its nearest neighbor belongs. The only required input for the algorithm is k. If we give a small k input, it may lead to over-fitting. On the other hand, if we give a large k input, it may result in under-fitting. To choose a proper k-value, one can count on cross-validation.

The advantages of knn are:

- The cost of the learning process is zero
- It is nonparametric, which means that you do not have to make the assumption of data distribution
- You can classify any data whenever you can find similarity measures of given instances

The main disadvantages of knn are:

- It is hard to interpret the classified result.
- It is an expensive computation for large datasets.
- The performance relies on the number of dimensions. Therefore, for a high dimension problem, you should reduce the dimension first to increase the process performance.

The use of knn does not vary significantly from applying a tree-based algorithm, mentioned in the previous recipes. However, while a tree-based algorithms may show you the decision tree model, the output produced by knn only reveals classification category factors. However, before building a classification model, one should replace the attribute with a string type to an integer since the k-nearest neighbor algorithm needs to calculate the distance between observations. Then, we build up a classification model by specifying *k=3*, which means choosing the three nearest neighbors. After the classification model is built, we can generate a classification table using predicted factors and the testing dataset label as the input.

Lastly, we can generate a confusion matrix from the classification table. The confusion matrix output reveals an accuracy result of (0.8723), which suggests that both the tree-based methods mentioned in previous recipes outperform the accuracy of the k-nearest neighbor classification method in this case. Still, we cannot determine which model is better depending merely on accuracy; one should also examine the specificity and sensitivity from the output.

See also

- There is another package named `kknn`, which provides a weighted k-nearest neighbor classification, regression, and clustering. You can learn more about the package by reading this document:
  `http://cran.r-project.org/web/packages/kknn/kknn.pdf`.

Classifying data with logistic regression

Logistic regression is a form of probabilistic statistical classification model, which can be used to predict class labels based on one or more features. The classification is done by using the `logit` function to estimate the outcome probability. One can use logistic regression by specifying the family as a binomial while using the `glm` function. In this recipe, we will introduce how to classify data using logistic regression.

Getting ready

You need to have completed the first recipe by generating training and testing datasets.

How to do it...

Perform the following steps to classify the churn data with logistic regression:

1. With the specification of family as a binomial, we apply the `glm` function on the dataset `trainset`, by using churn as a class label and the rest of the variables as input features:

   ```
   > fit = glm(churn ~ ., data = trainset, family=binomial)
   ```

2. Use the `summary` function to obtain summary information of the built logistic regression model:

```
> summary(fit)
```

```
Call:
glm(formula = churn ~ ., family = binomial, data = trainset)

Deviance Residuals:
   Min      1Q   Median      3Q      Max
-3.1519   0.1983   0.3460   0.5186   2.1284

Coefficients:
                               Estimate  Std. Error  z value  Pr(>|z|)
(Intercept)                    8.3462866   0.8364914    9.978  < 2e-16 ***
international_plan1            -2.0534243   0.1726694  -11.892  < 2e-16 ***
voice_mail_plan1               1.3445887   0.6618905    2.031  0.042211 *
number_vmail_messages         -0.0155101   0.0209220   -0.741  0.458496
total_day_minutes              0.2398946   3.9168466    0.061  0.951163
total_day_calls               -0.0014003   0.0032769   -0.427  0.669141
total_day_charge              -1.4855284  23.0402950   -0.064  0.948592
total_eve_minutes              0.3600678   1.9349825    0.186  0.852379
total_eve_calls               -0.0028484   0.0033061   -0.862  0.388928
total_eve_charge              -4.3204432  22.7644698   -0.190  0.849475
total_night_minutes            0.4431210   1.0478105    0.423  0.672367
total_night_calls              0.0003978   0.0033188    0.120  0.904588
total_night_charge            -9.9162795  23.2836376   -0.426  0.670188
total_intl_minutes             0.4587114   6.3524560    0.072  0.942435
total_intl_calls               0.1065264   0.0304318    3.500  0.000464 ***
total_intl_charge             -2.0803428  23.5262100   -0.088  0.929538
number_customer_service_calls -0.5109077   0.0476289  -10.727  < 2e-16 ***
---
Signif. codes:  0 '***' 0.001 '**' 0.01 '*' 0.05 '.' 0.1 ' ' 1

(Dispersion parameter for binomial family taken to be 1)

    Null deviance: 1938.8  on 2314  degrees of freedom
Residual deviance: 1515.3  on 2298  degrees of freedom
AIC: 1549.3

Number of Fisher Scoring iterations: 6
```

3. Then, we find that the built model contains insignificant variables, which would lead to misclassification. Therefore, we use significant variables only to train the classification model:

```
> fit = glm(churn ~ international_plan +
voice_mail_plan+total_intl_calls+number_customer_service_calls,
data = trainset, family=binomial)
> summary(fit)
Output
Call:
glm(formula = churn ~ international_plan + voice_mail_plan +
    total_intl_calls + number_customer_service_calls, family =
binomial,
```

```
data = trainset)

Deviance Residuals:
    Min 1Q Median 3Q Max
-2.7308 0.3103 0.4196 0.5381 1.6716

Coefficients:
                          Estimate Std. Error z value
(Intercept)                2.32304   0.16770 13.852
international_planyes -2.00346 0.16096 -12.447
voice_mail_planyes 0.79228 0.16380 4.837
total_intl_calls 0.08414 0.02862 2.939
number_customer_service_calls -0.44227 0.04451 -9.937
                        Pr(>|z|)
(Intercept) < 2e-16 ***
international_planyes < 2e-16 ***
voice_mail_planyes 1.32e-06 ***
total_intl_calls 0.00329 **
number_customer_service_calls < 2e-16 ***
---
Signif. codes:
0 es: des: **rvice_calls < '. es: de

(Dispersion parameter for binomial family taken to be 1)

    Null deviance: 1938.8 on 2314 degrees of freedom
Residual deviance: 1669.4 on 2310 degrees of freedom
            AIC: 1679.4

Number of Fisher Scoring iterations: 5
```

4. Then, you can then use a fitted model, `fit`, to predict the outcome of `testset`. You can also determine the class by judging whether the probability is above 0.5:

```
> pred = predict(fit,testset, type="response")
> Class = pred >.5
```

5. Next, the use of the `summary` function will show you the binary outcome count, and reveal whether the probability is above 0.5:

```
> summary(Class)
Output
    Mode    FALSE    TRUE    NA's
logical      29      989       0
```

6. You can generate the counting statistics based on the testing dataset label and predicted result:

```
> tb = table(testset$churn, Class)
> tb
 Output
        Class
     FALSE TRUE
  yes  18  123
  no   11  866
```

7. You can turn the statistics of the previous step into a classification table, and then generate the confusion matrix:

```
> churn.mod = ifelse(testset$churn == "yes", 1, 0)
> pred_class = churn.mod
> pred_class[pred<=.5] = 1- pred_class[pred<=.5]
> ctb = table(churn.mod, pred_class)
> ctb
Output
          pred_class
churn.mod 0 1
        0 866 11
        1 18 123
> confusionMatrix(ctb)
Output
Confusion Matrix and Statistics

          pred_class
churn.mod 0 1
        0 866 11
        1 18 123

               Accuracy : 0.9715
                 95% CI : (0.9593, 0.9808)
    No Information Rate : 0.8684
    P-Value [Acc > NIR] : <2e-16

                  Kappa : 0.8781
 Mcnemar's Test P-Value : 0.2652

            Sensitivity : 0.9796
            Specificity : 0.9179
         Pos Pred Value : 0.9875
         Neg Pred Value : 0.8723
             Prevalence : 0.8684
         Detection Rate : 0.8507
```

```
Detection Prevalence : 0.8615
   Balanced Accuracy : 0.9488

    'Positive' Class : 0
```

How it works...

Logistic regression is very similar to linear regression; the main difference is that the dependent variable in linear regression is continuous but the dependent variable in logistic regression is dichotomous (or nominal). The primary goal of logistic regression is to use logic to yield the probability of a nominal variable being related to the measurement variable. We can formulate logic in the following equation: *ln(P/(1-P))*, where *P* is the probability that a certain event occurs.

The advantage of logistic regression is that it is easy to interpret, it directs model logistic probability, and provides a confidence interval for the result. Unlike the decision tree, which makes it difficult to update the model, you can quickly update the classification model to incorporate new data in logistic regression. The main drawback of the algorithm is that it suffers from multicollinearity and, therefore, the explanatory variables must be linear independent. `glm` provides a generalized linear regression model, which enables specifying the model in an option family. If the family is specified to a binomial logistic, you can set the family as a binomial to classify the dependent variable of the category.

The classification process begins by generating a logistic regression model with the use of the training dataset by specifying `Churn` as the class label, the other variables as training features, and family set as binomial. We then use the `summary` function to generate the model's summary information. From the summary information, we may find some insignificant variables (*p-values* > 0.05), which may lead to misclassification. Therefore, we should consider only significant variables for the model.

Next, we use the `fit` function to predict the categorical dependent variable of the testing dataset, `testset`. The `fit` function outputs the probability of a class label with a result equal to 0.5 and below, suggesting that the predicted label does not match the label of the testing dataset, and a probability above 0.5, which indicates that the predicted label matches the label of the testing dataset. Further, we can use the `summary` function to obtain the statistics of whether the predicted label matches the label of the testing dataset. Lastly, in order to generate a confusion matrix, we first generate a classification table and then use `confusionMatrix` to generate the performance measurement.

See also

- For more information on how to use the `glm` function, please refer to `Chapter 4`, *Understanding Regression Analysis*, which covers how to interpret the output of the `glm` function

Classifying data with the Naïve Bayes classifier

The Naïve Bayes classifier is also a probability-based classifier, which is based on applying the Bayes theorem with a strong independent assumption. In this recipe, we will introduce how to classify data with the Naïve Bayes classifier.

Getting ready

You need to have the first recipe completed by generating training and testing datasets.

How to do it...

Perform the following steps to classify the churn data with the Naïve Bayes classifier:

1. Load the `e1071` library and employ the `naiveBayes` function to build the classifier:

```
> library(e1071)
> classifier=naiveBayes(trainset[, !names(trainset)
%in% c("churn")], trainset$churn)
```

2. Type `classifier` to examine the function call, a-priori probability, and conditional probability:

```
> classifier
Output
Naive Bayes Classifier for Discrete Predictors

Call:
naiveBayes.default(x = trainset[, !names(trainset) %in%
c("churn")],
```

```
        y = trainset$churn)

A-priori probabilities:
trainset$churn
        yes no
0.1477322 0.8522678

Conditional probabilities:
                international_plan
trainset$churn no yes
            yes 0.70467836 0.29532164
            no 0.93512418 0.06487582
```

3. Next, you can generate a classification table for the testing dataset:

```
> bayes.table = table(predict(classifier, testset[,
!names(testset) %in% c("churn")]), testset$churn)
> bayes.table
Output
        yes no
 yes 68 45
 no 73 832
```

4. Lastly, you can generate a confusion matrix from the classification table:

```
> confusionMatrix(bayes.table)
Output
Confusion Matrix and Statistics


        yes no
 yes 68 45
 no 73 832


                 Accuracy : 0.8841
                   95% CI : (0.8628, 0.9031)
     No Information Rate : 0.8615
     P-Value [Acc > NIR] : 0.01880

                    Kappa : 0.4701
 Mcnemar's Test P-Value : 0.01294

            Sensitivity : 0.4823
            Specificity : 0.9487
         Pos Pred Value : 0.6018
         Neg Pred Value : 0.9193
             Prevalence : 0.1385
         Detection Rate : 0.0668
```

```
Detection Prevalence : 0.1110
   Balanced Accuracy : 0.7155

    'Positive' Class : yes
```

How it works...

Naive Bayes assumes that features are conditionally independent, which the effect of a predictor(x) to class (c) is independent of the effect of other predictors to class(c). It computes the posterior probability, $P(c|x)$, as the following formula:

$$P(c|x) = \frac{P(x|c)P(c)}{P(x)}$$

Where $P(x|c)$ is called likelihood, $p(x)$ is called the marginal likelihood, and $p(c)$ is called the prior probability. If there are many predictors, we can formulate the posterior probability as follows:

$$P(c|x) = P(x_1|c) \times P(x_2|c) \times \ldots P(x_n|c) \times P(c)$$

The advantage of Naïve Bayes is that it is relatively simple and straightforward to use. It is suitable when the training set is relative small, and may contain some noisy and missing data. Moreover, you can easily obtain the probability for a prediction. The drawbacks of Naïve Bayes are that it assumes that all features are independent and equally important, which is very unlikely in real-world cases.

In this recipe, we use the Naïve Bayes classifier from the `e1071` package to build a classification model. First, we specify all the variables (excluding the `churn` class label) as the first input parameters, and specify the `churn` class label as the second parameter in the `naiveBayes` function call. Next, we assign the classification model into the variable classifier. Then, we print the variable classifier to obtain information, such as function call, A-priori probabilities, and conditional probabilities. We can also use the `predict` function to obtain the predicted outcome and the `table` function to retrieve the classification table of the testing dataset. Finally, we use a confusion matrix to calculate the performance measurement of the classification model.

Lastly, we list a comparison table of all the mentioned algorithms in this chapter:

Algorithm	Advantage	Disadvantage
Recursive partitioning tree	• Very flexible and easy to interpret • Works on both classification and regression problems • Nonparametric	• Prone to bias and over-fitting
Conditional inference tree	• Very flexible and easy to interpret • Works on both classification and regression problems • Nonparametric • Less prone to bias than a recursive partitioning tree	• Prone to over-fitting
K-nearest neighbor classifier	• The cost of the learning process is zero • Nonparametric • You can classify any data whenever you can find similarity measures of any given instances	• Hard to interpret the classified result • Computation is expensive for a large dataset • The performance relies on the number of dimensions
Logistic regression	• Easy to interpret • Provides model logistic probability • Provides confidence interval • You can quickly update the classification model to incorporate new data	• Suffers multicollinearity • Does not handle the missing value of continuous variables • Sensitive to extreme values of continuous variables
Naïve Bayes	• Relatively simple and straightforward to use • Suitable when the training set is relativly small • Can deal with some noisy and missing data • Can easily obtain the probability for a prediction	• Assumes all features are independent and equally important, which is very unlikely in real-world cases • Prone to bias when the number of training sets increases

See also

- To learn more about the Bayes theorem, you can refer to the following Wikipedia article: `http://en.wikipedia.org/wiki/Bayes'_theorem`

8
Classification 2 - Neural Network and SVM

In this chapter, we will cover the following recipes:

- Classifying data with a support vector machine
- Choosing the cost of a support vector machine
- Visualizing an SVM fit
- Predicting labels based on a model trained by a support vector machine
- Tuning a support vector machine
- The basics of neural network
- Training a neural network with `neuralnet`
- Visualizing a neural network trained by `neuralnet`
- Predicting labels based on a model trained by `neuralnet`
- Training a neural network with `nnet`
- Predicting labels based on a model trained by `nnet`

Introduction

Most research has shown that **Support Vector Machines (SVM)** and **Neural Networks (NN)** are powerful classification tools, which can be applied to several different areas. Unlike tree-based or probabilistic-based methods that were mentioned in the previous chapter, the process of how support vector machines and neural networks transform from input to output is less clear and can be hard to interpret. As a result, both support vector machines and neural networks are referred to as black box methods.

The development of a neural network is inspired by human brain activities. As such, this type of network is a computational model that mimics the pattern of the human mind. In contrast to this, support vector machines first map input data into a high dimension feature space defined by the kernel function and then find the optimum hyperplane that separates the training data by the maximum margin. In short, we can think of support vector machines as a linear algorithm in a high dimensional space.

The basic idea behind **Support Vector Machine (SVM)** is for binary classification. Think of input data as x and y. If we have two input data points, then we have two-dimensional space. The hyperplane is a line that splits the input in space. In some cases, separation seems to be easy, consider following figure:

Linear classification

As shown in the preceding figure, there is a lot space for separation and we can draw more than one line. So, the question arises: which will be best? Select a line that maximizes margin where the distance between the closest point and the line is at a minimum:

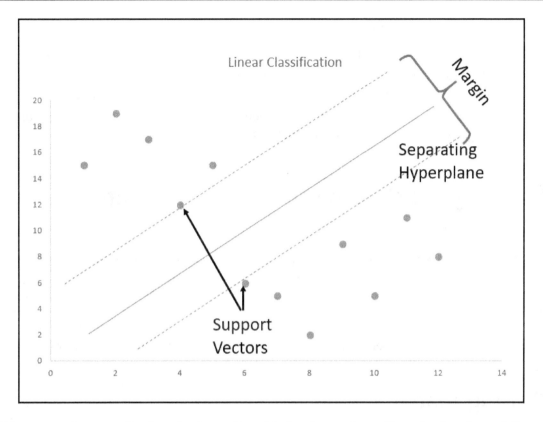

This approach seems fine but, in the real world, the data point will not be that far and linear separation may not be possible. A simple approach is to formulate a quadratic optimization problem and the program able to do this is SVM.

Both of these methods have advantages and disadvantages in solving classification problems. For example, support vector machine solutions are the global optimum, while neural networks may suffer from multiple local optimums. Thus, choosing between either depends on the characteristics of the dataset source. In this chapter, we will illustrate the following:

- How to train a support vector machine
- Observing how the choice of cost can affect the SVM classifier
- Visualizing the SVM fit
- Predicting the labels of a testing dataset based on the model trained by SVM
- Tuning the SVM

In the neural network section, we will cover:

- How to train a neural network
- How to visualize a neural network model
- Predicting the labels of a testing dataset based on a model trained by `neuralnet`
- Finally, we will show how to train a neural network with `nnet` and how to use it to predict the labels of a testing dataset

Classifying data with a support vector machine

The two most well-known and popular support vector machine tools are `libsvm` and `SVMLite`. For R users, you can find the implementation for `libsvm` in the e1071 package and `SVMLite` in the `klaR` package. Therefore, you can use the implemented function of these two packages to train support vector machines. In this recipe, we will focus on using the `svm` function (the `libsvm` implemented version) from the e1071 package to train a support vector machine based on the telecom customer churn data training dataset.

Getting ready

In this recipe, we will continue to use the telecom churn dataset as the input data source to train the support vector machine. For those who have not prepared the dataset, please refer to `Chapter 7`, *Classification 1 - Tree, Lazy, and Probabilistic*, for more details.

How to do it...

Perform the following steps to train the SVM:

1. Load the e1071 package:

    ```
    > library(e1071)
    ```

2. Train the support vector machine using the `svm` function with `trainset` as the input dataset and use `churn` as the classification category:

    ```
    > model  =svm(churn~., data = trainset, kernel="radial", cost=1,
    gamma = 1/ncol(trainset))
    ```

3. Finally, you can obtain overall information about the built model with `summary`:

```
> summary(model)
Output
Call:
svm(formula = churn ~ ., data = trainset, kernel = "radial",
cost = 1, gamma = 1/ncol(trainset))
Parameters:
SVM-Type:   C-classification
SVM-Kernel:   radial
     cost:   1
    gamma:   0.05882353
Number of Support Vectors:   691
( 394 297 )
Number of Classes:   2
Levels:
yes no
```

How it works...

The support vector machine constructs a hyperplane (or set of hyperplanes) that maximize the margin width between two classes in a high dimensional space. In these, the cases that define the hyperplane are support vectors, as shown in the following figure:

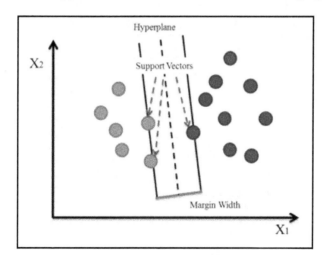

Support vector machine

The support vector machine starts by constructing a hyperplane that maximizes the margin width. Then, it extends the definition to a nonlinear separable problem. Lastly, it maps the data to a high dimensional space where the data can be more easily separated with a linear boundary.

The advantage of using SVM is that it builds a highly accurate model through an engineering problem-oriented kernel. Also, it makes use of the regularization term to avoid over-fitting. It also does not suffer from local optimal and multicollinearity. The main limitation of SVM is its speed and size in the training and testing time. Therefore, it is not suitable or efficient enough to construct classification models for data that is large in size. Also, since it is hard to interpret SVM, how does the determination of the kernel take place? Regularization is another problem that we need tackle.

In this recipe, we continue to use the telecom `churn` dataset as our example data source. We begin training a support vector machine using `libsvm` provided in the `e1071` package. Within the training function, `svm`, one can specify the `kernel` function, cost, and the `gamma` function. For the `kernel` argument, the default value is radial, and one can specify the kernel to a linear, polynomial, radial basis, and sigmoid. As for the `gamma` argument, the default value is equal to (1/data dimension), and it controls the shape of the separating hyperplane. Increasing the `gamma` argument usually increases the number of support vectors.

As for the cost, the default value is set to 1, which indicates that the regularization term is constant and the larger the value, the smaller the margin is. We will discuss more on how the cost can affect the SVM classifier in the next recipe. Once the support vector machine is built, the `summary` function can be used to obtain information, such as calls, parameters, number of classes, and the types of label.

See also

Another popular support vector machine tool is `SVMLight`. Unlike the `e1071` package, which provides the full implementation of `libsvm`, the `klaR` package simply provides an interface to `SVMLight`. To use `SVMLight`, one can perform the following steps:

1. Install the `klaR` package:

```
> install.packages("klaR")
> library(klaR)
```

2. Download the SVMLight source code and binary for your platform from
   http://svmlight.joachims.org/. For example, if your guest OS is Windows 64-bit, you should download the file from
   http://download.joachims.org/svm_light/current/svm_light_windows64.zip
   .

3. Then, you should unzip the file and put the workable binary in the working directory; you may check your working directory by using the getwd function:

   ```
   > getwd()
   ```

4. Train the support vector machine using the svmlight function:

   ```
   > model.light  = svmlight(churn~., data = trainset,
   kernel="radial", cost=1, gamma = 1/ncol(trainset))
   ```

Choosing the cost of a support vector machine

The support vector machines create an optimum hyperplane that separates the training data by the maximum margin. However, sometimes we would like to allow some misclassifications while separating categories. The SVM model has a cost function, which controls training errors and margins. For example, a small cost creates a large margin (a soft margin) and allows more misclassifications. On the other hand, a large cost creates a narrow margin (a hard margin) and permits fewer misclassifications. In this recipe, we will illustrate how the large and small cost will affect the SVM classifier.

Getting ready

In this recipe, we will use the iris dataset as our example data source.

How to do it...

Perform the following steps to generate two different classification examples with different costs:

1. Subset the `iris` dataset with columns named as `Sepal.Length`, `Sepal.Width`, `Species`, with species in `setosa` and `virginica`:

   ```
   > iris.subset = subset(iris, select=c("Sepal.Length",
   "Sepal.Width", "Species"), Species %in% c("setosa","virginica"))
   ```

2. Then, you can generate a scatter plot with `Sepal.Length` as the *x*-axis and the `Sepal.Width` as the *y*-axis:

   ```
   > plot(x=iris.subset$Sepal.Length,y=iris.subset$Sepal.Width,
   col=iris.subset$Species, pch=19)
   ```

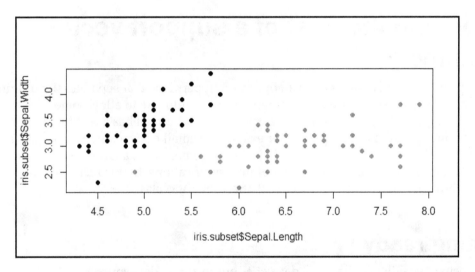

Scatter plot of Sepal.Length and Sepal.Width with subset of iris dataset

3. Next, you can train SVM based on `iris.subset` with the cost equal to 1:

   ```
   > svm.model = svm(Species ~ ., data=iris.subset, kernel='linear',
   cost=1, scale=FALSE)
   ```

4. Then, we can circle the support vector with blue circles:

```
> points(iris.subset[svm.model$index,c(1,2)],col="blue",cex=2)
```

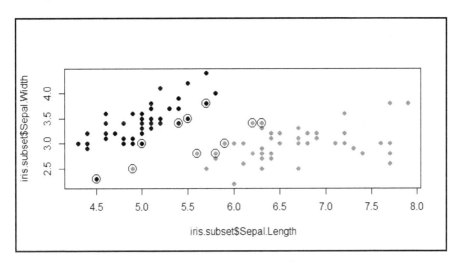

Circling support vectors with blue ring

5. Lastly, we can add a separation line to the plot:

```
> w = t(svm.model$coefs) %*% svm.model$SV
> b = -svm.model$rho
> abline(a=-b/w[1,2], b=-w[1,1]/w[1,2], col="red", lty=5)
```

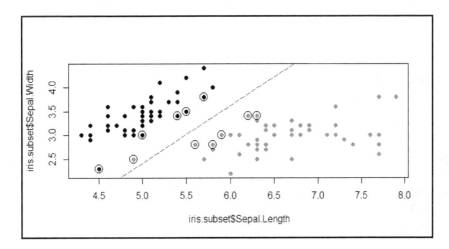

Add separation line to scatter plot

6. In addition to this, we create another SVM classifier where `cost = 10,000`:

```
> plot(x=iris.subset$Sepal.Length,y=iris.subset$Sepal.Width,
col=iris.subset$Species, pch=19)
> svm.model = svm(Species ~ ., data=iris.subset,
  type='C-classification',
kernel='linear', cost=10000, scale=FALSE)
> points(iris.subset[svm.model$index,c(1,2)],col="blue",cex=2)
> w = t(svm.model$coefs) %*% svm.model$SV
> b = -svm.model$rho
> abline(a=-b/w[1,2], b=-w[1,1]/w[1,2], col="red", lty=5)
```

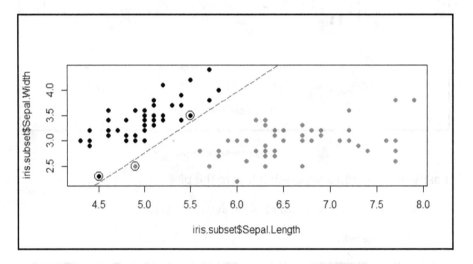

A classification example with large cost

How it works...

In this recipe, we demonstrate how different costs can affect the SVM classifier. First, we create an iris subset with the columns `Sepal.Length`, `Sepal.Width`, and `Species` containing the species, `setosa` and `virginica`. Then, in order to create a soft margin and allow some misclassification, we use an SVM with a small cost (where `cost = 1`) to train the support of the vector machine. Next, we circle the support vectors with blue circles and add the separation line. As per the preceding figure, one of the green points (`virginica`) is misclassified (it is classified to `setosa`) to the other side of the separation line due to the choice of the small cost.

In addition to this, we would like to determine how a large cost can affect the SVM classifier. Therefore, we choose a large cost (where `cost = 10,000`). From the preceding figure, we can see that the margin created is narrow (a hard margin) and no misclassification cases are present. As a result, the two examples show that the choice of different costs may affect the margin created and also affect the possibilities of misclassification.

See also

- The idea of soft margin, which allows misclassified examples, was suggested by Corinna Cortes and Vladimir N. Vapnik in 1995 in the following paper: Cortes, C., and Vapnik, V. (1995). *Support-vector networks. Machine learning*, 20(3), 273-297.

Visualizing an SVM fit

To visualize the built model, one can first use the plot function to generate a scatter plot of data input and the SVM fit. In this plot, support vectors and classes are highlighted through the color symbol. In addition to this, one can draw a contour filled plot of the class regions to easily identify misclassified samples from the plot.

Getting ready

In this recipe, we will use two datasets: the `iris` dataset and the telecom `churn` dataset. For the telecom `churn` dataset, one needs to have completed the previous recipe by training a support vector machine with SVM and to have saved the SVM fit model.

How to do it...

Perform the following steps to visualize the SVM fit object:

1. Use SVM to train the support vector machine based on the `iris` dataset and use the `plot` function to visualize the fitted model:

```
> data(iris)
> model.iris  = svm(Species~., iris)
> plot(model.iris, iris, Petal.Width ~ Petal.Length, slice =
list(Sepal.Width
```

```
= 3, Sepal.Length = 4))
```

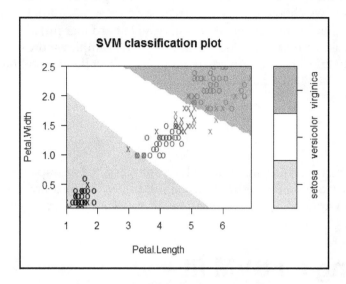

The SVM classification plot of trained SVM fit based on iris dataset

2. Visualize the SVM fit object, `model`, using the `plot` function with the dimensions of `total_day_minutes` and `total_intl_charge`:

```
> plot(model, trainset, total_day_minutes ~ total_intl_charge)
```

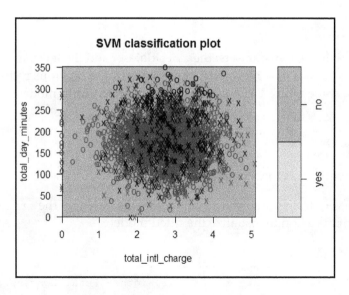

The SVM classification plot of trained SVM fit based on churn dataset

How it works...

In this recipe, we demonstrate how to use the `plot` function to visualize the SVM fit. In the first plot, we train a support vector machine using the `iris` dataset. Then, we use the `plot` function to visualize the fitted SVM.

In the argument list, we specify the fitted model in the first argument and the dataset (this should be the same data used to build the model) as the second parameter. The third parameter indicates the dimension used to generate the classification plot. By default, the `plot` function can only generate a scatter plot based on two dimensions (for the *x*-axis and *y*-axis). Therefore, we select the variables, `Petal.Length` and `Petal.Width` as the two dimensions to generate the scatter plot.

From the preceding figure, we find `Petal.Length` assigned to the *x*-axis, `Petal.Width` assigned to the *y*-axis, and data points with X and O symbols scattered on the plot. Within the scatter plot, the X symbol shows the support vector and the O symbol represents the data points. These two symbols can be altered through the configuration of the `svSymbol` and `dataSymbol` options. Both the support vectors and true classes are highlighted and colored depending on their label (green refers to **viginica**, red refers to **versicolor**, and black refers to **setosa**). The last argument, `slice`, is set when there are more than two variables. Therefore, in this example, we use the additional variables, `Sepal.width` and `Sepal.length`, by assigning a constant of 3 and 4.

Next, we take the same approach to draw the SVM fit based on customer churn data. In this example, we use `total_day_minutes` and `total_intl_charge` as the two dimensions used to plot the scatterplot. As per *The SVM classification plot of trained SVM fit based on churn dataset* figure, the support vectors and data points in red and black are scattered closely together in the central region of the plot, and there is no simple way to separate them.

See also

- There are other parameters, such as `fill`, `grid`, `symbolPalette`, and so on, that can be configured to change the layout of the plot. You can use the `help` function to view the following document for further information:

  ```
  > ?svm.plot
  ```

Predicting labels based on a model trained by a support vector machine

In the previous recipe, we trained an SVM based on the training dataset. The training process finds the optimum hyperplane that separates the training data by the maximum margin. We can then utilize the SVM fit to predict the label (category) of new observations. In this recipe, we will demonstrate how to use the `predict` function to predict values based on a model trained by SVM.

Getting ready

You need to have completed the previous recipe by generating a fitted SVM and save the fitted model in model.

How to do it...

Perform the following steps to predict the labels of the testing dataset:

1. Predict the label of the testing dataset based on the fitted SVM and attributes of the testing dataset:

```
> svm.pred = predict(model, testset[, !names(testset)
%in% c("churn")])
```

2. Then, you can use the `table` function to generate a classification table with the prediction result and labels of the testing dataset:

```
> svm.table=table(svm.pred, testset$churn)
> svm.table
Output
svm.pred yes no
yes 70 12
   no 71 865
```

3. Next, you can use `classAgreement` to calculate coefficients compared to the classification agreement:

```
> classAgreement(svm.table)
Output

 $diag
 [1] 0.9184676
$kappa
[1] 0.5855903

$rand
[1] 0.850083

$crand
[1] 0.5260472
```

4. Now, you can use `confusionMatrix` to measure the prediction performance based on the classification table:

```
> library(caret)
> confusionMatrix(svm.table)
Output
Confusion Matrix and Statistics

svm.pred yes no
 yes 70 12
     no 71 865

Accuracy : 0.9185
        95% CI : (0.8999, 0.9345)
    No Information Rate : 0.8615
    P-Value [Acc> NIR] : 1.251e-08

Kappa : 0.5856
Mcnemar's Test P-Value : 1.936e-10

Sensitivity : 0.49645
Specificity : 0.98632
PosPredValue : 0.85366
    Neg PredValue : 0.92415
Prevalence : 0.13851
        Detection Rate : 0.06876
 Detection Prevalence : 0.08055
        Balanced Accuracy : 0.74139

'Positive' Class : yes
```

How it works...

In this recipe, we first used the `predict` function to obtain the predicted labels of the testing dataset. Next, we used the `table` function to generate the classification table based on the predicted labels of the testing dataset. So far, the evaluation procedure is very similar to the evaluation process mentioned in the previous chapter.

We then introduced a new function, `classAgreement`, which computes several coefficients of agreement between the columns and rows of a two-way contingency table. The coefficients include `diag`, `kappa`, `rand`, and `crand`. The `diag` coefficient represents the percentage of data points in the main diagonal of the classification table, `kappa` refers to `diag`, which is corrected for an agreement by a change (the probability of random agreements), `rand` represents the `rand` index, which measures the similarity between two data clusters, and `crand` indicates the `rand` index, which is adjusted for the chance grouping of elements.

Finally, we used `confusionMatrix` from the `caret` package to measure the performance of the classification model. The accuracy of `0.9185` shows that the trained support vector machine can correctly classify most of the observations. However, accuracy alone is not a good measurement of a classification model. One should also reference sensitivity and specificity.

There's more...

Besides using SVM to predict the category of new observations, you can use SVM to predict continuous values. In other words, one can use SVM to perform regression analysis.

In the following example, we will show how to perform a simple regression prediction based on a fitted SVM with the type specified as `eps-regression`.

Perform the following steps to train a regression model with SVM:

1. Train a support vector machine based on a `Quartet` dataset:

```
> library(car)
> data(Quartet)
> model.regression = svm(Quartet$y1~Quartet$x,type="eps
-regression")
```

2. Use the `predict` function to obtain prediction results:

```
> predict.y = predict(model.regression, Quartet$x)
```

```
> predict.y
Output
        1         2         3         4         5
8.196894  7.152946  8.807471  7.713099  8.533578
        6         7         8
8.774046  6.186349  5.763689
        9        10        11
8.726925  6.621373  5.882946
```

3. Plot the predicted points as squares and the training data points as circles on the same plot:

```
> plot(Quartet$x, Quartet$y1, pch=19)
> points(Quartet$x, predict.y, pch=15, col="red")
```

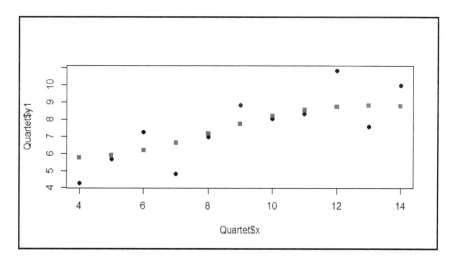

The scatter plot contains predicted data points and training data points

Tuning a support vector machine

Besides using different feature sets and the kernel function in support vector machines, one trick that you can use to tune its performance is to adjust the gamma and cost configured in the argument. One possible approach to test the performance of different gamma and cost combination values is to write a for loop to generate all the combinations of gamma and cost as inputs to train different support vector machines. Fortunately, SVM provides a tuning function, tune.svm, which makes the tuning much easier. In this recipe, we will demonstrate how to tune a support vector machine through the use of tune.svm.

Getting ready

Before completing this recipe, you need to have completed the previous recipe by preparing a training dataset, `trainset`.

How to do it...

Perform the following steps to tune the support vector machine:

1. First, tune the support vector machine using `tune.svm`:

```
> tuned = tune.svm(churn~., data = trainset, gamma = 10^(-6:-1),
cost = 10^(1:2))
```

2. Next, you can use the `summary` function to obtain the tuning result:

```
> summary(tuned)
Output
Parameter tuning of 'svm':

 - sampling method: 10-fold cross validation

 - best parameters:
gamma cost
0.01 100

 - best performance: 0.08077885

 - Detailed performance results:
   gamma cost error dispersion
1 1e-06 10 0.14774780 0.02399512
2 1e-05 10 0.14774780 0.02399512
3 1e-04 10 0.14774780 0.02399512
4 1e-03 10 0.14774780 0.02399512
5 1e-02 10 0.09245223 0.02046032
6 1e-01 10 0.09202306 0.01938475
7 1e-06 100 0.14774780 0.02399512
8 1e-05 100 0.14774780 0.02399512
9 1e-04 100 0.14774780 0.02399512
10 1e-03 100 0.11794484 0.02368343
11 1e-02 100 0.08077885 0.01858195
12 1e-01 100 0.12356135 0.01661508
```

3. After retrieving the best performance parameter from tuning the result, you can retrain the support vector machine with the best performance parameter:

```
> model.tuned = svm(churn~., data = trainset, gamma =
tuned$best.parameters$gamma, cost = tuned$best.parameters$cost)
> summary(model.tuned)
Output
Call:
svm(formula = churn ~ ., data = trainset, gamma = 10^-2, cost =
100)


Parameters:
   SVM-Type:  C-classification
 SVM-Kernel:  radial
       cost:  100
      gamma:  0.01

Number of Support Vectors: 547

( 304 243 )


Number of Classes: 2

Levels:
 yes no
```

4. Then, you can use the `predict` function to predict labels based on the fitted SVM:

```
> svm.tuned.pred = predict(model.tuned, testset[, !names(testset)
%in% c("churn")])
```

5. Next, generate a classification table based on the predicted and original labels of the testing dataset:

```
> svm.tuned.table=table(svm.tuned.pred, testset$churn)
> svm.tuned.table
Output
svm.tuned.pred yes no
yes 95 24
          no 46 853
```

6. Also, generate a class agreement to measure the performance:

```
> classAgreement(svm.tuned.table)
Output
$diag
[1] 0.9312377

$kappa
[1] 0.691678

$rand
[1] 0.871806

$crand
[1] 0.6303615
```

7. Finally, you can use a confusion matrix to measure the performance of the retrained model:

```
> confusionMatrix(svm.tuned.table)
Output
Confusion Matrix and Statistics


svm.tuned.pred yes no
yes 95 24
          no 46 853

Accuracy : 0.9312
                  95% CI : (0.9139, 0.946)
    No Information Rate : 0.8615
    P-Value [Acc> NIR] : 1.56e-12

Kappa : 0.6917
Mcnemar's Test P-Value : 0.01207

Sensitivity : 0.67376
Specificity : 0.97263
PosPredValue : 0.79832
        Neg PredValue : 0.94883
Prevalence : 0.13851
        Detection Rate : 0.09332
    Detection Prevalence : 0.11690
        Balanced Accuracy : 0.82320

    'Positive' Class : yes
```

How it works...

To tune the support vector machine, you can use a trial and error method to find the best gamma and cost parameters. In other words, one has to generate a variety of combinations of gamma and cost for the purpose of training different support vector machines.

In this example, we generate different gamma values from *10^-6* to *10^-1*, and cost with a value of either 10 or 100. Therefore, you can use the tuning function, `svm.tune`, to generate 12 sets of parameters. The function then makes 10 cross-validations and outputs the error dispersion of each combination. As a result, the combination with the least error dispersion is regarded as the best parameter set. From the summary table, we found that gamma with a value of 0.01 and cost with a value of 100 are the best parameters for the SVM fit.

After obtaining the best parameters, we can then train a new support vector machine with gamma equal to 0.01 and cost equal to 100. Additionally, we can obtain a classification table based on the predicted labels and labels of the testing dataset. We can also obtain a confusion matrix from the classification table. From the output of the confusion matrix, you can determine the accuracy of the newly trained model in comparison to the original model.

See also

- For more information about how to tune SVM with `svm.tune`, you can use the `help` function to access this document:

  ```
  > ?svm.tune
  ```

The basics of neural network

Neural Network concepts relies on how the brain works. In simple terms, the brain is composed of large numbers of interconnected neurons working together to solve a specific problem. Neurons, in turn, are inter-connected with dendrites that produce output signals based on the inputs through an axon to another neuron. Neural nets are used to teach or rather a computer learns to perform a task by analyzing some training examples provided, like object or pattern recognition.

Getting ready

You should have completed previous recipes and understood them before completing this recipe.

How to do it...

In this example, we will provide training data of a number and its square root. Using `neuralnet` we will generate the square root of any number. Perform the following steps in R:

```
> install.packages('neuralnet')
> library("neuralnet")
```

Once the package is installed and loaded, we will create sample data of 50 numbers and their square roots in input and output. We combine both in DataFrame using the `cbind` function:

```
> input <- as.data.frame(sample(1:100, 50))
> output <- sqrt(input)
> data <- cbind(input,output)
> colnames(data)<-c("Input", "Output")
```

Now, we will use `neuralnet` with 10 layers and a threshold for stopping:

```
> neuralsqrt = neuralnet(output~input,data,hidden=10, threshold =
0.01)
```

We will create a test DataFrame, which will have some values and using the preceding `neuralnet` object we will find the result:

```
> test=as.data.frame(c(25,64))
> result=compute(neuralsqrt,test)
> result$net.result
Output
            [,1]
[1,] 4.995759843
[2,] 7.997538172
```

We can see it produces a result near to the expected result.

Training a neural network with neuralnet

The neural network is constructed with an interconnected group of nodes, which involves the input, connected weights, processing element, and output. Neural networks can be applied to many areas, such as classification, clustering, and prediction. To train a neural network in R, you can use `neuralnet`, which is built to train multilayer perception in the context of regression analysis and contains many flexible functions to train forward neural networks. In this recipe, we will introduce how to use `neuralnet` to train a neural network.

Getting ready

In this recipe, we will use the `iris` dataset as our example dataset. We will first split the `iris` dataset into training and testing datasets, respectively.

How to do it...

Perform the following steps to train a neural network with `neuralnet`:

1. First, load the `iris` dataset and split the data into training and testing datasets:

   ```
   > data(iris)
   > ind = sample(2, nrow(iris), replace = TRUE, prob=c(0.7, 0.3))
   > trainset = iris[ind == 1,]
   > testset = iris[ind == 2,]
   ```

2. Then, install and load the `neuralnet` package:

   ```
   > install.packages("neuralnet")
   > library(neuralnet)
   ```

3. Add the columns `versicolor`, `setosa`, and `virginica` based on the name matched value in the `Species` column:

   ```
   > trainset$setosa = trainset$Species == "setosa"
   > trainset$virginica = trainset$Species == "virginica"
   > trainset$versicolor = trainset$Species == "versicolor"
   ```

4. Next, train the neural network with the `neuralnet` function with three hidden neurons in each layer. Notice that the results may vary with each training, so you might not get the same result. However, you can use set.seed at the beginning, so you can get the same result in every training process:

```
> network = neuralnet(versicolor + virginica + setosa~
Sepal.Length + Sepal.Width + Petal.Length + Petal.Width, trainset,
hidden=3)
> network
Output
Call: neuralnet(formula = versicolor + virginica + setosa ~
Sepal.Length + Sepal.Width + Petal.Length + Petal.Width, data =
trainset, hidden = 3)

1 repetition was calculated.

        Error Reached Threshold Steps
1 0.8156100175 0.009994274769 11063
```

5. Now, you can view the `summary` information by accessing the `result.matrix` attribute of the built neural network model:

```
> network$result.matrix
Output
                                        1
error                         0.815610017474
reached.threshold             0.009994274769
steps                     11063.000000000000
Intercept.to.1layhid1         1.686593311644
Sepal.Length.to.1layhid1      0.947415215237
Sepal.Width.to.1layhid1      -7.220058260187
Petal.Length.to.1layhid1      1.790333443486
Petal.Width.to.1layhid1       9.943109233330
Intercept.to.1layhid2         1.411026063895
Sepal.Length.to.1layhid2      0.240309549505
Sepal.Width.to.1layhid2       0.480654059973
Petal.Length.to.1layhid2      2.221435192437
Petal.Width.to.1layhid2       0.154879347818
Intercept.to.1layhid3        24.399329878242
Sepal.Length.to.1layhid3      3.313958088512
Sepal.Width.to.1layhid3       5.845670010464
Petal.Length.to.1layhid3     -6.337082722485
Petal.Width.to.1layhid3     -17.990352566695
Intercept.to.versicolor      -1.959842102421
1layhid.1.to.versicolor       1.010292389835
1layhid.2.to.versicolor       0.936519720978
1layhid.3.to.versicolor       1.023305801833
```

```
Intercept.to.virginica      -0.908909982893
1layhid.1.to.virginica      -0.009904635231
1layhid.2.to.virginica       1.931747950462
1layhid.3.to.virginica      -1.021438938226
Intercept.to.setosa          1.500533827729
1layhid.1.to.setosa         -1.001683936613
1layhid.2.to.setosa         -0.498758815934
1layhid.3.to.setosa         -0.001881935696
```

6. Lastly, you can view the generalized weight by accessing it in the network:

```
> head(network$generalized.weights[[1]])
```

How it works...

The neural network is a network made up of artificial neurons (or nodes). There are three types of neurons within the network: input neurons, hidden neurons, and output neurons. In the network, neurons are connected; the connection strength between neurons is called weight. If the weight is greater than zero, it is in an excitation status. Otherwise, it is in an inhibition status. Input neurons receive the input information; the higher the input value, the greater the activation. Then, the activation value is passed through the network in regard to weights and transfer functions in the graph. The hidden neurons (or output neurons) then sum up the activation values and modify the summed values with the transfer function. The activation value then flows through hidden neurons and stops when it reaches the output nodes. As a result, one can use the output value from the output neurons to classify the data:

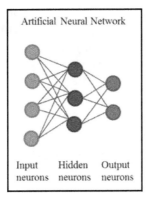

Artificial neural network

The advantages of a neural network are: first, that it can detect nonlinear relationships between the dependent and independent variable. Second, one can efficiently train large datasets using the parallel architecture. Third, it is a nonparametric model so that one can eliminate errors in the estimation of parameters. The main disadvantages of a neural network are that it often converges on the local minimum, rather than the global minimum. Also, it might over-fit when the training process goes on for too long.

In this recipe, we demonstrate how to train a neural network. First, we split the `iris` dataset into training and testing datasets, and then install the `neuralnet` package and load the library into an R session. Next, we add the columns `versicolor`, `setosa`, and `virginica` based on the name matched value in the `Species` column, respectively. We then use the `neuralnet` function to train the network model. Besides specifying the label (the column where the name equals to `versicolor`, `virginica`, and `setosa`) and training attributes in the function, we also configure the number of hidden neurons (vertices) as three in each layer.

Then, we examine the basic information about the training process and the trained network saved in the network. From the output message, it shows the training process needed 11,063 steps until all the absolute partial derivatives of the error function were lower than 0.01 (specified in the threshold). The error refers to the likelihood of calculating **Akaike Information Criterion** (**AIC**). To see detailed information on this, you can access the `result.matrix` of the built neural network to see the estimated weight. The output reveals that the estimated weight ranges from -18 to 24.40; the intercepts of the first hidden layer are 1.69, 1.41 and 24.40, and the two weights leading to the first hidden neuron are estimated as 0.95 (`Sepal.Length`), -7.22 (`Sepal.Width`), 1.79 (`Petal.Length`), and 9.94 (`Petal.Width`). We can lastly determine that the trained neural network information includes generalized weights, which express the effect of each covariate. In this recipe, the model generates 12 generalized weights, which are the combination of four covariates (`Sepal.Length`, `Sepal.Width`, `Petal.Length`, `Petal.Width`) to three responses (`setosa`, `virginica`, `versicolor`).

See also

- For a more detailed introduction on neuralnet, one can refer to the following paper: Günther, F. and Fritsch, S. (2010). *Neuralnet: Training of Neural Networks. The R Journal*, 2(1), 30-38.

Visualizing a neural network trained by neuralnet

The package, `neuralnet`, provides the `plot` function to visualize a built neural network and the `gwplot` function to visualize generalized weights. In following recipe, we will cover how to use these two functions.

Getting ready

You need to have completed the previous recipe by training a neural network and have all the basic information saved in the network in order to complete this recipe.

How to do it...

Perform the following steps to visualize the neural network and the generalized weights:

1. You can visualize the trained neural network with the `plot` function:

    ```
    > plot(network)
    ```

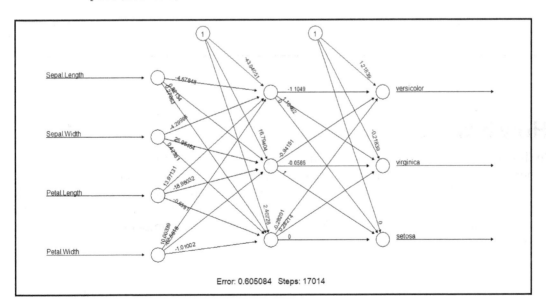

The plot of the trained neural network

2. Furthermore, you can use `gwplot` to visualize the generalized weights:

```
> par(mfrow=c(2,2))
> gwplot(network,selected.covariate="Petal.Width")
> gwplot(network,selected.covariate="Sepal.Width")
> gwplot(network,selected.covariate="Petal.Length")
> gwplot(network,selected.covariate="Petal.Width")
```

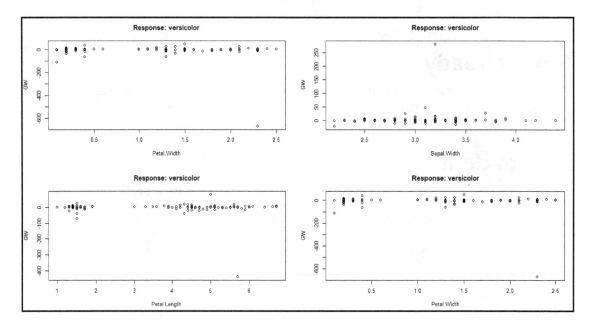

The plot of generalized weights

How it works...

In this recipe, we demonstrate how to visualize the trained neural network and the generalized weights of each trained attribute. As per *The plot of the trained neural network* figure, the plot displays the network topology of the trained neural network. Also, the plot includes the estimated weight, intercepts and basic information about the training process. At the bottom of the figure, one can find the overall error and number of steps required to converge.

The preceding figure presents the generalized weight plot in regard to `network$generalized.weights`. The four plots in the preceding figure display the four covariates: `Petal.Width`, `Sepal.Width`, `Petal.Length`, and `Petal.Width`, in regard to the versicolor response. If all the generalized weights are close to zero on the plot, it means the covariate has little effect. However, if the overall variance is greater than one, it means the covariate has a nonlinear effect.

See also

- For more information about `gwplot`, one can use the `help` function to access the following document:

  ```
  > ?gwplot
  ```

Predicting labels based on a model trained by neuralnet

Similar to other classification methods, we can predict the labels of new observations based on trained neural networks. Furthermore, we can validate the performance of these networks through the use of a confusion matrix. In the following recipe, we will introduce how to use the `compute` function in a neural network to obtain a probability matrix of the testing dataset labels, and use a table and confusion matrix to measure the prediction performance.

Getting ready

To complete this recipe, you need to have completed the previous recipe by generating the training dataset, `trainset`, and the testing dataset, `testset`. The trained neural network needs to be saved in the network.

How to do it...

Perform the following steps to measure the prediction performance of the trained neural network:

1. First, generate a prediction probability matrix based on a trained neural network and the testing dataset, `testset`:

```
> net.predict = compute(network, testset[-5])$net.result
```

2. Then, obtain other possible labels by finding the column with the greatest probability:

```
> net.prediction = c("versicolor", "virginica",
"setosa")[apply(net.predict, 1, which.max)]
```

3. Generate a classification table based on the predicted labels and the labels of the testing dataset:

```
> predict.table = table(testset$Species, net.prediction)
> predict.table
Output
                  prediction
       setosa versicolor virginica
setosa         20  0  0
  versicolor    0 19  1
    virginica   0  2 16
```

4. Next, generate `classAgreement` from the classification table:

```
> classAgreement (predict.table)
Output
$diag
[1] 0.9444444444

$kappa
[1] 0.9154488518

$rand
[1] 0.9224318658

$crand
[1] 0.8248251737
```

5. Finally, use `confusionMatrix` to measure the prediction performance:

```
> confusionMatrix(predict.table)
Output
Confusion Matrix and Statistics

                prediction
setosa versicolor virginica
setosa 20 0 0
  versicolor 0 19 1
  virginica 0 2 16

Overall Statistics

Accuracy : 0.9482759
                  95% CI : (0.8561954, 0.9892035)
    No Information Rate : 0.362069
    P-Value [Acc> NIR] :< 0.00000000000000022204

Kappa : 0.922252
Mcnemar's Test P-Value : NA

Statistics by Class:

        Class: setosa Class: versicolor Class: virginica
Sensitivity             1.0000000 0.9047619 0.9411765
Specificity             1.0000000 0.9729730 0.9512195
PosPred Value           1.0000000 0.9500000 0.8888889
Neg Pred Value          1.0000000 0.9473684 0.9750000
Prevalence              0.3448276 0.3620690 0.2931034
Detection Rate          0.3448276 0.3275862 0.2758621
Detection Prevalence 0.3448276 0.3448276 0.3103448
Balanced Accuracy       1.0000000 0.9388674 0.9461980
```

How it works...

In this recipe, we demonstrate how to predict labels based on a model trained by `neuralnet`. Initially, we use the `compute` function to create an output probability matrix based on the trained neural network and the testing dataset. Then, to convert the probability matrix to class labels, we use the `which.max` function to determine the class label by selecting the column with the maximum probability within the row. Next, we use a table to generate a classification matrix based on the labels of the testing dataset and the predicted labels. As we have created the classification table, we can employ a confusion matrix to measure the prediction performance of the built neural network.

See also

- In this recipe, we use the net.result function, which is the overall result of the neural network, used to predict the labels of the testing dataset. Apart from examining the overall result by accessing net.result, the compute function also generates the output from neurons in each layer. You can examine the output of neurons to get a better understanding of how compute works:

```
> compute(network, testset[-5])
```

Training a neural network with nnet

The nnet package is another package that can deal with artificial neural networks. This package provides the functionality to train feed-forward neural networks with traditional backpropagation. As you can find most of the neural network function implemented in the neuralnet package, in this recipe we provide a short overview of how to train neural networks with nnet.

Getting ready

In this recipe, we do not use the trainset and trainset generated from the previous step; please reload the iris dataset again.

How to do it...

Perform the following steps to train the neural network with nnet:

1. First, install and load the nnet package:

```
> install.packages("nnet")
> library(nnet)
```

2. Next, split the dataset into training and testing datasets:

```
> data(iris)
> set.seed(2)
> ind = sample(2, nrow(iris), replace = TRUE,
prob=c(0.7, 0.3))
> trainset = iris[ind == 1,]
> testset = iris[ind == 2,]
```

3. Then, train the neural network with nnet:

```
> iris.nn = nnet(Species ~ ., data = trainset, size = 2, rang =
0.1, decay = 5e-4, maxit = 200)
Output:
# weights:   19
initial  value 165.086674
iter  10 value 70.447976
iter  20 value 69.667465
iter  30 value 69.505739
iter  40 value 21.588943
iter  50 value 8.691760
iter  60 value 8.521214
iter  70 value 8.138961
iter  80 value 7.291365
iter  90 value 7.039209
iter 100 value 6.570987
iter 110 value 6.355346
iter 120 value 6.345511
iter 130 value 6.340208
iter 140 value 6.337271
iter 150 value 6.334285
iter 160 value 6.333792
iter 170 value 6.333578
iter 180 value 6.333498
final  value 6.333471
converged
```

4. Use the summary to obtain information about the trained neural network:

```
> summary(iris.nn)
Output:
a 4-2-3 network with 19 weights
options were - softmaxmodelling decay=0.0005
b->h1 i1->h1 i2->h1 i3->h1 i4->h1
-0.38 -0.63 -1.96 3.13 1.53
b->h2 i1->h2 i2->h2 i3->h2 i4->h2
8.95 0.52 1.42 -1.98 -3.85
```

```
b->o1 h1->o1 h2->o1
3.08 -10.78 4.99
b->o2 h1->o2 h2->o2
-7.41 6.37 7.18
b->o3 h1->o3 h2->o3
4.33 4.42 -12.16
```

How it works...

In this recipe, we demonstrate steps to train a neural network model with the `nnet` package. We first use `nnet` to train the neural network. With this function, we can set the classification formula, the source of data, the number of hidden units in the `size` parameter, the initial random weight in the `rang` parameter, the parameter for weight decay in the `decay` parameter, and the maximum iteration in the `maxit` parameter. As we set `maxit` to 200, the training process repeatedly runs till the value of the fitting criterion plus the decay term converge. Finally, we use the `summary` function to obtain information about the built neural network, which reveals that the model is built with 4-2-3 networks with 19 weights. Also, the model shows a list of weight transitions from one node to another at the bottom of the printed message.

See also

For those who are interested in the background theory of `nnet` and how it is made, please refer to the following articles:

- Ripley, B. D. (1996) *Pattern Recognition and Neural Networks*. Cambridge
- Venables, W. N., and Ripley, B. D. (2002). *Modern Applied Statistics with S. Fourth edition*. Springer

Predicting labels based on a model trained by nnet

As we have trained a neural network with `nnet` in the previous recipe, we can now predict the labels of the testing dataset based on the trained neural network. Furthermore, we can assess the model with a confusion matrix adapted from the `caret` package.

Getting ready

To complete this recipe, you need to have completed the previous recipe by generating the training dataset, `trainset`, and the testing dataset, `testset`, from the `iris` dataset. The trained neural network also needs to be saved as `iris.nn`.

How to do it...

Perform the following steps to predict labels based on the trained neural network:

1. Generate the predictions of the testing dataset based on the model, `iris.nn`:

   ```
   > iris.predict = predict(iris.nn, testset, type="class")
   ```

2. Generate a classification table based on the predicted labels and labels of the testing dataset:

   ```
   > nn.table = table(testset$Species, iris.predict)
   iris.predict
           setosa versicolor virginica
   setosa 17 0 0
     versicolor 0 14 0
     virginica 0 1 14
   ```

3. Lastly, generate a confusion matrix based on the classification table:

   ```
   > confusionMatrix(nn.table)
   Output:
   Confusion Matrix and Statistics

   iris.predict
   setosa versicolor virginica
   setosa          17    0    0
     versicolor    0   14    0
     virginica     0    1   14


   Overall Statistics

   Accuracy : 0.9782609
           95% CI : (0.8847282, 0.9994498)
       No Information Rate : 0.3695652
       P-Value [Acc> NIR] :< 0.00000000000000022204

   Kappa : 0.9673063
   Mcnemar's Test P-Value : NA
   ```

```
Statistics by Class:

                Class: setosa Class: versicolor
Sensitivity              1.0000000        0.9333333
Specificity              1.0000000        1.0000000
PosPred Value            1.0000000        1.0000000
Neg Pred Value           1.0000000        0.9687500
Prevalence               0.3695652        0.3260870
Detection Rate           0.3695652        0.3043478
Detection Prevalence 0.3695652            0.3043478
Balanced Accuracy    1.0000000            0.9666667
           Class: virginica
Sensitivity          1.0000000
Specificity          0.9687500
PosPred Value        0.9333333
Neg Pred Value       1.0000000
Prevalence           0.3043478
Detection Rate       0.3043478
Detection Prevalence 0.3260870
Balanced Accuracy 0.9843750
```

How it works...

Similar to other classification methods, one can also predict labels based on the neural networks trained by nnet. First, we use the predict function to generate the predicted labels based on a testing dataset, testset. Within the predict function, we specify the type argument to the class, so the output will be class labels instead of a probability matrix. Next, we use the table function to generate a classification table based on predicted labels and labels written in the testing dataset. Finally, as we have created the classification table, we can employ a confusion matrix from the caret package to measure the prediction performance of the trained neural network.

See also

- For the predict function, if the type argument to class is not specified,
  it will, by default, generate a probability matrix as a prediction result. This is very
  similar to net.result generated from the compute function within the
  neuralnet package:

  ```
  > head(predict(iris.nn, testset))
  ```

9
Model Evaluation

In this chapter, we will cover the following topics:

- Why do models need to be evaluated?
- Different methods for model evaluation
- Estimating model performance with k-fold cross-validation
- Estimating model performance with Leave One Out Cross Validation
- Performing cross-validation with the `e1071` package
- Performing cross-validation with the `caret` package
- Ranking the variable importance with the `caret` package
- Ranking the variable importance with the `rminer` package
- Finding highly correlated features with the `caret` package
- Selecting features using the `caret` package
- Measuring the performance of a regression model
- Measuring the prediction performance with the confusion matrix
- Measuring the prediction performance using ROCR
- Comparing an ROC curve using the `caret` package
- Measuring performance differences between models with the `caret` package

Introduction

Model evaluation is performed to ensure that a fitted model can accurately predict responses for future or unknown subjects. Without model evaluation, we might train models that over-fit in the training data. To prevent overfitting, we can employ packages, such as `caret`, `rminer`, and `rocr` to evaluate the performance of the fitted model.

In the following chapter, we will discuss how one can implement a simple R script or use one of the packages (for example, `caret` or `rminer`) to evaluate the performance of a fitted model.

Why do models need to be evaluated?

Whenever we are building a model, it needs to be tested and evaluated to ensure that it will not only work on trained data, but also on unseen data and can generate results with accuracy. A model should not generate a random result though some noise is permitted. If the model is not evaluated properly then the chances are that the result produced with unseen data is not accurate. Furthermore, model evaluation can help select the optimum model, which is more robust and can accurately predict responses for future subjects.

Different methods of model evaluation

There are various ways by which a model can be evaluated:

- **Split test**: In a split test, the dataset is divided into two parts, one is the training set and the other is test dataset. Once data is split the algorithm will use the training set and a model is created. The accuracy of a model is tested using the test dataset. The ratio of dividing the dataset in training and test can be decided on basis of the size of the dataset. It is fast and great when the dataset is of large size or the dataset is expensive. It can produce different result on how the dataset is divided into the training and test dataset. If the date set is divided in 80% as a training set and 20% as a test set, 60% as a training set and 40%, both will generate different results. We can go for multiple split tests, where the dataset is divided in different ratios and the result is found and compared for accuracy.

- **Cross validation**: In cross validation, the dataset is divided in number of parts, for example, dividing the dataset in 10 parts. An algorithm is run on 9 subsets and holds one back for test. This process is repeated 10 times. Based on different results generated on each run, the accuracy is found. It is known as k-fold cross validation is where k is the number in which a dataset is divided. Selecting the k is very crucial here, which is dependent on the size of dataset.

- **Bootstrap**: We start with some random samples from the dataset, and an algorithm is run on dataset. This process is repeated for n times until we have all covered the full dataset. In aggregate, the result provided in all repetition shows the model performance.
- **Leave One Out Cross Validation**: As the name suggests, only one data point from the dataset is left out, an algorithm is run on the rest of the dataset and it is repeated for each point. As all points from the dataset are covered it is less biased, but it requires higher execution time if the dataset is large.

Estimating model performance with k-fold cross-validation

The k-fold cross-validation technique is a common technique used to estimate the performance of a classifier as it overcomes the problem of over-fitting. For k-fold cross-validation, the method does not use the entire dataset to build the model; instead it splits the data into a training dataset and a testing dataset. Therefore, the model built with a training dataset can then be used to assess the performance of the model on the testing dataset. By performing *n* repeats of the k-fold validation, we can then use the average of *n* accuracies to truly assess the performance of the built model. In this recipe, we will illustrate how to perform a k-fold cross-validation.

Getting ready

In this recipe, we will continue to use the telecom `churn` dataset as the input data source to train the support vector machine. For those who have not prepared the dataset, please refer to `Chapter 7`, *Classification 1 - Tree, Lazy, and Probabilistic*, for detailed information.

How to do it...

Perform the following steps to cross-validate the telecom `churn` dataset:

1. Split the index into `10` fold using the `cut` function:

```
> ind = cut(1:nrow(churnTrain), breaks=10, labels=F)
```

2. Next, use the `for` loop to perform a 10 fold cross-validation, repeated 10 times:

```
> accuracies = c()
> for (i in 1:10) {+    fit = svm(churn ~., churnTrain[ind != i,])
+    predictions = predict(fit, churnTrain[ind == i,
! names(churnTrain) %in% c("churn")])
+    correct_count = sum(predictions == churnTrain[ind ==
i,c("churn")])
+    accuracies = append(correct_count / nrow(churnTrain[ind ==
i,]), accuracies)
+ }
```

3. You can then print the accuracies:

```
> accuracies
Output
 [1] 0.9341317 0.8948949 0.8978979 0.9459459 0.9219219 0.9281437
 0.9219219 0.9249249 0.9189189 0.9251497
```

4. Lastly, you can generate average accuracies with the `mean` function:

```
> mean(accuracies)
Output
[1] 0.9213852
```

How it works...

In this recipe, we implement a simple script performing 10-fold cross-validations. We first generate an index with 10 fold with the `cut` function. Then, we implement a `for` loop to perform a 10-fold cross-validation 10 times. Within the loop, we first apply `svm` on 9 folds of data as the training set. We then use the fitted model to predict the label of the rest of the data (the testing dataset). Next, we use the sum of the correctly predicted labels to generate the accuracy. As a result of this, the loop stores 10 generated accuracies. Finally, we use the `mean` function to retrieve the average of the accuracies.

There's more...

If you wish to perform the k-fold validation with the use of other models, simply replace the line to generate the `fit` variable to whatever classifier you prefer. For example, if you would like to assess the Naïve Bayes model with a 10-fold cross-validation, you just need to replace the calling function from `svm` to `naiveBayes`:

```
> for (i in 1:10) {
+    fit = naiveBayes(churn ~., churnTrain[ind != i,])
+    predictions = predict(fit, churnTrain[ind == i, ! names(churnTrain)
%in% c("churn")])
+    correct_count = sum(predictions == churnTrain[ind == i,c("churn")])
+    accuracies = append(correct_count / nrow(churnTrain[ind == i,]),
accuracies)
+ }
```

Estimating model performance with Leave One Out Cross Validation

We have already seen k-fold cross validation, **Leave One Out Cross Validation** (LOOCV) is a special case of k-fold cross validation where the number of folds is same as number of observation. In this case the set contains a single observation. It uses an entire model except the single point and later it is used to make a prediction. Once the prediction is made using the model, it is compared with the actual value.

Getting ready

In this recipe, we will continue to use the telecom `churn` dataset as the input data source to perform Leave One Out Cross Validation. We will use the `caret` and C50 package.

How to do it...

Perform the following steps:

1. We need a `caret` and C50 library:

```
> install.packages("caret")
> install.packages("C50")
> library(caret)
> library(C50)
```

2. From the previous chapters, we have a `churn` dataset ready:

```
> train_control <- trainControl(method="LOOCV")
 The following command will take some time and may give out some
 warnings
 > model<- train(churn~., trControl=train_control, method="nb")
 > model
Output
Naive Bayes

 3333 samples
 19 predictor
 2 classes: 'yes', 'no'

 No pre-processing
 Resampling: Leave-One-Out Cross-Validation
 Summary of sample sizes: 3332, 3332, 3332, 3332, 3332, 3332, ...
 Resampling results across tuning parameters:

  usekernel Accuracy Kappa
  FALSE 0.6066606661 0.1091075239
  TRUE 0.8550855086 0.0000000000

 Tuning parameter 'fL' was held constant at a value of 0
 Tuning parameter 'adjust' was
 held constant at a value of 1
 Accuracy was used to select the optimal model using the
 largest value.
 The final values used for the model were fL = 0, usekernel = TRUE
 and adjust = 1.
```

How it works...

In the preceding example, we have seen how to use the LOOCV by using the `train` function, which is a part of the `caret` package. This function can be used to train a model on basis of the parameters provided. It will do all the work of sampling and finding the performance and gives the summarized result. In the preceding recipe, we have used LOOCV as `trainControl` and the method as Naive Bayes specified as `nb`.

See also

- For more details refer to the `train` function help using the following command:

```
> ?train
```

Performing cross-validation with the e1071 package

Besides implementing a `loop` function to perform the k-fold cross-validation, you can use the `tuning` function (for example, `tune.nnet`, `tune.randomForest`, `tune.rpart`, `tune.svm`, and `tune.knn`.) within the `e1071` package to obtain the minimum error value. In this recipe, we will illustrate how to use `tune.svm` to perform the 10-fold cross-validation and obtain the optimum classification model.

Getting ready

In this recipe, we continue to use the telecom `churn` dataset as the input data source to perform 10-fold cross-validation.

How to do it...

Perform the following steps to retrieve the minimum estimation error using cross-validation:

1. Apply `tune.svm` on the training dataset, `trainset`, with the 10-fold cross-validation as the tuning control (if you find an error message, such as `could not find function predict.func`, please clear the workspace, restart the R session, and reload the `e1071` library again):

```
> tuned = tune.svm(churn~., data = trainset, gamma = 10^-2, cost
= 10^2, tunecontrol=tune.control(cross=10))
```

2. Next, you can obtain the summary information of the model, tuned:

```
> summary(tuned)
Output
Error estimation of 'svm' using 10-fold cross validation:
0.08164651
```

3. Then, you can access the performance details of the tuned model:

```
> tuned$performances
Output
  gamma cost      error dispersion
1  0.01  100 0.08164651 0.02437228
```

4. Lastly, you can use the optimum model to generate a classification table:

```
> svmfit = tuned$best.model
> table(trainset[,c("churn")], predict(svmfit))
Output
      yes   no
yes   234  108
no     13 1960
```

How it works...

The e1071 package provides miscellaneous functions to build and assess models; therefore, you do not need to reinvent the wheel to evaluate a fitted model. In this recipe, we use the tune.svm function to tune the svm model with the given formula, dataset, gamma, cost, and control functions. Within the tune.control options, we configure the option as cross=10, which performs a 10-fold cross validation during the tuning process. The tuning process will eventually return the minimum estimation error, performance detail, and the best model during the tuning process. Therefore, we can obtain the performance measures of the tuning and further use the optimum model to generate a classification table.

See also

- In the e1071 package, the tune function uses a grid search to tune parameters
- For those interested in other tuning functions, use the help function to view the tune document:

```
> ?e1071::tune
```

Performing cross-validation with the caret package

The `caret` (classification and regression training) package contains many functions in regard to the training process for regression and classification problems. Similar to the `e1071` package, it also contains a function to perform the k-fold cross validation. In this recipe, we will demonstrate how to perform the k-fold cross validation using the `caret` package.

Getting ready

In this recipe, we will continue to use the telecom `churn` dataset as the input data source to perform the k-fold cross validation.

How to do it...

Perform the following steps to perform the k-fold cross-validation with the `caret` package:

1. First, set up the `control` parameter to train the 10-fold cross validation in 3 repetitions:

```
> control = trainControl(method="repeatedcv", number=10,
repeats=3)
```

2. Then, you can train the classification model using the telecom `churn` data with `rpart`:

```
> model = train(churn~., data=trainset, method="rpart",
preProcess="scale", trControl=control)
```

3. Finally, you can examine the output of the generated model:

```
> model
Ouput
CART
2315 samples
  16 predictor
   2 classes: 'yes', 'no'
Pre-processing: scaled
Resampling: Cross-Validated (10 fold, repeated 3 times)
Summary of sample sizes: 2084, 2083, 2082, 2084, 2083, 2084, ...
```

```
Resampling results across tuning parameters:
  cp        Accuracy  Kappa  Accuracy SD  Kappa SD
  0.0556    0.904     0.531  0.0236       0.155
  0.0746    0.867     0.269  0.0153       0.153
  0.0760    0.860     0.212  0.0107       0.141
Accuracy was used to select the optimal model using the largest
value.
The final value used for the model was cp = 0.05555556.
```

How it works...

In this recipe, we demonstrate how convenient it is to conduct the k-fold cross-validation using the caret package. In the first step, we set up the training control and select the option to perform the 10-fold cross-validation in three repetitions. The process of repeating the k-fold validation is called repeated k-fold validation, which is used to test the stability of the model. If the model is stable, one should get a similar test result. Then, we apply rpart on the training dataset with the option to scale the data and to train the model with the options configured in the previous step.

After the training process is complete, the model outputs three resampling results. Of these results, the model with cp=0.05555556 has the largest accuracy value (0.904), and is therefore selected as the optimal model for classification.

See also

- You can configure the resampling function in trainControl, in which you can specify boot, boot632, cv, repeatedcv, LOOCV, LGOCV, none, oob, adaptive_cv, adaptive_boot, or adaptive_LGOCV. To view more detailed information of how to choose the resampling method, view the trainControl document:

    ```
    > ?trainControl
    ```

Ranking the variable importance with the caret package

After building a supervised learning model, we can estimate the importance of features. This estimation employs a sensitivity analysis to measure the effect on the output of a given model when the inputs are varied. In this recipe, we will show you how to rank the variable importance with the caret package.

Getting ready

You need to have completed the previous recipe by storing the fitted rpart object in the model variable.

How to do it...

Perform the following steps to rank the variable importance with the caret package:

1. First, you can estimate the variable importance with the varImp function:

```
> importance = varImp(model, scale=FALSE)
> importance
Output
rpart variable importance
                                 Overall
number_customer_service_calls    116.015
total_day_minutes                106.988
total_day_charge                 100.648
international_planyes              86.789
voice_mail_planyes                25.974
total_eve_charge                  23.097
total_eve_minutes                 23.097
number_vmail_messages             19.885
total_intl_minutes                 6.347
total_eve_calls                    0.000
total_day_calls                    0.000
total_night_charge                 0.000
total_intl_calls                   0.000
total_intl_charge                  0.000
total_night_minutes                0.000
total_night_calls                  0.000
```

2. Then, you can generate the variable importance plot with the `plot` function:

```
> plot(importance)
```

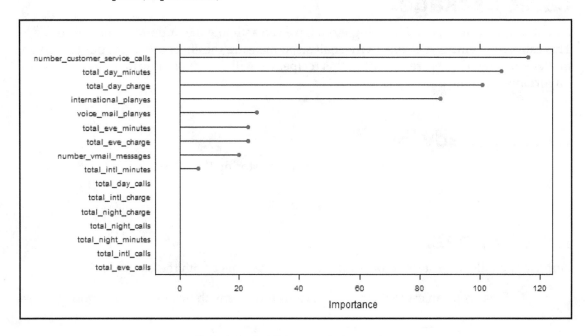

The visualization of variable importance using the caret package

How it works...

In this recipe, we first use the `varImp` function to retrieve the variable importance and obtain the summary. The overall results show the sensitivity measure of each attribute. Next, we plot the variable importance in terms of rank, which shows that the `number_customer_service_calls` attribute is the most important variable in the sensitivity measure.

There's more...

In some classification packages, such as `rpart`, the object generated from the training model contains the variable importance. We can examine the variable importance by accessing the `output` object:

```
> library(rpart)
> model.rp = rpart(churn~., data=trainset)
> model.rp$variable.importance
Output
            total_day_minutes                  total_day_charge
                   111.645286                        110.881583
 number_customer_service_calls                 total_intl_minutes
                    58.486651                         48.283228
             total_intl_charge                  total_eve_charge
                    47.698379                         47.166646
             total_eve_minutes                 international_plan
                    47.166646                         42.194508
              total_intl_calls               number_vmail_messages
                    36.730344                         19.884863
               voice_mail_plan                  total_night_calls
                    19.884863                          7.195828
               total_eve_calls                 total_night_charge
                     3.553423                          1.754547
            total_night_minutes                  total_day_calls
                     1.754547                          1.494986
```

Ranking the variable importance with the rminer package

Besides using the caret package to generate variable importance, you can use the rminer package to generate the variable importance of a classification model. In the following recipe, we will illustrate how to use rminer to obtain the variable importance of a fitted model.

Getting ready

In this recipe, we will continue to use the telecom churn dataset as the input data source to rank the variable importance.

How to do it...

Perform the following steps to rank the variable importance with `rminer`:

1. Install and load the package, `rminer`:

```
> install.packages("rminer")
> library(rminer)
```

2. Fit the svm model with the training set:

```
> model=fit(churn~.,trainset,model="svm")
```

3. Use the `Importance` function to obtain the variable importance:

```
> VariableImportance=Importance(model,trainset,method="sensv")
```

4. Plot the variable importance ranked by the variance:

```
>
L=list(runs=1,sen=t(VariableImportance$imp),sresponses=
VariableImportance$sresponses)
> mgraph(L,graph="IMP",leg=names(trainset),col="gray",Grid=10)
```

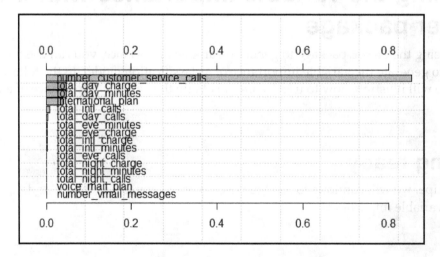

The visualization of variable importance using the rminer package

How it works...

Similar to the `caret` package, the `rminer` package can also generate the variable importance of a classification model. In this recipe, we first train the svm model on the training dataset, `trainset`, with the `fit` function. Then, we use the `Importance` function to rank the variable importance with a sensitivity measure. Finally, we use `mgraph` to plot the rank of the variable importance. Similar to the result obtained from using the `caret` package, `number_customer_service_calls` is the most important variable in the measure of sensitivity.

See also

- The `rminer` package provides many classification models for one to choose from. If you are interested in using models other than svm, you can view these options with the following command:

```
> ?rminer::fit
```

Finding highly correlated features with the caret package

When performing regression or classification, some models perform better if highly correlated attributes are removed. The `caret` package provides the `findCorrelation` function, which can be used to find attributes that are highly correlated to each other. In this recipe, we will demonstrate how to find highly correlated features using the `caret` package.

Getting ready

In this recipe, we will continue to use the telecom `churn` dataset as the input data source to find highly correlated features.

How to do it...

Perform the following steps to find highly correlated attributes:

1. Remove the features that are not coded in numeric characters:

   ```
   > new_train = trainset[,! names(churnTrain) %in% c("churn",
   "international_plan", "voice_mail_plan")]
   ```

2. Then, you can obtain the correlation of each attribute:

   ```
   >cor_mat = cor(new_train)
   ```

3. Next, we use findCorrelation to search for highly correlated attributes with a cut off equal to 0.75:

   ```
   > highlyCorrelated = findCorrelation(cor_mat, cutoff=0.75)
   ```

4. We then obtain the name of highly correlated attributes:

   ```
   > names(new_train)[highlyCorrelated]
   Output
   [1] "total_intl_minutes"   "total_day_charge"
   "total_eve_minutes"    "total_night_minutes"
   ```

How it works...

In this recipe, we search for highly correlated attributes using the caret package. In order to retrieve the correlation of each attribute, one should first remove non-numeric attributes. Then, we perform correlation to obtain a correlation matrix. Next, we use findCorrelation to find highly correlated attributes with the cut off set to 0.75. We finally obtain the names of highly correlated (with a correlation coefficient over 0.75) attributes, which are total_intl_minutes, total_day_charge, total_eve_minutes, and total_night_minutes. You can consider removing some highly correlated attributes and keep one or two attributes for better accuracy.

See also

- In addition to the caret package, you can use the leaps, genetic, and anneal functions in the subselect package to achieve the same goal

Selecting features using the caret package

The feature selection method searches the subset of features with minimized predictive errors. We can apply feature selection to identify which attributes are required to build an accurate model. The caret package provides a recursive feature elimination function, rfe, which can help automatically select the required features. In the following recipe, we will demonstrate how to use the caret package to perform feature selection.

Getting ready

In this recipe, we will continue to use the telecom churn dataset as the input data source for feature selection.

How to do it...

Perform the following steps to select features:

1. Transform the feature named as international_plan from the training dataset, trainset, to intl_yes and intl_no:

   ```
   > intl_plan = model.matrix(~ trainset.international_plan - 1,
   data=data.frame(trainset$international_plan))
   > colnames(intl_plan) =
   c("trainset.international_planno"="intl_no",
   "trainset.international_planyes"= "intl_yes")
   ```

2. Transform the feature named as voice_mail_plan from the training dataset, trainset, to voice_yes and voice_no:

   ```
   > voice_plan = model.matrix(~ trainset.voice_mail_plan - 1,
   data=data.frame(trainset$voice_mail_plan))
   > colnames(voice_plan) =
   c("trainset.voice_mail_planno" ="voice_no",
   "trainset.voice_mail_planyes"="voidce_yes")
   ```

3. Remove the international_plan and voice_mail_plan attributes and combine the training dataset, trainset, with the data frames, intl_plan and voice_plan:

   ```
   > trainset$international_plan = NULL
   > trainset$voice_mail_plan = NULL
   > trainset = cbind(intl_plan, voice_plan, trainset)
   ```

4. Transform the feature named as `international_plan` from the testing dataset, `testset`, to `intl_yes` and `intl_no`:

```
> intl_plan = model.matrix(~ testset.international_plan - 1,
data=data.frame(testset$international_plan))
> colnames(intl_plan) = c("testset.international_planno"="intl_no",
"testset.international_planyes"= "intl_yes")
```

5. Transform the feature named as `voice_mail_plan` from the training dataset, `trainset`, to `voice_yes` and `voice_no`:

```
> voice_plan = model.matrix(~ testset.voice_mail_plan - 1,
data=data.frame(testset$voice_mail_plan))
> colnames(voice_plan) = c("testset.voice_mail_planno"
="voice_no", "testset.voice_mail_planyes"="voidce_yes")
```

6. Remove the `international_plan` and `voice_mail_plan` attributes and combine the testing dataset, `testset`, with the data frames, `intl_plan` and `voice_plan`:

```
> testset$international_plan = NULL
> testset$voice_mail_plan = NULL
> testset = cbind(intl_plan,voice_plan, testset)
```

7. We then create a feature selection algorithm using linear discriminant analysis:

```
> ldaControl = rfeControl(functions = ldaFuncs, method = "cv")
```

8. Next, we perform a backward feature selection on the training dataset, `trainset`, using subsets from 1 to 18:

```
> ldaProfile = rfe(trainset[, !names(trainset) %in% c("churn")],
trainset[,c("churn")],sizes = c(1:18), rfeControl = ldaControl)
> ldaProfile
Output
Recursive feature selection
Outer resampling method: Cross-Validated (10 fold)
Resampling performance over subset size:
 Variables Accuracy  Kappa AccuracySD KappaSD Selected
         1   0.8523 0.0000   0.001325 0.00000
         2   0.8523 0.0000   0.001325 0.00000
         3   0.8423 0.1877   0.015468 0.09787
         4   0.8462 0.2285   0.016593 0.09610
         5   0.8466 0.2384   0.020710 0.09970
         6   0.8466 0.2364   0.019612 0.09387
         7   0.8458 0.2315   0.017551 0.08670
```

```
   8    0.8458 0.2284    0.016608 0.09536
   9    0.8475 0.2430    0.016882 0.10147
  10    0.8514 0.2577    0.014281 0.08076
  11    0.8518 0.2587    0.014124 0.08075
  12    0.8544 0.2702    0.015078 0.09208       *
  13    0.8544 0.2721    0.015352 0.09421
  14    0.8531 0.2663    0.018428 0.11022
  15    0.8527 0.2652    0.017958 0.10850
  16    0.8531 0.2684    0.017897 0.10884
  17    0.8531 0.2684    0.017897 0.10884
  18    0.8531 0.2684    0.017897 0.10884
The top 5 variables (out of 12):
   total_day_charge, total_day_minutes, intl_no,
 number_customer_service_calls, total_eve_charge
```

9. Next, we can plot the selection result:

```
> plot(ldaProfile, type = c("o", "g"))
```

The feature selection result

10. We can then examine the best subset of the variables:

```
> ldaProfile$optVariables
Output
 [1] "total_day_charge"
 [2] "total_day_minutes"
 [3] "intl_no"
 [4] "number_customer_service_calls"
 [5] "total_eve_charge"
 [6] "total_eve_minutes"
 [7] "voidce_yes"
 [8] "total_intl_calls"
 [9] "number_vmail_messages"
[10] "total_intl_charge"
[11] "total_intl_minutes"
[12] "total_night_minutes"
```

11. Now, we can examine the fitted model:

```
> ldaProfile$fit
Output
Call:
lda(x, y)
Prior probabilities of groups:
      yes        no
0.1477322 0.8522678
Group means:
    total_day_charge total_day_minutes   intl_no
yes         35.00143          205.8877 0.7046784
no          29.62402          174.2555 0.9351242
    number_customer_service_calls total_eve_charge
yes                      2.204678         18.16702
no                       1.441460         16.96789
    total_eve_minutes voidce_yes total_intl_calls
yes         213.7269   0.1666667         4.134503
no          199.6197   0.2954891         4.514445
    number_vmail_messages total_intl_charge
yes              5.099415          2.899386
no               8.674607          2.741343
    total_intl_minutes total_night_minutes
yes           10.73684            205.4640
no            10.15119            201.4184
Coefficients of linear discriminants:
                                        LD1
total_day_charge               0.715025524
total_day_minutes             -0.130486470
intl_no                        2.259889324
number_customer_service_calls -0.421997335
```

```
total_eve_charge               -2.390372793
total_eve_minutes               0.198406977
voidce_yes                      0.660927935
total_intl_calls                0.066240268
number_vmail_messages          -0.003529233
total_intl_charge               2.315069869
total_intl_minutes             -0.693504606
total_night_minutes            -0.002127471
```

12. Finally, we can calculate the performance across resamples:

```
> postResample(predict(ldaProfile, testset[, !names(testset) %in%
c("churn")]), testset[,c("churn")])
Output
Accuracy       Kappa
0.8605108  0.2672027
```

How it works...

In this recipe, we perform feature selection using the caret package. As there are factor-coded attributes within the dataset, we first use a function called model.matrix to transform the factor-coded attributes into multiple binary attributes. Therefore, we transform the international_plan attribute to intl_yes and intl_no. Additionally, we transform the voice_mail_plan attribute to voice_yes and voice_no.

Next, we set up control parameters for training using the cross-validation method, cv, with the linear discriminant function, ldaFuncs. Then, we use the recursive feature elimination, rfe, to perform feature selection with the use of the control function, ldaFuncs. The rfe function generates the summary of feature selection, which contains resampling a performance over the subset size and top variables.

We can then use the obtained model information to plot the number of variables against accuracy. From the preceding figure, it is obvious that using 12 features can obtain the best accuracy. In addition to this, we can retrieve the best subset of the variables in (12 variables in total) the fitted model. Lastly, we can calculate the performance across resamples, which yields an accuracy of 0.86 and a kappa of 0.27.

See also

- In order to specify the algorithm used to control feature selection, one can change the control function specified in `rfeControl`. Here are some of the options you can use:

```
    caretFuncs       SVM (caret)
lmFuncs         lm (base)
rfFuncs         RF (randomForest)
treebagFuncs    DT (ipred)
ldaFuncs        lda(base)
nbFuncs         NB (klaR)
gamFuncs        gam (gam)
```

Measuring the performance of the regression model

To measure the performance of a regression model, we can calculate the distance from predicted output and the actual output as a quantifier of the performance of the model. Here, we often use the **Root Mean Square Error (RMSE)**, **Relative Square Error (RSE)**, and R-Square as common measurements. In the following recipe, we will illustrate how to compute these measurements from a built regression model.

Getting ready

In this recipe, we will use the `Quartet` dataset, which contains four regression datasets as our input data source.

How to do it...

Perform the following steps to measure the performance of the regression model:

1. Load the `Quartet` dataset from the `car` package:

```
> library(car)
> data(Quartet)
```

2. Plot the attribute, y3, against x using the lm function:

```
> plot(Quartet$x, Quartet$y3)
> lmfit = lm(Quartet$y3~Quartet$x)
> abline(lmfit, col="red")
```

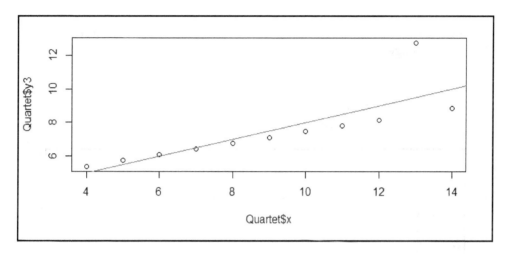

The linear regression plot

3. You can retrieve predicted values by using the predict function:

```
> predicted= predict(lmfit, newdata=Quartet[c("x")])
```

4. Now, you can calculate the root mean square error:

```
> actual = Quartet$y3
> rmse = (mean((predicted - actual)^2))^0.5
> rmse
Output
[1] 1.118286
```

5. You can calculate the relative square error:

```
> mu = mean(actual)
> rse = mean((predicted - actual)^2) / mean((mu - actual)^2)
> rse
Output
[1] 0.333676
```

6. Also, you can use R-Square as a measurement:

```
> rsquare = 1 - rse
> rsquare
Output
[1] 0.666324
```

7. Then, you can plot attribute, y3, against x using the rlm function from the MASS package:

```
> library(MASS)
> plot(Quartet$x, Quartet$y3)
> rlmfit = rlm(Quartet$y3~Quartet$x)
> abline(rlmfit, col="red")
```

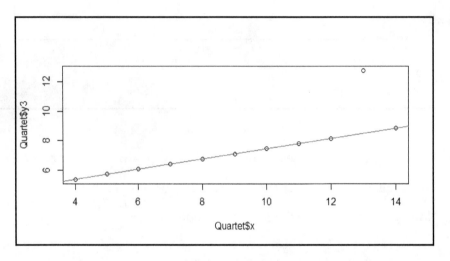

The robust linear regression plot on the Quartet dataset

8. You can then retrieve the predicted value using the predict function:

```
> predicted = predict(rlmfit, newdata=Quartet[c("x")])
```

9. Next, you can calculate the root mean square error using the distance of the predicted and actual value:

```
> actual = Quartet$y3
> rmse = (mean((predicted - actual)^2))^0.5
> rmse
Output
[1] 1.279045
```

10. Calculate the relative square error between the predicted and actual labels:

```
> mu = mean(actual)
> rse =mean((predicted - actual)^2) / mean((mu - actual)^2)
> rse
Output
[1] 0.4365067
```

11. Now, you can calculate the R-Square value:

```
> rsquare = 1 - rse
> rsquare
Output
[1] 0.5634933
```

How it works...

The measurement of the performance of the regression model employs the distance between the predicted value and the actual value. We often use these three measurements, root mean square error, relative square error, and R-Square, as the quantifier for the performance of regression models. In this recipe, we first load the Quartet data from the car package. We then use the lm function to fit the linear model, and add the regression line on a scatter plot of the x variable against the y3 variable. Next, we compute the predicted value using the predict function, and begin to compute the **Root Mean Square Error (RMSE)**, **Relative Square Error (RSE)**, and R-Square for the built model.

As this dataset has an outlier at x=13, we would like to quantify how the outlier affects the performance measurement. To achieve this, we first train a regression model using the rlm function from the MASS package. Similar to the previous step, we then generate a performance measurement of the root square mean error, relative square error, and R-Square. From the output measurement, it is obvious that the mean square error and the relative square errors of the lm model are smaller than the model built by rlm, and the score of R-Square shows that the model built with lm has a greater prediction power. However, for the actual scenario, we should remove the outlier at x=13. This comparison shows that the outlier may be biased toward the performance measure and may lead us to choose the wrong model.

There's more...

If you would like to perform cross-validation on a linear regression model, you can use the `tune` function within the e1071 package:

```
> tune(lm, y3~x, data = Quartet)
Output
Error estimation of 'lm' using 10-fold cross validation: 2.33754
```

Other than the e1071 package, you can use the `train` function from the caret package to perform cross-validation. In addition to this, you can also use `cv.lm` from the DAAG package to achieve the same goal.

Measuring prediction performance with a confusion matrix

To measure the performance of a classification model, we can first generate a classification table based on our predicted label and actual label. Then, we can use a confusion matrix to obtain performance measures such as precision, recall, specificity, and accuracy. In this recipe, we will demonstrate how to retrieve a confusion matrix using the caret package.

Getting ready

In this recipe, we will continue to use the telecom churn dataset as our example dataset.

How to do it...

Perform the following steps to generate a classification measurement:

1. Train an svm model using the training dataset:

```
> svm.model= train(churn ~ .,
+                 data = trainset,
+                 method = "svmRadial")
```

2. You can then predict labels using the fitted model, svm.model:

```
> svm.pred = predict(svm.model, testset[,! names(testset)
%in% c("churn")])
```

3. Next, you can generate a classification table:

```
> table(svm.pred, testset[,c("churn")])
Output
svm.pred yes   no
     yes  73   16
     no   68  861
```

4. Lastly, you can generate a confusion matrix using the prediction results and the actual labels from the testing dataset:

```
> confusionMatrix(svm.pred, testset[,c("churn")])
Output
Confusion Matrix and Statistics
          Reference
Prediction yes   no
      yes   73   16
      no    68  861

               Accuracy : 0.9175
                 95% CI : (0.8989, 0.9337)
    No Information Rate : 0.8615
    P-Value [Acc > NIR] : 2.273e-08
                  Kappa : 0.5909
 Mcnemar's Test P-Value : 2.628e-08
            Sensitivity : 0.51773
            Specificity : 0.98176
         Pos Pred Value : 0.82022
         Neg Pred Value : 0.92680
             Prevalence : 0.13851
         Detection Rate : 0.07171
   Detection Prevalence : 0.08743
      Balanced Accuracy : 0.74974
       'Positive' Class : yes
```

How it works...

In this recipe, we demonstrate how to obtain a confusion matrix to measure the performance of a classification model. First, we use the `train` function from the `caret` package to train an svm model. Next, we use the `predict` function to extract the predicted labels of the svm model using the testing dataset. Then, we perform the `table` function to obtain the classification table based on the predicted and actual labels. Finally, we use the `confusionMatrix` function from the `caret` package to generate a confusion matrix to measure the performance of the classification model.

See also

- If you are interested in the available methods that can be used in the `train` function, you can refer to this website:
  `http://topepo.github.io/caret/modelList.html`

Measuring prediction performance using ROCR

A **Receiver Operating Characteristic** (**ROC**) curve is a plot that illustrates the performance of a binary classifier system, and plots the true positive rate against the false positive rate for different cut points. We most commonly use this plot to calculate the **Area Under Curve** (**AUC**) to measure the performance of a classification model. In this recipe, we will demonstrate how to illustrate an ROC curve and calculate the AUC to measure the performance of a classification model.

Getting ready

In this recipe, we will continue using the telecom `churn` dataset as our example dataset.

How to do it...

Perform the following steps to generate two different classification examples with different costs:

1. First, you should install and load the ROCR package:

   ```
   > install.packages("ROCR")
   > library(ROCR)
   ```

2. Train the svm model using the training dataset with a probability equal to TRUE:

   ```
   > svmfit=svm(churn~ ., data=trainset, prob=TRUE)
   ```

3. Make predictions based on the trained model on the testing dataset with the probability set as TRUE:

```
>pred=predict(svmfit,testset[, !names(testset) %in% c("churn")],
  probability=TRUE)
```

4. Obtain the probability of labels with `yes`:

```
> pred.prob = attr(pred, "probabilities")
> pred.to.roc = pred.prob[, 2]
```

5. Use the `prediction` function to generate a prediction result:

```
> pred.rocr = prediction(pred.to.roc, testset$churn)
```

6. Use the `performance` function to obtain the performance measurement:

```
> perf.rocr = performance(pred.rocr, measure = "auc", x.measure =
"cutoff")
> perf.tpr.rocr = performance(pred.rocr, "tpr","fpr")
```

7. Visualize the ROC curve using the `plot` function:

```
> plot(perf.tpr.rocr, colorize=T,
main=paste("AUC:", (perf.rocr@y.values)))
```

The ROC curve for the svm classifier performance

How it works...

In this recipe, we demonstrated how to generate an ROC curve to illustrate the performance of a binary classifier. First, we should install and load the library, ROCR. Then, we use svm, from the e1071 package, to train a classification model, and then use the model to predict labels for the testing dataset. Next, we use the prediction function (from the package, ROCR) to generate prediction results. We then adapt the performance function to obtain the performance measurement of the true positive rate against the false positive rate. Finally, we use the plot function to visualize the ROC plot, and add the value of AUC to the title. In this example, the AUC value is 0.92, which indicates that the svm classifier performs well in classifying telecom user churn datasets.

See also

- For those interested in the concept and terminology of ROC, you can refer to http://en.wikipedia.org/wiki/Receiver_operating_characteristic.

Comparing an ROC curve using the caret package

In previous chapters, we introduced many classification methods; each method has its own advantages and disadvantages. However, when it comes to the problem of how to choose the best fitted model, you need to compare all the performance measures generated from different prediction models. To make the comparison easy, the caret package allows us to generate and compare the performance of models. In this recipe, we will use the function provided by the caret package to compare different algorithm trained models on the same dataset.

Getting ready

Here, we will continue to use telecom dataset as our input data source.

How to do it...

Perform the following steps to generate an ROC curve of each fitted model:

1. Install and load the library, pROC:

```
> install.packages("pROC")
> library("pROC")
```

2. Set up the training control with a 10-fold cross-validation in three repetitions:

```
> control = trainControl(method = "repeatedcv",
+                        number = 10,
+                        repeats = 3,
+                        classProbs = TRUE,
+                        summaryFunction = twoClassSummary)
```

3. Then, you can train a classifier on the training dataset using glm:

```
> glm.model= train(churn ~ .,
+                   data = trainset,
+                   method = "glm",
+                   metric = "ROC",
+                   trControl = control)
```

4. Also, you can train a classifier on the training dataset using svm:

```
> svm.model= train(churn ~ .,
+                   data = trainset,
+                   method = "svmRadial",
+                   metric = "ROC",
+                   trControl = control)
```

5. To see how rpart performs on the training data, we use the rpart function:

```
> rpart.model= train(churn ~ .,
+                     data = trainset,
+                     method = "rpart",
+                     metric = "ROC",
+                     trControl = control)
```

6. You can make predictions separately based on different trained models:

```
> glm.probs = predict(glm.model, testset[,! names(testset) %in%
c("churn")], type = "prob")
> svm.probs = predict(svm.model, testset[,! names(testset) %in%
c("churn")], type = "prob")
> rpart.probs = predict(rpart.model, testset[,! names(testset) %in%
c("churn")], type = "prob")
```

7. You can generate the ROC curve of each model, and plot the curve on the same figure:

```
> glm.ROC = roc(response = testset[,c("churn")],
+ predictor =glm.probs$yes,
+ levels = levels(testset[,c("churn")]))
> plot(glm.ROC, type="S", col="red")
Output
Call:
roc.default(response = testset[, c("churn")], predictor =
glm.probs$yes, levels = levels(testset[, c("churn")]))

Data: glm.probs$yes in 141 controls (testset[, c("churn")] yes) >
877 cases (testset[, c("churn")] no).
Area under the curve: 0.82

> svm.ROC = roc(response = testset[,c("churn")],
+              predictor =svm.probs$yes,
+              levels = levels(testset[,c("churn")]))
> plot(svm.ROC, add=TRUE, col="green")
Output
Call:
roc.default(response = testset[, c("churn")], predictor =
svm.probs$yes, levels = levels(testset[, c("churn")]))

Data: svm.probs$yes in 141 controls (testset[, c("churn")] yes) >
877 cases (testset[, c("churn")] no).
Area under the curve: 0.9233

> rpart.ROC = roc(response = testset[,c("churn")],
+              predictor =rpart.probs$yes,
+              levels = levels(testset[,c("churn")]))
> plot(rpart.ROC, add=TRUE, col="blue")
Output
Call:
roc.default(response = testset[, c("churn")], predictor =
rpart.probs$yes, levels = levels(testset[, c("churn")]))

Data: rpart.probs$yes in 141 controls (testset[, c("churn")] yes) >
```

```
877 cases (testset[, c("churn")] no).
Area under the curve: 0.7581
```

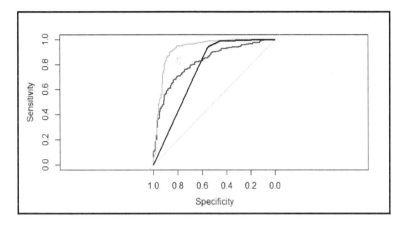

The ROC curve for the performance of three classifiers

How it works...

Here, we demonstrate how we can compare fitted models by illustrating their ROC curve in one figure. First, we set up the control of the training process with a 10-fold cross validation in three repetitions with the performance evaluation in `twoClassSummary`. After setting up control of the training process, we then apply `glm`, `svm`, and `rpart` algorithms on the training dataset to fit the classification models. Next, we can make a prediction based on each generated model and plot the ROC curve, respectively. Within the generated figure, we find that the model trained by svm has the largest area under curve, which is 0.9233 (plotted in green), the AUC of the `glm` model (red) is 0.82, and the AUC of the `rpart` model (blue) is 0.7581. From *Figure 7*, it is obvious that `svm` performs the best among all the fitted models on this training dataset (without requiring tuning).

See also

- We use another ROC visualization package, pROC, which can be employed to display and analyze ROC curves. If you would like to know more about the package, please use the `help` function:

```
> help(package="pROC")
```

Measuring performance differences between models with the caret package

In the previous recipe, we introduced how to generate ROC curves for each generated model, and have the curve plotted on the same figure. Apart from using an ROC curve, one can use the resampling method to generate statistics of each fitted model in ROC, sensitivity, and specificity metrics. Therefore, we can use these statistics to compare the performance differences between each model. In the following recipe, we will introduce how to measure performance differences between fitted models with the caret package.

Getting ready

One needs to have completed the previous recipe by storing the glm fitted model, svm fitted model, and the rpart fitted model into glm.model, svm.model, and rpart.model, respectively.

How to do it...

Perform the following steps to measure performance differences between each fitted model:

1. Resample the three generated models:

```
> cv.values = resamples(list(glm = glm.model, svm=svm.model,
rpart = rpart.model))
```

2. Then, you can obtain a summary of the resampling result:

```
> summary(cv.values)
Output
Call:
summary.resamples(object = cv.values)
Models: glm, svm, rpart
Number of resamples: 30
ROC
        Min. 1st Qu. Median    Mean 3rd Qu.    Max. NA's
glm    0.7206  0.7847 0.8126 0.8116  0.8371 0.8877     0
svm    0.8337  0.8673 0.8946 0.8929  0.9194 0.9458     0
rpart 0.2802  0.7159 0.7413 0.6769  0.8105 0.8821     0
Sens
         Min. 1st Qu. Median    Mean 3rd Qu.    Max. NA's
glm    0.08824  0.2000 0.2286 0.2194  0.2517 0.3529     0
```

```
svm    0.44120   0.5368 0.5714 0.5866   0.6424 0.7143      0
rpart  0.20590   0.3742 0.4706 0.4745   0.5929 0.6471      0
Spec
         Min. 1st Qu. Median   Mean 3rd Qu.   Max. NA's
glm    0.9442   0.9608 0.9746 0.9701   0.9797 0.9949      0
svm    0.9442   0.9646 0.9746 0.9740   0.9835 0.9949      0
rpart  0.9492   0.9709 0.9797 0.9780   0.9848 0.9949      0
```

3. Use `dotplot` to plot the resampling result in the ROC metric:

```
> dotplot(cv.values, metric = "ROC")
```

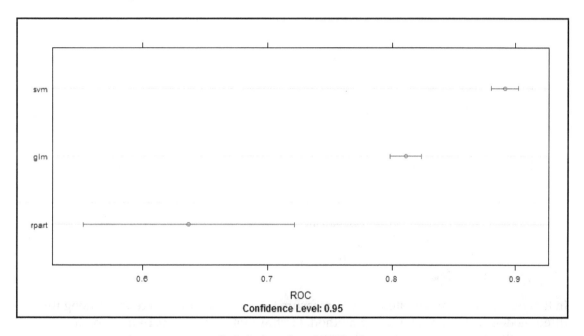

The dotplot of resampling result in ROC metric

4. Also, you can use a box-whisker plot to plot the resampling result:

```
> bwplot(cv.values, layout = c(3, 1))
```

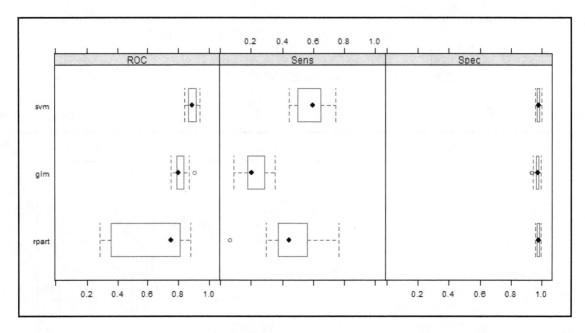

The box-whisker plot of resampling result

How it works...

In this recipe, we demonstrated how to measure the performance differences among three fitted models using the resampling method. First, we use the `resample` function to generate the statistics for each fitted model (`svm.model`, `glm.model`, and `rpart.model`). Then, we can use the `summary` function to obtain the statistics of these three models in the ROC, sensitivity, and specificity metrics. Next, we can apply a `dotplot` on the resampling result to see how ROC varied between each model. Last, we use a box-whisker plot on the resampling results to show the box-whisker plot for different models in the ROC, sensitivity, and specificity metrics on a single plot.

See also

- Besides using `dotplot` and `bwplot` to measure performance differences, one can use `densityplot`, `splom`, and `xyplot` to visualize the performance differences for each fitted model in the ROC, sensitivity, and specificity metrics.

10
Ensemble Learning

In this chapter, we will cover the following topics:

- Using the Super Learner algorithm
- Train and test Super Learner
- Using ensemble to train and test
- Classifying data with the `bagging` method
- Performing cross-validation with the `bagging` method
- Classifying data with the `boosting` method
- Performing cross-validation with the `boosting` method
- Classifying data with gradient boosting
- Calculating the margins of a classifier
- Calculating the error evolution of the ensemble method
- Classifying the data with random forest
- Estimating the prediction errors of different classifiers

Introduction

Ensemble learning is a method for combining results produced by different learners into one format, with the aim of producing better classification results and regression results. In previous chapters, we discussed several classification methods. These methods take different approaches, but they all have the same goal, that is, finding an optimum classification model.

However, a single classifier may be imperfect, as it misclassify data in certain categories. As not all classifiers are imperfect, a better approach is to average the results by voting. In other words, if we average the prediction results of every classifier with the same input, we may create a superior model compared to using an individual method.

In ensemble learning, `bagging`, `boosting`, and random forest are the three most common methods:

- Bagging is a voting method, which first uses Bootstrap to generate a different training set, and then uses the training set to make different base learners. The `bagging` method employs a combination of base learners to make a better prediction.
- Boosting is similar to the `bagging` method. However, what makes boosting different is that it first constructs the base learning in sequence, where each successive learner is built for the prediction residuals of the preceding learner. With the means to create a complementary learner, it uses the mistakes made by previous learners to train the next base learner.
- Random forest uses the classification results voted from many classification trees. The idea is simple; a single classification tree will obtain a single classification result with a single input vector. However, a random forest grows many classification trees, obtaining multiple results from a single input. Therefore, a random forest will use the majority of votes from all the decision trees to classify data or use an average output for regression.
- Stacking or Super Learner algorithm multiple models are used and stacked over one another, predictions are passed from one layer to another and to the top layer. It is a loss-based supervised learning method.

In the following recipes, we will discuss how to use `bagging` and `boosting` to classify data. We can then perform cross-validation to estimate the error rate of each classifier. In addition to this, we'll introduce the use of a margin to measure the certainty of a model. Next, we will cover random forests, similar to the `bagging` and `boosting` methods, and introduce how to train the model to classify data and use margins to estimate the model certainty. Lastly, we'll demonstrate how to estimate the error rate of each classifier, and use the error rate to compare the performance of different classifiers.

Using the Super Learner algorithm

Super Learner is an algorithm that uses various learning prediction models and finds the optimal combination of collection of algorithms. It learns best optimal fits. Ensemble methods use multiple learning algorithms to obtain better performance.

Getting ready

In this recipe, we will use the `SuperLearner` package.

How to do it...

1. Perform the following steps in R:

```
> install.packages("SuperLearner")
> install.packages("caret")
> install.packages("glmnet")
> install.packages("xgboost")
> install.packages("randomForest")
> library(SuperLearner)
```

2. To list all the available wrappers for predictions and screening, execute the following:

```
> listWrappers()
```

It will list all prediction algorithms and screening algorithms as follows:

```
All prediction algorithm wrappers in SuperLearner:

 [1] "SL.bartMachine"    "SL.bayesglm"       "SL.biglasso"        "SL.caret"          "SL.caret.rpart"
 [6] "SL.cforest"        "SL.dbarts"         "SL.earth"           "SL.extraTrees"     "SL.gam"
[11] "SL.gbm"            "SL.glm"            "SL.glm.interaction" "SL.glmnet"         "SL.ipredbagg"
[16] "SL.kernelKnn"      "SL.knn"            "SL.ksvm"            "SL.lda"            "SL.leekasso"
[21] "SL.lm"             "SL.loess"          "SL.logreg"          "SL.mean"           "SL.nnet"
[26] "SL.nnls"           "SL.polymars"       "SL.qda"             "SL.randomForest"   "SL.ranger"
[31] "SL.ridge"          "SL.rpart"          "SL.rpartPrune"      "SL.speedglm"       "SL.speedlm"
[36] "SL.step"           "SL.step.forward"   "SL.step.interaction" "SL.stepAIC"       "SL.svm"
[41] "SL.template"       "SL.xgboost"

All screening algorithm wrappers in SuperLearner:

[1] "All"
[1] "screen.corP"       "screen.corRank"     "screen.glmnet"      "screen.randomForest" "screen.SIS"
[6] "screen.template"   "screen.ttest"       "write.screen.template"
```

```
> data(Boston, package="MASS")
> training = sample(nrow(Boston), 100)
```

```
> X = Boston[training, ]
> X_Hold = Boston[-training, ]
> Y = Boston$medv[training, ]
> Y_Hold = Boston$medv[-training, ]
We can fit single model using the SuperLearner
> sl_glm = SuperLearner(Y = Y, X = X, family = gaussian(),
SL.library = "SL.glmnet")
> sl_glm
Output

Call: SuperLearner(Y = Y, X = X, family = gaussian(), SL.library
= "SL.glmnet")


 Risk Coef
SL.glmnet_All 0.08537136 1

> sl_randomf = SuperLearner(Y = Y, X = X, family = gaussian(),
SL.library = "SL.randomForest")
> sl_randomf
Output

Call:
SuperLearner(Y = Y, X = X, family = gaussian(), SL.library
= "SL.randomForest")


 Risk Coef
SL.randomForest_All 10.66687 1
```

How it works...

We have used Super Learner to fit the single model. We can specify more models also. We tried with random forest and glment with family as gaussian for a continuous outcome. For a binary outcome family is binomial. Risk shows model accuracy or performance--the lower the risk, the better the model. It shows that the model is predicting more accurate values. The coefficient column tells the weight of a model.

Using ensemble to train and test

We can fit more than one model in Super Learner and it will tell which is best from all the applied models. It also creates a weighted average for all the models.

Getting ready

You have completed all the recipes, and you have dataset X,Y, X_Hold, and Y_Hold created from the previous recipes.

How to do it...

Perform the following steps in R:

```
> install.packages("SuperLearner")
> library(SuperLearner)
> sl_models = c("SL.xgboost", "SL.randomForest", "SL.glmnet",
"SL.nnet", "SL.rpartPrune", "SL.lm", "SL.mean")
> superlearner = SuperLearner(Y = Y, X = X, family = gaussian (),
                        SL.library = sl_models)
> superlearner
Output
Call: SuperLearner(Y = Y, X = X, family = gaussian(), SL.library
= sl_lib)


                        Risk           Coef
SL.xgboost_All         7.606564e+00  0.000000e+00
SL.randomForest_All    1.027187e+01  2.907956e-16
SL.glmnet_All          8.641940e-02  0.000000e+00
SL.nnet_All            8.442002e+01  0.000000e+00
SL.rpartPrune_All      1.198280e+01  0.000000e+00
SL.lm_Al               1 9.947536e-30  1.000000e+00
SL.mean_All            8.443262e+01  7.768893e-17

> r = CV.SuperLearner(Y = Y, X = X, family = gaussian(),
                    + SL.library = sl_lib)
> plot(r)
```

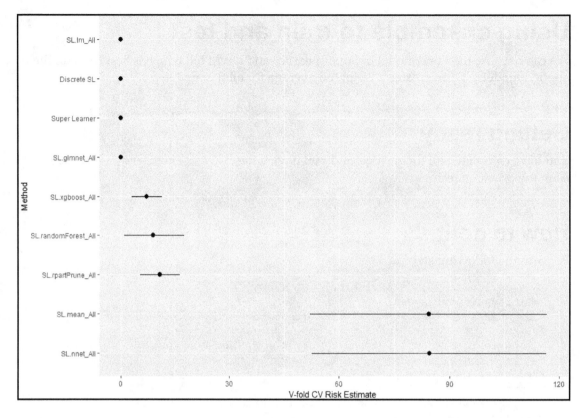

We can predict using the data we removed from the training set to see if its predicted correctly or not (recall the X and X_Hold variable we created in beginning):

```
> pred = predict(superlearner, X_Hold, onlySL = T)
```

How it works...

Ensemble learning means using multiple learning algorithms so that we can predict better. We created a vector of different models we want to ensemble. We used that vector in Super Learner in SL.Library. Super Learner will provide the risk and coefficient for all the models. Using .cv we get V fold cross validated risk for Super Learner, which can be easily plotted to see the risk estimate of all the modes.

Classifying data with the bagging method

The `adabag` package implements both `boosting` and `bagging` methods. For the `bagging` method, the package implements Breiman's Bagging algorithm, which first generates multiple versions of classifiers and then obtains an aggregated classifier. In this recipe, we will illustrate how to use the `bagging` method from `adabag` to generate a classification model using the telecom `churn` dataset.

Getting ready

In this recipe, we will continue to use the telecom `churn` dataset as the input data source for the `bagging` method. For those who have not prepared the dataset, please refer to Chapter 7, *Classification 1 - Tree, Lazy, and Probabilistic*, for detailed information.

How to do it...

Perform the following steps to generate a classification model for the telecom `churn` dataset:

1. First, you need to install and load the `adabag` package (it might take a while to install `adabag`):

   ```
   > install.packages("adabag")
   > library(adabag)
   ```

2. Next, you can use the `bagging` function to train a training dataset (the result may vary during the training process):

   ```
   > set.seed(2)
   > churn.bagging = bagging(churn ~ ., data=trainset, mfinal=10)
   ```

3. Access the variable importance from the bagging result:

   ```
   > churn.bagging$importance
   Output:
      international_plan number_customer_service_calls
           10.4948380                    16.4260510
   number_vmail_messages total_day_calls
            0.5319143                     0.3774190
       total_day_charge total_day_minutes
            0.0000000                    28.7545042
       total_eve_calls total_eve_charge
   ```

```
        0.1463585                0.0000000
    total_eve_minutes total_intl_calls
       14.2366754                8.7733895
    total_intl_charge total_intl_minutes
        0.0000000                9.7838256
    total_night_calls total_night_charge
        0.4349952                0.0000000
  total_night_minutes voice_mail_plan
        2.3379622                7.7020671
```

4. After generating the classification model, you can use the predicted results from the testing dataset:

```
> churn.predbagging= predict.bagging(churn.bagging,
newdata=testset)
```

5. From the predicted results, you can obtain a classification table:

```
> churn.predbagging$confusion
Output:

               Observed Class
Predicted Class yes no
           no 35 866
          yes 106 11
```

6. Finally, you can retrieve the average error of the bagging result:

```
> churn.predbagging$error
Output
[1] 0.0451866
```

How it works...

Bagging is derived from the name Bootstrap aggregating, which is a stable, accurate, and easy to implement model for data classification and regression. The definition of bagging is as follows: given a training dataset of size n, bagging performs Bootstrap sampling and generates m new training sets, Di, each of size n. Finally, we can fit m Bootstrap samples to m models and combine the result by averaging the output (for regression) or voting (for classification):

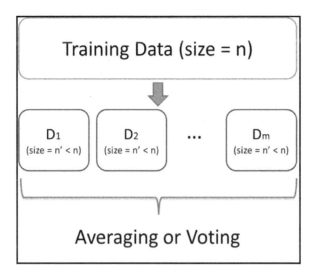

An illustration of the bagging method

The advantage of using bagging is that it is a powerful learning method which is easy to understand and implement. However, the main drawback of this technique is that it is hard to analyze the result.

In this recipe, we use the `boosting` method from `adabag` to classify the telecom churn data. Similar to other classification methods discussed in previous chapters, you can train a `boosting` classifier with a formula and a training dataset. Additionally, you can set the number of iterations to 10 in the `mfinal` argument. Once the classification model is built, you can examine the importance of each attribute. Ranking the attributes by importance reveals that the number of customer service calls plays a crucial role in the classification model.

Next, with a fitted model, you can apply the `predict.bagging` function to predict the labels of the testing dataset. Therefore, you can use the labels of the testing dataset and predicted results to generate a classification table and obtain the average error, which is 0.045 in this example.

There's more...

Besides `adabag`, the `ipred` package provides a `bagging` method for a classification tree. We demonstrate here how to use the `bagging` method of the `ipred` package to train a classification model:

1. First, you need to install and load the `ipred` package:

```
> install.packages("ipred")
> library(ipred)
```

2. You can then use the `bagging` method to fit the classification method:

```
> churn.bagging = bagging(churn ~ ., data = trainset, coob = T)
> churn.bagging
Output
Bagging classification trees with 25 bootstrap replications
Call: bagging.data.frame(formula = churn ~ ., data = trainset, coob
  = T)
Out-of-bag estimate of misclassification error:  0.0605
```

3. Obtain an out of bag estimate of misclassification of the errors:

```
> mean(predict(churn.bagging) != trainset$churn)
Output
[1] 0.06047516
```

4. You can then use the `predict` function to obtain the predicted labels of the testing dataset:

```
> churn.prediction = predict(churn.bagging, newdata=testset,
type="class")
```

5. Obtain the classification table from the labels of the testing dataset and prediction results:

```
> prediction.table = table(churn.prediction, testset$churn)
Output
churn.prediction yes   no
            no    31 869
            yes  110    8
```

Performing cross-validation with the bagging method

To assess the prediction power of a classifier, you can run a cross-validation method to test the robustness of the classification model. In this recipe, we will introduce how to use `bagging.cv` to perform cross-validation with the `bagging` method.

Getting ready

In this recipe, we continue to use the telecom `churn` dataset as the input data source to perform a k-fold cross-validation with the `bagging` method.

How to do it...

Perform the following steps to retrieve the minimum estimation errors by performing cross-validation with the `bagging` method:

1. First, we use `bagging.cv` to make a 10-fold classification on the training dataset with 10 iterations:

   ```
   > churn.baggingcv = bagging.cv(churn ~ ., v=10, data=trainset,
   mfinal=10)
   ```

2. You can then obtain the confusion matrix from the cross-validation results:

   ```
   > churn.baggingcv$confusion
   Output
                   Observed Class
   Predicted Class   yes    no
               no    100  1938
               yes   242    35
   ```

3. Lastly, you can retrieve the minimum estimation errors from the cross-validation results:

   ```
   > churn.baggingcv$error
   Output
   [1] 0.05831533
   ```

How it works...

The `adabag` package provides a function to perform the k-fold validation with either the `bagging` or `boosting` method. In this example, we use `bagging.cv` to make the k-fold cross-validation with the bagging method. We first perform a 10-fold cross validation with 10 iterations by specifying `v=10` and `mfinal=10`. Please note that this is quite time consuming due to the number of iterations. After the cross-validation process is complete, we can obtain the confusion matrix and average errors (0.058 in this case) from the cross-validation results.

See also

- For those interested in tuning the parameters of `bagging.cv`, please view the `bagging.cv` document by using the `help` function:

```
> help(bagging.cv)
```

Classifying data with the boosting method

Similar to the `bagging` method, boosting starts with a simple or weak classifier and gradually improves it by reweighting the misclassified samples. Thus, the new classifier can learn from previous classifiers. The `adabag` package provides implementation of the **AdaBoost.M1** and **SAMME** algorithms. Therefore, one can use the `boosting` method in `adabag` to perform ensemble learning. In this recipe, we will use the `boosting` method in `adabag` to classify the telecom `churn` dataset.

Getting ready

In this recipe, we will continue to use the telecom churn dataset as the input data source to perform classifications with the `boosting` method. Also, you need to have the `adabag` package loaded in R before commencing the recipe.

How to do it...

Perform the following steps to classify the telecom `churn` dataset with the `boosting` method:

1. You can use the `boosting` function from the `adabag` package to train the classification model:

```
> set.seed(2)
> churn.boost = boosting(churn ~.,data=trainset,mfinal=10,
coeflearn="Freund", boos=FALSE , control=rpart.control(maxdepth=3))
```

2. You can then make a prediction based on the boosted model and testing dataset:

```
> churn.boost.pred = predict.boosting(churn.boost,newdata=testset)
```

3. Next, you can retrieve the classification table from the predicted results:

```
> churn.boost.pred$confusion
Output
                Observed Class
Predicted Class yes   no
            no    41  858
           yes   100   19
```

4. Finally, you can obtain the average errors from the predicted results:

```
> churn.boost.pred$error
Output
[1] 0.0589391
```

How it works...

The idea of boosting is to *boost* weak learners (for example, a single decision tree) into strong learners. Assuming that we have n points in our training dataset, we can assign a weight, Wi ($0 <= i <n$), for each point. Then, during the iterative learning process (we assume the number of iterations is m), we can reweigh each point in accordance with the classification result in each iteration. If the point is correctly classified, we should decrease the weight. Otherwise, we increase the weight of the point. When the iteration process is finished, we can then obtain the m fitted model, $f_i(x)$ ($0 <= i <n$).

Finally, we can obtain the final prediction through the weighted average of each tree's prediction, where the weight, b, is based on the quality of each tree:

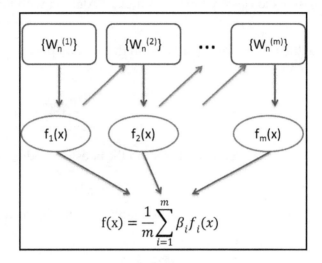

An illustration of the boosting method

Both `bagging` and `boosting` are ensemble methods which combine the prediction power of each single learner into a strong learner. The difference between `bagging` and `boosting` is that the `bagging` method combines independent models but boosting performs an iterative process to reduce the errors of preceding models by predicting them with successive models.

In this recipe, we demonstrate how to fit a classification model within the `boosting` method. Similar to `bagging`, one has to specify the formula and the training dataset used to train the classification model. In addition, one can specify parameters, such as the number of iterations (`mfinal`), the weight update coefficient (`coeflearn`), the weight of how each observation is used (`boos`), and the control for `rpart` (a single decision tree). In this recipe, we set the iteration to 10, using `Freund` (the AdaBoost.M1 algorithm implemented method) as `coeflearn`, `boos` set to false and max depth set to 3 for `rpart` configuration.

We use the boosting method to fit the classification model and then save it in `churn.boost`. We can then obtain predicted labels using the `prediction` function. Furthermore, we can use the `table` function to retrieve a classification table based on the predicted labels and testing the dataset labels. Lastly, we can get the average errors of the predicted results.

There's more...

In addition to using the boosting function in the adabag package, one can also use the caret package to perform a classification with the boosting method:

1. First, load the mboost and pROC package:

   ```
   > library(mboost)
   > install.packages("pROC")
   > library(pROC)
   ```

2. We can then set the training control with the trainControl function and use the train function to train the classification model with AdaBoost.M1:

   ```
   > set.seed(2)
   > ctrl = trainControl(method = "repeatedcv", repeats = 1, class
   Probs = TRUE, summaryFunction = twoClassSummary)
   > ada.train = train(churn ~ ., data = trainset, method = "ada",
   metric = "ROC", trControl = ctrl)
   ```

3. Use the summary function to obtain the details of the classification model:

   ```
   > ada.train$result
   Output
   nu maxdepth iter       ROC       Sens        Spec         ROCSD
   SensSD       SpecSD
   1 0.1       1   50 0.8571988 0.9152941 0.012662155 0.03448418
   0.04430519 0.007251045
   4 0.1       2   50 0.8905514 0.7138655 0.006083679 0.03538445
   0.10089887 0.006236741
   7 0.1       3   50 0.9056456 0.4036134 0.007093780 0.03934631
   0.09406015 0.006407402
   2 0.1       1  100 0.8550789 0.8918487 0.015705276 0.03434382
   0.06190546 0.006503191
   5 0.1       2  100 0.8907720 0.6609244 0.009626724 0.03788941
   0.11403364 0.006940001
   8 0.1       3  100 0.9077750 0.3832773 0.005576065 0.03601187
   0.09630026 0.003738978
   3 0.1       1  150 0.8571743 0.8714286 0.016720505 0.03481526
   0.06198773 0.006767313
   6 0.1       2  150 0.8929524 0.6171429 0.011654617 0.03638272
   0.11383803 0.006777465
   9 0.1       3  150 0.9093921 0.3743697 0.007093780 0.03258220
   0.09504202 0.005446136
   ```

4. Use the `plot` function to plot the ROC curve within different iterations:

    ```
    > plot(ada.train)
    ```

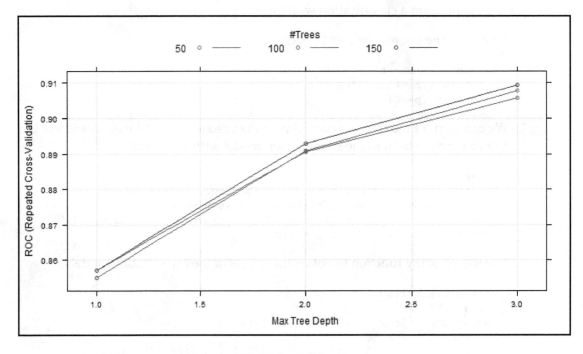

The repeated cross validation plot

5. Finally, we can make predictions using the `predict` function and view the classification table:

    ```
    > ada.predict = predict(ada.train, testset, "prob")
    > ada.predict.result = ifelse(ada.predict[1] > 0.5, "yes", "no")
    > table(testset$churn, ada.predict.result)
    Output
            ada.predict.result
             no yes
      yes    40 101
      no    872   5
    ```

Performing cross-validation with the boosting method

Similar to the `bagging` function, `adabag` provides a cross-validation function for the boosting method named `boosting.cv`. In this recipe, we will demonstrate how to perform cross-validation using `boosting.cv` from the package `adabag`.

Getting ready

In this recipe, we continue to use the telecom `churn` dataset as the input data source to perform a k-fold cross-validation with the `boosting` method.

How to do it...

Perform the following steps to retrieve the minimum estimation errors via cross-validation with the `boosting` method:

1. First, you can use `boosting.cv` to cross-validate the training dataset:

   ```
   > churn.boostcv = boosting.cv(churn ~ ., v=10, data=trainset,
   mfinal=5,control=rpart.control(cp=0.01))
   ```

2. You can then obtain the confusion matrix from the boosting results:

   ```
   > churn.boostcv$confusion
   Output
                   Observed Class
   Predicted Class  yes   no
               no   119 1940
               yes  223   33
   ```

3. Finally, you can retrieve the average errors of the `boosting` method:

   ```
   > churn.boostcv$error
   Output
   [1] 0.06565875
   ```

How it works...

Similar to `bagging.cv`, we can perform cross-validation with the `boosting` method using `boosting.cv`. If v is set to `10` and `mfinal` is set to `5`, the `boosting` method will perform 10-fold cross-validations with five iterations. Also, one can set the control of the `rpart` fit within the parameter. We can set the complexity parameter to 0.01 in this example. Once the training is complete, the confusion matrix and average errors of the boosted results will be obtained.

See also

- For those who require more information on tuning the parameters of `boosting.cv`, please view the `boosting.cv` document by using the `help` function:

  ```
  > help(boosting.cv) by
  ```

Classifying data with gradient boosting

Gradient boosting ensembles weak learners and creates a new base learner that maximally correlates with the negative gradient of the loss function. One may apply this method on either regression or classification problems, and it will perform well in different datasets. In this recipe, we will introduce how to use `gbm` to classify a telecom `churn` dataset.

Getting ready

In this recipe, we continue to use the telecom `churn` dataset as the input data source for the `bagging` method. For those who have not prepared the dataset, please refer to `Chapter 7`, *Classification 1 - Tree, Lazy, and Probabilistic,* for detailed information.

How to do it...

Perform the following steps to calculate and classify data with the gradient boosting method:

1. First, install and load the package gbm:

```
> install.packages("gbm")
> library(gbm)
```

2. The gbm function only uses responses ranging from 0 to 1; therefore, you should transform yes/no responses to numeric responses (0/1):

```
> trainset$churn = ifelse(trainset$churn == "yes", 1, 0)
```

3. Next, you can use the gbm function to train a training dataset:

```
> set.seed(2)
> churn.gbm = gbm(formula = churn ~ .,distribution = "bernoulli"
,data = trainset,n.trees = 1000,interaction.depth = 7,shrinkage
= 0.01, cv.folds=3)
```

4. Then, you can obtain the summary information from the fitted model:

```
> summary(churn.gbm)
```

```
                                                    var       rel.inf
total_day_minutes                         total_day_minutes 28.1217146858
total_eve_minutes                         total_eve_minutes 16.8097150728
number_customer_service_calls number_customer_service_calls 12.7894463723
total_intl_minutes                       total_intl_minutes  9.4515821668
total_intl_calls                           total_intl_calls  8.1379826341
international_plan                         international_plan  8.0703899754
total_night_minutes                     total_night_minutes  4.0805152939
number_vmail_messages                 number_vmail_messages  3.9173514880
voice_mail_plan                             voice_mail_plan  2.5501479818
total_night_calls                         total_night_calls  2.1357970481
total_day_calls                             total_day_calls  1.7367887716
total_eve_calls                             total_eve_calls  1.4398047425
total_eve_charge                           total_eve_charge  0.5457485756
total_night_charge                       total_night_charge  0.2130151913
total_day_charge                           total_day_charge  0.0000000000
total_intl_charge                         total_intl_charge  0.0000000000
```

Relative influence plot of a fitted model

5. You can obtain the best iteration using cross-validation:

```
> churn.iter = gbm.perf(churn.gbm,method="cv")
```

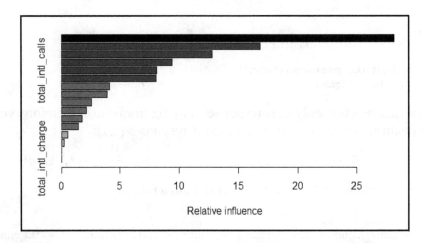

6. Then, you can retrieve the odd value of the log returned from the Bernoulli `loss` function:

```
> churn.predict = predict(churn.gbm, testset, n.trees = churn.iter)
> str(churn.predict)
Output
  num [1:1018] -3.31 -2.91 -3.16 -3.47 -3.48 ...
```

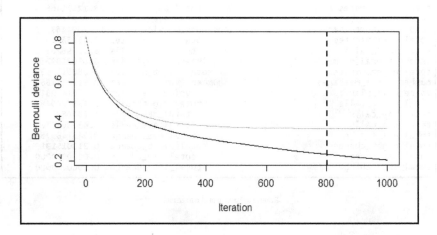

The performance measurement plot

7. Next, you can plot the ROC curve and get the best cut off that will have maximum accuracy:

```
> churn.roc = roc(testset$churn, churn.predict)
> plot(churn.roc)
Output
Call:
roc.default(response = testset$churn, predictor = churn.predict)
Data: churn.predict in 141 controls (testset$churn yes) > 877
cases (testset$churn no).
Area under the curve: 0.9393
```

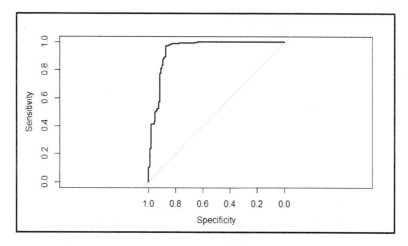

The ROC curve of a fitted model

8. You can retrieve the best cut off with the `coords` function and use this cut off to obtain the predicted label:

```
> coords(churn.roc, "best")
Output
  threshold specificity sensitivity
 -0.9495258   0.8723404   0.9703535
> churn.predict.class = ifelse(churn.predict > coords(churn.roc,
"best")["threshold"], "yes", "no")
```

9. Lastly, you can obtain the classification table from the predicted results:

```
> table( testset$churn,churn.predict.class)
Output
        churn.predict.class
          no  yes
    yes   18  123
    no    851  26
```

How it works...

The algorithm of gradient boosting involves, first, the process computing the deviation of residuals for each partition, and then, determining the best data partitioning in each stage. Next, the successive model will fit the residuals from the previous stage and build a new model to reduce the residual variance (an error). The reduction of the residual variance follows the functional gradient descent technique, in which it minimizes the residual variance by going down its derivative, as show here:

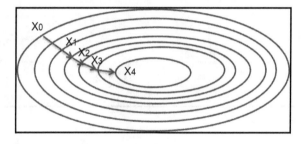

Gradient descent method

In this recipe, we use the gradient `boosting` method from `gbm` to classify the telecom `churn` dataset. To begin the classification, we first install and load the `gbm` package. Then, we use the `gbm` function to train the classification model. Here, as our prediction target is the `churn` attribute, which is a binary outcome, we set the distribution as `bernoulli` in the `distribution` argument. Also, we set the 1,000 trees to fit in the `n.tree` argument, the maximum depth of the variable interaction to 7 in `interaction.depth`, the learning rate of the step size reduction to 0.01 in `shrinkage`, and the number of cross-validations to 3 in `cv.folds`. After the model is fitted, we can use the summary function to obtain the relative influence information of each variable in the table and figure. The relative influence shows the reduction attributable to each variable in the sum of the square error. Here, we can find that `total_day_minutes` is the most influential one in reducing the loss function.

Next, we use the `gbm.perf` function to find the optimum iteration. Here, we estimate the optimum number with cross-validation by specifying the `method` argument to `cv`. The function further generates two plots, where the black line plots the training error and the green one plots the validation error. The error measurement here is a `bernoulli` distribution, which we defined earlier in the training stage. The blue dash line on the plot shows where the optimum iteration is.

Then, we use the `predict` function to obtain the odd value of a log in each testing case returned from the Bernoulli `loss` function. In order to get the best prediction result, one can set the `n.trees` argument to an optimum iteration number. However, as the returned value is an odd value log, we still have to determine the best cut off to determine the label. Therefore, we use the `roc` function to generate an ROC curve and get the cut off with the maximum accuracy.

Finally, we can use the function `coords` to retrieve the best cut off threshold and use the `ifelse` function to determine the class label from the odd value of the log. Now, we can use the `table` function to generate the classification table and see how accurate the classification model is.

There's more...

In addition to using the `boosting` function in the `gbm` package, one can also use the `mboost` package to perform classifications with the gradient `boosting` method:

1. First, install and load the `mboost` package:

```
> install.packages("mboost")
> library(mboost)
```

2. The `mboost` function only uses numeric responses; therefore, you should transform yes/no responses to numeric responses (0/1):

```
> trainset$churn = ifelse(trainset$churn == "yes", 1, 0)
```

3. Also, you should remove nonnumerical attributes, such as `voice_mail_plan` and `international_plan`:

```
> trainset$voice_mail_plan = NULL
> trainset$international_plan = NULL
```

4. We can then use `mboost` to train the classification model:

```
> churn.mboost = mboost(churn ~ ., data=trainset,  control =
boost_control(mstop = 10))
```

5. Use the `summary` function to obtain the details of the classification model:

```
> summary(churn.mboost)
Output
    Model-based Boosting

Call:
mboost(formula = churn ~ ., data = trainset, control =
boost_control(mstop = 10))


  Squared Error (Regression)

Loss function: (y - f)^2


Number of boosting iterations: mstop = 10
Step size: 0.1
Offset: 1.147732
Number of baselearners: 14

Selection frequencies:
          bbs(total_day_minutes)
bbs(number_customer_service_calls)
          0.6                                    0.4
```

6. Lastly, use the `plot` function to draw a partial contribution plot of each attribute:

```
> par(mfrow=c(1,2))
> plot(churn.mboost)
```

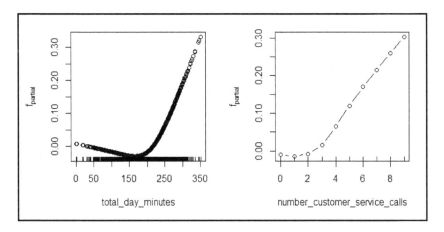

The partial contribution plot of important attributes

Calculating the margins of a classifier

A margin is a measure of the certainty of classification. This method calculates the difference between the support of a correct class and the maximum support of an incorrect class. In this recipe, we will demonstrate how to calculate the margins of the generated classifiers.

Getting ready

You need to have completed the previous recipe by storing a fitted bagging model in the variables, `churn.bagging` and `churn.predbagging`. Also, put the fitted `boosting` classifier in both `churn.boost` and `churn.boost.pred`.

How to do it...

Perform the following steps to calculate the margin of each ensemble learner:

1. First, use the `margins` function to calculate the margins of the `boosting` classifiers:

```
> boost.margins = margins(churn.boost, trainset)
> boost.pred.margins = margins(churn.boost.pred, testset)
```

2. You can then use the `plot` function to plot a marginal cumulative distribution graph of the `boosting` classifiers:

```
> plot(sort(boost.margins[[1]]),
(1:length(boost.margins[[1]]))/length(boost.margins[[1]]),
type="l",xlim=c(-1,1),main="Boosting: Margin cumulative
distribution graph", xlab="margin", ylab="% observations",
col = "blue")
> lines(sort(boost.pred.margins[[1]])
(1:length(boost.pred.margins[[1]]))/length(boost.pred.margins[[1]])
, type="l", col = "green")
> abline(v=0, col="red",lty=2)
```

The margin cumulative distribution graph of using the boosting method

3. You can then calculate the percentage of negative margin matches training errors and the percentage of negative margin matches test errors:

```
> boosting.training.margin = table(boost.margins[[1]] > 0)
> boosting.negative.training =
as.numeric(boosting.training.margin[1]/
boosting.training.margin[2])
> boosting.negative.training
Output
[1] 0.06387868
> boosting.testing.margin =
table(boost.pred.margins[[1]] > 0)
> boosting.negative.testing =
as.numeric(boosting.testing.margin[1]/boosting.testing.margin[2])
> boosting.negative.testing
Output
[1] 0.06263048
```

4. Also, you can calculate the margins of the `bagging` classifiers. You might see the warning message showing `no non-missing argument to min`. The message simply indicates that the `min/max` function is applied to the numeric of the `0` length argument:

```
> bagging.margins = margins(churn.bagging, trainset)
> bagging.pred.margins = margins(churn.predbagging, testset)
```

5. You can then use the `plot` function to plot a margin cumulative distribution graph of the `bagging` classifiers:

```
> plot(sort(bagging.margins[[1]]),
(1:length(bagging.margins[[1]]))/length(bagging.margins[[1]]),
type="l",xlim=c(-1,1),main="Bagging: Margin cumulative
distribution graph", xlab="margin", ylab="% observations",
col = "blue")
> lines(sort(bagging.pred.margins[[1]]),
(1:length(bagging.pred.margins[[1]]))/length(bagging.pred.margins
[[1]]), type="l", col = "green")
> abline(v=0, col="red",lty=2)
```

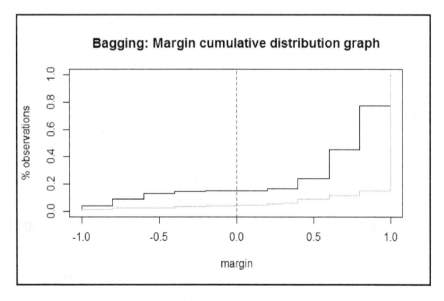

The margin cumulative distribution graph of the bagging method

6. Finally, you can then compute the percentage of negative margin matches training errors and the percentage of negative margin matches test errors:

```
> bagging.training.margin = table(bagging.margins[[1]] > 0)
> bagging.negative.training =
as.numeric(bagging.training.margin[1]/bagging.training.margin[2])
> bagging.negative.training
Output
[1] 0.1733401
> bagging.testing.margin =
 table(bagging.pred.margins[[1]] > 0)
> bagging.negative.testing =
as.numeric(bagging.testing.margin[1]/bagging.testing.margin[2])
> bagging.negative.testing
Output
[1] 0.04303279
```

How it works...

A margin is the measurement of certainty of the classification; it is computed by the support of the correct class and the maximum support of the incorrect class. The formula of margins can be formulated as:

$$\text{margin}(x_i) = support_c(x_i) - \max_{j \neq c} support_j(x_i)$$

Here, the margin of the xi sample equals the support of a correctly classified sample (c denotes the correct class) minus the maximum support of a sample that is classified to class j (where $j \neq c$ and $j=1...k$). Therefore, correctly classified examples will have positive margins and misclassified examples will have negative margins. If the margin value is close to one, it means that correctly classified examples have a high degree of confidence. On the other hand, examples of uncertain classifications will have small margins.

The `margins` function calculates the margins of AdaBoost.M1, AdaBoost-SAMME, or the `bagging` classifier, which returns a vector of a margin. To visualize the margin distribution, one can use a margin cumulative distribution graph. In these graphs, the x-axis shows the margin and the y-axis shows the percentage of observations where the margin is less than or equal to the margin value of the x-axis. If every observation is correctly classified, the graph will show a vertical line at the margin equal to 1 (where margin = 1).

For the margin cumulative distribution graph of the `boosting` classifiers, we can see that there are two lines plotted on the graph, in which the green line denotes the margin of the testing dataset, and the blue line denotes the margin of the training set. The figure shows about 6.39 percent of negative margins match the training error, and 6.26 percent of negative margins match the test error. On the other hand, we can find that 17.33% of negative margins match the training error and 4.3 percent of negative margins match the test error in the margin cumulative distribution graph of the `bagging` classifiers. Normally, the percentage of negative margins matching the training error should be close to the percentage of negative margins that match the test error. As a result of this, we should then examine the reason why the percentage of negative margins that match the training error is much higher than the negative margins that match the test error.

See also

- If you are interested in more details on margin distribution graphs, please refer to the following source: *Kuncheva LI (2004), Combining Pattern Classifiers: Methods and Algorithms, John Wiley & Sons.*

Calculating the error evolution of the ensemble method

The `adabag` package provides the `errorevol` function for a user to estimate the ensemble method errors in accordance with the number of iterations. In this recipe, we will demonstrate how to use `errorevol` to show the evolution of errors of each ensemble classifier.

Getting ready

You need to have completed the previous recipe by storing the fitted bagging model in the `churn.bagging` variable. Also, put the fitted `boosting` classifier in `churn.boost`.

How to do it...

Perform the following steps to calculate the error evolution of each ensemble learner:

1. First, use the `errorevol` function to calculate the error evolution of the `boosting` classifiers:

```
> boosting.evol.train = errorevol(churn.boost, trainset)
> boosting.evol.test = errorevol(churn.boost, testset)
> plot(boosting.evol.test$error, type = "l", ylim = c(0, 1),
+        main = "Boosting error versus number of trees", xlab =
"Iterations",
+        ylab = "Error", col = "red", lwd = 2)
> lines(boosting.evol.train$error, cex = .5, col =
"blue", lty = 2, lwd = 2)
> legend("topright", c("test", "train"), col = c("red", "blue"),
lty = 1:2, lwd = 2)
```

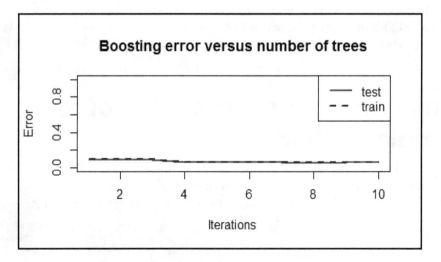

Boosting error versus number of trees

2. Next, use the `errorevol` function to calculate the error evolution of the `bagging` classifiers:

```
> bagging.evol.train = errorevol(churn.bagging, trainset)
> bagging.evol.test = errorevol(churn.bagging, testset)
> plot(bagging.evol.test$error, type = "l", ylim = c(0, 1),
+        main = "Bagging error versus number of trees", xlab =
"Iterations",
+        ylab = "Error", col = "red", lwd = 2)
> lines(bagging.evol.train$error, cex = .5, col = "blue",
```

```
  lty = 2, lwd = 2)
> legend("topright", c("test", "train"), col = c("red", "blue"),
  lty = 1:2, lwd = 2)
```

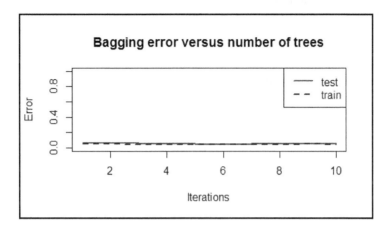

Bagging error versus number of trees

How it works...

The `errorest` function calculates the error evolution of AdaBoost.M1, AdaBoost-SAMME, or the `bagging` classifiers and returns a vector of error evolutions. In this recipe, we use the boosting and bagging models to generate error evolution vectors and graph the error versus number of trees.

The resulting graph reveals the error rate of each iteration. The trend of the error rate can help measure how fast the errors reduce, while the number of iterations increases. In addition to this, the graphs may show whether the model is over-fitted.

See also

- If the ensemble model is over-fitted, you can use the `predict.bagging` and `predict.boosting` functions to prune the ensemble model. For more information, please use the `help` function to refer to `predict.bagging` and `predict.boosting`:

    ```
    > help(predict.bagging)
    > help(predict.boosting)
    ```

Classifying data with random forest

Random forest is another useful ensemble learning method that grows multiple decision trees during the training process. Each decision tree will output its own prediction results corresponding to the input. The forest will use the voting mechanism to select the most voted class as the prediction result. In this recipe, we will illustrate how to classify data using the randomForest package.

Getting ready

In this recipe, we will continue to use the telecom churn dataset as the input data source to perform classifications with the random forest method.

How to do it...

Perform the following steps to classify data with random forest:

1. First, you have to install and load the randomForest package:

```
> install.packages("randomForest")
> library(randomForest)
```

2. You can then fit the random forest classifier with a training set:

```
> churn.rf = randomForest(churn ~ ., data = trainset, importance = T)
> churn.rf
Output
Call:
 randomForest(formula = churn ~ ., data = trainset, importance = T)
               Type of random forest: classification
                     Number of trees: 500
No. of variables tried at each split: 4
        OOB estimate of  error rate: 4.88%
Confusion matrix:
     yes      no class.error
 yes 247     95 0.277777778
 no   18 1955 0.009123163
```

3. Next, make predictions based on the fitted model and testing dataset:

```
> churn.prediction = predict(churn.rf, testset)
```

4. Similar to other classification methods, you can obtain the classification table:

```
> table(churn.prediction, testset$churn)
Output
churn.prediction yes   no
           yes 110    7
           no   31  870
```

5. You can use the `plot` function to plot the mean square error of the forest object:

```
> plot(churn.rf)
```

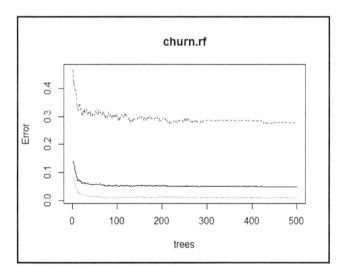

The mean square error of the random forest

6. You can then examine the importance of each attribute within the fitted classifier:

```
> importance(churn.rf)
Output
                             yes          no
international_plan       66.55206691  56.5100647
voice_mail_plan         19.98337191  15.2354970
number_vmail_messages   21.02976166  14.0707195
total_day_minutes       28.05190188  27.7570444
```

7. Next, you can use the `varImpPlot` function to obtain the plot of variable importance:

```
> varImpPlot(churn.rf)
```

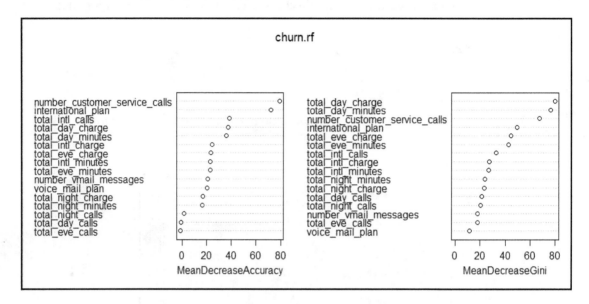

The visualization of variable importance

8. You can also use the `margin` function to calculate the margins and plot the margin cumulative distribution:

```
> margins.rf=margin(churn.rf,trainset)
> plot(margins.rf)
```

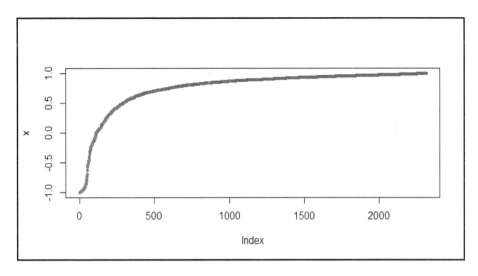

The margin cumulative distribution graph for the random forest method

9. Furthermore, you can use a histogram to visualize the margin distribution of the random forest:

```
> hist(margins.rf,main="Margins of Random Forest for churn
dataset")
```

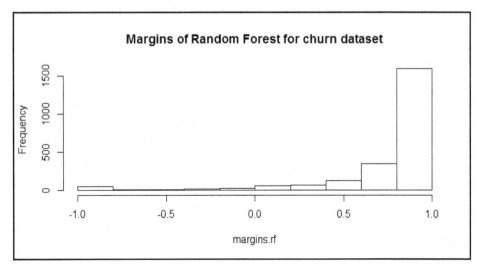

The histogram of margin distribution

10. You can also use `boxplot` to visualize the margins of the random forest by class:

```
> boxplot(margins.rf~trainset$churn, main="Margins of Random Forest
for churn dataset by class")
```

Margins of the random forest by class

How it works...

The purpose of random forest is to ensemble weak learners (for example, a single decision tree) into a strong learner. The process of developing a random forest is very similar to the `bagging` method, assuming that we have a training set containing N samples with M features. The process first performs bootstrap sampling, which samples N cases at random, with the replacement as the training dataset of each single decision tree. Next, in each node, the process first randomly selects m variables (where $m \ll M$), and then finds the predictor variable that provides the best split among m variables. Next, the process grows the full tree without pruning. In the end, we can obtain the predicted result of an example from each single tree. As a result, we can get the prediction result by taking an average or weighted average (for regression) of an output or taking a majority vote (for classification):

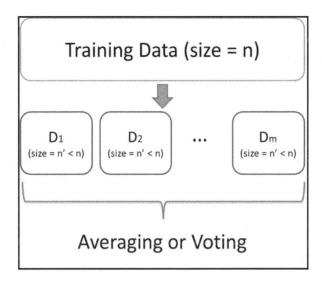

A random forest uses two parameters: **ntree** (the number of trees) and **mtry** (the number of features used to find the best feature), while the `bagging` method only uses `ntree` as a parameter. Therefore, if we set mtry equal to the number of features within a training dataset, then the random forest is equal to the `bagging` method.

The main advantages of random forest are that it is easy to compute, it can efficiently process data, and it is fault tolerant to missing or unbalanced data. The main disadvantage of random forest is that it cannot predict the value beyond the range of a training dataset. Also, it is prone to over-fitting of noisy data.

In this recipe, we employ the random forest method adapted from the `randomForest` package to fit a classification model. First, we install and load `randomForest` into an R session. We then use the random forest method to train a classification model. We set `importance = T`, which will ensure that the importance of the predictor is assessed.

Similar to the `bagging` and `boosting` methods, once the model is fitted, one can perform predictions using a fitted model on the testing dataset and, furthermore, obtain the classification table.

In order to assess the importance of each attribute, the `randomForest` package provides the importance and `varImpPlot` functions to either list the importance of each attribute in the fitted model or visualize the importance using either mean decrease accuracy or mean decrease `gini`.

Similar to `adabag`, which contains a method to calculate the margins of the `bagging` and `boosting` methods, `randomForest` provides the `margin` function to calculate the margins of the forest object. With the `plot`, `hist`, and `boxplot` functions, you can visualize the margins in different aspects to the proportion of correctly classified observations.

There's more...

Apart from the `randomForest` package, the `party` package also provides an implementation of random forest. In the following steps, we illustrate how to use the `cforest` function within the `party` package to perform classifications:

1. First, install and load the `party` package:

```
> install.packages("party")
> library(party)
```

2. You can then use the `cforest` function to fit the classification model:

```
> churn.cforest = cforest(churn ~ ., data = trainset, con-
trols=cforest_unbiased(ntree=1000, mtry=5))
> churn.cforest
Output
Random Forest using Conditional Inference Trees

Number of trees: 1000

Response: churn
Inputs: international_plan, voice_mail_plan, num-
ber_vmail_messages, total_day_minutes, total_day_calls, to-
tal_day_charge, total_eve_minutes,
total_eve_calls, to-tal_eve_charge, total_night_minutes,
total_night_calls, to-tal_night_charge, total_intl_minutes,
total_intl_calls, to-tal_intl_charge, number_customer_service_calls
Number of observations: 2315
```

3. You can make predictions based on the built model and the testing dataset:

```
> churn.cforest.prediction = predict(churn.cforest, testset,
OOB=TRUE, type = "response")
```

4. Finally, obtain the classification table from the predicted labels and the labels of the testing dataset:

```
> table(churn.cforest.prediction, testset$churn)
Output
churn.cforest.prediction yes   no
                    yes   91    3
                    no    50  874
```

Estimating the prediction errors of different classifiers

At the beginning of this chapter, we discussed why we use ensemble learning and how it can improve prediction performance compared to using just a single classifier. We will now validate whether the ensemble model performs better than a single decision tree by comparing the performance of each method. In order to compare the different classifiers, we can perform a 10-fold cross-validation on each classification method to estimate test errors using `erroreset` from the `ipred` package.

Getting ready

In this recipe, we will continue to use the telecom `churn` dataset as the input data source to estimate the prediction errors of the different classifiers.

How to do it...

Perform the following steps to estimate the prediction errors of each classification method:

1. You can estimate the error rate of the bagging model:

```
> churn.bagging= errorest(churn ~ ., data = trainset, model =
  bagging)
> churn.bagging
Output
Call:
errorest.data.frame(formula = churn ~ ., data = trainset, model
= bagging)
    10-fold cross-validation estimator of misclassification error
Misclassification error:   0.0583
```

2. You can then estimate the error rate of the `boosting` method:

```
> install.packages("ada")
> library(ada)
> churn.boosting= errorest(churn ~ ., data = trainset, model =
ada)
> churn.boosting
Output
Call:
errorest.data.frame(formula = churn ~ ., data = trainset, model
= ada)
     10-fold cross-validation estimator of misclassification error
Misclassification error:   0.0475
```

3. Next, estimate the error rate of the random forest model:

```
> churn.rf= errorest(churn ~ ., data = trainset, model =
randomForest)
> churn.rf
Output
Call:
errorest.data.frame(formula = churn ~ ., data = trainset, model
= randomForest)
     10-fold cross-validation estimator of misclassification error
  Misclassification error:   0.051
```

4. Finally, make a prediction function using `churn.predict`, and then use the function to estimate the error rate of the single decision tree:

```
> churn.predict = function(object, newdata) {predict(object, new
data = newdata, type = "class")}
> churn.tree= errorest(churn ~ ., data = trainset, model =
rpart,predict = churn.predict)
> churn.tree
Output
Call:
errorest.data.frame(formula = churn ~ ., data = trainset, model
= rpart,
     predict = churn.predict)
     10-fold cross-validation estimator of misclassification error
Misclassification error:   0.0674
```

How it works...

In this recipe, we estimated the error rates of four different classifiers using the `errorest` function from the `ipred` package. We compared the boosting, bagging, and random forest methods, and the single decision tree classifier. The `errorest` function performs a 10-fold cross-validation on each classifier and calculates the misclassification error. The estimation results from the four chosen models reveal that the `boosting` method performs the best with the lowest error rate (0.0475). The random forest method has the second lowest error rate (0.051), while the `bagging` method has an error rate of 0.0583. The single decision tree classifier, `rpart`, performs the worst among the four methods with an error rate equal to 0.0674. These results show that all three ensemble learning methods, boosting, bagging, and random forest, outperform a single decision tree classifier.

See also

- In this recipe, we mentioned the `ada` package, which contains a method to perform stochastic boosting. For those interested in this package, please refer to: *Additive Logistic Regression: A Statistical View of Boosting by Friedman, et al. (2000).*

11
Clustering

In this chapter, we will cover the following topics:

- Clustering data with hierarchical clustering
- Cutting a tree into clusters
- Clustering data with the k-means method
- Drawing a bivariate cluster plot
- Comparing clustering methods
- Extracting silhouette information from clustering
- Obtaining optimum clusters for k-means
- Clustering data with the density-based method
- Clustering data with the model-based method
- Visualizing a dissimilarity matrix
- Validating clusters externally

Introduction

Clustering is a technique used to group similar objects (close in terms of distance) together in the same group (cluster). Unlike supervised learning methods (for example, classification and regression) covered in the previous chapters, a clustering analysis does not use any label information, but simply uses the similarity between data features to group them into clusters.

Clustering can be widely adapted in the analysis of businesses. For example, a marketing department can use clustering to segment customers by personal attributes. As a result of this, different marketing campaigns targeting various types of customers can be designed.

The four most common types of clustering methods are hierarchical clustering, k-means clustering, model-based clustering, and density-based clustering:

- **Hierarchical clustering**: This creates a hierarchy of clusters, and presents the hierarchy in a dendrogram. This method does not require the number of clusters to be specified at the beginning.
- **k-means clustering**: This is also referred to as flat clustering. Unlike hierarchical clustering, it does not create a hierarchy of clusters, and it requires the number of clusters as an input. However, its performance is faster than hierarchical clustering.
- **Model-based clustering**: Both hierarchical clustering and k-means clustering use a heuristic approach to construct clusters, and do not rely on a formal model. Model-based clustering assumes a data model and applies an EM algorithm to find the most likely model components and the number of clusters.
- **Density-based clustering**: This constructs clusters in relation to the density measurement. Clusters in this method have a higher density than the remainder of the dataset.

In the following recipes, we will discuss how to use these four clustering techniques to cluster data. We will discuss how to validate clusters internally, using within clusters the sum of squares, average silhouette width, and externally, with ground truth.

Clustering data with hierarchical clustering

Hierarchical clustering adopts either an agglomerative or divisive method to build a hierarchy of clusters. Regardless of which approach is adopted, both first use a distance similarity measure to combine or split clusters. The recursive process continues until there is only one cluster left or you cannot split more clusters. Eventually, we can use a dendrogram to represent the hierarchy of clusters. In this recipe, we will demonstrate how to cluster customers with hierarchical clustering.

Getting ready

In this recipe, we will perform hierarchical clustering on customer data, which involves segmenting customers into different groups. You can download the data from this GitHub page: https://github.com/ywchiu/ml_R_cookbook/tree/master/CH9.

How to do it...

Perform the following steps to cluster customer data into a hierarchy of clusters:

1. First, you need to load data from `customer.csv` and save it into `customer`:

```
> customer= read.csv('customer.csv', header=TRUE)
> head(customer)
Output
  ID Visit.Time Average.Expense Sex Age
1  1          3             5.7   0  10
2  2          5            14.5   0  27
3  3         16            33.5   0  32
4  4          5            15.9   0  30
5  5         16            24.9   0  23
6  6          3            12.0   0  15
```

2. You can then examine the dataset structure:

```
> str(customer)
Output
'data.frame':   60 obs. of  5 variables:
 $ ID             : int  1 2 3 4 5 6 7 8 9 10 ...
 $ Visit.Time     : int  3 5 16 5 16 3 12 14 6 3 ...
 $ Average.Expense: num  5.7 14.5 33.5 15.9 24.9 12 28.5 18.8
23.8 5.3 ...
 $ Sex            : int  0 0 0 0 0 0 0 0 0 0 ...
 $ Age            : int  10 27 32 30 23 15 33 27 16 11 ...
```

3. Next, you should normalize the customer data into the same scale:

```
> customer = scale(customer[,-1])
```

4. You can then use agglomerative hierarchical clustering to cluster the customer data:

```
> hc = hclust(dist(customer, method="euclidean"), method=
"ward.D2")
> hc
Output
Call:
hclust(d = dist(customer, method = "euclidean"), method =
"ward.D2")
Cluster method    : ward.D2
Distance          : euclidean
Number of objects: 60
```

5. Lastly, you can use the `plot` function to plot the dendrogram:

```
> plot(hc, hang = -0.01, cex = 0.7)
```

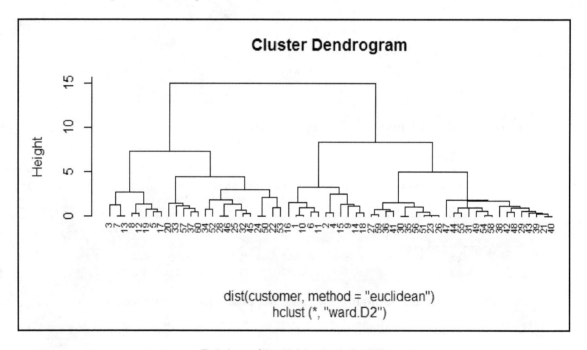

The dendrogram of hierarchical clustering using "ward.D2"

6. Additionally, you can use the single method to perform hierarchical clustering and see how the generated dendrogram differs from the previous:

```
> hc2 = hclust(dist(customer), method="single")
> plot(hc2, hang = -0.01, cex = 0.7)
```

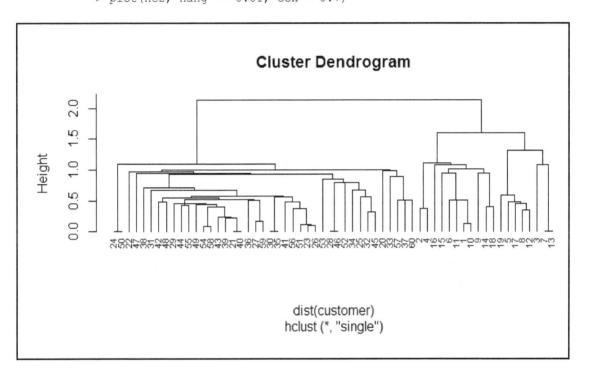

The dendrogram of hierarchical clustering using "single"

How it works...

Hierarchical clustering is a clustering technique that tries to build a hierarchy of clusters iteratively. Generally, there are two approaches to building hierarchical clusters:

- **Agglomerative hierarchical clustering**: This is a bottom-up approach. Each observation starts in its own cluster. We can then compute the similarity (or the distance) between each cluster and then merge the two most similar ones at each iteration until there is only one cluster left.

- **Divisive hierarchical clustering**: This is a top-down approach. All observations start in one cluster, and then we split the cluster into the two least dissimilar clusters recursively until there is one cluster for each observation:

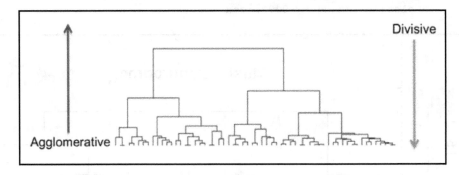

An illustration of hierarchical clustering

Before performing hierarchical clustering, we need to determine how similar the two clusters are. Here, we list some common distance functions used for the measurement of similarity:

- **Single linkage**: This refers to the shortest distance between two points in each cluster:

$$\text{dist}\left(C_i, C_j\right) = \min_{a \in C_i, b \in C_j} dist\left(a, b\right)$$

- **Complete linkage**: This refers to the longest distance between two points in each cluster:

$$\text{dist}\left(C_i, C_j\right) = \max_{a \in C_i, b \in C_j} dist\left(a, b\right)$$

- **Average linkage**: This refers to the average distance between two points in each cluster (where is the size of cluster and is the size of cluster):

$$\text{dist}\left(C_i, C_j\right) = \frac{1}{|C_i||C_j|} \sum_{a \in C_i, b \in C_j} dist\left(a, b\right)$$

- **Ward method**: This refers to the sum of the squared distance from each point to the mean of the merged clusters (where is the mean vector of):

$$\text{dist}\left(C_i, C_j\right) = \sum_{a \in C_i \cup C_j} \|a - \mu\|$$

In this recipe, we perform hierarchical clustering on customer data. First, we load the data from `customer.csv`, and then load it into the customer DataFrame. Within the data, we find five variables of customer account information, which are ID, number of visits, average expense, sex, and age. As the scale of each variable varies, we use the scale function to normalize the scale.

After the scales of all the attributes are normalized, we perform hierarchical clustering using the `hclust` function. We use the Euclidean distance as distance metrics, and use Ward's minimum variance method to perform agglomerative clustering.

Finally, we use the `plot` function to plot the dendrogram of hierarchical clusters. We specify `hang` to display labels at the bottom of the dendrogram, and use `cex` to shrink the label to 70 percent of the normal size. In order to compare the differences using the `ward.D2` and `single` methods to generate a hierarchy of clusters, we draw another dendrogram using `single` in the preceding figure (*step 6*).

There's more...

You can choose a different distance measure and method while performing hierarchical clustering. For more details, you can refer to the documents for `dist` and `hclust`:

```
> ? dist
> ? hclust
```

In this recipe, we use `hclust` to perform agglomerative hierarchical clustering; if you would like to perform divisive hierarchical clustering, you can use the `diana` function:

1. First, you can use `diana` to perform divisive hierarchical clustering:

   ```
   > dv = diana(customer, metric = "euclidean")
   ```

2. Then, you can use `summary` to obtain the summary information:

   ```
   > summary(dv)
   ```

3. Lastly, you can plot a dendrogram and banner with the `plot` function:

   ```
   > plot(dv)
   ```

If you are interested in drawing a horizontal dendrogram, you can use the dendextend package. Use the following procedure to generate a horizontal dendrogram:

1. First, install and load the dendextend and magrittr packages (if your R version is 3.1 or higher, you do not have to install and load the magrittr package):

```
> install.packages("dendextend")
> library(dendextend)
> install.packages("margrittr")
> library(magrittr)
```

2. Set up the dendrogram:

```
> dend = customer %>% dist %>% hclust %>% as.dendrogram
```

3. Finally, plot the horizontal dendrogram:

```
dend %>% plot(horiz=TRUE, main = "Horizontal Dendrogram")
```

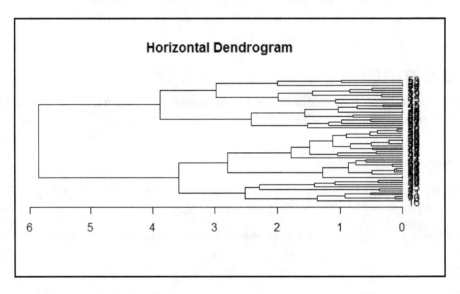

The horizontal dendrogram

Cutting trees into clusters

In a dendrogram, we can see the hierarchy of clusters, but we have not grouped data into different clusters yet. However, we can determine how many clusters are within the dendrogram and cut the dendrogram at a certain tree height to separate the data into different groups. In this recipe, we will demonstrate how to use the cutree function to separate the data into a given number of clusters.

Getting ready

In order to perform the cutree function, you need to have the previous recipe completed by generating the hclust object, hc.

How to do it...

Perform the following steps to cut the hierarchy of clusters into a given number of clusters:

1. First, categorize the data into four groups:

```
> fit = cutree(hc, k = 4)
```

2. You can then examine the cluster labels for the data:

```
> fit
Output
 [1] 1 1 2 1 2 1 2 2 1 1 1 2 2 1 1 1 2 1 2 3 4 3 4 3 3 4 4 3 4
[30] 4 4 3 3 3 4 4 3 4 4 4 4 4 4 4 3 3 4 4 4 3 4 3 3 4 4 4 3 4
[59] 4 3
```

3. Count the amount of data within each cluster:

```
> table(fit)
Output
fit
 1  2  3  4
11  8 16 25
```

4. Finally, you can visualize how data is clustered with a red rectangle border:

```
> plot(hc)
> rect.hclust(hc, k = 4 , border="red")
```

Using the red rectangle border to distinguish different clusters within the dendrogram

How it works...

We can determine the number of clusters from the dendrogram in the preceding figure. In this recipe, we determine that there should be four clusters within the tree. Therefore, we specify the number of clusters as 4 in the cutree function. Besides using the number of clusters to cut the tree, you can specify the height as the cut tree parameter.

Next, we can output the cluster labels of the data and use the table function to count the amount of data within each cluster. From the counting table, we find that most of the data is in cluster 4. Lastly, we can draw red rectangles around the clusters to show how data is categorized into the four clusters with the rect.hclust function.

There's more...

Besides drawing rectangles around all hierarchical clusters, you can place a red rectangle around a certain cluster:

```
> rect.hclust(hc, k = 4 , which =2, border="red")
```

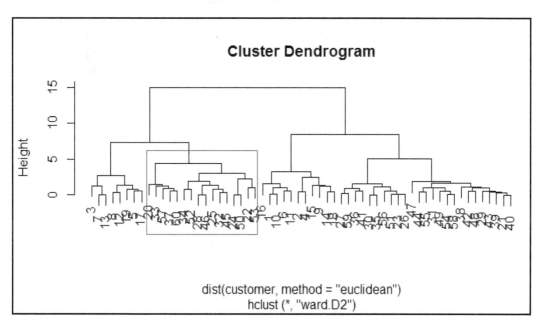

Drawing a red rectangle around a certain cluster

Also, you can color clusters in different colors with a red rectangle around the clusters by using the dendextend package. You have to complete the instructions outlined in the *There's more...* section of the previous recipe and perform the following steps:

1. Color the branch according to the cluster it belongs to:

```
> dend %>% color_branches(k=4) %>% plot(horiz=TRUE, main =
"Horizontal Dendrogram")
```

2. You can then add a red rectangle around the clusters:

```
> dend %>% rect.dendrogram(k=4,horiz=TRUE)
```

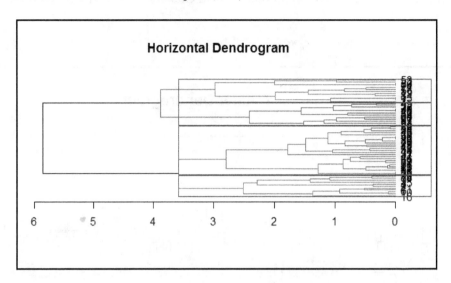

Drawing red rectangles around clusters within a horizontal dendrogram

3. Finally, you can add a line to show the tree cutting location:

```
> abline(v = heights_per_k.dendrogram(dend)["4"] + .1, lwd = 2,
lty = 2, col = "blue")
```

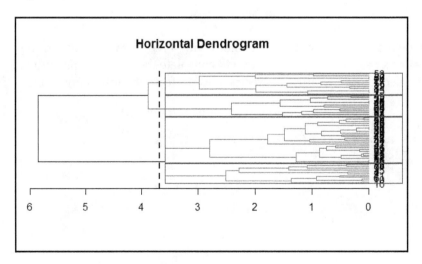

Drawing a cutting line within a horizontal dendrogram

Clustering data with the k-means method

k-means clustering is a flat clustering technique, which produces only one partition with *k* clusters. Unlike hierarchical clustering, which does not require a user to determine the number of clusters at the beginning, the k-means method requires this to be determined first. However, k-means clustering is much faster than hierarchical clustering as the construction of a hierarchical tree is very time consuming. In this recipe, we will demonstrate how to perform k-means clustering on the customer dataset.

Getting ready

In this recipe, we will continue to use the customer dataset as the input data source to perform k-means clustering.

How to do it...

Perform the following steps to cluster the customer dataset with the k-means method:

1. First, you can use kmeans to cluster the customer data:

```
> set.seed(22)
> fit = kmeans(customer, 4)
> fit
Output
K-means clustering with 4 clusters of sizes 8, 11, 16, 25
Cluster means:
   Visit.Time Average.Expense      Sex        Age
1   1.3302016       1.0155226 -1.4566845  0.5591307
2  -0.7771737      -0.5178412 -1.4566845 -0.4774599
3   0.8571173       0.9887331  0.6750489  1.0505015
4  -0.6322632      -0.7299063  0.6750489 -0.6411604
Clustering vector:
 [1] 2 2 1 2 1 2 1 1 2 2 2 1 1 2 2 2 1 2 1 3 4 3 4 3 3 4 4 3
[29] 4 4 4 3 3 3 4 4 3 4 4 4 4 4 4 4 3 3 4 4 4 3 4 3 3 4 4 4
[57] 3 4 4 3
Within cluster sum of squares by cluster:
[1]  5.90040 11.97454 22.58236 20.89159
 (between_SS / total_SS =  74.0 %)
Available components:
[1] "cluster"      "centers"      "totss"
[4] "withinss"     "tot.withinss" "betweenss"
[7] "size"         "iter"         "ifault
```

2. You can then inspect the center of each cluster using `barplot`:

```
> barplot(t(fit$centers), beside = TRUE, xlab="cluster",
ylab="value")
```

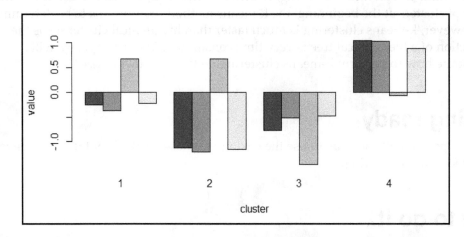

The barplot of centers of different attributes in four clusters

3. Lastly, you can draw a scatter plot of the data and color the points according to the clusters:

```
> plot(customer, col = fit$cluster)
```

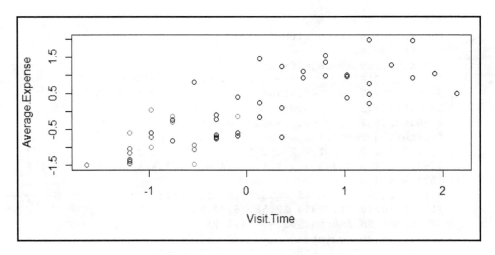

The scatter plot showing data colored with regard to its cluster label

How it works...

k-means clustering is a method of partitioning clustering. The goal of the algorithm is to partition n objects into k clusters, where each object belongs to the cluster with the nearest mean. The objective of the algorithm is to minimize the **Within-cluster Sum of Squares (WCSS)**. Assuming x is the given set of observations, $S =$ denotes k partitions, and is the mean of , then we can formulate the WCSS function as follows:

$$f = \sum_{i=1}^{k} \sum_{x \in S_i} \|x - \mu_i\|^2$$

The process of k-means clustering can be illustrated by the following five steps:

1. Specify the number of k clusters.
2. Randomly create k partitions.
3. Calculate the center of the partitions.
4. Associate objects closest to the cluster center.
5. Repeat steps 2, 3, and 4 until the WCSS changes very little (or is minimized).

In this recipe, we demonstrate how to use k-means clustering to cluster customer data. In contrast to hierarchical clustering, k-means clustering requires the user to input the number of K. In this example, we use $K=4$. Then, the output of a fitted model shows the size of each cluster, the cluster means of four generated clusters, the cluster vectors with regard to each data point, the within cluster sum of squares by the clusters, and other available components.

Furthermore, you can draw the centers of each cluster in a bar plot, which will provide more details on how each attribute affects the clustering. Lastly, we plot the data point in a scatter plot and use the fitted cluster labels to assign colors with regard to the cluster label.

See also

- In k-means clustering, you can specify the algorithm used to perform clustering analysis. You can specify either Hartigan-Wong, Lloyd, Forgy, or MacQueen as the clustering algorithm. For more details, please use the `help` function to refer to the document for the `kmeans` function:

  ```
  >help(kmeans)
  ```

Drawing a bivariate cluster plot

In the previous recipe, we employed the k-means method to fit data into clusters. However, if there are more than two variables, it is impossible to display how data is clustered in two dimensions. Therefore, you can use a bivariate cluster plot to first reduce variables into two components, and then use components, such as axis and circle, as clusters to show how data is clustered. In this recipe, we will illustrate how to create a bivariate cluster plot.

Getting ready

In this recipe, we will continue to use the `customer` dataset as the input data source to draw a bivariate cluster plot.

How to do it...

Perform the following steps to draw a bivariate cluster plot:

1. Install and load the cluster package:

    ```
    > install.packages("cluster")
    > library(cluster)
    ```

2. You can then draw a bivariate cluster plot:

    ```
    > clusplot(customer, fit$cluster, color=TRUE, shade=TRUE)
    ```

The bivariate clustering plot of the customer dataset

3. You can also zoom into the bivariate cluster plot:

```
> par(mfrow= c(1,2))
> clusplot(customer, fit$cluster, color=TRUE, shade=TRUE)
> rect(-0.7,-1.7, 2.2,-1.2, border = "orange", lwd=2)
> clusplot(customer, fit$cluster, color = TRUE, xlim = c(-0.7,2.2),
ylim = c(-1.7,-1.2))
```

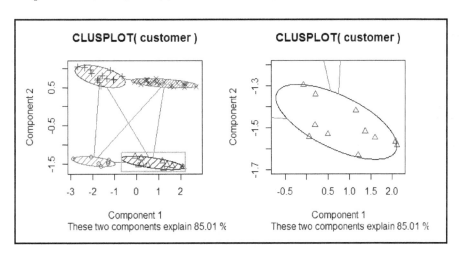

The zoom-in of the bivariate clustering plot

How it works...

In this recipe, we draw a bivariate cluster plot to show how data is clustered. To draw a bivariate cluster plot, we first need to install the cluster package and load it into R. We then use the clusplot function to draw a bivariate cluster plot from a customer dataset. In the clustplot function, we can set shade to TRUE and color to TRUE to display a cluster with colors and shades. As per the preceding figure (*step 2*), we found that the bivariate uses two components, which explains 85.01 percent of point variability, as the *x*-axis and *y*-axis. The data points are then scattered on the plot in accordance with component 1 and component 2. Data within the same cluster is circled in the same color and shade.

Besides drawing the four clusters in a single plot, you can use rect to add a rectangle around a specific area within a given x-axis and y-axis range. You can then zoom into the plot to examine the data within each cluster by using xlim and ylim in the clusplot function.

There's more...

The `clusplot` function uses `princomp` and `cmdscale` to reduce the original feature dimension to the principal component. Therefore, one can see how data is clustered in a single plot with these two components as the *x*-axis and *y*-axis. To learn more about `princomp` and `cmdscale`, one can use the `help` function to view related documents:

```
> help(cmdscale)
> help(princomp)
```

For those interested in how to use `cmdscale` to reduce the dimensions, please perform the following steps:

```
> mds = cmdscale(dist(customer), k = 2)
> plot(mds, col = fit$cluster)
```

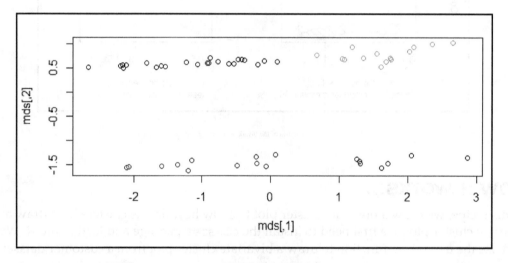

The scatter plot of data with regard to scaled dimensions

Comparing clustering methods

After fitting data into clusters using different clustering methods, you may wish to measure the accuracy of the clustering. In most cases, you can use either intracluster or intercluster metrics as measurements. We will now introduce how to compare different clustering methods using `cluster.stat` from the `fpc` package.

Getting ready

In order to perform a clustering method comparison, one needs to have the previous recipe completed by generating the `customer` dataset.

How to do it...

Perform the following steps to compare clustering methods:

1. First, install and load the `fpc` package:

```
> install.packages("fpc")
> library(fpc)
```

2. You then need to use hierarchical clustering with the `single` method to cluster customer data and generate the object `hc_single`:

```
> single_c =  hclust(dist(customer), method="single")
> hc_single = cutree(single_c, k = 4)
```

3. Use hierarchical clustering with the `complete` method to cluster customer data and generate the object `hc_complete`:

```
> complete_c =  hclust(dist(customer), method="complete")
> hc_complete =  cutree(complete_c, k = 4)
```

4. You can then use k-means clustering to cluster customer data and generate the object `km`:

```
> set.seed(22)
> km = kmeans(customer, 4)
```

5. Next, retrieve the cluster validation statistics of either clustering method:

```
> cs = cluster.stats(dist(customer), km$cluster)
```

6. Most often, we focus on using `within.cluster.ss` and `avg.silwidth` to validate the clustering method:

```
> cs[c("within.cluster.ss","avg.silwidth")]
Output
$within.cluster.ss
[1]  61.3489
$avg.silwidth
```

```
[1] 0.4640587
```

7. Finally, we can generate the cluster statistics of each clustering method and list them in a table:

```
> sapply(list(kmeans = km$cluster, hc_single = hc_single,
hc_complete = hc_complete), function(c)
clus-ter.stats(dist(customer),
c)[c("within.cluster.ss","avg.silwidth")])
Output
                    kmeans hc_single hc_complete
within.cluster.ss 61.3489 136.0092 65.94076
avg.silwidth      0.4640587 0.2481926 0.4255961
```

How it works...

In this recipe, we demonstrate how to validate clusters. To validate a clustering method, we often employ two techniques: intercluster distance and intracluster distance. In these techniques, the higher the intercluster distance, the better it is, and the lower the intracluster distance, the better it is. In order to calculate related statistics, we can apply `cluster.stat` from the fpc package on the fitted clustering object.

From the output, the `within.cluster.ss` measurement stands for the within clusters sum of squares, and `avg.silwidth` represents the average silhouette width. The `within.cluster.ss` measurement shows how closely related objects are in clusters; the smaller the value, the more closely related objects are within the cluster. On the other hand, a silhouette is a measurement that considers how closely related objects are within the cluster and how clusters are separated from each other. Mathematically, we can define the silhouette width for each point x as follows:

$$\text{Silhouette}(x) = \frac{b(x)-a(x)}{\max([b(x),a(x)])}$$

In the preceding equation, $a(x)$ is the average distance between x and all other points within the cluster, and $b(x)$ is the minimum of the average distances between x and the points in the other clusters. The silhouette value usually ranges from 0 to 1; a value closer to 1 suggests the data is better clustered.

The summary table generated in the last step shows that the complete hierarchical clustering method outperforms a single hierarchical clustering method and k-means clustering in `within.cluster.ss` and `avg.silwidth`.

See also

- The `kmeans` function also outputs statistics (for example, `withinss` and `betweenss`) for users to validate a clustering method:

```
> set.seed(22)
> km = kmeans(customer, 4)
> km$withinss
Output
[1]   5.90040 11.97454 22.58236 20.89159
> km$betweenss
Output
[1]  174.6511
```

Extracting silhouette information from clustering

Silhouette information is a measurement to validate a cluster of data. In the previous recipe, we mentioned that the measurement of a cluster involves the calculation of how closely the data is clustered within each cluster, and measures how far different clusters are apart from each other. The silhouette coefficient combines the measurement of the intracluster and intercluster distance. The output value typically ranges from *0* to *1*; the closer to *1*, the better the cluster is. In this recipe, we will introduce how to compute silhouette information.

Getting ready

In order to extract the silhouette information from a cluster, you need to have the previous recipe completed by generating the `customer` dataset.

How to do it...

Perform the following steps to compute the silhouette information:

1. Use `kmeans` to generate a k-means object, `km`:

```
> set.seed(22)
> km = kmeans(customer, 4)
```

2. You can then compute the silhouette information:

```
> kms = silhouette(km$cluster,dist(customer))
> summary(kms)
Output
Silhouette of 60 units in 4 clusters from silhouette.default(x =
km$cluster, dist = dist(customer)) :
 Cluster sizes and average silhouette widths:
        8         11         16         25
0.5464597 0.4080823 0.3794910 0.5164434
Individual silhouette widths:
   Min. 1st Qu.  Median    Mean 3rd Qu.    Max.
 0.1931  0.4030  0.4890  0.4641  0.5422  0.6333
```

3. Next, you can plot the silhouette information:

```
> plot(kms)
```

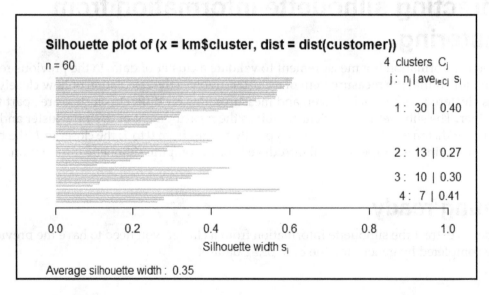

The silhouette plot of the k-means clustering result

How it works...

In this recipe, we demonstrate how to use the silhouette plot to validate clusters. You can first retrieve the silhouette information, which shows cluster sizes, the average silhouette widths, and individual silhouette widths. The silhouette coefficient is a value ranging from 0 to 1; the closer to 1, the better the quality of the cluster.

Lastly, we use the `plot` function to draw a silhouette plot. The left-hand side of the plot shows the number of horizontal lines, which represent the number of clusters. The right-hand column shows the mean similarity of the plot of its own cluster minus the mean similarity of the next similar cluster. The average silhouette width is presented at the bottom of the plot.

See also

- For those interested in how silhouettes are computed, please refer to the wikipedia entry for **Silhouette Value**:
  http://en.wikipedia.org/wiki/Silhouette_%28clustering%29

Obtaining the optimum number of clusters for k-means

While k-means clustering is fast and easy to use, it requires k to be the input at the beginning. Therefore, we can use the sum of squares to determine which k value is best for finding the optimum number of clusters for k-means. In the following recipe, we will discuss how to find the optimum number of clusters for the k-means clustering method.

Getting ready

In order to find the optimum number of clusters, you need to have the previous recipe completed by generating the `customer` dataset.

How to do it...

Perform the following steps to find the optimum number of clusters for the k-means clustering:

1. First, calculate the within sum of squares (`withinss`) of different numbers of clusters:

```
> nk = 2:10
> set.seed(22)
> WSS = sapply(nk, function(k) {
```

```
+        kmeans(customer, centers=k)$tot.withinss
+ })
> WSS
Output
[1] 123.49224   88.07028   61.34890   48.76431   47.20813
[6]   45.48114   29.58014   28.87519   23.21331
```

2. You can then use a line plot to plot the within sum of squares with a different number of k:

```
> plot(nk, WSS, type="l", xlab= "number of k", ylab="within sum of
squares")
```

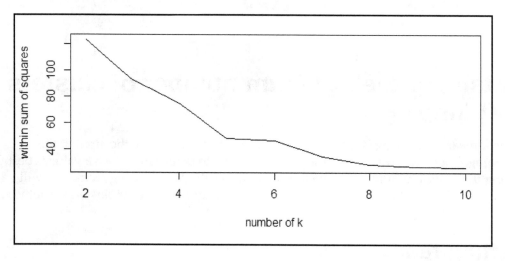

The line plot of the within sum of squares with regard to the different number of k

3. Next, you can calculate the average silhouette width (avg.silwidth) of different numbers of clusters:

```
> SW = sapply(nk, function(k) {
+    cluster.stats(dist(customer), kmeans(customer,
centers=k)$cluster)$avg.silwidth
+ })
> SW
Output
[1] 0.4203896 0.4278904 0.4640587 0.4308448 0.3481157
[6] 0.3320245 0.4396910 0.3417403 0.4070539
```

4. You can then use a line plot to plot the average silhouette width with a different number of k:

```
> plot(nk, SW, type="l", xlab="number of clusers", ylab="average
silhouette width")
```

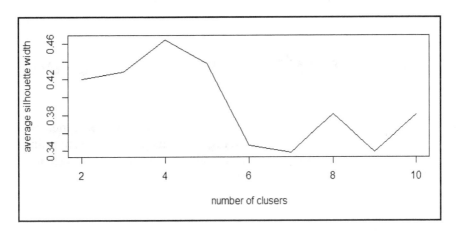

The line plot of average silhouette width with regard to the different number of k

5. Retrieve the maximum number of clusters:

```
> nk[which.max(SW)]
Output
[1] 4
```

How it works...

In this recipe, we demonstrate how to find the optimum number of clusters by iteratively getting within the sum of squares and the average silhouette value. For the within sum of squares, lower values represent clusters with better quality. By plotting the within sum of squares in regard to different numbers of k, we find that the elbow of the plot is at k=4.

On the other hand, we also compute the average silhouette width based on the different numbers of clusters using cluster.stats. Also, we can use a line plot to plot the average silhouette width with regard to the different numbers of clusters. The preceding figure (*step 4*) shows the maximum average silhouette width appears at k=4. Lastly, we use which.max to obtain the value of *k* to determine the location of the maximum average silhouette width.

See also

- For those interested in how the within sum of squares is computed, please refer to the Wikipedia entry for **K-means clustering**:
  `http://en.wikipedia.org/wiki/K-means_clustering`

Clustering data with the density-based method

As an alternative to distance measurement, you can use a density-based measurement to cluster data. This method finds an area with a higher density than the remaining area. One of the most famous methods is DBSCAN. In the following recipe, we will demonstrate how to use DBSCAN to perform density-based clustering.

Getting ready

In this recipe, we will use simulated data generated from the `mlbench` package.

How to do it...

Perform the following steps to perform density-based clustering:

1. First, install and load the `fpc` and `mlbench` packages:

```
> install.packages("mlbench")
> library(mlbench)
> install.packages("fpc")
> library(fpc)
```

2. You can then use the `mlbench` library to draw a Cassini problem graph:

```
> set.seed(2)
> p = mlbench.cassini(500)
> plot(p$x)
```

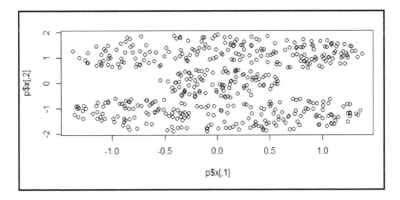

The Cassini problem graph

3. Next, you can cluster data with regard to its density measurement:

```
> ds = dbscan(dist(p$x),0.2, 2, countmode=NULL, method="dist")
> ds
Output
dbscan Pts=500 MinPts=2 eps=0.2
          1    2    3
seed    200  200  100
total   200  200  100
```

4. Plot the data in a scatter plot with different cluster labels as the color:

```
> plot(ds, p$x)
```

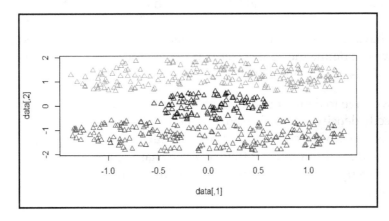

The data scatter plot colored with regard to the cluster label

5. You can also use `dbscan` to predict which cluster the data point belongs to. In this example, first make three inputs in the matrix `p`:

```
> y = matrix(0,nrow=3,ncol=2)
> y[1,] = c(0,0)
> y[2,] = c(0,-1.5)
> y[3,] = c(1,1)
> y
Output
      [,1] [,2]
[1,]    0  0.0
[2,]    0 -1.5
[3,]    1  1.0
```

6. You can then predict which cluster the data belongs to:

```
> predict(ds, p$x, y)
[1] 3 1 2
```

How it works...

Density-based clustering uses the idea of density reachability and density connectivity, which makes it very useful in discovering a cluster in nonlinear shapes. Before discussing the process of density-based clustering, some important background concepts must be explained. Density-based clustering takes two parameters into account: `eps` and `MinPts`. `eps` stands for the maximum radius of the neighborhood; `MinPts` denotes the minimum number of points within the `eps` neighborhood. With these two parameters, we can define the core point as having points more than `MinPts` within `eps`. Also, we can define the board point as having points less than `MinPts`, but it is in the neighborhood of the core points. Then, we can define the core object as if the number of points in the `eps`-neighborhood of p is more than `MinPts`.

Furthermore, we have to define the reachability between two points. We can say that a point, p, is directly density reachable from another point, q, if q is within the `eps`-neighborhood of p and p is a core object. Then, we can define that a point, p, is generic and density reachable from the point, q, if there exists a chain of points, $p_1, p_2..., p_n$, where $p_1 = q$, $p_n = p$, and p_i+1 is directly density reachable from p_i with regard to `eps` and `MinPts` for $1 <= i <= n$:

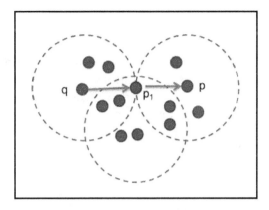

Point p and q is density reachable

With a preliminary concept of density-based clustering, we can then illustrate the process of DBSCAN, the most popular density-based clustering, as shown in these steps:

1. Randomly select a point, p.
2. Retrieve all the points that are density-reachable from p with regard to eps and MinPts.
3. If p is a core point, then a cluster is formed. Otherwise, if it is a board point and no points are density reachable from p, the process will mark the point as noise and continue visiting the next point.
4. Repeat the process until all points have been visited.

In this recipe, we demonstrate how to use the DBSCAN density-based method to cluster customer data. First, we have to install and load the mlbench and fpc libraries. The mlbench package provides many methods to generate simulated data with different shapes and sizes. In this example, we generate a Cassini problem graph.

Next, we perform dbscan on a Cassini dataset to cluster the data. We specify the reachability distance as 0.2, the minimum reachability number of points to 2, the progress reporting as null, and use distance as a measurement. The clustering method successfully clusters data into three clusters with sizes of 200, 200, and 100. By plotting the points and cluster labels on the plot, we see that three sections of the Cassini graph are separated in different colors.

The fpc package also provides a predict function, and you can use this to predict the cluster labels of the input matrix. Point $c(0,0)$ is classified into cluster 3, point $c(0, -1.5)$ is classified into cluster 1, and point $c(1,1)$ is classified into cluster 2.

See also

- The `fpc` package contains flexible procedures of clustering, and has useful clustering analysis functions. For example, you can generate a discriminant projection plot using the `plotcluster` function. For more information, please refer to the following document:

```
> help(plotcluster)
```

Clustering data with the model-based method

In contrast to hierarchical clustering and k-means clustering, which use a heuristic approach and do not depend on a formal model, model-based clustering techniques assume varieties of data models and apply an EM algorithm to obtain the most likely model, and further use the model to infer the most likely number of clusters. In this recipe, we will demonstrate how to use the model-based method to determine the most likely number of clusters.

Getting ready

In order to perform a model-based method to cluster customer data, you need to have the previous recipe completed by generating the customer dataset.

How to do it...

Perform the following steps to perform model-based clustering:

1. First, please install and load the `mclust` library:

```
> install.packages("mclust")
> library(mclust)
```

2. You can then perform model-based clustering on the `customer` dataset:

```
> mb = Mclust(customer)
> plot(mb)
```

3. Then, you can press the *1* key to obtain the BIC against a number of components:

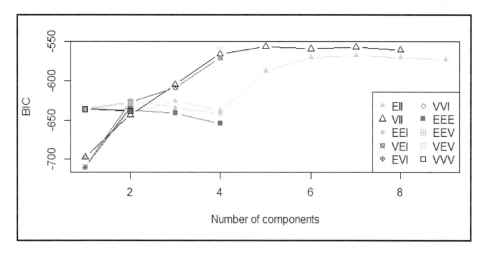

Plot of BIC against a number of components

4. Then, you can press the *2* key to show the classification with regard to different combinations of features:

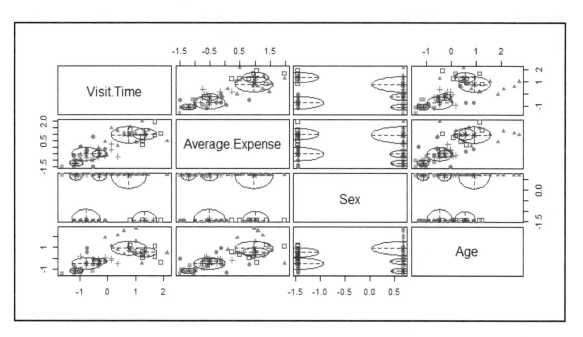

Plot showing classification with regard to different combinations of features

5. Press the *3* key to show the classification uncertainty with regard to different combinations of features:

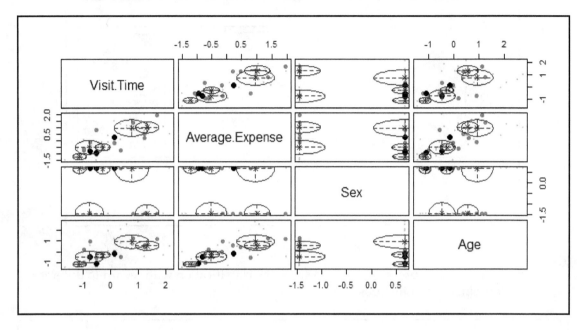

Plot showing classification uncertainty with regard to different combinations of features

6. Next, press the 4 key to plot the density estimation:

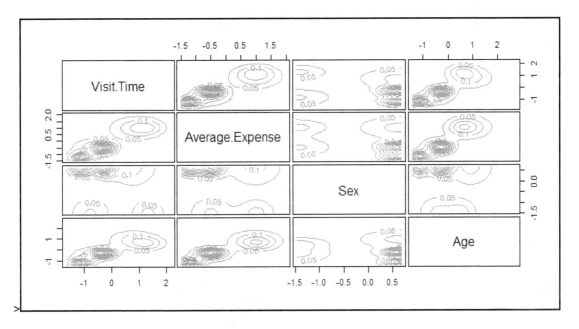

A plot of density estimation

7. Then, you can press the *0* key to plot density to exit the plotting menu.

8. Lastly, use the `summary` function to obtain the most likely model and number of clusters:

```
> summary(mb)
Output
--------------------------------------------------
Gaussian finite mixture model fitted by EM algorithm
--------------------------------------------------
Mclust VII (spherical, varying volume) model with 5 components:
 log.likelihood  n df        BIC        ICL
      -218.6891 60 29 -556.1142 -557.2812
Clustering table:
  1  2  3  4  5
 11  8 17 14 10
```

How it works...

Instead of taking a heuristic approach to building a cluster, model-based clustering uses a probability-based approach. Model-based clustering assumes that the data is generated by an underlying probability distribution and tries to recover the distribution from the data. One common model-based approach is using finite mixture models, which provide a flexible modeling framework for the analysis of the probability distribution. Finite mixture models are a linearly weighted sum of component probability distribution. Assume the data $y=(y_1,y_2...y_n)$ contains n independent and multivariable observations; G is the number of components; the likelihood of finite mixture models can be formulated as:

$$L_{MIX}\left(\theta_1,\cdots\theta_G\mid y\right)=\prod_{i=1}^{n}\prod_{k=1}^{G}\tau_k f_k\left(y_i\mid\theta_k\right)$$

Where and are the density and parameters of the kth component in the mixture, and (and) is the probability that an observation belongs to the kth component.

The process of model-based clustering has several steps: First, the process selects the number and types of component probability distribution. Then, it fits a finite mixture model and calculates the posterior probabilities of a component membership. Lastly, it assigns the membership of each observation to the component with the maximum probability.

In this recipe, we demonstrate how to use model-based clustering to cluster data. We first install and load the `Mclust` library into R. We then fit the customer data into the model-based method by using the `Mclust` function.

After the data is fit into the model, we plot the model based on clustering results. There are four different plots: BIC, classification, uncertainty, and density plots. The BIC plot shows the BIC value, and one can use this value to choose the number of clusters. The classification plot shows how data is clustered in regard to different dimension combinations. The uncertainty plot shows the uncertainty of classifications in regard to different dimension combinations. The density plot shows the density estimation in contour.

You can also use the `summary` function to obtain the most likely model and the hidhest possible number of clusters. For this example, the highest possible number of clusters is five, with a BIC value equal to -556.1142.

See also

- For those interested in detail on how `Mclust` works, please refer to the following source: C. Fraley, A. E. Raftery, T. B. Murphy and L. Scrucca (2012). *mclust Version 4 for R: Normal Mixture Modeling for Model-Based Clustering, Classification, and Density Estimation. Technical Report No. 597*, Department of Statistics, University of Washington.

Visualizing a dissimilarity matrix

A dissimilarity matrix can be used as a measurement for the quality of a cluster. To visualize the matrix, we can use a heat map on a distance matrix. Within the plot, entries with low dissimilarity (or high similarity) are plotted darker, which is helpful to identify hidden structures in the data. In this recipe, we will discuss some techniques that are useful for visualizing a dissimilarity matrix.

Getting ready

In order to visualize the dissimilarity matrix, you need to have the previous recipe completed by generating the customer dataset. In addition to this, a k-means object needs to be generated and stored in the `km` variable.

How to do it...

Perform the following steps to visualize the dissimilarity matrix:

1. First, install and load the `seriation` package:

```
> install.packages("seriation")
> library(seriation)
```

2. You can then use `dissplot` to visualize the dissimilarity matrix in a heat map:

```
> dissplot(dist(customer), labels=km$cluster,
options=list(main="Kmeans Clustering With k=4"))
```

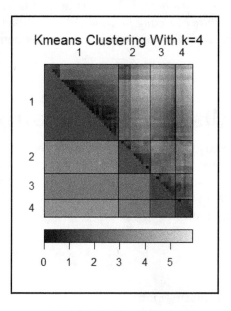

A dissimilarity plot of k-means clustering

3. Next, apply `dissplot` on hierarchical clustering in the heat map:

```
> complete_c =  hclust(dist(customer), method="complete")
> hc_complete =  cutree(complete_c, k = 4)
> dissplot(dist(customer), labels=hc_complete,
options=list(main="Hierarchical Clustering"))
```

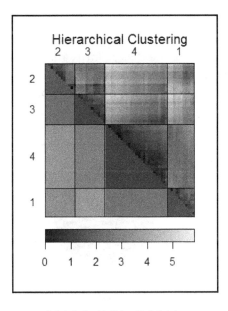

A dissimilarity plot of hierarchical clustering

How it works...

In this recipe, we use a dissimilarity plot to visualize the dissimilarity matrix. We first install and load the `seriation` package, and then apply the `dissplot` function on the k-means clustering output, generating the preceding figure (*step 2*).

It shows that clusters similar to each other are plotted darker, and dissimilar combinations are plotted lighter. Therefore, we can see clusters against their corresponding clusters (such as cluster 4 to cluster 4) are plotted diagonally and darker. On the other hand, clusters dissimilar to each other are plotted lighter and away from the diagonal.

Likewise, we can apply the `dissplot` function on the output of hierarchical clustering. The generated plot in the figure (*step 3*) shows the similarity of each cluster in a single heat map.

There's more...

Besides using `dissplot` to visualize the dissimilarity matrix, one can also visualize a distance matrix by using the `dist` and `image` functions. In the resulting graph, closely related entries are plotted in red. Less related entries are plotted closer to white:

```
> image(as.matrix(dist(customer)))
```

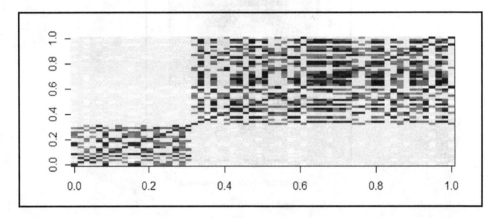

A distance matrix plot of customer dataset

In order to plot both a dendrogram and heat map to show how data is clustered, you can use the `heatmap` function:

```
> cd=dist(customer)
> hc=hclust(cd)
> cdt=dist(t(customer))
> hcc=hclust(cdt)
> heatmap(customer, Rowv=as.dendrogram(hc), Colv=as.dendrogram(hcc))
```

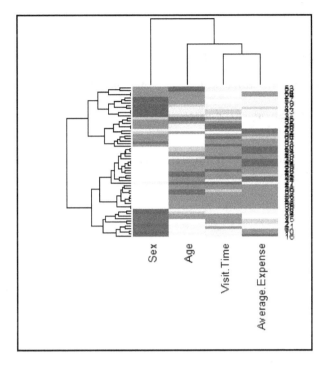

A heat map with dendrogram on the column and row side

Validating clusters externally

Besides generating statistics to validate the quality of the generated clusters, you can use known data clusters as the ground truth to compare different clustering methods. In this recipe, we will demonstrate how clustering methods differ with regard to data with known clusters.

Getting ready

In this recipe, we will continue to use handwriting digits as clustering inputs; you can find the figure at the author's GitHub page:

`https://github.com/ywchiu/ml_R_cookbook/tree/master/CH9.`

How to do it...

Perform the following steps to cluster digits with different clustering techniques:

1. First, you need to install and load the png package:

```
> install.packages("png")
> library(png)
```

2. Then, please read images from handwriting.png and transform the read data into a scatter plot:

```
> img2 = readPNG("handwriting.png", TRUE)
> img3 = img2[,nrow(img2):1]
> b = cbind(as.integer(which(img3 < -1) %% 28), which(img3 < -1)
/ 28)
> plot(b, xlim=c(1,28), ylim=c(1,28))
```

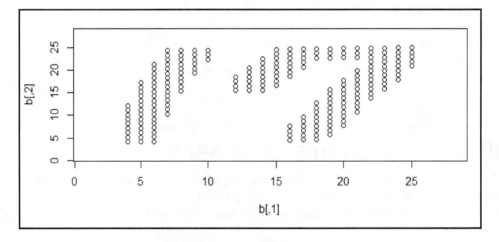

A scatter plot of handwriting digits

3. Perform a k-means clustering method on the handwriting digits:

```
> set.seed(18)
> fit = kmeans(b, 2)
> plot(b, col=fit$cluster)
> plot(b, col=fit$cluster,  xlim=c(1,28), ylim=c(1,28))
```

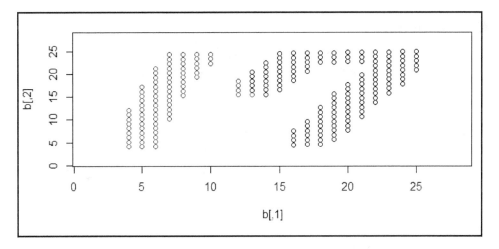

k-means clustering result on handwriting digits

4. Next, perform the `dbscan` clustering method on the handwriting digits:

```
> ds = dbscan(b, 2)> ds
Output
dbscan Pts=212 MinPts=5 eps=2
         1    2
seed   75  137
total  75  137
> plot(ds, b,  xlim=c(1,28), ylim=c(1,28))
```

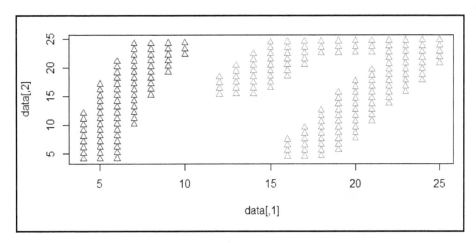

DBSCAN clustering result on handwriting digits

How it works...

In this recipe, we demonstrate how different clustering methods work in regard to a handwriting dataset. The aim of the clustering is to separate 1 and 7 into different clusters. We perform different techniques to see how data is clustered in regard to the k-means and DBSCAN methods.

To generate the data, we use the Windows application `paint.exe` to create a PNG file with dimensions of 28 x 28 pixels. We then read the PNG data using the `readPNG` function and transform the read PNG data points into a scatter plot, which shows the handwriting digits in 17.

After the data is read, we perform clustering techniques on the handwriting digits. First, we perform k-means clustering, where `k=2` on the dataset. Since k-means clustering employs distance measures, the constructed clusters cover the area of both the 1 and 7 digits. We then perform DBSCAN on the dataset. As DBSCAN is a density-based clustering technique, it successfully separates digit 1 and digit 7 into different clusters.

See also

- If you are interested in how to read various graphic formats in R, you may refer to the following document:

```
> help(package="png")
```

12
Association Analysis and Sequence Mining

In this chapter, we will cover the following topics:

- Transforming data into transactions
- Displaying transactions and associations
- Mining associations with the Apriori rule
- Pruning redundant rules
- Visualizing associations rules
- Mining frequent itemsets with Eclat
- Creating transactions with temporal information
- Mining frequent sequential patterns with cSPADE
- Using the `TraMineR` package for sequence analysis
- Visualizing sequence, Chronogram, and Traversal Statistics

Introduction

Enterprises accumulate a large amount of transaction data (for example, sales orders from retailers, invoices, and shipping documentations) from daily operations. Finding hidden relationships in the data can be useful, such as *What products are often bought together?* or *What are the subsequent purchases after buying a cell phone?* To answer these two questions, we need to perform association analysis and frequent sequential pattern mining on a transaction dataset.

Association analysis is an approach to find interesting relationships within a transaction dataset. A famous association between products is *customers who buy diapers also buy beer*. While this association may sound unusual, if retailers can use this kind of information or rule to cross-sell products to their customers, there is a high likelihood that they can increase their sales.

Association analysis is used to finding a correlation between **itemsets**, but what if you want to find out the order in which items are frequently purchased? To achieve this, you can adopt frequent sequential pattern mining to find frequent subsequences from transaction datasets with temporal information. You can then use the mined frequent subsequences to predict customer shopping sequence orders, web click streams, biological sequences, and usages in other applications.

In this chapter, we will cover recipes to create and inspect transaction datasets, performing association analysis with an Apriori algorithm, visualizing associations in various graph formats, and finding frequent itemsets using the **Eclat** algorithm. Lastly, we will create transactions with temporal information and use the **cSPADE** algorithm to discover frequent sequential patterns.

Transforming data into transactions

Before creating a mining association rule, you need to transform the data into transactions. In the following recipe, we will introduce how to transform either a list, matrix, or DataFrame into transactions.

Getting ready

In this recipe, we will generate three different datasets in a list, matrix, or DataFrame. We can then transform the generated dataset into transactions.

How to do it...

Perform the following steps to transform different formats of data into transactions:

1. First, you have to install and load the `arule` package:

```
> install.packages("arules")
> library(arules)
```

2. You can then make a list with three vectors containing purchase records:

```
> tr_list = list(c("Apple", "Bread", "Cake"),
+                c("Apple", "Bread", "Milk"),
+                c("Bread", "Cake", "Milk"))
> names(tr_list) = paste("Tr",c(1:3), sep = "")
```

3. Next, you can use the `as` function to transform the DataFrame into transactions:

```
> trans = as(tr_list, "transactions")
> trans
Output
transactions in sparse format with
 3 transactions (rows) and
 4 items (columns)
```

4. You can also transform the matrix format data into transactions:

```
> tr_matrix = matrix(
+    c(1,1,1,0,
+      1,1,0,1,
+      0,1,1,1), ncol = 4)
> dimnames(tr_matrix) =  list(
+    paste("Tr",c(1:3), sep = ""),
+    c("Apple","Bread","Cake", "Milk")
+    )
> trans2 =  as(tr_matrix, "transactions")
> trans2
Output
transactions in sparse format with
 3 transactions (rows) and
 4 items (columns)
```

5. Lastly, you can transform the DataFrame format datasets into transactions:

```
> Tr_df = data.frame(
+   TrID= as.factor(c(1,2,1,1,2,3,2,3,2,3)),
+   Item = as.factor(c("Apple","Milk","Cake","Bread",
+                      "Cake","Milk","Apple","Cake",
+                      "Bread","Bread"))
+ )
> trans3 = as(split(Tr_df[,"Item"], Tr_df[,"TrID"]),
"transactions")
> trans3
 Output
transactions in sparse format with
 3 transactions (rows) and
 4 items (columns)
```

How it works...

Before mining frequent itemsets or using the association rule, it is important to prepare the dataset by the class of transactions. In this recipe, we will demonstrate how to transform a dataset from a list, matrix, and DataFrame format to transactions. In the first step, we generate the dataset in a list format containing three vectors of purchase records. Then, after we have assigned a transaction ID to each transaction, we transform the data into transactions using the as function.

Next, we demonstrate how to transform the data from the matrix format into transactions. To denote how items are purchased, one should use a binary incidence matrix to record the purchase behavior of each transaction with regard to different items purchased. Likewise, we can use an as function to transform the dataset from the matrix format into transactions.

Lastly, we illustrate how to transform the dataset from the DataFrame format into transactions. The DataFrame contains two factor-type vectors: one is a transaction ID named TrID, while the other shows purchased items (named in Item) with regard to different transactions. Also, one can use the as function to transform the DataFrame format data into transactions.

See also

- The transactions class is used to represent transaction data for rules or frequent pattern mining. It is an extension of the itemMatrix class. If you are interested in how to use the two different classes to represent transaction data, please use the help function to refer to the following documents:

```
> help(transactions)
> help(itemMatrix)
```

Displaying transactions and associations

The arule package uses its own transactions class to store transaction data. As such, we must use the generic function provided by arule to display transactions and association rules. In this recipe, we will illustrate how to display transactions and association rules via various functions in the arule package.

Getting ready

Ensure that you have completed the previous recipe by generating transactions and storing these in the `trans` variable.

How to do it...

Perform the following steps to display transactions and associations:

1. First, you can obtain a `LIST` representation of the transaction data:

   ```
   > LIST(trans)
   Output
   $Tr1
   [1] "Apple" "Bread" "Cake"
   $Tr2
   [1] "Apple" "Bread" "Milk"
   $Tr3
   [1] "Bread" "Cake"  "Milk"
   ```

2. Next, you can use the `summary` function to show a summary of the statistics and details of the transactions:

   ```
   > summary(trans)
   Output
   transactions as itemMatrix in sparse format with
    3 rows (elements/itemsets/transactions) and
    4 columns (items) and a density of 0.75

   most frequent items:
    Bread Apple Cake Milk (Other)
        3     2    2    2      0

    element (itemset/transaction) length distribution:
   sizes
   3
   3

       Min. 1st Qu. Median Mean 3rd Qu. Max.
          3       3      3    3       3    3

   includes extended item information - examples:
     labels
   1 Apple
   2 Bread
   ```

```
3 Cake

  includes extended transaction information - examples:
transactionID
1 Tr1
2 Tr2
3 Tr3
```

3. You can then display transactions using the `inspect` function:

```
> inspect(trans)
Output
   items     transactionID
 1 {Apple,
   Bread,
Cake}              Tr1
 2 {Apple,
   Bread,
Milk}              Tr2
 3 {Bread,
     Cake,
Milk}              Tr3
```

4. In addition to this, you can filter the transactions by size:

```
> filter_trains = trans[size(trans) >=3]
> inspect(filter_trains)
Output
   items     transactionID
1 {Apple,
   Bread,
Cake}              Tr1
2 {Apple,
   Bread,
Milk}              Tr2
3 {Bread,
   Cake,
Milk}              Tr3
```

5. Also, you can use the image function to visually inspect the transactions:

```
> image(trans)
```

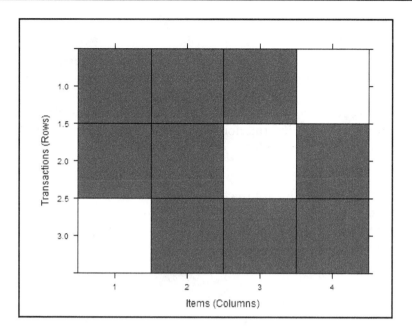

Visual inspection of transactions

6. To visually show the frequency/support bar plot, one can use `itemFrequenctPlot`:

```
> itemFrequencyPlot (trans)
```

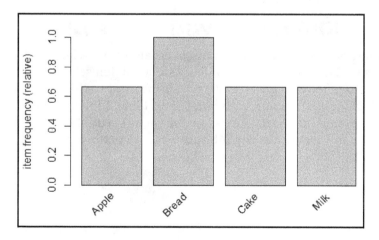

Item frequency bar plot of transactions

How it works...

As the transaction data is the base for mining associations and frequent patterns, we have to learn how to display the associations to gain insights and determine how associations are built. The `arules` package provides various methods to inspect transactions. First, we use the `LIST` function to obtain the list representation of the transaction data. We can then use the `summary` function to obtain information, such as basic descriptions, most frequent items, and the transaction length distribution.

Next, we use the `inspect` function to display the transactions. Besides displaying all transactions, one can first filter the transactions by size and then display the associations by using the `inspect` function. Furthermore, we can use the `image` function to visually inspect the transactions. Finally, we illustrate how to use the frequency/support bar plot to display the relative item frequency of each item.

See also

- Besides using `itemFrequencyPlot` to show the frequency/bar plot, you can use the `itemFrequency` function to show the support distribution. For more details, please use the `help` function to view the following document:

  ```
  > help(itemFrequency)
  ```

Mining associations with the Apriori rule

Association mining is a technique that can discover interesting relationships hidden in transaction datasets. This approach first finds all frequent itemsets and generates strong association rules from frequent itemsets. Apriori is the most well-known association mining algorithm which identifies frequent individual items first and then performs a breadth-first search strategy to extend individual items to larger itemsets until larger frequent itemsets cannot be found. In this recipe, we will introduce how to perform association analysis using the Apriori rule.

Getting ready

In this recipe, we will use the built-in transaction dataset `Groceries` to demonstrate how to perform association analysis with the Apriori algorithm in the `arules` package. Please make sure that the `arules` package is installed and loaded first.

How to do it...

Perform the following steps to analyze the association rules:

1. First, you need to load the `Groceries` dataset:

   ```
   > data(Groceries)
   ```

2. You can then examine the summary of the `Groceries` dataset:

   ```
   > summary(Groceries)
   ```

3. Next, you can use `itemFrequencyPlot` to examine the relative item frequency of itemsets:

   ```
   > itemFrequencyPlot(Groceries, support = 0.1, cex.names=0.8,
   topN=5)
   ```

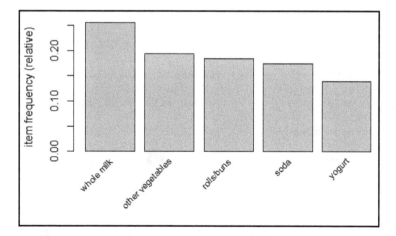

The top five item frequency bar plot of groceries transactions

4. Use `apriori` to discover rules with support over 0.001 and confidence over 0.5:

```
> rules = apriori(Groceries, parameter = list(supp = 0.001, conf =
0.5, target= "rules"))
> summary(rules)
Output
set of 5668 rules
rule length distribution (lhs + rhs):sizes
   2    3    4    5    6
  11 1461 3211  939   46
   Min. 1st Qu. Median    Mean 3rd Qu.    Max.
   2.00    3.00   4.00    3.92    4.00    6.00
summary of quality measures:
     support            confidence            lift
 Min.   :0.001017   Min.   :0.5000   Min.   : 1.957
 1st Qu.:0.001118   1st Qu.:0.5455   1st Qu.: 2.464
 Median :0.001322   Median :0.6000   Median : 2.899
 Mean   :0.001668   Mean   :0.6250   Mean   : 3.262
 3rd Qu.:0.001729   3rd Qu.:0.6842   3rd Qu.: 3.691
 Max.   :0.022267   Max.   :1.0000   Max.   :18.996
mining info:
      data ntransactions support confidence
 Groceries         9835    0.001         0.5
```

5. We can then inspect the first few rules:

```
> inspect(head(rules))
Output
lhsrhs                  support confidence     lift
1 {honey}            => {whole milk} 0.001118454  0.7333333
2.870009
2 {tidbits}          => {rolls/buns} 0.001220132  0.5217391
2.836542
3 {cocoa drinks}     => {whole milk} 0.001321810  0.5909091
2.312611
4 {pudding powder}   => {whole milk} 0.001321810  0.5652174
2.212062
5 {cooking chocolate} => {whole milk} 0.001321810  0.5200000
2.035097
6 {cereals}          => {whole milk} 0.003660397  0.6428571
2.515917
```

6. You can sort rules by confidence and inspect the first few rules:

```
> rules=sort(rules, by="confidence", decreasing=TRUE)
> inspect(head(rules))
Output
lhsrhs support confidence lift
```

```
1 {rice,
sugar} => {whole milk} 0.001220132 1 3.913649
2 {canned fish,
hygiene articles} => {whole milk} 0.001118454 1 3.913649
3 {root vegetables,
   butter,
rice} => {whole milk} 0.001016777 1 3.913649
4 {root vegetables,
   whipped/sour cream,
flour} => {whole milk} 0.001728521 1 3.913649
5 {butter,
   soft cheese,
   domestic eggs} => {whole milk} 0.001016777 1 3.913649
6 {citrus fruit,
   root vegetables,
   soft cheese} => {other vegetables} 0.001016777 1 5.168156
```

How it works...

The purpose of association mining is to discover associations among items from the transactional database. Typically, the process of association mining proceeds by finding itemsets that have support greater than the minimum support. Next, the process uses the frequent itemsets to generate strong rules (for example, `milk` => `bread` a customer who buys milk is likely to buy bread) that have confidence greater than minimum confidence. By definition, an association rule can be expressed in the form of X=>Y, where X and Y are disjointed itemsets. We can measure the strength of associations between two terms: support and confidence. Support shows how much of the percentage of a rule is applicable within a dataset, while confidence indicates the probability of both X and Y appearing in the same transaction:

- Support = $\dfrac{\sigma(x \cup y)}{N}$

- Confidence = $\dfrac{\sigma(x \cup y)}{\sigma(x)}$

Here, X and Y refers to the frequency of a particular itemset; N denotes the populations.

As support and confidence are metrics for the strength rule only, you might still obtain many redundant rules with high support and confidence. Therefore, we can use the third measure, lift, to evaluate the quality (ranking) of the rule. By definition, lift indicates the strength of a rule over the random co-occurrence of X and Y, so we can formulate lift in the following form:

$$\text{Lift} = \frac{\sigma(x \cup y)}{\sigma(x) \times \sigma(y)}$$

Apriori is the best known algorithm for mining associations which performs a level-wise, breadth-first algorithm to count the candidate itemsets. The process of Apriori starts by finding frequent itemsets (a set of items that have minimum support) level-wisely. For example, the process starts with finding frequent 1-itemsets. Then, the process continues by using frequent 1-itemsets to find frequent 2-itemsets. The process iteratively discovers new frequent k+1-itemsets from frequent k-itemsets until no frequent itemsets are found.

Finally, the process utilizes frequent itemsets to generate association rules:

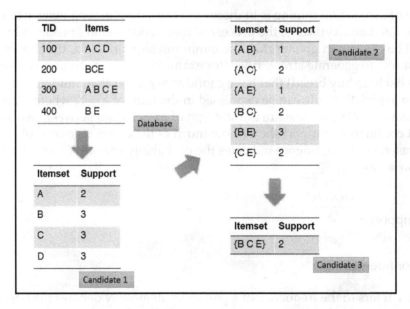

An illustration of the Apriori algorithm (where support = 2)

In this recipe, we use the Apriori algorithm to find association rules within transactions. We use the built-in `Groceries` dataset, which contains one month of real-world point-of-sale transaction data from a typical grocery outlet. We then use the `summary` function to obtain the summary statistics of the `Groceries` dataset. The summary statistics shows that the dataset contains 9,835 transactions which are categorized into 169 categories. In addition to this, the summary shows information, such as most frequent items, itemset distribution, and example extended item information within the dataset. We can then use `itemFrequencyPlot` to visualize the five most frequent items with support over 0.1.

Next, we apply the Apriori algorithm to search for rules with support over 0.001 and confidence over 0.5. We then use the `summary` function to inspect detailed information on the generated rules. From the output summary, we find that the Apriori algorithm generates 5,668 rules with support over 0.001 and confidence over 0.5. Furthermore, we can find the rule length distribution, summary of quality measures, and mining information. In the summary of the quality measurement we find descriptive statistics of three measurements, which are support, confidence, and lift. Support is the proportion of transactions containing a certain itemset. Confidence is the correct percentage of the rule. Lift is the response target association rule divided by the average response.

To explore some generated rules, we can use the `inspect` function to view the first six rules of the 5,668 generated rules. Lastly, we can sort rules by confidence and list rules with the most confidence. Therefore, we find that `rich sugar` associated to `whole milk` is the most confident rule with support equal to 0.001220132, confidence equal to 1, and lift equal to 3.913649.

See also

For those interested in the research results using the `Groceries` dataset and how the support, confidence, and lift measurements are defined, you can refer to the following papers:

- Michael Hahsler, Kurt Hornik, and Thomas Reutterer (2006) *Implications of Probabilistic Data Modeling for Mining Association Rules. In M. Spiliopoulou, R. Kruse, C. Borgelt, A*
- Nuernberger, and W. Gaul, editors, *From Data and Information Analysis to Knowledge Engineering, Studies in Classification, Data Analysis, and Knowledge Organization, pages 598-605. Springer-Verlag*

Also, in addition to using the `summary` and `inspect` functions to inspect association rules, you can use `interestMeasure` to obtain additional interest measures:

```
> head(interestMeasure(rules, c("support", "chiSquare", "confidence",
"conviction","cosine", "coverage", "leverage", "lift","oddsRatio"),
 Groceries))
```

Pruning redundant rules

Among the generated rules, we sometimes find repeated or redundant rules (for example, one rule is the super rule or subset of another rule). In this recipe, we will show you how to prune (or remove) repeated or redundant rules.

Getting ready

In this recipe, you have to complete the previous recipe by generating rules and have them stored in the `rules` variable.

How to do it...

Perform the following steps to prune redundant rules:

1. First, follow these steps to find redundant rules:

```
> rules.sorted = sort(rules, by="lift")
> subset.matrix = is.subset(rules.sorted, rules.sorted)
> subset.matrix[lower.tri(subset.matrix, diag=T)] = NA
> redundant = colSums(subset.matrix, na.rm=T) >= 1
```

2. You can then remove redundant rules:

```
> rules.pruned = rules.sorted[!redundant]
> inspect(head(rules.pruned))
Output
lhsrhs                     support confidence       lift
1 {Instant food products,
soda}                   => {hamburger meat} 0.001220132  0.6315789
18.99565
2 {soda,
popcorn}                => {salty snack}    0.001220132  0.6315789
16.69779
```

```
 3 {flour,
baking powder}         => {sugar}          0.001016777  0.5555556
16.40807
 4 {ham,
processed cheese}      => {white bread}    0.001931876  0.6333333
15.04549
 5 {whole milk,
Instant food products} => {hamburger meat} 0.001525165  0.5000000
15.03823
 6 {other vegetables,
curd,
yogurt,
whipped/sour cream}    => {cream cheese }  0.001016777  0.5882353
14.83409
```

How it works...

The two main constraints of association mining are to the choices regarding support and confidence. For example, if you use a high support threshold, you might remove rare item rules without considering whether these rules have a high confidence value. On the other hand, if you choose to use a low support threshold, the association mining can produce huge sets of redundant association rules, making them difficult to utilize and analyze. Therefore, we need to prune redundant rules so we can discover meaningful information from these generated rules.

In this recipe, we demonstrate how to prune redundant rules. First, we search for redundant rules. We sort the rules by a lift measure and then find subsets of the sorted rules using the is.subset function, which will generate an itemMatrix object. We can then set the lower triangle of the matrix to NA. Lastly, we compute colSums of the generated matrix, of which colSums>=1 indicates that the specific rule is redundant.

After we have found the redundant rules, we can prune these rules from the sorted rules. Lastly, we can examine the pruned rules using the inspect function.

See also

- In order to find subsets or supersets of rules, you can use the `is.superset` and `is.subset` functions on the association rules. These two methods may generate an `itemMatrix` object to show which rule is the superset or subset of other rules. You can refer to the `help` function for more information:

```
> help(is.superset)
> help(is.subset)
```

Visualizing association rules

Besides listing rules as text, you can visualize association rules, making it easier to find the relationship between itemsets. In the following recipe, we will introduce how to use the `arulesViz` package to visualize the association rules.

Getting ready

In this recipe, we will continue using the `Groceries` dataset. You need to have completed the previous recipe by generating the pruned rule `rules.pruned`.

How to do it...

Perform the following steps to visualize the association rule:

1. First, you need to install and load the `arulesViz` package:

```
> install.packages("arulesViz")
> library(arulesViz)
```

2. You can then make a scatter plot from the pruned rules:

```
> plot(rules.pruned)
```

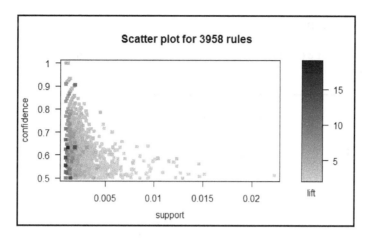

The scatter plot of pruned association rules

3. Additionally, to prevent overplotting, you can add jitter to the scatter plot:

```
> plot(rules.pruned, shading="order", control=list(jitter=6))
```

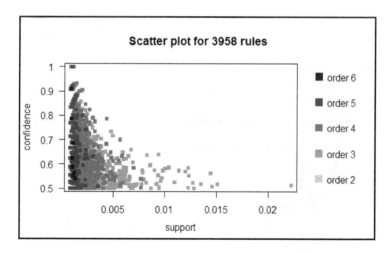

The scatter plot of pruned association rules with jitters

4. We then produce new rules with `soda` on the left-hand side using the Apriori algorithm:

```
> soda_rule=apriori(data=Groceries, parameter=list(supp=0.001,conf
= 0.1, minlen=2), appearance = list(default="rhs",lhs="soda"))
```

5. Next, you can plot `soda_rule` in a graph plot:

```
> plot(sort(soda_rule, by="lift"), method="graph",
  control=list(type="items"))
```

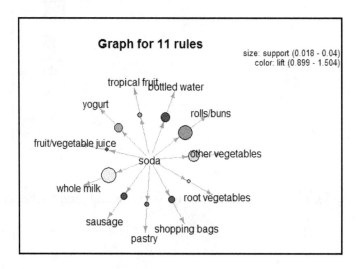

Graph plot of association rules

6. Also, the association rules can be visualized in a balloon plot:

```
> plot(soda_rule, method="grouped")
```

Balloon plot of association rules

How it works...

Besides presenting association rules as text, one can use `arulesViz` to visualize association rules. The `arulesViz` is an `arules` extension package which provides many visualization techniques to explore association rules. To start using `arulesViz`, first install and load the `arulesViz` package. We then use the pruned rules generated in the previous recipe to make a scatter plot. As per the figure in *step 2*, we find the rules are shown as points within the scatter plot, with the x-axis in support and y-axis in confidence. The shade of color shows the lift of the rule; the darker the shade, the higher the lift. Next, in order to prevent overplotting points, we can include the jitter as an argument in the control list. The plot with the jitter added is provided in the figure in *step 3*.

In addition to plotting the rules in a scatter plot, `arulesViz` enables you to plot rules in a graph and grouped matrix. Instead of printing all the rules on a single plot, we choose to produce new rules with `soda` on the left-hand side. We then sort the rules by using the lift and visualize the rules in the graph in the figure in *step 4*. From the graph, every itemset is presented in a vertex and their relationship is presented in an edge. The figure (*step 4*) shows it is clear that the rule with `soda` on the left-hand side to `whole milk` on the right-hand side has the maximum support, for the size of the node is greatest. Also, the rule shows that `soda` on the left-hand side to `bottled water` on the right-hand side has the maximum lift as the shade of color in the circle is the darkest. We can then use the same data with `soda` on the left-hand side to generate a grouped matrix, which is a balloon plot shown in the figure in *step 5*, with the left-hand side rule as column labels and the right-hand side as row labels. Similar to the graph plot, in the figure in *step 4*, the size of the balloon in the figure in *step 5* shows the support of the rule, and the color of the balloon shows the lift of the rule.

See also

- In this recipe, we introduced three visualization methods to plot association rules. However, `arulesViz` also provides features to plot parallel coordinate plots, double-decker plots, mosaic plots, and other related charts. For those who are interested in how these plots work, you may refer to: Hahsler, M., and Chelluboina, S. (2011). *Visualizing association rules: Introduction to the R-extension package arulesViz. R project module.*

- In addition to generating a static plot, you can generate an interactive plot by setting interactive equal to TRUE through the following steps:

```
> plot(rules.pruned,interactive=TRUE)
```

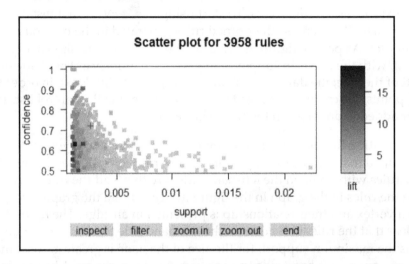

The interactive scatter plots

Mining frequent itemsets with Eclat

In addition to the Apriori algorithm, you can use the Eclat algorithm to generate frequent itemsets. As the Apriori algorithm performs a breadth-first search to scan the complete database, the support counting is rather time consuming. Alternatively, if the database fits into the memory, you can use the Eclat algorithm, which performs a depth-first search to count the supports. The Eclat algorithm, therefore, performs quicker than the Apriori algorithm. In this recipe, we will introduce how to use the Eclat algorithm to generate frequent itemsets.

Getting ready

In this recipe, we will continue using the Groceries dataset as our input data source.

How to do it...

Perform the following steps to generate a frequent itemset using the Eclat algorithm:

1. Similar to the Apriori method, we can use the `eclat` function to generate the frequent itemset:

```
>
frequentsets=eclat(Groceries,parameter=list(support=0.05,
maxlen=10))
```

2. We can then obtain the summary information from the generated frequent itemset:

```
> summary(frequentsets)
Output
set of 31 itemsets
most frequent items:
      whole milk other vegetables              yogurt
               4               2                   2
      rolls/buns       frankfurter           (Other)
               2               1                  23
element (itemset/transaction) length distribution:sizes
1   2
28  3
   Min. 1st Qu.  Median    Mean 3rd Qu.     Max.
  1.000   1.000   1.000   1.097   1.000    2.000
summary of quality measures:
    support
 Min.    :0.05236
 1st Qu.:0.05831
 Median :0.07565
 Mean   :0.09212
 3rd Qu.:0.10173
 Max.   :0.25552
includes transaction ID lists: FALSE
mining info:
       data ntransactions support
  Groceries          9835    0.05
```

3. Lastly, we can examine the top 10 support frequent itemsets:

```
> inspect(sort(frequentsets,by="support")[1:10])
Output
    items                    support
1   {whole milk}          0.25551601
2   {other vegetables}    0.19349263
```

```
 3  {rolls/buns}       0.18393493
 4  {soda}             0.17437722
 5  {yogurt}           0.13950178
 6  {bottled water}    0.11052364
 7  {root vegetables}  0.10899847
 8  {tropical fruit}   0.10493137
 9  {shopping bags}    0.09852567
10  {sausage}          0.09395018
```

How it works...

In this recipe, we introduce another algorithm, Eclat, to perform frequent itemset generation. Though Apriori is a straightforward and easy to understand association mining method, the algorithm has the disadvantage of generating huge candidate sets and performs inefficiently in support counting, for it takes multiple scans of databases. In contrast to Apriori, Eclat uses equivalence classes, depth-first searches, and set intersections, which greatly improve the speed in support counting.

In Apriori, the algorithm uses a horizontal data layout to store transactions. On the other hand, Eclat uses a vertical data layout to store a list of transaction IDs (tid) for each item. Then, Eclat determines the support of any k+1-itemset by intersecting tid-lists of two k-itemsets. Lastly, Eclat utilizes frequent itemsets to generate association rules:

An illustration of the Eclat algorithm

Similar to the recipe using the Apriori algorithm, we can use the eclat function to generate a frequent itemset with a given support (assume support = 2 in this case) and maximum length:

Generating frequent itemset

We can then use the `summary` function to obtain summary statistics, which include: most frequent items, itemset length distributions, summary of quality measures, and mining information. Finally, we can sort frequent itemsets by the support and inspect the top 10 support frequent itemsets.

See also

- Besides Apriori and Eclat, another popular association mining algorithm is **FP-Growth**. Similar to Eclat, this takes a depth-first search to count supports. However, there is no existing R package that you can download from CRAN that contains this algorithm. However, if you are interested in knowing how to apply the FP-growth algorithm in your transaction dataset, you can refer to Christian Borgelt's page at `http://www.borgelt.net/fpgrowth.html` for more information.

Creating transactions with temporal information

In addition to mining interesting associations within the transaction database, we can mine interesting sequential patterns using transactions with temporal information. In the following recipe, we will demonstrate how to create transactions with temporal information.

Getting ready

In this recipe, we will generate transactions with temporal information. We can use the generated transactions as the input source for frequent sequential pattern mining.

How to do it...

Perform the following steps to create transactions with temporal information:

1. First, you need to install and load the `arulesSequences` package:

```
> install.packages("arulesSequences")
> library(arulesSequences)
```

2. You can first create a list with purchasing records:

```
> tmp_data=list(c("A"),
+                c("A","B","C"),
+                c("A","C"),
+                c("D"),
+                c("C","F"),
+                c("A","D"),
+                c("C"),
+                c("B","C"),
+                c("A","E"),
+                c("E","F"),
+                c("A","B"),
+                c("D","F"),
+                c("C"),
+                c("B"),
+                c("E"),
+                c("G"),
+                c("A","F"),
+                c("C"),
+                c("B"),
+                c("C"))
```

3. You can then turn the list into transactions and add temporal information:

```
> names(tmp_data) = paste("Tr",c(1:20), sep = "")
> trans =  as(tmp_data,"transactions")
> transactionInfo(trans)$sequenceID=c(1,1,1,1,1,2,2,2,2,3,3,3,3,3,3,4
,4,4,4,4,4)
> transactionInfo(trans)$eventID=c(10,20,30,40,50,10,20,30,40,10,20
,30,40,50,10,20,30,40,50,60)
> trans
Output
transactions in sparse format with
 20 transactions (rows) and
 7 items (columns)
```

4. Next, you can use the `inspect` function to inspect the transactions:

```
> inspect(head(trans))
Output
  items transactionIDsequenceIDeventID
1 {A}             Tr1           1        10
2 {A,
   B,
   C}             Tr2           1        20
3 {A,
   C}             Tr3           1        30
4 {D}             Tr4           1        40
5 {C,
F}          Tr5            1      50
6 {A,
   D}             Tr6           2        10
```

5. You can then obtain the summary information of the transactions with the temporal information:

```
> summary(trans)
Output
transactions as itemMatrix in sparse format with
 20 rows (elements/itemsets/transactions) and
 7 columns (items) and a density of 0.2214286
most frequent items:
       C        A        B        F        D  (Other)
       8        7        5        4        3        4
element (itemset/transaction) length distribution:
sizes
1  2  3
10  9  1
   Min. 1st Qu.  Median   Mean 3rd Qu.    Max.
   1.00    1.00    1.50    1.55    2.00    3.00
includes extended item information - examples:
  labels
1      A
2      B
3      C
includes extended transaction information - examples:
transactionIDsequenceIDeventID
1             Tr1           1        10
2             Tr2           1        20
3             Tr3           1        30
```

6. You can also read the transaction data in a basket format:

```
> zaki=read_baskets(con = system.file("misc", "zaki.txt", package
= "arulesSequences"), info = c("sequenceID","eventID","SIZE"))
>as(zaki, "data.frame")
Output
transactionID.sequenceIDtransactionID.eventIDtransactionID.SIZE
items
1                              1                  10
2        {C,D}
2                              1                  15
3    {A,B,C}
3                              1                  20
3    {A,B,F}
4                              1                  25
4 {A,C,D,F}
5                              2                  15
3    {A,B,F}
6                              2                  20
1        {E}
7                              3                  10
3    {A,B,F}
8                              4                  10
3    {D,G,H}
9                              4                  20
2       {B,F}
10                             4                  25
3    {A,G,H}
```

How it works...

Before mining frequent sequential patterns, you are required to create transactions with the temporal information. In this recipe, we introduce two methods to obtain transactions with temporal information. In the first method, we create a list of transactions and assign a transaction ID for each transaction. We use the `as` function to transform the list data into a transaction dataset. We then add `eventID` and `sequenceID` as temporal information; `sequenceID` is the sequence that the event belongs to, and `eventID` indicates when the event occurred. After generating transactions with temporal information, one can use this dataset for frequent sequential pattern mining.

In addition to creating your own transactions with temporal information, if you already have data stored in a text file, you can use the `read_basket` function from `arulesSequences` to read the transaction data into the basket format. We can also read the transaction dataset for further frequent sequential pattern mining.

See also

- The `arulesSequences` function provides two additional data structures, `sequences` and `timedsequences`, to present pure sequence data and sequence data with time information. For those who are interested in these two collections, please use the `help` function to view the following documents:

  ```
  > help("sequences-class")
  > help("timedsequences-class")
  ```

Mining frequent sequential patterns with cSPADE

In contrast to association mining, which only discovers relationships between itemsets, we may be interested in exploring patterns shared among transactions where a set of itemsets occur sequentially.

One of the most famous frequent sequential pattern mining algorithms is the **Sequential PAttern Discovery using Equivalence Classes** (**SPADE**) algorithm, which employs the characteristics of a vertical database to perform an intersection on an ID list with an efficient lattice search and allows us to place constraints on mined sequences. In this recipe, we will demonstrate how to use cSPADE to mine frequent sequential patterns.

Getting ready

In this recipe, you have to complete the previous recipes by generating transactions with the temporal information and have it stored in the `trans` variable.

How to do it...

Perform the following steps to mine the frequent sequential patterns:

1. First, you can use the `cspade` function to generate frequent sequential patterns:

   ```
   > s_result=cspade(trans,parameter = list(support = 0.75),control =
   list(verbose = TRUE))
   ```

2. You can then examine the summary of the frequent sequential patterns:

```
> summary(s_result)
Output
set of 14 sequences with
most frequent items:
       C       A       B       D       E (Other)
       8       5       5       2       1       1
most frequent elements:
     {C}     {A}     {B}     {D}     {E} (Other)
       8       5       5       2       1       1
element (sequence) size distribution:
sizes
1 2 3
6 6 2
sequence length distribution:
lengths
1 2 3
6 6 2
summary of quality measures:
     support
 Min.    :0.7500
 1st Qu.:0.7500
 Median :0.7500
 Mean    :0.8393
 3rd Qu.:1.0000
 Max.    :1.0000
includes transaction ID lists: FALSE
mining info:
   data ntransactionsnsequences support
 trans               20           4    0.75
```

3. You then transform a generated sequence format data back to the DataFrame:

```
> as(s_result, "data.frame")
          sequence support
1             <{A}>    1.00
2             <{B}>    1.00
3             <{C}>    1.00
4             <{D}>    0.75
5             <{E}>    0.75
6             <{F}>    0.75
7        <{A},{C}>    1.00
8        <{B},{C}>    0.75
9        <{C},{C}>    0.75
10       <{D},{C}>    0.75
11 <{A},{C},{C}>    0.75
12       <{A},{B}>    1.00
```

```
13      <{C},{B}>      0.75
14  <{A},{C},{B}>      0.75
```

How it works...

The object of sequential pattern mining is to discover sequential relationships or patterns in transactions. You can use the pattern mining result to predict future events or recommend items to users.

One popular method of sequential pattern mining is SPADE. SPADE uses a vertical data layout to store a list of IDs. In these, each input sequence in the database is called SID, and each event in a given input sequence is called EID. The process of SPADE is performed by generating patterns level-wisely by an Apriori candidate generation. In detail, SPADE generates subsequent n-sequences from joining (n-1)-sequences from the intersection of ID lists. If the number of sequences is greater than the **minimum support (minsup)**, we can consider the sequence to be frequent enough. The algorithm stops until the process cannot find any more frequent sequences:

Database			Frequent Sequences (minsup=2)				
SID	**EID**	**Items**	**Frequent 1 – Sequences**			**Frequent 3 – Sequences**	
1	100	C D	A	4		ABF	3
1	150	A B C	B	4		BF->A	2
1	200	A B F	D	2		D->BF	2
1	250	A C D F	F	4		D->B->A	2
2	150	A B F				D->F->A	2
2	200	E	**Frequent 2 – Sequences**				
3	100	A B F	AB	3		**Frequent 4 – Sequences**	
4	100	D G H	AF	3		D->BF->A	2
4	200	B F	B->A	2			
4	250	A G H	BF	4			
			D->A	2			
			D->B	2			
			D->F	2			
			F->A	2			

An illustration of the SPADE algorithm

In this recipe, we illustrate how to use a frequent sequential pattern mining algorithm, cSPADE, to mine frequent sequential patterns. First, as we have transactions with temporal information loaded in the `trans` variable, we can use the `cspade` function with the support over 0.75 to generate frequent sequential patterns in the `sequences` format. We can then obtain summary information, such as most frequent items, sequence size distributions, a summary of quality measures, and mining information. Lastly, we can transform the generated `sequence` information back to the DataFrame format, so we can examine the sequence and support of frequent sequential patterns with the support over 0.75.

See also

- If you are interested in the concept and design of the SPADE algorithm, you can refer to the original published paper: M. J. Zaki. (2001). *SPADE: An Efficient Algorithm for Mining Frequent Sequences. Machine Learning Journal*, 42, 31-60.

Using the TraMineR package for sequence analysis

TraMineR stands for *Tra*jectory *Mine*r in R. It is used to explore, render, and analyze the categorical sequence data. Its primary aim is to discover insights from event or states sequences describing life courses mainly from longitudinal data. Longitudinal data refers to data that is recorded repeatedly over time. A more formal definition is *A dataset is longitudinal if it tracks the same type of information on the same subjects at multiple points in time* (http://www.caldercenter.org/whatis.cfm). Alphabet is the list of the states allowed in the sequence.

Getting ready

In this recipe, we will install the required package and have a look into longitudinal data.

How to do it...

Perform the following steps in R:

```
>install.packages("TraMineR")
> library(TraMineR)
> data("mvad")
> head(mvad)
>alphabet = seqstatl(mvad[,17:86])
Output
    [1] "employment" "FE" "HE" "joblessness" "school"
    "training"
    > fulllabel<- c("employment", "further education",
    "higher education","joblessness", "school", "training")
    > shortlabel<- c("EM", "FE", "HE", "JL", "SC", "TR")
    > seq_mvad<- seqdef(mvad[, 17:86], alphabet = alphabet,
    states = shortlabel, labels = fulllabel, weights = mvad$weight,
    xtstep = 6)
    Output
    [>] state coding:
     [alphabet] [label] [long label]
    1 employment EM employment
    2 FEFE further education
    3 HEHE higher education
    4 joblessness JL joblessness
    5 school SC school
    6 training TR training
     [>] sum of weights: 711.57 - min/max: 0.13/4.46
     [>] 712 sequences in the data set
     [>] min/max sequence length: 70/70
    > seq_mvad[1:2,]
    Output
    Sequence
    1 EM-EM-EM-EM-TR-TR-EM-EM-EM-EM-EM-EM-EM-EM-EM-EM-EM
    -EM-EM-EM-EM-EM-EM-EM-EM-EM-EM-EM-EM-EM-EM-EM-EM-EM-
    EM-EM-EM-EM-EM-EM-EM-EM-EM-EM-EM-EM-EM-EM-EM-EM-EM-EM
    -EM-EM-EM-EM-EM-EM-EM-EM-EM-EM-EM-EM-EM-EM-EM-EM-EM-EM
    2 FE-FE-FE-FE-FE-FE-FE-FE-FE-FE-FE-FE-FE-FE-FE-FE-FE-
    FE-FE-FE-FE-FE-FE-FE-FE-FE-FE-FE-FE-FE-FE-FE-FE-FE-FE-
    FE-HE-HE-HE-HE-HE-HE-HE-HE-HE-HE-HE-HE-HE-HE-HE-HE-
    HE-HE-HE-HE-HE-HE-HE-HE-HE-HE-HE-HE-HE-HE-HE-HE
    > print(seq_mvad[1:2,],format="SPS")
    Output
     Sequence
    [1] (EM,4)-(TR,2)-(EM,64)
    [2] (FE,36)-(HE,34)
```

How it works...

The `mvad` contains data about the transition from school to work. It is recorded for July 1993 to June 1999. States are `EM`, `FE`, `HE`, `JL`, `SC`, and `TR`, which indicate employment, further education, higher education, joblessness, school, and training. There are other additional variables such as male, catholic, grammar school. `Belfast` shows location of school, `funemp` shows father employment status, `fmpr` shows father's current or recent job, `livboth` shows living both parents, `gcse5eq` shows qualification gained, followed by monthly status. The data is stored in **STS** format, that is, **State Sequence format**. In STS format, each sequence is given as a row of consecutive states. We can see that using the `head` command to print the first six sequences in STS format.

Using the `seqstatl` function we find all the states. We store short labels and long labels in two different vectors. Using the `seqdef` function we create state sequence objects. Once we create the state sequence object we display the sequence in a different format, that is, STS (default) or **SPS** (**State Performance Sequence**).

Before mining frequent sequential patterns, you are required to create transactions with the temporal information. In this recipe, we introduce two methods to obtain transactions with temporal information. In the first method, we create a list of transactions, and assign a transaction ID for each transaction. We use the `as` function to transform the list data into a transaction dataset. We then add `eventID` and `sequenceID` as temporal information; `sequenceID` is the sequence that the event belongs to, and `eventID` indicates when the event occurred. After generating transactions with temporal information, one can use this dataset for frequent sequential pattern mining.

In addition to creating your own transactions with temporal information, if you already have data stored in a text file, you can use the `read_basket` function from `arulesSequences` to read the transaction data into the basket format. We can also read the transaction dataset for further frequent sequential pattern mining:

```
> help("timedsequences-class")
```

Visualizing sequence, Chronogram, and Traversal Statistics

Once we have created the state sequence object, we can visualize it to get some insights into the data.

Getting ready

In this recipe, we will visualize the state sequence objects, based on the previous recipe.

How to do it...

Perform the following steps in R:

```
> seqiplot(seq_mvad)
```

```
> seqfplot(seq_mvad)
```

```
> seqdplot(seq_mvad)
```

```
> seqmtplot(seq_mvad)
```

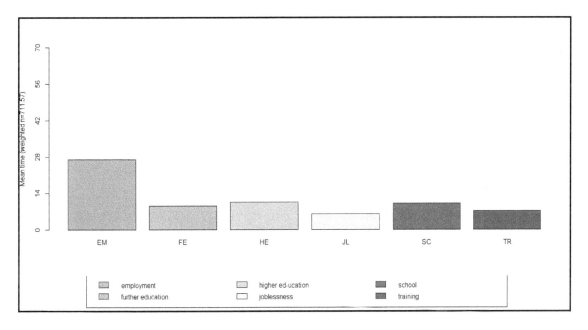

```
> seqiplot(seq_mvad, group = mvad$male)
```

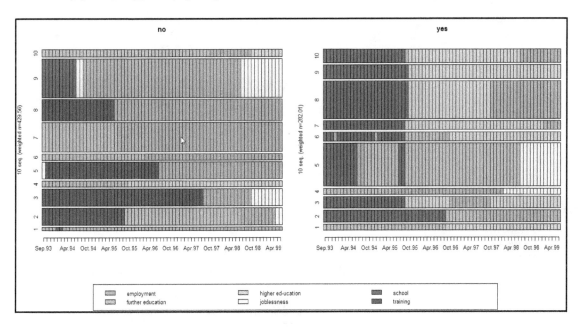

```
> seqmtplot(seq_mvad, group = mvad$male)
```

```
> seqHtplot(seq_mvad)
```

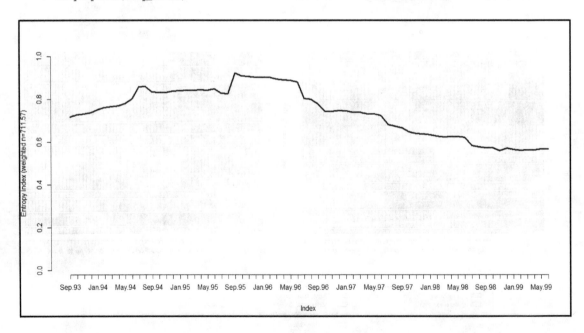

```
> seqHtplot(seq_mvad, group = mvad$male)
```

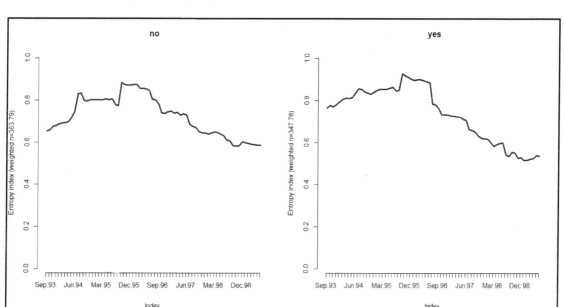

How it works...

Using different types of plots, we can now visualize the state sequence object. seqplot is a generic function for plotting the state sequence objects. Different functions will produce plots in different manners. The following is a brief description:

- seqiplot: Sequence is rendered as a horizontal stack bar showing the states over a period over time
- seqfplot: Renders the sequence in a horizontal bar, displaying the most frequent sequence
- seqdplot: Renders the sequence in cross-sectional state frequencies
- seqmtplot: Displays the mean time spent in each state
- seqHtplot: Displays the evolution over positions of the transversal entropies

When used with group argument to product the group wise plots.

See also

- Use the `help` function for `seqplot` to get more details about different types of combinations and results.

13
Dimension Reduction

In this chapter, we will cover the following topics:

- Why reduce dimension?
- Performing feature selection with `FSelector`
- Performing dimension reduction with PCA
- Determining the number of principal components using a scree test
- Determining the number of principal components using the Kaiser method
- Visualizing multivariate data using biplot
- Performing dimension reduction with MDS
- Reducing dimensions with SVD
- Compressing images with SVD
- Performing nonlinear dimension reduction with ISOMAP
- Performing nonlinear dimension deduction with Local Linear Embedding

Introduction

Most datasets contain features (such as attributes or variables) that are highly redundant. In order to remove irrelevant and redundant data to reduce the computational cost and avoid overfitting, you can reduce the features into a smaller subsets without a significant loss of information. The mathematical procedure of reducing features is known as dimension reduction. Dimension reduction is the process of converting data with large dimensions in to data will fewer relevant dimensions.

Nowadays, there has been an explosion of dataset sizes due to the continuous collection of data by sensors, cameras, GPS sensors, setup boxes, phones, and so on. With more data with many dimensions, processing has become difficult and some dimensions may not be relevant for all case studies.

Dimension reduction gives the following benefits:

- The reduction of features can increase the efficiency of data processing, as fast computation will be possible
- Data will be compressed, which reduces the storage requirements
- It improves the model performance by removing the redundant data
- It plays an important role in noise removal, improving the performance of the model

Dimension reduction is, therefore, widely used in the fields of pattern recognition, text retrieval, and machine learning. Dimension reduction can be divided into two parts: feature extraction and feature selection. Feature extraction is a technique that uses a lower dimension space to represent data in a higher dimension space. Feature selection is used to find a subset of the original variables.

The objective of feature selection is to select a set of relevant features to construct the model. The techniques for feature selection can be categorized into feature ranking and feature selection. Feature ranking ranks features with certain criteria and then selects features that are above a defined threshold. On the other hand, feature selection searches the optimal subset from a space of feature subsets.

In feature extraction, the problem can be categorized as linear or nonlinear. The linear method searches an affine space that best explains the variation of data distribution. In contrast, the nonlinear method is a better option for data that is distributed on a highly nonlinear curved surface. Here, we list some common linear and nonlinear methods.

Here are some common linear methods:

- **PCA**: Principal component analysis maps data to a lower dimension, so that the variance of the data in a low dimension representation is maximized.
- **MDS**: Multidimensional scaling is a method that allows you to visualize how near (pattern proximities) objects are to each other and can produce a representation of your data with lower dimension space. PCA can be regarded as the simplest form of MDS if the distance measurement used in MDS equals the covariance of the data.

- **SVD**: Singular value decomposition removes redundant features that are linear correlated from the perspective of linear algebra. PCA can also be regarded as a specific case of SVD.

Here are some common nonlinear methods:

- **ISOMAP**: ISOMAP can be viewed as an extension of MDS, which uses the distance metric of geodesic distances. In this method, geodesic distance is computed by graphing the shortest path distances.
- **LLE**: Locally linear embedding performs local PCA and global eigen-decomposition. LLE is a local approach, which involves selecting features for each category of the class feature. In contrast, ISOMAP is a global approach, which involves selecting features for all features.

In this chapter, we will first discuss how to perform feature ranking and selection. Next, we will focus on the topic of feature extraction and cover recipes in performing dimension reduction with both linear and nonlinear methods. For linear methods, we will look at how to perform PCA, determine the number of principal components, and discuss its visualization. We then move on to MDS and SVD. Furthermore, we will discuss the application of SVD to compress images. For nonlinear methods, we will look at how to perform dimension reduction with ISOMAP and LLE.

Why to reduce the dimension?

The following are the reasons to reduce the dimension:

1. When we have data with high dimensions, it will always add or increase the computational cost.
2. Considering all dimensions may lead to overfitting the model.
3. Not all the dimensions are required for analysis; some dimensions have not much effect.
4. Almost all data mining algorithms consider dimensions.
5. It reduces storage requirements.
6. Fewer dimensions means better visualization of data is possible.

Performing feature selection with FSelector

The FSelector package provides two approaches to select the most influential features from the original feature set. Firstly, rank features using certain criteria and select the ones that are above a defined threshold. Secondly, search for optimum feature subsets from a space of feature subsets. In this recipe, we will introduce how to perform feature selection with the FSelector package.

Getting ready

In this recipe, we will continue to use the telecom churn dataset as the input data source to train the support vector machine. For those who have not prepared the dataset, please refer to Chapter 7, *Classification 1 - Tree, Lazy, and Probabilistic*, for detailed information.

How to do it...

Perform the following steps to perform feature selection on a churn dataset:

1. First, install and load the package, FSelector:

```
> install.packages("FSelector")
> library(FSelector)
```

2. Then, we can use random.forest.importance to calculate the weight for each attribute, where we set the importance type to 1:

```
> weights = random.forest.importance(churn~., trainset,
importance.type = 1)
> print(weights)
Output
attr_importance
international_plan                       96.3255882
voice_mail_plan                          24.8921239
number_vmail_messages                    31.5420332
total_day_minutes                        51.9365357
total_day_calls                          -0.1766420
total_day_charge                         53.7930096
total_eve_minutes                        33.2006078
total_eve_calls                          -2.2270323
total_eve_charge                         32.4317375
total_night_minutes                      22.0888120
total_night_calls                         0.3407087
```

```
total_night_charge                    21.6368855
total_intl_minutes                    32.4984413
total_intl_calls                      51.1154046
total_intl_charge                     32.4855194
number_customer_service_calls        114.2566676
```

3. Next, we can use the `cutoff` function to obtain the attributes of the top five weights:

```
> subset = cutoff.k(weights, 5)
> f = as.simple.formula(subset, "Class")
> print(f)
Output
Class ~ number_customer_service_calls + international_plan +
total_day_charge + total_day_minutes + total_intl_calls
<environment: 0x00000000269a28e8>
```

4. Next, we can make an evaluator to select the feature subsets:

```
> evaluator = function(subset) {
+    k = 5
+    set.seed(2)
+    ind = sample(5, nrow(trainset), replace = TRUE)
+    results = sapply(1:k, function(i) {
+      train = trainset[ind ==i,]
+      test  = trainset[ind !=i,]
+      tree  =rpart(as.simple.formula(subset, "churn"), trainset)
+      error.rate = sum(test$churn != predict(tree, test,
type="class")) / nrow(test)
+      return(1 - error.rate)
+    })
+    return(mean(results))
+ }
```

5. Finally, we can find the optimum feature subset using a hill climbing search:

```
> attr.subset =
 hill.climbing.search(names(trainset)[!names(trainset)
%in% "churn"], evaluator)
> f = as.simple.formula(attr.subset, "churn")
> print(f)
Output
churn ~ international_plan + voice_mail_plan +
number_vmail_messages +
total_day_minutes + total_day_calls + total_eve_minutes +
total_eve_charge + total_intl_minutes + total_intl_calls +
total_intl_charge + number_customer_service_calls
<environment: 0x000000002224d3d0>
```

How it works...

In this recipe, we present how to use the `FSelector` package to select the most influential features. We first demonstrate how to use the feature ranking approach. In the feature ranking approach, the algorithm first employs a `weight` function to generate weights for each feature. Here, we use the random forest algorithm with the mean decrease in accuracy (where `importance.type = 1`) as the importance measurement to gain the weights of each attribute. Besides the random forest algorithm, you can select other feature ranking algorithms (for example, `chi.squared`, `information.gain`) from the `FSelector` package. Then, the process sorts attributes by their weight. Finally, we can obtain the top five features from the sorted feature list with the `cutoff` function. In this case, `number_customer_service_calls, international_plan, total_day_charge, total_day_minutes,` and `total_intl_calls` are the five most important features.

Next, we illustrate how to search for optimum feature subsets. First, we need to make a five-fold cross-validation function to evaluate the importance of feature subsets. Then, we use the hill climbing searching algorithm to find the optimum feature subsets from the original feature sets. Besides the hill-climbing method, one can select other feature selection algorithms (for example, `forward.search`) from the `FSelector` package. Lastly, we can find that `international_plan + voice_mail_plan + number_vmail_messages + total_day_minutes + total_day_calls + total_eve_minutes + total_eve_charge + total_intl_minutes + total_intl_calls + total_intl_charge + number_customer_service_calls` are optimum feature subsets.

See also

- You can also use the `caret` package to perform feature selection. As we have discussed related recipes in the model assessment chapter, you can refer to `Chapter 9`, *Model Evaluation*, for more detailed information.
- For both feature ranking and optimum feature selection, you can explore the package, `FSelector`, for more related functions:

    ```
    > help(package="FSelector")
    ```

Performing dimension reduction with PCA

Principal Component Analysis (PCA) is the most widely used linear method in dealing with dimension reduction problems. It is useful when data contains many features, and there is redundancy (correlation) within these features. To remove redundant features, PCA maps high dimension data into lower dimensions by reducing features into a smaller number of principal components that account for most of the variance of the original features. In this recipe, we will look at how to perform dimension reduction with the PCA method.

Getting ready

In this recipe, we will use the `swiss` dataset as our target to perform PCA. The `swiss` dataset includes standardized fertility measures and socio-economic indicators from around the year 1888 for each of the 47 French-speaking provinces of Switzerland.

How to do it...

Perform the following steps to perform principal component analysis on the `swiss` dataset:

1. First, load the `swiss` dataset:

    ```
    > data(swiss)
    ```

2. Exclude the first column of the `swiss` data:

    ```
    > swiss = swiss[,-1]
    ```

3. You can then perform principal component analysis on the `swiss` data:

    ```
    > swiss.pca = prcomp(swiss,
    + center = TRUE,
    + scale  = TRUE)
    >swiss.pca
    Output
    Standard deviations:
    [1] 1.6228065 1.0354873 0.9033447 0.5592765 0.4067472
    Rotation:
                         PC1         PC2         PC3         PC4
      PC5
    Agriculture     0.52396452 -0.25834215  0.003003672 -0.8090741
    0.06411415
    ```

```
Examination     -0.57185792 -0.01145981 -0.039840522 -0.4224580
-0.70198942
Education       -0.49150243  0.19028476  0.539337412 -0.3321615
0.56656945
Catholic         0.38530580  0.36956307  0.725888143 0.1007965
-0.42176895
Infant.Mortality 0.09167606 0.87197641 -0.424976789 -0.2154928
0.06488642
```

4. Obtain a summary from the PCA results:

```
> summary(swiss.pca)
Output
Importance of components:
                           PC1    PC2    PC3     PC4     PC5
Standard deviation      1.6228 1.0355 0.9033 0.55928 0.40675
Proportion of Variance  0.5267 0.2145 0.1632 0.06256 0.03309
Cumulative Proportion   0.5267 0.7411 0.9043 0.96691 1.00000
```

5. Lastly, you can use the `predict` function to output the value of the principal component with the first row of data:

```
> predict(swiss.pca, newdata=head(swiss, 1))
Output
                    PC1        PC2        PC3      PC4       PC5
Courtelary -0.9390479 0.8047122 -0.8118681 1.000307 0.4618643
```

How it works...

Since the feature selection method may remove some correlated but informative features, you have to consider combining these correlated features into a single feature with the feature extraction method. PCA is one of the feature extraction methods that performs orthogonal transformation to convert possibly correlated variables into principal components. Also, you can use these principal components to identify the directions of variance.

The process of PCA involves the following steps: firstly, find the mean vector, $\mu = \frac{1}{n}\sum_{i=1}^{n} x_i$ where x_i indicates the data point, and n denotes the number of points. Secondly, compute the covariance matrix using the equation, $C = \frac{1}{n}\sum_{i=1}^{n}(x_i - \mu)(x_i - \mu)^T$. Thirdly, compute the eigenvectors, φ and the corresponding eigenvalues.

In the fourth step, we rank and choose the top *k* eigenvectors. In the fifth step, we construct a *d* x *k* dimensional eigenvector matrix, U. Here, *d* is the number of original dimensions and *k* is the number of eigenvectors. Finally, we can transform data samples to a new subspace in the equation, $y = U^T \cdot x$.

The following figure illustrates that we can use two principal components, φ_1 , and φ_2 to transform the data point from a two-dimensional space to new two-dimensional subspace:

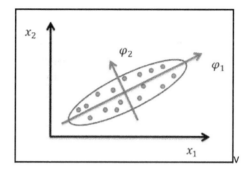

A sample illustration of PCA

In this recipe, we use the `prcomp` function from the `stats` package to perform PCA on the `swiss` dataset. First, we remove the standardized fertility measures and use the rest of the predictors as input to the function, `prcomp`. In addition to this, we set `swiss` as an input dataset; the variable should be shifted to the zero center by specifying `center=TRUE`. Scale variables into the unit variance with the option, `scale=TRUE`, and store the output in the variable, `swiss.pca`.

Then, as we print out the value stored in `swiss.pca`, we can find the standard deviation and rotation of the principal component. The standard deviation indicates the square root of the eigenvalues of the covariance/correlation matrix. On the other hand, the rotation of the principal components shows the coefficient of the linear combination of the input features. For example, PC1 equals *Agriculture * 0.524 + Examination * -0.572 + Education * -0.492 + Catholic* 0.385 + Infant.Mortality * 0.092*. Here, we can find that the attribute, *Agriculture*, contributes the most for PC1, as it has the highest coefficient.

Additionally, we can use the `summary` function to obtain the importance of components. The first row shows the standard deviation of each principal component, the second row shows the proportion of variance explained by each component, and the third row shows the cumulative proportion of the explained variance. Finally, you can use the `predict` function to obtain principal components from the input features. Here, we input the first row of the dataset, and retrieve five principal components.

There's more...

Another principal component analysis function is `princomp`. In this function, the calculation is performed by using eigen on a correlation or covariance matrix instead of a single value decomposition used in the `prcomp` function. In general practice, using `prcomp` is preferable; however, we cover how to use `princomp` here:

1. First, use `princomp` to perform PCA:

```
> swiss.princomp = princomp(swiss,
+ center = TRUE,
+ scale  = TRUE)
>swiss.princomp
Output
Call:
princomp(x = swiss, center = TRUE, scale = TRUE)
Standard deviations:
    Comp.1    Comp.2    Comp.3    Comp.4    Comp.5
42.896335 21.201887  7.587978  3.687888  2.721105
 5 variables and 47 observations.
```

2. You can then obtain the summary information:

```
> summary(swiss.princomp)
Output
Importance of components:
                            Comp.1     Comp.2     Comp.3
Comp.4        Comp.5
Standard deviation     42.8963346 21.2018868 7.58797830
3.687888330 2.721104713
Proportion of Variance  0.7770024  0.1898152 0.02431275
0.005742983 0.003126601
Cumulative Proportion   0.7770024  0.9668177 0.99113042
0.996873399 1.000000000
```

3. You can use the `predict` function to obtain principal components from the input features:

```
> predict(swiss.princomp, swiss[1,])
Output
                Comp.1    Comp.2   Comp.3   Comp.4   Comp.5
Courtelary  -38.95923 -20.40504 12.45808 4.713234 -1.46634
```

In addition to the `prcomp` and `princomp` functions from the `stats` package, you can use the `principal` function from the `psych` package:

1. First, install and load the `psych` package:

```
> install.packages("psych")
> install.packages("GPArotation")
> library(psych)
```

2. You can then use the `principal` function to retrieve the principal components:

```
> swiss.principal = principal(swiss, nfactors=5, rotate="none")
> swiss.principal
Output
Principal Components Analysis
Call: principal(r = swiss, nfactors = 5, rotate = "none")
Standardized loadings (pattern matrix) based upon correlation
matrix
                   PC1   PC2   PC3   PC4   PC5 h2        u2
Agriculture      -0.85 -0.27  0.00  0.45 -0.03  1 -6.7e-16
Examination       0.93 -0.01 -0.04  0.24  0.29  1  4.4e-16
Education         0.80  0.20  0.49  0.19 -0.23  1  2.2e-16
Catholic         -0.63  0.38  0.66 -0.06  0.17  1 -2.2e-16
Infant.Mortality -0.15  0.90 -0.38  0.12 -0.03  1 -8.9e-16
                   PC1   PC2   PC3   PC4   PC5
SS loadings       2.63  1.07  0.82  0.31  0.17
Proportion Var    0.53  0.21  0.16  0.06  0.03
Cumulative Var    0.53  0.74  0.90  0.97  1.00
Proportion Explained 0.53 0.21 0.16 0.06 0.03
Cumulative Proportion 0.53 0.74 0.90 0.97 1.00
Test of the hypothesis that 5 components are sufficient.
The degrees of freedom for the null model are 10 and the objective
function was 2.13
The degrees of freedom for the model are -5  and the objective
function was  0
The total number of observations was  47  with MLE Chi Square =  0
with prob<  NA
Fit based upon off diagonal values = 1
```

Determining the number of principal components using the scree test

As we only need to retain the principal components that account for most of the variance of the original features, we can either use the Kaiser method, scree test, or the percentage of variation explained as the selection criteria. The main purpose of a scree test is to graph the component analysis results as a scree plot and find where the obvious change in the slope (elbow) occurs. In this recipe, we will demonstrate how to determine the number of principal components using a scree plot.

Getting ready

Ensure that you have completed the previous recipe by generating a principal component object and save it in the variable, `swiss.pca`.

How to do it...

Perform the following steps to determine the number of principal components with the scree plot:

1. First, you can generate a bar plot by using `screeplot`:

    ```
    > screeplot(swiss.pca, type="barplot")
    ```

    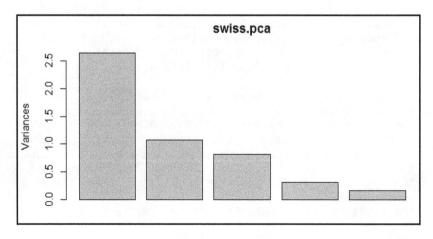

    The scree plot in bar plot form

2. You can also generate a line plot by using `screeplot`:

```
> screeplot(swiss.pca, type="line")
```

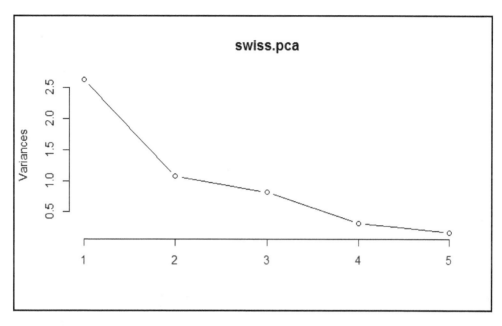

The scree plot in line plot form

How it works...

In this recipe, we demonstrate how to use a scree plot to determine the number of principal components. In a scree plot, there are two types of plots, namely, bar plots and line plots. As both generated scree plots reveal, the obvious change in slope (the so-called elbow or knee) occurs at component 2. As a result, we should retain component 1, where the component is in a steep curve before component 2, which is where the flat line trend commences. However, as this method can be ambiguous, you can use other methods (such as the Kaiser method) to determine the number of components.

There's more...

By default, if you use the `plot` function on a generated principal component object, you can also retrieve the scree plot. For more details on `screeplot`, please refer to the following document:

```
> help(screeplot)
```

You can also use `nfactors` to perform parallel analysis and non-graphical solutions to the Cattell scree test:

```
> install.packages("nFactors")
> library(nFactors)
> ev = eigen(cor(swiss))
> ap = parallel(subject=nrow(swiss),var=ncol(swiss),rep=100,cent=.05)
> nS = nScree(x=ev$values, aparallel=ap$eigen$qevpea)
> plotnScree(nS)
```

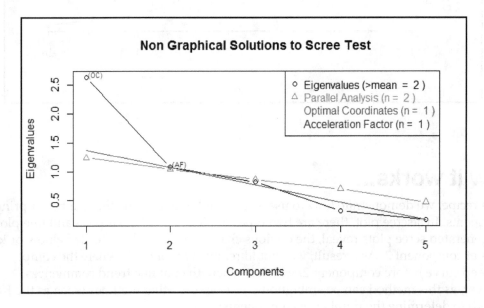

Non-graphical solution to scree test

Determining the number of principal components using the Kaiser method

In addition to the scree test, you can use the Kaiser method to determine the number of principal components. In this method, the selection criteria retains eigenvalues greater than 1. In this recipe, we will demonstrate how to determine the number of principal components using the Kaiser method.

Getting ready

Ensure that you have completed the previous recipe by generating a principal component object and save it in the variable, swiss.pca.

How to do it...

Perform the following steps to determine the number of principal components with the Kaiser method:

1. First, you can obtain the standard deviation from swiss.pca:

```
> swiss.pca$sdev
Output
[1] 1.6228065 1.0354873 0.9033447 0.5592765 0.4067472
```

2. Next, you can obtain the variance from swiss.pca:

```
> swiss.pca$sdev ^ 2
output
[1] 2.6335008 1.0722340 0.8160316 0.3127902 0.1654433
```

3. Select components with a variance above 1:

```
> which(swiss.pca$sdev ^ 2> 1)
Output
[1] 1 2
```

4. You can also use the scree plot to select components with a variance above 1:

```
> screeplot(swiss.pca, type="line")
> abline(h=1, col="red", lty= 3)
```

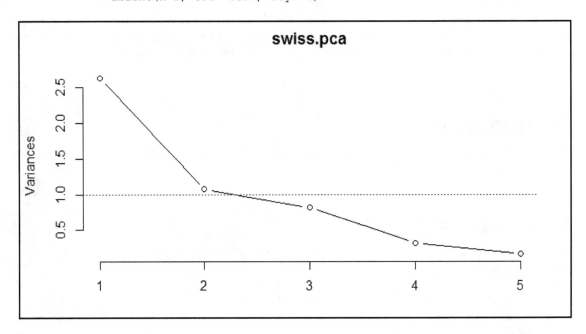

Select components with variance above 1

How it works...

You can also use the Kaiser method to determine the number of components. As the computed principal component object contains the standard deviation of each component, we can compute the variance as the standard deviation, which is the square root the of variance. From the computed variance, we find both component 1 and 2 have a variance above 1.

Therefore, we can determine the number of principal components as 2 (both component 1 and 2). Also, we can draw a red line on the scree plot (as shown in the preceding figure) to indicate that we need to retain component 1 and 2 in this case.

See also

In order to determine which principal components to retain, please refer to:

- Ledesma, R. D., and Valero-Mora, P. (2007), *Determining the Number of Factors to Retain in EFA: an easy-to-use computer program for carrying out Parallel Analysis. Practical Assessment, Research & Evaluation*, 12(2), 1-11.

Visualizing multivariate data using biplot

In order to find out how data and variables are mapped in regard to the principal component, you can use `biplot`, which plots data and the projections of original features on to the first two components. In this recipe, we will demonstrate how to use `biplot` to plot both variables and data on the same figure.

Getting ready

Ensure that you have completed the previous recipe by generating a principal component object and save it in the variable, `swiss.pca`.

How to do it...

Perform the following steps to create a biplot:

1. You can create a scatter plot using component 1 and 2:

```
> plot(swiss.pca$x[,1], swiss.pca$x[,2], xlim=c(-4,4))
> text(swiss.pca$x[,1], swiss.pca$x[,2], rownames(swiss.pca$x),
cex=0.7, pos=4, col="red")
```

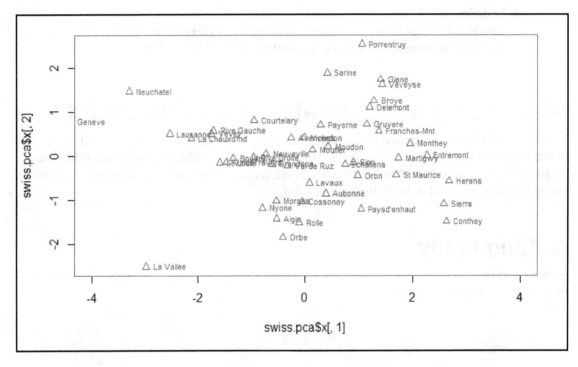

The scatter plot of first two components from PCA result

2. If you would like to add features to the plot, you can create a `biplot` using the generated principal component object:

```
> biplot(swiss.pca)
```

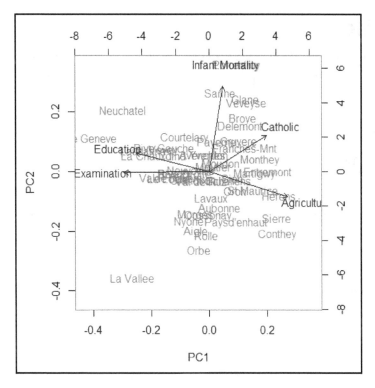

A biplot using PCA result

How it works...

In this recipe, we demonstrate how to use `biplot` to plot data and projections of original features for the first two components. In the first step, we demonstrate that we can actually use the first two components to create a scatter plot. Furthermore, if you want to add variables on the same plot, you can use `biplot`. In `biplot`, you can see the provinces with higher indicators in the agriculture variable, lower indicators in the education variable, and examination variables scores that are higher in **PC1**. On the other hand, the provinces with higher infant mortality indicators and lower agriculture indicators score higher in **PC2**.

There's more...

Besides `biplot` in the `stats` package, you can also use `ggbiplot`. However, you may not find this package in CRAN; you have to first install `devtools` and then install `ggbiplot` from GitHub:

```
> install.packages("devtools")
> library(ggbiplot)
> g = ggbiplot(swiss.pca, obs.scale = 1, var.scale = 1,
+ ellipse = TRUE,
+ circle = TRUE)
> print(g)
```

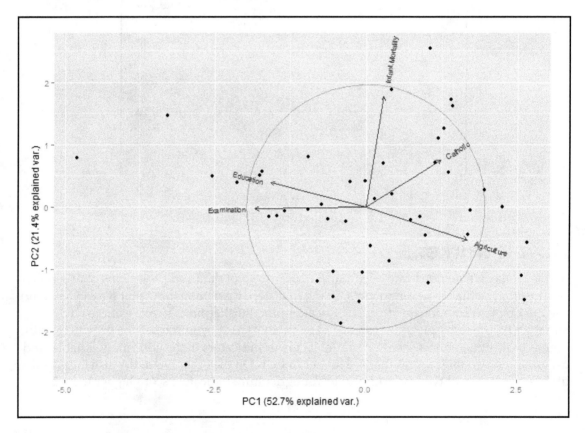

The ggbiplot using PCA result

Performing dimension reduction with MDS

Multidimensional Scaling (MDS) is a technique to create a visual presentation of similarities or dissimilarities (distance) for a number of objects. The *multi* prefix indicates that one can create a presentation map in one, two, or more dimensions. However, we most often use MDS to present the distance between data points in one or two dimensions.

In MDS, you can either use a metric or a nonmetric solution. The main difference between the two solutions is that metric solutions try to reproduce the original metric, while nonmetric solutions assume that the ranks of the distance are known. In this recipe, we will illustrate how to perform MDS on the `swiss` dataset.

Getting ready

In this recipe, we will continue using the `swiss` dataset as our input data source.

How to do it...

Perform the following steps to perform multidimensional scaling using the metric method:

1. First, you can perform metric MDS with a maximum of two dimensions:

```
> swiss.dist =dist(swiss)
> swiss.mds = cmdscale(swiss.dist, k=2)
```

2. You can then plot the `swiss` data in a two-dimension scatter plot:

```
> plot(swiss.mds[,1], swiss.mds[,2], type = "n", main = "cmdscale
(stats)")
> text(swiss.mds[,1], swiss.mds[,2], rownames(swiss), cex = 0.9,
xpd = TRUE)
```

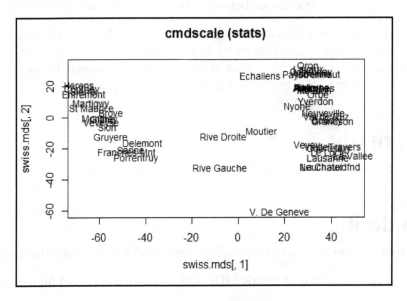

The two-dimension scatter plot from cmdscale object

3. In addition, you can perform nonmetric MDS with `isoMDS`:

```
> library(MASS)
> swiss.nmmds = isoMDS(swiss.dist, k=2)
initial   value 2.979731
iter    5 value 2.431486
iter   10 value 2.343353
final   value 2.338839
converged
```

4. You can also plot the data points in a two-dimension scatter plot:

```
> plot(swiss.nmmds$points, type = "n", main = "isoMDS (MASS)")
> text(swiss.nmmds$points, rownames(swiss), cex = 0.9, xpd = TRUE)
```

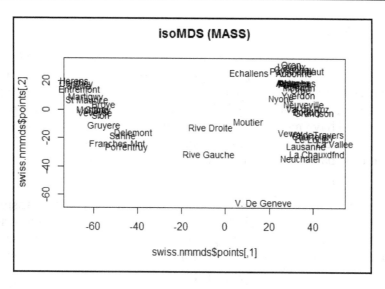

The two-dimension scatter plot from isoMDS object

5. You can then plot the data points in a two-dimension scatter plot:

```
> swiss.sh = Shepard(swiss.dist, swiss.mds)
> plot(swiss.sh, pch = ".")
> lines(swiss.sh$x, swiss.sh$yf, type = "S")
```

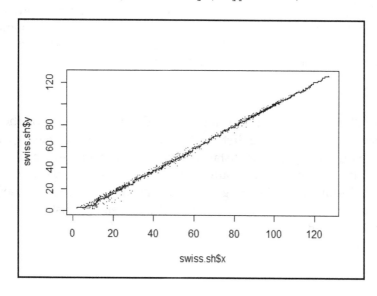

The Shepard plot from isoMDS object

How it works...

MDS reveals the structure of the data by providing a visual presentation of similarities among a set of objects. In more detail, MDS places an object in an n-dimensional space, where the distances between pairs of points corresponds to the similarities among the pairs of objects. Usually, the dimensional space is a two-dimensional Euclidean space, but it may be non-Euclidean and have more than two dimensions. In accordance with the meaning of the input matrix, MDS can be mainly categorized into two types: metric MDS, where the input matrix is metric-based, and nonmetric MDS, where the input matrix is nonmetric-based.

Metric MDS is also known as principal coordinate analysis, which first transforms a distance into similarities. In the simplest form, the process linearly projects original data points to a subspace by performing principal components analysis on similarities. On the other hand, the process can also perform a nonlinear projection on similarities by minimizing the stress value, $S = \sum_{k \neq l} \left[d(k,l) - d'(k,l) \right]^2$ where $d(k,l)$ is the distance measurement between the two points, x_k and x_l, and $d'(k,l)$ is the similarity measure of two projected points, x'_k and x'_l as a result, we can represent the relationship among objects in the Euclidean space.

In contrast to metric MDS, which uses a metric-based input matrix, a nonmetric-based MDS is used when the data is measured at the ordinal level. As only the rank order of the distances between the vectors is meaningful, nonmetric MDS applies a monotonically increasing function, f, on the original distances and projects the distance to new values that preserve the rank order. The normalized equation can be formulated as

$$S = \frac{1}{\sum_{k \neq l} \left[d'(k,l) \right]^2} \sum_{k \neq l} \left[f(d(k,l)) - d'(k,l) \right]^2 .$$

In this recipe, we illustrate how to perform metric and nonmetric MDS on the `swiss` dataset. To perform metric MDS, we first need to obtain the distance metric from the `swiss` data. In this step, you can replace the distance measure to any measure as long as it produces a similarity/dissimilarity measure of data points. You can use `cmdscale` to perform metric multidimensional scaling. Here, we specify k = 2, so the maximum generated dimensions equals 2. You can also visually present the distance of the data points on a two-dimensional scatter plot.

Next, you can perform nonmetric MDS with `isoMDS`. In nonmetric MDS, we do not match the distances, but only arrange them in order. We also set `swiss` as an input dataset with maximum dimensions of two. Similar to the metric MDS example, we can plot the distance between data points on a two-dimensional scatter plot. Then, we use a Shepard plot, which shows how well the projected distances match those in the distance matrix. As per the figure in step 4, the projected distance matches well in the distance matrix.

There's more...

Another visualization method is to present an MDS object as a graph. A sample code is listed here:

```
> library(igraph)
> swiss.sample = swiss[1:10,]
> g = graph.full(nrow(swiss.sample))
> V(g)$label = rownames(swiss.sample)
> layout = layout.mds(g, dist = as.matrix(dist(swiss.sample)))
> plot(g, layout = layout, vertex.size = 3)
```

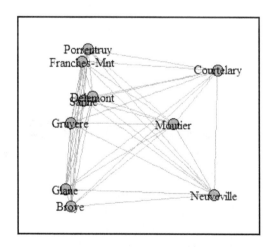

The graph presentation of MDS object

You can also compare differences between the generated results from MDS and PCA. You can compare their differences by drawing the projected dimensions on the same scatter plot. If you use a Euclidean distance on MDS, the projected dimensions are exactly the same as the ones projected from PCA:

```
> swiss.dist = dist(swiss)
> swiss.mds = cmdscale(swiss.dist, k=2)
> plot(swiss.mds[,1], swiss.mds[,2], type="n")
```

```
> text(swiss.mds[,1], swiss.mds[,2], rownames(swiss), cex = 0.9, xpd =
TRUE)
> swiss.pca = prcomp(swiss)
> text(-swiss.pca$x[,1],-swiss.pca$x[,2], rownames(swiss),
+        ,col="blue", adj = c(0.2,-0.5),cex = 0.9, xpd = TRUE)
```

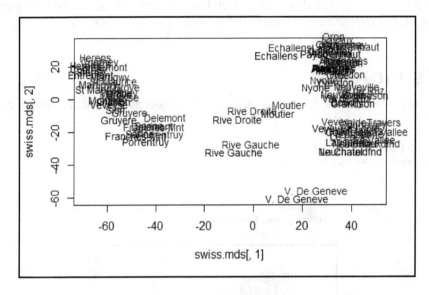

The comparison between MDS and PCA

Reducing dimensions with SVD

Singular Value Decomposition (SVD) is a type of matrix factorization (decomposition), which can factorize matrices into two orthogonal matrices and diagonal matrices. You can multiply the original matrix back using these three matrices. SVD can reduce redundant data that is linear dependent from the perspective of linear algebra. Therefore, it can be applied to feature selection, image processing, clustering, and many other fields. In this recipe, we will illustrate how to perform dimension reduction with SVD.

Getting ready

In this recipe, we will continue using the dataset, `swiss`, as our input data source.

How to do it...

Perform the following steps to perform dimension reduction using SVD:

1. First, you can perform `svd` on the `swiss` dataset:

   ```
   > swiss.svd = svd(swiss)
   ```

2. You can then plot the percentage of variance explained and the cumulative variance explained in accordance with the SVD column:

   ```
   > plot(swiss.svd$d^2/sum(swiss.svd$d^2), type="l", xlab=" Singular
   vector", ylab = "Variance explained")
   ```

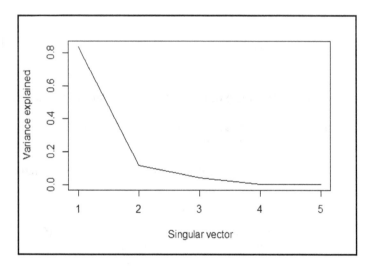

The percent of variance explained

```
> plot(cumsum(swiss.svd$d^2/sum(swiss.svd$d^2)), type="l",
xlab="Singular vector", ylab = "Cumulative percent of variance
explained")
```

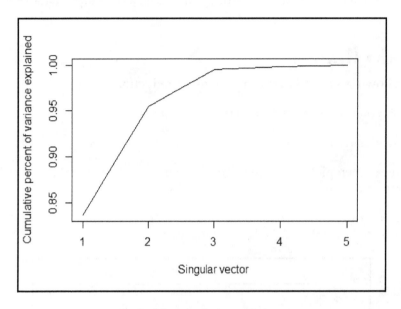

Cumulative percent of variance explained

3. Next, you can reconstruct the data with only one singular vector:

```
> swiss.recon = swiss.svd$u[,1] %*% diag(swiss.svd$d[1], length(1),
length(1)) %*% t(swiss.svd$v[,1])
```

4. Lastly, you can compare the original dataset with the constructed dataset in an image:

```
> par(mfrow=c(1,2))
> image(as.matrix(swiss), main="swiss data Image")
> image(swiss.recon,  main="Reconstructed Image")
```

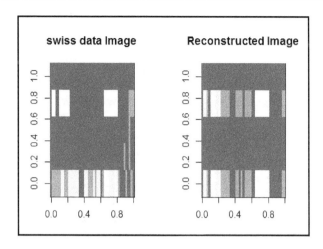

The comparison between original dataset and re-constructed dataset

How it works...

SVD is a factorization of a real or complex matrix. In detail, the SVD of *m x n* matrix, *A*, is the factorization of *A* into the product of three matrices, $A = UDV^T$. Here, *U* is an *m x m* orthonormal matrix, *D* has singular values and is an *m x n* diagonal matrix, and V^T is an *n x n* orthonormal matrix.

In this recipe, we demonstrate how to perform dimension reduction with SVD. First, you can apply the svd function on the swiss dataset to obtain factorized matrices. You can then generate two plots: one shows the variance explained in accordance to a singular vector, the other shows the cumulative variance explained in accordance to a singular vector.

The preceding figure shows that the first singular vector can explain 80 percent of variance. We now want to compare the differences from the original dataset and the reconstructed dataset with a single singular vector. We, therefore, reconstruct the data with a single singular vector and use the image function to present the original and reconstructed datasets side-by-side and see how they differ from each other. The next figure reveals that these two images are very similar.

See also

- As we mentioned earlier, PCA can be regarded as a specific case of SVD. Here, we generate the orthogonal vector from the `swiss` data from SVD and obtain the rotation from `prcomp`. We can see that the two generated matrices are the same:

```
> svd.m = svd(scale(swiss))
> svd.m$v
Output
              [,1]         [,2]         [,3]         [,4]         [,5]
[1,]   0.52396452 -0.25834215  0.003003672 -0.8090741  0.06411415
[2,]  -0.57185792 -0.01145981 -0.039840522 -0.4224580 -0.70198942
[3,]  -0.49150243  0.19028476  0.539337412 -0.3321615  0.56656945
[4,]   0.38530580  0.36956307  0.725888143  0.1007965 -0.42176895
[5,]   0.09167606  0.87197641 -0.424976789 -0.2154928  0.06488642
> pca.m = prcomp(swiss,scale=TRUE)
> pca.m$rotation
 Output
                        PC1          PC2          PC3          PC4
 PC5
Agriculture      0.52396452 -0.25834215  0.003003672 -0.8090741
0.06411415
Examination     -0.57185792 -0.01145981 -0.039840522 -0.4224580
-0.70198942
Education       -0.49150243  0.19028476  0.539337412 -0.3321615
0.56656945
Catholic         0.38530580  0.36956307  0.725888143  0.1007965
-0.42176895
Infant.Mortality 0.09167606 0.87197641 -0.424976789 -0.2154928
0.06488642
```

Compressing images with SVD

In the previous recipe, we demonstrated how to factorize a matrix with SVD and then reconstruct the dataset by multiplying the decomposed matrix. Furthermore, the application of matrix factorization can be applied to image compression. In this recipe, we will demonstrate how to perform SVD on the classic image processing material, Lenna.

Getting ready

In this recipe, you should download the image of Lenna beforehand (refer to `http://www.ece.rice.edu/~wakin/images/lena512.bmp` for this), or you can prepare an image of your own to see how image compression works.

How to do it...

Perform the following steps to compress an image with SVD:

1. First, install and load `bmp`:

   ```
   > install.packages("bmp")
   > library(bmp)
   ```

2. You can then read the image of Lenna as a numeric matrix with the `read.bmp` function. When the reader downloads the image, the default name is `lena512.bmp`:

   ```
   > lenna = read.bmp("lena512.bmp")
   ```

3. Rotate and plot the image:

   ```
   > lenna = t(lenna)[,nrow(lenna):1]
   > image(lenna)
   ```

The picture of Lenna

4. Next, you can perform SVD on the read numeric matrix and plot the percentage of variance explained:

```
> lenna.svd = svd(scale(lenna))
> plot(lenna.svd$d^2/sum(lenna.svd$d^2), type="l", xlab="
Singular
vector", ylab = "Variance explained")
```

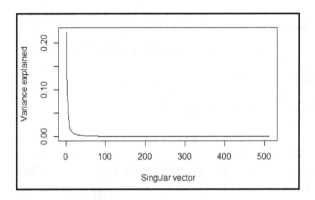

The percentage of variance explained

5. Next, you can obtain the number of dimensions to reconstruct the image:

```
> length(lenna.svd$d)
Output
[1] 512
```

6. Obtain the point at which the singular vector can explain more than 90 percent of the variance:

```
> min(which(cumsum(lenna.svd$d^2/sum(lenna.svd$d^2))> 0.9))
Output
[1] 18
```

7. You can also wrap the code into a function, `lenna_compression`, and you can then use this function to plot the compressed Lenna:

```
> lenna_compression = function(dim){
+        u=as.matrix(lenna.svd$u[, 1:dim])
+        v=as.matrix(lenna.svd$v[, 1:dim])
+        d=as.matrix(diag(lenna.svd$d)[1:dim, 1:dim])
+        image(u%*%d%*%t(v))
+ }
```

8. Also, you can use 18 vectors to reconstruct the image:

```
> lenna_compression(18)
```

The reconstructed image with 18 components

9. You can obtain the point at which the singular vector can explain more than 99 percent of the variance:

```
> min(which(cumsum(lenna.svd$d^2/sum(lenna.svd$d^2))> 0.99))
Output
[1] 92
> lenna_compression(92)
```

The reconstructed image with 92 components

How it works...

In this recipe, we demonstrate how to compress an image with SVD. In the first step, we use the package, `bmp`, to load the image, Lenna, to an R session. Then, as the read image is rotated, we can rotate the image back and use the `plot` function to plot Lenna in R (as shown in the figure in step 3). Next, we perform SVD on the image matrix to factorize the matrix. We then plot the percentage of variance explained in regard to the number of singular vectors.

Further, as we discover that we can use 18 components to explain 90 percent of the variance, we then use these 18 components to reconstruct Lenna. Thus, we make a function named `lenna_compression` with the purpose of reconstructing the image by matrix multiplication. As a result, we enter 18 as the input to the function, which returns a rather blurry Lenna image (as shown in the figure in *step 8*). However, we can at least see an outline of the image. To obtain a clearer picture, we discover that we can use 92 components to explain 99 percent of the variance. We, therefore, set the input to the function, `lenna_compression`, as 92. The figure in step 9 shows that this generates a clearer picture than the one constructed using merely 18 components.

See also

- The Lenna picture is one of the most widely used standard test images for compression algorithms. For more details on the Lenna picture, please refer to `http://www.cs.cmu.edu/~chuck/lennapg/`.

Performing nonlinear dimension reduction with ISOMAP

ISOMAP is one of the approaches for manifold learning, which generalizes linear framework to nonlinear data structures. Similar to MDS, ISOMAP creates a visual presentation of similarities or dissimilarities (distance) of a number of objects. However, as the data is structured in a nonlinear format, the Euclidian distance measure of MDS is replaced by the geodesic distance of a data manifold in ISOMAP. In this recipe, we will illustrate how to perform a nonlinear dimension reduction with ISOMAP.

Getting ready

In this recipe, we will use the `digits` data from `RnavGraphImageData` as our input source.

How to do it...

Perform the following steps to perform nonlinear dimension reduction with ISOMAP:

1. First, install and load the `RnavGraphImageData` and `vegan` packages:

```
> install.packages("RnavGraphImageData")
> install.packages("vegan")
> library(RnavGraphImageData)
> library(vegan)
```

2. You can then load the dataset, `digits`:

```
> data(digits)
```

3. Rotate and plot the image:

```
> sample.digit = matrix(digits[,3000],ncol = 16, byrow=FALSE)
> image(t(sample.digit)[,nrow(sample.digit):1])
```

A sample image from the digits dataset

4. Next, you can randomly sample 300 digits from the population:

```
> set.seed(2)
> digit.idx = sample(1:ncol(digits),size = 600)
> digit.select = digits[,digit.idx]
```

5. Transpose the selected digit data and then compute the dissimilarity between objects using `vegdist`:

```
> digits.Transpose = t(digit.select)
> digit.dist = vegdist(digits.Transpose, method="euclidean")
```

6. Next, you can use `isomap` to perform dimension reduction:

```
> digit.isomap = isomap(digit.dist,k = 8, ndim=6, fragmentedOK
= TRUE)
> plot(digit.isomap)
```

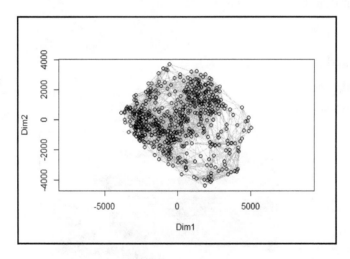

A two-dimension scatter plot from ISOMAP object

7. Finally, you can overlay the scatter plot with the minimum spanning tree, marked in red:

```
> digit.st = spantree(digit.dist)
> digit.plot = plot(digit.isomap, main="isomap k=8")
> lines(digit.st, digit.plot, col="red")
```

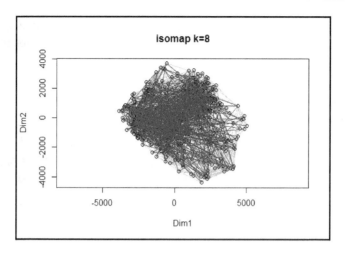

A two-dimension scatter plot overlay with minimum spanning tree

How it works...

ISOMAP is a nonlinear dimension reduction method and a representative of isometric mapping methods. ISOMAP can be regarded as an extension of the metric MDS, where pairwise, the Euclidean distance among data points is replaced by geodesic distances induced by a neighborhood graph.

The description of the ISOMAP algorithm is shown in four steps. First, determine the neighbor of each point. Secondly, construct a neighborhood graph. Thirdly, compute the shortest distance path between two nodes. Finally, find a low dimension embedding of the data by performing MDS.

In this recipe, we demonstrate how to perform a nonlinear dimension reduction using ISOMAP. First, we load the digits data from `RnavGraphImageData`. Then, after we select one digit and plot its rotated image, we can see an image of the handwritten digit (the numeral 3, in the figure in *step 3*).

Next, we randomly sample 300 digits as our input data to ISOMAP. We then transpose the dataset to calculate the distance between each image object. Once the data is ready, we calculate the distance between each object and perform a dimension reduction. Here, we use `vegdist` to calculate the dissimilarities between each object using a Euclidean measure. We then use ISOMAP to perform a nonlinear dimension reduction on the `digits` data with the dimension set as 6 and the number of shortest dissimilarities retained for a point as 8, and ensure that you analyze the largest connected group by specifying `fragmentedOK` as TRUE.

Finally, we can use the generated ISOMAP object to make a two-dimension scatter plot (figure in *step 6*), and also overlay the minimum spanning tree with lines in red on the scatter plot (figure in *step 7*).

There's more...

You can also use the `RnavGraph` package to visualize high dimensional data (digits in this case) using graphs as a navigational infrastructure. For more information, please refer to `http://www.icesi.edu.co/CRAN/web/packages/RnavGraph/vignettes/RnavGraph.pdf`.

Here is a description of how you can use `RnavGraph` to visualize high dimensional data in a graph:

1. First, install and load the `RnavGraph` and `graph` packages:

```
> install.packages("RnavGraph")
> source("http://bioconductor.org/biocLite.R")
> biocLite("graph")
> library(RnavGraph)
```

2. You can then create an `NG_data` object from the `digit` data:

```
> digit.group = rep(c(1:9,0), each = 1100)
> digit.ng_data = ng_data(name = "ISO_digits",
+ data = data.frame(digit.isomap$points),
+ shortnames = paste('i',1:6, sep = ''),
+ group = digit.group[digit.idx],
+ labels = as.character(digits.group[digit.idx]))
```

3. Create an `NG_graph` object from `NG_data`:

```
>  V = shortnames(digit.ng_data)
>  G = completegraph(V)
>  LG =linegraph(G)
> LGnot = complement(LG)
> ng.LG = ng_graph(name = "3D Transition", graph = LG)
> ng.LGnot = ng_graph(name = "4D Transition", graph = LGnot)
```

4. Finally, you can visualize the graph in the `tk2d` plot:

```
> ng.i.digits = ng_image_array_gray('USPS Handwritten Digits',
+ digit.select,16,16,invert = TRUE,
+ img_in_row = FALSE)
> vizDigits1 = ng_2d(data = digit.ng_data, graph = ng.LG, images
 = ng.i.digits)
> vizDigits2 = ng_2d(data = digit.ng_data, graph = ng.LGnot, images
 = ng.i.digits)
> nav = navGraph(data = digit.ng_data, graph
 = list(ng.LG, ng.LGnot), viz = list(vizDigits1, vizDigits2))
```

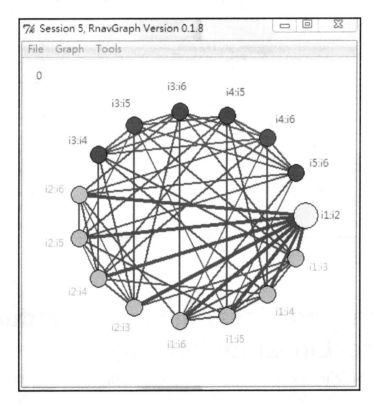

A 3D transition graph plot

5. One can also view a 4D transition graph plot:

A 4D transition graph plot

Performing nonlinear dimension reduction with Local Linear Embedding

Local Linear Embedding (LLE) is an extension of PCA, which reduces data that lies on a manifold embedded in a high dimensional space into a low dimensional space. In contrast to ISOMAP, which is a global approach for nonlinear dimension reduction, LLE is a local approach that employs a linear combination of the k-nearest neighbor to preserve local properties of data. In this recipe, we will give a short introduction of how to use LLE for s-curve data.

Getting ready

In this recipe, we will use digit data from `lle_scurve_data` within the `lle` package as our input source.

How to do it...

Perform the following steps to perform nonlinear dimension reduction with LLE:

1. First, you need to install and load the package, `lle`:

   ```
   > install.packages("lle")
   > library(lle)
   ```

2. You can then load `ll_scurve_data` from `lle`:

   ```
   > data( lle_scurve_data )
   ```

3. Next, perform `lle` on `lle_scurve_data`:

   ```
   > X = lle_scurve_data
   > results = lle( X=X , m=2, k=12,  id=TRUE)
   Output
   finding neighbours
   calculating weights
   intrinsic dim: mean=2.47875, mode=2
   computing coordinates
   ```

4. Examine the result with the `str` and `plot` function:

   ```
   > str( results )
   Output
   List of 4
    $ Y     :num [1:800, 1:2] -1.586 -0.415 0.896 0.513 1.477 ...
    $ X     :num [1:800, 1:3] 0.955 -0.66 -0.983 0.954 0.958 ...
    $ choise: NULL
    $ id    :num [1:800] 3 3 2 3 2 2 2 3 3 3 ...
   > plot( results$Y, main="embedded data", xlab=expression(y[1]),
   ylab=expression(y[2]) )
   ```

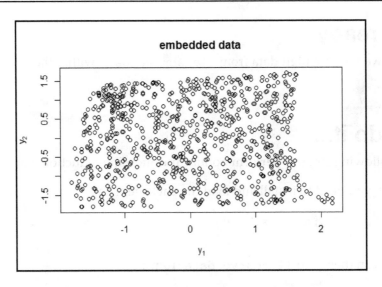

A 2-D scatter plot of embedded data

5. Lastly, you can use `plot_lle` to plot the LLE result:

```
> plot_lle( results$Y, X, FALSE, col="red", inter=TRUE )
```

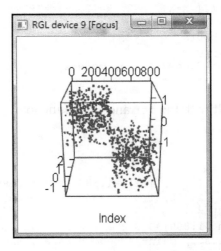

A LLE plot of LLE result

How it works...

LLE is a nonlinear dimension reduction method, which computes a low dimensional neighborhood, preserving embeddings of high dimensional data. The algorithm of LLE can be illustrated in these steps: first, LLE computes the k-neighbors of each data point. Secondly, it computes a set of weights for each point, which minimizes the residual sum of errors, which can best reconstruct each data point from its neighbors. The residual sum of errors can be described as $RSS(w) = \sum_{i=1}^{n} \left\| x_i - \sum_{j \neq i} w_{ij} x_j \right\|^2$, where $w_{ij} = 0$ if x_j is not one of x_i's k-nearest neighbor, and for each i, $\sum_i w_{ij} = 1$. Finally, find the vector, Y, which is best reconstructed by the weight, W. The cost function can be illustrated as

$$\varphi(Y) = \sum_{i=1}^{n} \left\| y_i - \sum_{j \neq i} w_{ij} y_j \right\|^2$$, with the constraint that $\sum_i Y_{ij} = 0$, and $Y^T Y = I$.

In this recipe, we demonstrate how to perform nonlinear dimension reduction using LLE. First, we load `lle_scurve_data` from `lle`. We then perform `lle` with two dimensions and 12 neighbors, and list the dimensions for every data point by specifying `id` =TRUE. The LLE has three steps, including: building a neighborhood for each point in the data, finding the weights for linearly approximating the data in that neighborhood, and finding the low dimensional coordinates.

Next, we can examine the data using the `str` and `plot` functions. The `str` function returns X,Y, choice, and ID. Here, X represents the input data, Y stands for the embedded data, choice indicates the index vector of the kept data, while subset selection and ID show the dimensions of every data input. The `plot` function returns the scatter plot of the embedded data. Lastly, we use `plot_lle` to plot the result. Here, we enable the interaction mode by setting the inter equal to TRUE.

See also

- Another useful package for nonlinear dimension reduction is RDRToolbox, which is a package for nonlinear dimension reduction with ISOMAP and LLE. You can use the following command to install RDRToolbox:

```
> source("http://bioconductor.org/biocLite.R")
> biocLite("RDRToolbox")
> library(RDRToolbox)
```

14
Big Data Analysis (R and Hadoop)

In this chapter, we will cover the following topics:

- Preparing the RHadoop environment
- Installing `rmr2`
- Installing `rhdfs`
- Operating HDFS with `rhdfs`
- Implementing a word count problem with RHadoop
- Comparing the performance between an R MapReduce program and a standard R program
- Testing and debugging the `rmr2` program
- Installing `plyrmr`
- Manipulating data with `plyrmr`
- Conducting machine learning with RHadoop
- Configuring RHadoop clusters on Amazon EMR

Introduction

RHadoop is a collection of R packages that enables users to process and analyze big data with Hadoop. Before understanding how to set up RHadoop and put it in to practice, we have to know why we need to use machine learning to scale big-data.

In the previous chapters, we have mentioned how useful R is when performing data analysis and machine learning. In traditional statistical analysis, the focus is on performing analysis on historical samples (small data), which may ignore rarely occurring but valuable events and results to uncertain conclusions.

The emergence of cloud technology has made real-time interaction between customers and businesses much more frequent; therefore, the focus of machine learning has now shifted to the development of accurate predictions for various customers. For example, businesses can provide real-time personal recommendations or online advertisements based on personal behavior via the use of a real-time prediction model.

However, if the data (for example, behaviors of all online users) is too large to fit in the memory of a single machine, you have no choice but to use a supercomputer or some other scalable solution. The most popular scalable big-data solution is Hadoop, which is an open source framework able to store and perform parallel computations across clusters. As a result, you can use RHadoop, which allows R to leverage the scalability of Hadoop, helping to process and analyze big data. In RHadoop, there are five main packages, which are:

- `rmr`: This is an interface between R and Hadoop MapReduce, which calls the Hadoop streaming MapReduce API to perform MapReduce jobs across Hadoop clusters. To develop an R MapReduce program, you only need to focus on the design of the map and reduce functions, and the remaining scalability issues will be taken care of by Hadoop itself.
- `rhdfs`: This is an interface between R and HDFS, which calls the HDFS API to access the data stored in HDFS. The use of `rhdfs` is very similar to the use of the Hadoop shell, which allows users to manipulate HDFS easily from the R console.
- `rhbase`: This is an interface between R and HBase, which accesses Hbase and is distributed in clusters through a Thrift server. You can use `rhbase` to read/write data and manipulate tables stored within HBase.

- `plyrmr`: This is a higher-level abstraction of MapReduce, which allows users to perform common data manipulation in a plyr-like syntax. This package greatly lowers the learning curve of big data manipulation.
- `ravro`: This allows users to read `avro` files in R, or write `avro` files. It allows R to exchange data with HDFS.

In this chapter, we will start by preparing the Hadoop environment, so that you can install RHadoop. We then cover the installation of three main packages: `rmr`, `rhdfs`, and `plyrmr`. Next, we will introduce how to use `rmr` to perform MapReduce from R, operate an HDFS file through `rhdfs`, and perform a common data operation using `plyrmr`. Further, we will explore how to perform machine learning using RHadoop. Lastly, we will look at how to deploy multiple RHadoop clusters on Amazon EC2.

Preparing the RHadoop environment

As RHadoop requires an R and Hadoop integrated environment, we must first prepare an environment with both R and Hadoop installed. Instead of building a new Hadoop system, we can use the **Cloudera QuickStart VM** (the VM is free), which contains a single node Apache Hadoop Cluster and R. In this recipe, we will demonstrate how to download the Cloudera QuickStart VM.

Getting ready

To use the Cloudera QuickStart VM, it is suggested that you should prepare a 64-bit guest OS with either VMWare, VirtualBox, or the KVM installed.

If you choose to use VMWare, you should prepare a player compatible with WorkStation 8.x or higher: Player 4.x or higher, ESXi 5.x or higher, or Fusion 4.x or higher.

Note, 4 GB of RAM is required to start VM, with an available disk space of at least 3 GB.

How to do it...

Perform the following steps to set up a Hadoop environment using the Cloudera QuickStart VM:

1. Visit the Cloudera QuickStart VM download site (you may need to update the link as Cloudera upgrades its VMs; the current version of CDH is 5.3) at `http://www.cloudera.com/content/cloudera/en/downloads/quickstart_vms/cdh-5-3-x.html`:

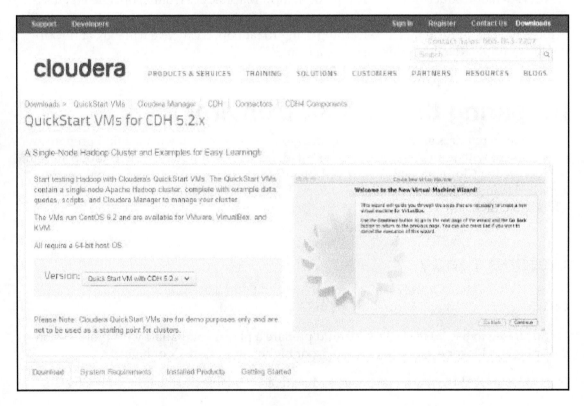

A screenshot of the Cloudera QuickStart VM download site

2. Depending on the virtual machine platform installed on your OS, choose the appropriate link (you may need to update the link as Cloudera upgrades its VMs) to download the VM file:

- **To download VMWare**: You can visit
  https://downloads.cloudera.com/demo_vm/vmware/cloudera-quicks
  tart-vm-5.2.0-0-vmware.7z

- **To download KVM**: You can visit
  https://downloads.cloudera.com/demo_vm/kvm/cloudera-quickstar
  t-vm-5.2.0-0-kvm.7z

- **To download VirtualBox**: You can visit
  https://downloads.cloudera.com/demo_vm/virtualbox/cloudera-qu
  ickstart-vm-5.2.0-0-virtualbox.7z

3. Next, you can start the QuickStart VM using the virtual machine platform installed on your OS. You should see the desktop of Centos 6.2 in a few minutes:

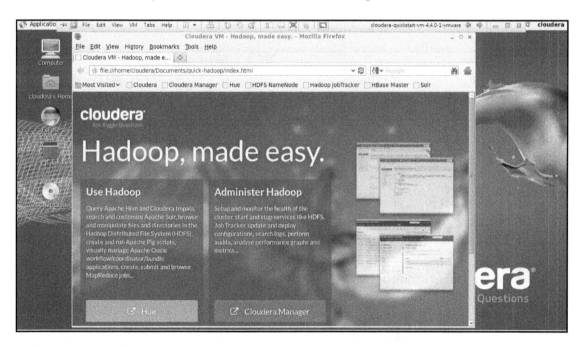

The screenshot of Cloudera QuickStart VM.

4. You can then open a terminal and type `hadoop`, which will display a list of functions that can operate a Hadoop cluster:

```
[cloudera@quickstart ~]$ hadoop
Usage: hadoop [--config confdir] COMMAND
       where COMMAND is one of:
  fs                    run a generic filesystem user client
  version               print the version
  jar <jar>             run a jar file
  checknative [-a|-h]   check native hadoop and compression libraries availa
bility
  distcp <srcurl> <desturl> copy file or directories recursively
  archive -archiveName NAME -p <parent path> <src>* <dest> create a hadoop
archive
  classpath             prints the class path needed to get the
                        Hadoop jar and the required libraries
  daemonlog             get/set the log level for each daemon
 or
  CLASSNAME             run the class named CLASSNAME

Most commands print help when invoked w/o parameters.
[cloudera@quickstart ~]$ ▐
```

The terminal screenshot after typing hadoop

5. Open a terminal and type `R`. Access an R session and check whether version 3.1.1 is already installed in the Cloudera QuickStart VM. If you cannot find R installed in the VM, please use the following command to install R:

```
$ yum install R R-core R-core-devel R-devel
```

How it works...

Instead of building a Hadoop system on your own, you can use the Hadoop VM application provided by Cloudera (the VM is free). The QuickStart VM runs on CentOS 6.2 with a single node Apache Hadoop cluster, Hadoop Ecosystem module, and R installed. This helps you to save time, instead of requiring you to learn how to install and use Hadoop.

The QuickStart VM requires you to have a computer with a 64-bit guest OS, at least 4 GB of RAM, 3 GB of disk space, and either VMWare, VirtualBox, or KVM installed. As a result, you may not be able to use this version of VM on some computers. As an alternative, you could consider using Amazon's Elastic MapReduce instead. We will illustrate how to prepare a RHadoop environment in EMR in the last recipe of this chapter.

Setting up the Cloudera QuickStart VM is simple. Download the VM from the download site and then open the built image with either VMWare, VirtualBox, or KVM. Once you can see the desktop of CentOS, you can then access the terminal and type `hadoop` to see whether Hadoop is working; then, type `R` to see whether R works in the QuickStart VM.

See also

- Besides using the Cloudera QuickStart VM, you may consider using a Sandbox VM provided by Hontonworks or MapR. You can find Hontonworks Sandbox at `http://hortonworks.com/products/hortonworks-sandbox/#install` and mapR Sandbox at `https://www.mapr.com/products/mapr-sandbox-hadoop/download`.

Installing rmr2

The `rmr2` package allows you to perform big data processing and analysis via MapReduce on a Hadoop cluster. To perform MapReduce on a Hadoop cluster, you have to install R and `rmr2` on every task node. In this recipe, we will illustrate how to install `rmr2` on a single node of a Hadoop cluster.

Getting ready

Ensure that you have completed the previous recipe by starting the Cloudera QuickStart VM and connecting the VM to the internet, so that you can proceed with downloading and installing the `rmr2` package.

How to do it...

Perform the following steps to install `rmr2` on the QuickStart VM:

1. First, open the terminal within the Cloudera QuickStart VM.
2. Use the permission of the root to enter an R session:

   ```
   $ sudo R
   ```

3. You can then install dependent packages before installing `rmr2`:

   ```
   > install.packages(c("codetools", "Rcpp", "RJSONIO", "bitops",
   "digest", "functional", "stringr", "plyr", "reshape2", "rJava",
   "caTools"))
   ```

4. Quit the R session:

```
> q()
```

5. Next, you can download rmr-3.3.0 to the QuickStart VM. You may need to update the link if Revolution Analytics upgrades the version of rmr2:

```
$ wget --no-check-certificate
https://raw.githubusercontent.com/RevolutionAnalytics/rmr2/3.3.0/
build/rmr2_3.3.0.tar.gz
```

6. You can then install rmr-3.3.0 to the QuickStart VM:

```
$ sudo R CMD INSTALL rmr2_3.3.0.tar.gz
```

7. Lastly, you can enter an R session and use the library function to test whether the library has been successfully installed:

```
$ R
> library(rmr2)
```

How it works...

In order to perform MapReduce on a Hadoop cluster, you have to install R and RHadoop on every task node. Here, we illustrate how to install rmr2 on a single node of a Hadoop cluster. First, open the terminal of the Cloudera QuickStart VM. Before installing rmr2, we first access an R session with root privileges and install dependent R packages.

Next, after all the dependent packages are installed, quit the R session and use the wget command in the Linux shell to download rmr-3.3.0 from GitHub to the local filesystem. You can then begin the installation of rmr2. Lastly, you can access an R session and use the library function to validate whether the package has been installed.

See also

- To see more information and read updates about RHadoop, you can refer to the RHadoop wiki page hosted on GitHub:
  https://github.com/RevolutionAnalytics/RHadoop/wiki.

Installing rhdfs

The rhdfs package is the interface between R and HDFS, which allows users to access HDFS from an R console. Similar to rmr2, one should install rhdfs on every task node, so that one can access HDFS resources through R. In this recipe, we will look at how to install rhdfs on the Cloudera QuickStart VM.

Getting ready

Ensure that you have completed the previous recipe by starting the Cloudera QuickStart VM and connecting the VM to the internet, so that you can proceed with downloading and installing the rhdfs package.

How to do it...

Perform the following steps to install rhdfs:

1. First, you can download rhdfs 1.0.8 from GitHub. You may need to update the link if Revolution Analytics upgrades the version of rhdfs:

    ```
    $wget --no-check-certificate
    https://raw.github.com/RevolutionAnalytics/rhdfs/master/
    build/rhdfs_1.0.8.tar.gz
    ```

2. Next, you can install rhdfs under the command-line mode:

    ```
    $ sudo HADOOP_CMD=/usr/bin/hadoop  R CMD INSTALL
    rhdfs_1.0.8.tar.gz
    ```

3. You can then set up JAVA_HOME. The configuration of JAVA_HOME depends on the installed Java version within the VM:

    ```
    $ sudo JAVA_HOME=/usr/java/jdk1.7.0_67-cloudera R CMD javareconf
    ```

4. Last, you can set up the system environment and initialize `rhdfs`. You may need to update the environment setup if you use a different version of QuickStart VM:

```
$ R
> Sys.setenv(HADOOP_CMD="/usr/bin/hadoop")
> Sys.setenv(HADOOP_STREAMING="/usr/lib/hadoop-mapreduce/hadoop
-streaming-2.5.0-cdh5.2.0.jar")
> library(rhdfs)
> hdfs.init()
```

How it works...

The package, `rhdfs`, provides functions so that users can manage HDFS using R. Similar to `rmr2`, you should install `rhdfs` on every task node, so that one can access HDFS through the R console.

To install `rhdfs`, you should first download `rhdfs` from GitHub. You can then install `rhdfs` in R by specifying where the HADOOP_CMD is located. You must configure R with Java support through the command, `javareconf`.

Next, you can access R and configure where HADOOP_CMD and HADOOP_STREAMING are located. Lastly, you can initialize `rhdfs` via the `rhdfs.init` function, which allows you to begin operating HDFS through `rhdfs`.

See also

- To find where HADOOP_CMD is located, you can use the `which hadoop` command in the Linux shell. In most Hadoop systems, HADOOP_CMD is located at `/usr/bin/hadoop`.
- As for the location of HADOOP_STREAMING, the streaming JAR file is often located in `/usr/lib/hadoop-mapreduce/`. However, if you cannot find the directory, `/usr/lib/Hadoop-mapreduce`, in your Linux system, you can search the streaming JAR by using the `locate` command. For example:

```
$ sudo updatedb
$ locate streaming | grep jar | more
```

Operating HDFS with rhdfs

The `rhdfs` package is an interface between Hadoop and R, which can call an HDFS API in the backend to operate HDFS. As a result, you can easily operate HDFS from the R console through the use of the `rhdfs` package. In the following recipe, we will demonstrate how to use the `rhdfs` function to manipulate HDFS.

Getting ready

To proceed with this recipe, you need to have completed the previous recipe by installing `rhdfs` into R, and validate that you can initialize HDFS via the `hdfs.init` function.

How to do it...

Perform the following steps to operate files stored on HDFS:

1. Initialize the `rhdfs` package:

   ```
   > Sys.setenv(HADOOP_CMD="/usr/bin/hadoop")
   > Sys.setenv(HADOOP_STREAMING="/usr/lib/hadoop-mapreduce/hadoop-
   streaming-2.5.0-cdh5.2.0.jar")
   > library(rhdfs)
   > hdfs.init ()
   ```

2. You can then manipulate files stored on HDFS, as follows:
   - `hdfs.put`: Copy a file from the local filesystem to HDFS:

   ```
   > hdfs.put('word.txt', './')
   ```

   - `hdfs.ls`: Read the list of directory from HDFS:

   ```
   > hdfs.ls('./')
   ```

   - `hdfs.copy`: Copy a file from one HDFS directory to another:

   ```
   > hdfs.copy('word.txt', 'wordcnt.txt')
   ```

   - `hdfs.move` : Move a file from one HDFS directory to another:

   ```
   > hdfs.move('wordcnt.txt', './data/wordcnt.txt')
   ```

- `hdfs.delete`: Delete an HDFS directory from R:

```
> hdfs.delete('./data/')
```

- `hdfs.rm`: Delete an HDFS directory from R:

```
> hdfs.rm('./data/')
```

- `hdfs.get`: Download a file from HDFS to a local filesystem:

```
> hdfs.get(word.txt', '/home/cloudera/word.txt')
```

- `hdfs.rename`: Rename a file stored on HDFS:

```
> hdfs.rename('./test/q1.txt','./test/test.txt')
```

- `hdfs.chmod`: Change the permissions of a file or directory:

```
> hdfs.chmod('test', permissions= '777')
```

- `hdfs.file.info`: Read the meta information of the HDFS file:

```
> hdfs.file.info('./')
```

3. Also, you can write streams to the HDFS file:

```
> f = hdfs.file("iris.txt","w")
> data(iris)
> hdfs.write(iris,f)
> hdfs.close(f)
```

4. Lastly, you can read streams from the HDFS file:

```
> f = hdfs.file("iris.txt", "r")
> dfserialized = hdfs.read(f)
> df = unserialize(dfserialized)
> df
> hdfs.close(f)
```

How it works...

In this recipe, we demonstrate how to manipulate HDFS using the `rhdfs` package. Normally, you can use the Hadoop shell to manipulate HDFS, but if you would like to access HDFS from R, you can use the `rhdfs` package.

Before you start using `rhdfs`, you have to initialize `rhdfs` with `hdfs.init()`. After initialization, you can operate HDFS through the functions provided in the `rhdfs` package.

Besides manipulating HDFS files, you can exchange streams to HDFS through `hdfs.read` and `hdfs.write`. We, therefore, demonstrate how to write a data frame in R to an HDFS file, `iris.txt`, using `hdfs.write`. Lastly, you can recover the written file back to the data frame using the `hdfs.read` function and the `unserialize` function.

See also

- To initialize `rhdfs`, you have to set `HADOOP_CMD` and `HADOOP_STREAMING` in the system environment. Instead of setting the configuration each time you're using `rhdfs`, you can put the configurations in the `.rprofile` file. Therefore, every time you start an R session, the configuration will be automatically loaded.

Implementing a word count problem with RHadoop

To demonstrate how MapReduce works, we illustrate the example of a word count, which counts the number of occurrences of each word in a given input set. In this recipe, we will demonstrate how to use `rmr2` to implement a word count problem.

Getting ready

In this recipe, we will need an input file as our word count program input. You can download the example input from
`https://github.com/ywchiu/ml_R_cookbook/tree/master/CH12`.

How to do it...

Perform the following steps to implement the word count program:

1. First, you need to configure the system environment, and then load `rmr2` and `rhdfs` into an R session. You may need to update the use of the JAR file if you use a different version of QuickStart VM:

```
> Sys.setenv(HADOOP_CMD="/usr/bin/hadoop")
> Sys.setenv(HADOOP_STREAMING="/usr/lib/hadoop-mapreduce/hadoop
-streaming-2.5.0-cdh5.2.0.jar ")
> library(rmr2)
> library(rhdfs)
> hdfs.init()
```

2. You can then create a directory on HDFS and put the input file into the newly created directory:

```
> hdfs.mkdir("/user/cloudera/wordcount/data")
> hdfs.put("wc_input.txt", "/user/cloudera/wordcount/data")
```

3. Next, you can create a `map` function:

```
> map = function(.,lines) { keyval(
+    unlist(
+      strsplit(
+        x = lines,
+        split = " +")),
+    1)}
```

4. Create a `reduce` function:

```
> reduce = function(word, counts) {
+    keyval(word, sum(counts))
+ }
```

5. Call the `MapReduce` program to count the words within a document:

```
> hdfs.root = 'wordcount'
> hdfs.data = file.path(hdfs.root, 'data')
> hdfs.out = file.path(hdfs.root, 'out')
> wordcount = function (input, output=NULL) {
+    mapreduce(input=input, output=output, input.format="text",
map=map,
+    reduce=reduce)
+ }
> out = wordcount(hdfs.data, hdfs.out)
```

6. Lastly, you can retrieve the top 10 occurring words within the document:

```
> results = from.dfs(out)
> results$key[order(results$val, decreasing = TRUE)][1:10]
```

How it works...

In this recipe, we demonstrate how to implement a word count using the `rmr2` package. First, we need to configure the system environment and load `rhdfs` and `rmr2` into R. Then, we specify the input of our word count program from the local filesystem into the HDFS directory, `/user/cloudera/wordcount/data`, via the `hdfs.put` function.

Next, we begin implementing the MapReduce program. Normally, we can divide the MapReduce program into the `map` and `reduce` functions. In the `map` function, we first use the `strsplit` function to split each line into words. Then, as the `strsplit` function returns a list of words, we can use the `unlist` function to characterize vectors. Lastly, we can return key-value pairs with each word as a key and the value as 1. As the `reduce` function receives the key-value pair generated from the `map` function, the `reduce` function sums the count and returns the number of occurrences of each word (or key).

After we have implemented the `map` and `reduce` functions, we can submit our job via the `mapreduce` function. Normally, the `mapreduce` function requires four inputs, which are the HDFS input path, the HDFS output path, the map function, and the reduce function. In this case, we specify the input as `wordcount/data`, the output as `wordcount/out`, the mapfunction as `map`, the reduce function as `reduce`, and wrap the `mapreduce` call in the function, `wordcount`. Lastly, we call the function, `wordcount`, and store the output path in the variable, `out`.

We can use the `from.dfs` function to load the HDFS data into the `results` variable, which contains the mapping of words and number of occurrences. We can then generate the top 10 occurring words from the `results` variable.

See also

- In this recipe, we demonstrate how to write an R MapReduce program to solve a word count problem. However, if you are interested in how to write a native Java MapReduce program, you can refer to
  `http://hadoop.apache.org/docs/current/hadoop-mapreduce-client/hadoop-mapreduce-client-core/MapReduceTutorial.html`.

Comparing the performance between an R MapReduce program and a standard R program

Those not familiar with how Hadoop works may often see Hadoop as a remedy for big data processing. Some might believe that Hadoop can return the processed results for any size of data within a few milliseconds. In this recipe, we will compare the performance between an R MapReduce program and a standard R program to demonstrate that Hadoop does not perform as quickly as some may believe.

Getting ready

In this recipe, you should have completed the previous recipe by installing rmr2 into the R environment.

How to do it...

Perform the following steps to compare the performance of a standard R program and an R MapReduce program:

1. First, you can implement a standard R program to have all numbers squared:

```
> a.time = proc.time()
> small.ints2=1:100000
> result.normal = sapply(small.ints2, function(x) x^2)
> proc.time() - a.time
```

2. To compare the performance, you can implement an R MapReduce program to have all numbers squared:

```
> b.time = proc.time()
> small.ints= to.dfs(1:100000)
> result = mapreduce(input = small.ints, map = function(k,v)
cbind(v,v^2))
> proc.time() - b.time
```

How it works...

In this recipe, we implement two programs to square all the numbers. In the first program, we use a standard R function, `sapply`, to square the sequence from 1 to 100,000. To record the program execution time, we first record the processing time before the execution in `a.time`, and then subtract `a.time` from the current processing time after the execution. Normally, the execution takes no more than 10 seconds. In the second program, we use the `rmr2` package to implement a program in the R MapReduce version. In this program, we also record the execution time. Normally, this program takes a few minutes to complete a task.

The performance comparison shows that a standard R program outperforms the MapReduce program when processing small amounts of data. This is because a Hadoop system often requires time to spawn daemons, job coordination between daemons, and fetching data from data nodes. Therefore, a MapReduce program often takes a few minutes to a couple of hours to finish the execution. As a result, if you can fit your data in the memory, you should write a standard R program to solve the problem. Otherwise, if the data is too large to fit in the memory, you can implement a MapReduce solution.

See also

- In order to check whether a job will run smoothly and efficiently in Hadoop, you can run a MapReduce benchmark, MRBench, to evaluate the performance of the job:

```
$ hadoop jar /usr/lib/hadoop-0.20-mapreduce/hadoop-test.jar
mrbench -numRuns 50
```

Testing and debugging the rmr2 program

Since running a MapReduce program will require a considerable amount of time, varying from a few minutes to several hours, testing and debugging become very important. In this recipe, we will illustrate some techniques you can use to troubleshoot an R MapReduce program.

Getting ready

In this recipe, you should have completed the previous recipe by installing `rmr2` into an R environment.

How to do it...

Perform the following steps to test and debug an R MapReduce program:

1. First, you can configure the backend as local in `rmr.options`:

   ```
   > rmr.options(backend = 'local')
   ```

2. Again, you can execute the number squared MapReduce program mentioned in the previous recipe:

   ```
   > b.time = proc.time()
   > small.ints= to.dfs(1:100000)
   > result = mapreduce(input = small.ints, map = function(k,v)
   cbind(v,v^2))
   > proc.time() - b.time
   ```

3. In addition to this, if you want to print the structure information of any variable in the MapReduce program, you can use the `rmr.str` function:

   ```
   > out = mapreduce(to.dfs(1), map = function(k, v) rmr.str(v))
   Dotted pair list of 14
    $ : language mapreduce(to.dfs(1), map = function(k, v)
   rmr.str(v))
    $ : language mr(map = map, reduce = reduce, combine = combine,
   vectorized.reduce, in.folder = if (is.list(input)) {    lap-
   ply(input, to.dfs.path) ...
    $ : language c.keyval(do.call(c, lapply(in.folder, func-
   tion(fname) { kv = get.data(fname) ...
    $ : language do.call(c, lapply(in.folder, function(fname) {
   kv = get.data(fname) ...
    $ : language lapply(in.folder, function(fname) {
   kv = get.data(fname) ...
    $ : language FUN("/tmp/Rtmp813BFJ/file25af6e85cfde"[[1L]], ...)
    $ : language unname(tapply(1:lkv, ceil-
   ing((1:lkv)/(lkv/(object.size(kv)/10^6))), function(r) {
   kvr = slice.keyval(kv, r) ...
    $ : language tapply(1:lkv, ceil-
   ing((1:lkv)/(lkv/(object.size(kv)/10^6))), function(r) { kvr
   = slice.keyval(kv, r) ...
   ```

```
$ : language lapply(X = split(X, group), FUN = FUN, ...)
$ : language FUN(X[[1L]], ...)
$ : language as.keyval(map(keys(kvr), values(kvr)))
$ : language is.keyval(x)
$ : language map(keys(kvr), values(kvr))
$ :length 2 rmr.str(v)
..- attr(*, "srcref")=Class 'srcref' atomic [1:8] 1 34 1 58 34 58
1 1
.. .. ..- attr(*, "srcfile")=Classes 'srcfilecopy', 'srcfile'
<environment: 0x3f984f0>
v
num 1
```

How it works...

In this recipe, we introduced some debugging and testing techniques you can use while implementing the MapReduce program. First, we introduced the technique to test a MapReduce program in a local mode. If you would like to run the MapReduce program in a pseudo-distributed or fully-distributed mode, it would take you a few minutes to several hours to complete the task, which would involve a lot of wastage of time while troubleshooting your MapReduce program. Therefore, you can set the backend to the local mode in rmr.options so that the program will be executed in the local mode, which takes lesser time to execute.

Another debugging technique is to list the content of the variable within the map or reduce function. In an R program, you can use the str function to display the compact structure of a single variable. In rmr2, the package also provides a function named rmr.str, which allows you to print out the content of a single variable onto the console. In this example, we use rmr.str to print the content of variables within a MapReduce program.

See also

- For those who are interested in the option settings for the rmr2 package, you can refer to the help document of rmr.options:

  ```
  > help(rmr.options)
  ```

Installing plyrmr

The `plyrmr` package provides common operations (as found in `plyr` or `reshape2`) for users to easily perform data manipulation through the MapReduce framework. In this recipe, we will look at how to install `plyrmr` on the Hadoop system.

Getting ready

Ensure that you have completed the previous recipe by starting the Cloudera QuickStart VM and connecting the VM to the internet. Also, you need to have the `rmr2` package installed beforehand.

How to do it...

Perform the following steps to install `plyrmr` on the Hadoop system:

1. First, you should install `libxml2-devel` and `curl-devel` in the Linux shell:

   ```
   $ yum install libxml2-devel
   $ sudo yum install curl-devel
   ```

2. You can then access R and install the dependent packages:

   ```
   $ sudo R
   > Install.packages(c(" Rcurl", "httr"),  dependencies = TRUE
   > Install.packages("devtools", dependencies = TRUE)
   > library(devtools)
   > install_github("pryr", "hadley")
   > install.packages(c(" R.methodsS3", "hydroPSO"),  dependencies
   = TRUE)
   > q()
   ```

3. Next, you can download `plyrmr 0.5.0` and install it on Hadoop VM. You may need to update the link if Revolution Analytics upgrades the version of `plyrmr`:

   ```
   $ wget —no-check-certificate
   https://raw.github.com/RevolutionAnalytics/plyrmr/master/
   build/plyrmr_0.5.0.tar.gz
   $ sudo R CMD INSTALL plyrmr_0.5.0.tar.gz
   ```

4. Lastly, validate the installation:

```
$ R
> library(plyrmr)
```

How it works...

Besides writing an R MapReduce program using the `rmr2` package, you can use the `plyrmr` to manipulate data. The `plyrmr` package is similar to hive and pig in the Hadoop ecosystem, which is the abstraction of the MapReduce program. Therefore, we can implement an R MapReduce program in `plyr` style instead of implementing the `map` and `reduce` functions.

To install `plyrmr`, first install the package of `libxml2-devel` and `curl-devel`, using the `yum install` command. Then, access R and install the dependent packages. Lastly, download the file from GitHub and install `plyrmr` in R.

See also

- To read more information about `plyrmr`, you can use the `help` function to refer to the following document:

  ```
  > help(package=plyrmr)
  ```

Manipulating data with plyrmr

While writing a MapReduce program with `rmr2` is much easier than writing a native Java version, it is still hard for non-developers to write a MapReduce program. Therefore, you can use `plyrmr`, a high-level abstraction of the MapReduce program, so that you can use plyr-like operations to manipulate big data. In this recipe, we will introduce some operations you can use to manipulate data.

Getting ready

In this recipe, you should have completed the previous recipes by installing `plyrmr` and `rmr2` in R.

How to do it...

Perform the following steps to manipulate data with `plyrmr`:

1. First, you need to load both `plyrmr` and `rmr2` into R:

```
> library(rmr2)
> library(plyrmr)
```

2. You can then set the execution mode to the local mode:

```
> plyrmr.options(backend="local")
```

3. Next, load the `Titanic` dataset into R:

```
> data(Titanic)
> titanic = data.frame(Titanic)
```

4. Begin the operation by filtering the data:

```
> where(
+      Titanic,
+ Freq >=100)
```

5. You can also use a pipe operator to filter the data:

```
> titanic %|% where(Freq >=100)
```

6. Put the `Titanic` data into HDFS and load the path of the data to the variable, `tidata`:

```
> tidata = to.dfs(data.frame(Titanic), output = '/tmp/titanic')
> tidata
```

7. Next, you can generate a summation of the frequency from the `Titanic` data:

```
> input(tidata) %|% transmute(sum(Freq))
```

8. You can also group the frequency by sex:

```
> input(tidata) %|% group(Sex) %|% transmute(sum(Freq))
```

9. You can then sample 10 records out of the population:

```
> sample(input(tidata), n=10)
```

10. In addition to this, you can use plyrmr to join two datasets:

```
> convert_tb = data.frame(Label=c("No","Yes"), Symbol=c(0,1))
ctb = to.dfs(convert_tb, output = 'convert')
> as.data.frame(plyrmr::merge(input(tidata), input(ctb),
by.x="Survived", by.y="Label"))
> file.remove('convert')
```

How it works...

In this recipe, we introduce how to use `plyrmr` to manipulate data. First, we need to load the `plyrmr` package into R. Then, similar to `rmr2`, you have to set the backend option of `plyrmr` as the local mode. Otherwise, you will have to wait anywhere between a few minutes to several hours if `plyrmr` is running on the Hadoop mode (the default setting).

Next, we can begin the data manipulation with data filtering. You can choose to call the function nested inside the other function call in *step 4*. On the other hand, you can use the pipe operator, `%|%`, to chain multiple operations. Therefore, we can filter data similar to *step 4*, using pipe operators in *step 5*.

Next, you can input the dataset into either the HDFS or local filesystem, using `to.dfs` in accordance with the current running mode. The function will generate the path of the dataset and save it in the variable, `tidata`. By knowing the path, you can access the data using the `input` function. Next, we illustrate how to generate a summation of the frequency from the Titanic dataset with the `transmute` and `sum` functions. Also, `plyrmr` allows users to sum up the frequency by gender.

Additionally, in order to sample data from a population, you can also use the `sample` function to select 10 records out of the Titanic dataset. Lastly, we demonstrate how to join two datasets using the `merge` function from `plyrmr`.

See also

Here we list some functions that can be used to manipulate data with `plyrmr`. You may refer to the `help` function for further details on their usage and functionalities:

- Data manipulation:
    - `bind.cols`: This adds new columns
    - `select`: This is used to select columns
    - `where`: This is used to select rows
    - `transmute`: This uses all of the aforementioned plus their summaries
- From `reshape2`:
    - `melt` and `dcast`: This converts long and wide DataFrames
- Summary:
    - `count`
    - `quantile`
    - `sample`
- Extract:
    - `top.k`
    - `bottom.k`

Conducting machine learning with RHadoop

In the previous chapters, we have demonstrated how powerful R is when used to solve machine learning problems. Also, we have shown that the use of Hadoop allows R to process big data in parallel. At this point, some may believe that the use of RHadoop can easily solve machine learning problems of big data via numerous existing machine learning packages. However, you cannot use most of these to solve machine learning problems as they cannot be executed in the MapReduce mode. In the following recipe, we will demonstrate how to implement a MapReduce version of linear regression and compare this version with the one using the `lm` function.

Getting ready

In this recipe, you should have completed the previous recipe by installing `rmr2` into the R environment.

How to do it...

Perform the following steps to implement a linear regression in MapReduce:

1. First, load the `cats` dataset from the `MASS` package:

```
> library(MASS)
> data(cats)
> X = matrix(cats$Bwt)
> y = matrix(cats$Hwt)
```

2. You can then generate a linear regression model by calling the `lm` function:

```
> model = lm(y~X)
> summary(model)
Call:
lm(formula = y ~ X)
Residuals:
    Min      1Q  Median      3Q     Max
-3.5694 -0.9634 -0.0921  1.0426  5.1238
Coefficients:
            Estimate Std. Error t value Pr(>|t|)
(Intercept)  -0.3567     0.6923  -0.515    0.607
X             4.0341     0.2503  16.119   <2e-16 ***
---
Signif. codes:
0 '***' 0.001 '**' 0.01 '*' 0.05 '.' 0.1 ' ' 1
Residual standard error: 1.452 on 142 degrees of freedom
Multiple R-squared:  0.6466,  Adjusted R-squared:  0.6441
F-statistic: 259.8 on 1 and 142 DF,  p-value: < 2.2e-16
```

3. You can now make a regression plot with the given data points and model:

```
> plot(y~X)
> abline(model, col="red")
```

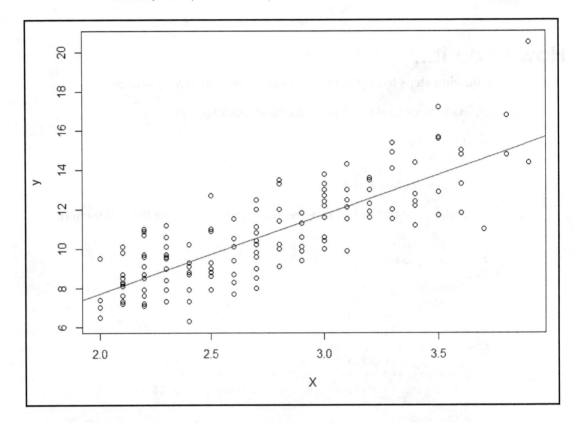

Linear regression plot of cats dataset

4. Load `rmr2` into R:

```
> Sys.setenv(HADOOP_CMD="/usr/bin/hadoop")
> Sys.setenv(HADOOP_STREAMING="/usr/lib/hadoop-mapreduce/hadoop->
streaming-2.5.0-cdh5.2.0.jar")
> library(rmr2)
> rmr.options(backend="local")
```

5. You can then set up X and y values:

```
> X = matrix(cats$Bwt)
> X.index = to.dfs(cbind(1:nrow(X), X))
> y = as.matrix(cats$Hwt)
```

6. Make a Sum function to sum up the values:

```
> Sum =
+    function(., YY)
+       keyval(1, list(Reduce('+', YY)))
```

7. Compute XtX in MapReduce, Job1:

```
> XtX =
+    values(
+       from.dfs(
+          mapreduce(
+             input = X.index,
+             map =
+                function(., Xi) {
+                   Xi = Xi[,-1]
+                   keyval(1, list(t(Xi) %*% Xi))},
+             reduce = Sum,
+             combine = TRUE)))[[1]]
```

8. You can then compute Xty in MapReduce, Job2:

```
Xty =
+    values(
+       from.dfs(
+          mapreduce(
+             input = X.index,
+             map = function(., Xi) {
+                yi = y[Xi[,1],]
+                Xi = Xi[,-1]
+                keyval(1, list(t(Xi) %*% yi))},
+             reduce = Sum,
+             combine = TRUE)))[[1]]
```

9. Lastly, you can derive the coefficient from XtX and Xty:

```
> solve(XtX, Xty)
          [,1]
[1,] 3.907113
```

How it works...

In this recipe, we demonstrate how to implement linear logistic regression in a MapReduce fashion in R. Before we start the implementation, we review how traditional linear models work. We first retrieve the `cats` dataset from the `MASS` package. We then load X as the body weight (`Bwt`) and y as the heart weight (`Hwt`).

Next, we begin to fit the data into a linear regression model using the `lm` function. We can then compute the fitted model and obtain the summary of the model. The summary shows that the coefficient is 4.0341 and the intercept is -0.3567. Furthermore, we draw a scatter plot in accordance with the given data points and then draw a regression line on the plot.

As we cannot perform linear regression using the `lm` function in the MapReduce form, we have to rewrite the regression model in a MapReduce fashion. Here, we would like to implement a MapReduce version of linear regression in three steps, which are: calculate the Xtx value with the MapReduce, `job1`, calculate the Xty value with MapReduce, `job2`, and then derive the coefficient value:

1. In the first step, we pass the matrix, X, as the input to the `map` function. The `map` function then calculates the cross-product of the transposed matrix, X, and, X. The `reduce` function then performs the sum operation defined in the previous section.
2. In the second step, the procedure of calculating Xty is similar to calculating XtX. The procedure calculates the cross-product of the transposed matrix, X, and, y. The `reduce` function then performs the sum operation.
3. Lastly, we use the `solve` function to derive the coefficient, which is 3.907113.

As the results show, the coefficients computed by `lm` and MapReduce differ slightly. Generally speaking, the coefficient computed by the `lm` model is more accurate than the one calculated by MapReduce. However, if your data is too large to fit in the memory, you have no choice but to implement linear regression in the MapReduce version.

See also

- You can access more information on machine learning algorithms at: `https://github.com/RevolutionAnalytics/rmr2/tree/master/pkg/tests`.

Configuring RHadoop clusters on Amazon EMR

Until now, we have only demonstrated how to run a RHadoop program in a single Hadoop node. In order to test our RHadoop program on a multi-node cluster, the only thing you need to do is to install RHadoop on all the task nodes (nodes with either task tracker for MapReduce version 1 or node manager for MapReduce version 2) of Hadoop clusters. However, the deployment and installation is time consuming. On the other hand, you can choose to deploy your RHadoop program on Amazon EMR, so that you can deploy multi-node clusters and RHadoop on every task node in only a few minutes. In the following recipe, we will demonstrate how to configure RHadoop cluster on an Amazon EMR service.

Getting ready

In this recipe, you must register and create an account on AWS, and you also must know how to generate a EC2 key-pair before using Amazon EMR.

For those who seek more information on how to start using AWS, please refer to the tutorial provided by Amazon at `http://docs.aws.amazon.com/AWSEC2/latest/UserGuide/EC2_GetStarted.html`.

How to do it...

Perform the following steps to configure RHadoop on Amazon EMR:

1. First, you can access the console of the Amazon Web Service (refer to https://us-west-2.console.aws.amazon.com/console/) and find EMR in the analytics section. Then, click on **EMR**:

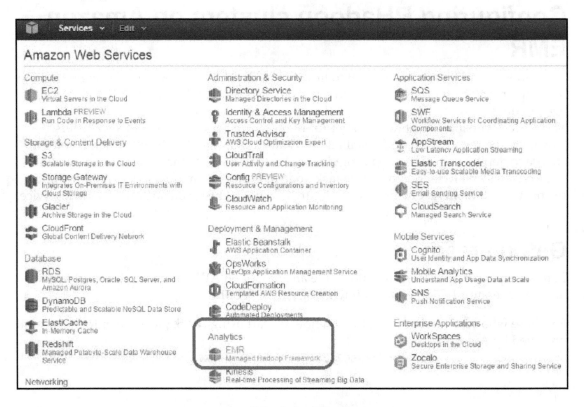

Access EMR service from AWS console.

2. You should find yourself in the cluster list of the EMR dashboard (refer to
   `https://us-west-2.console.aws.amazon.com/elasticmapreduce/home?region=`
   `us-west-2#cluster-list::`). Click on **Create cluster**:

Cluster list of EMR

3. Then, you should find yourself on the **Create cluster** page (refer to
   `https://us-west-2.console.aws.amazon.com/elasticmapreduce/home?region=`
   `us-west-2#create-cluster:`).

4. Next, you should specify the **Cluster name** and **Log folder S3 location** in the
   cluster configuration:

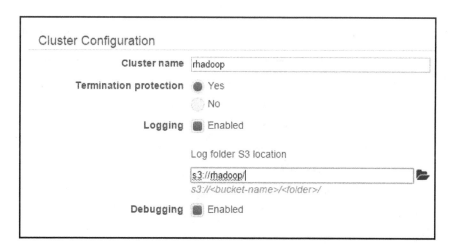

Cluster configuration in the create cluster page

5. You can then configure the Hadoop distribution on **Software Configuration**:

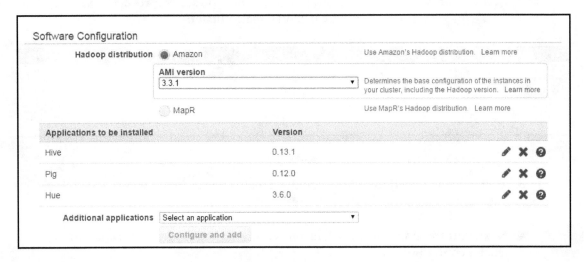

Configure the software and applications

6. Next, you can configure the number of nodes within the Hadoop cluster:

Configure the hardware within Hadoop cluster

7. You can then specify the EC2 key-pair for the master node login:

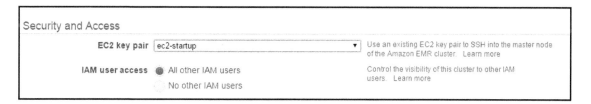

Security and access to the master node of the EMR cluster

8. To set up RHadoop, one has to perform bootstrap actions to install RHadoop on every task node. Please write a file named bootstrapRHadoop.sh, and insert the following lines within the file:

```
echo 'install.packages(c("codetools", "Rcpp", "RJSONIO",
"bitops", "digest", "functional", "stringr", "plyr",
"reshape2", "rJava", "caTools"),
repos="http://cran.us.r-project.org")'
> /home/hadoop/installPackage.R
sudo Rscript /home/hadoop/installPackage.R
wget --no-check-certificate https://raw.githubusercontent.com/
RevolutionAnalytics/rmr2/master/build/rmr2_3.3.0.tar.gz
sudo R CMD INSTALL rmr2_3.3.0.tar.gz
wget --no-check-certificate https://raw.github.com/
RevolutionAnalytics/rhdfs/master/build/rhdfs_1.0.8.tar.gz
sudo HADOOP_CMD=/home/hadoop/bin/hadoop R CMD INSTALL
rhdfs_1.0.8.tar.gz
```

9. You should upload bootstrapRHadoop.sh to S3.

10. You now need to add the bootstrap action with Custom action, and add s3://<location>/bootstrapRHadoop.sh within the S3 location:

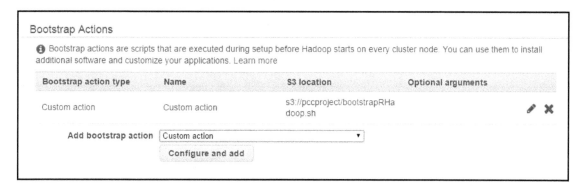

Set up the bootstrap action

11. Next, you can click on **Create cluster** to launch the Hadoop cluster:

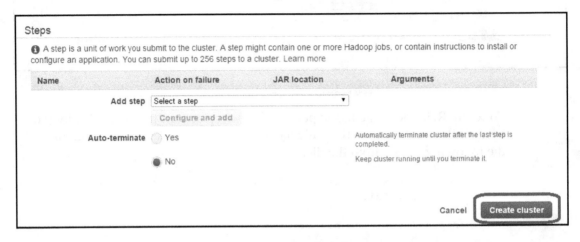

Create the cluster

12. Lastly, you should see the master public DNS when the cluster is ready. You can now access the terminal of the master node with your EC2-key pair:

A screenshot of the created cluster

How it works...

In this recipe, we demonstrate how to set up RHadoop on Amazon EMR. The benefit of this is that you can quickly create a scalable, on-demand Hadoop with just a few clicks within a few minutes. This helps save you time from building and deploying a Hadoop application. However, you have to pay for the number of running hours for each instance. Before using Amazon EMR, you should create an AWS account and know how to set up the EC2 key-pair and the S3. You can then start installing RHadoop on Amazon EMR.

In the first step, access the EMR cluster list and click on **Create cluster**. You can see a list of configurations on the **Create cluster** page. You should then set up the cluster name and log folder in the S3 location in the cluster configuration.

Next, you can set up the software configuration and choose the Hadoop distribution you would like to install. Amazon provides both its own distribution and the MapR distribution. Normally, you would skip this section unless you have concerns about the default Hadoop distribution.

You can then configure the hardware by specifying the master, core, and task node. By default, there is only one master node, and two core nodes. You can add more core and task nodes if you like. You should then set up the key-pair to log in to the master node.

You should next make a file containing all the start scripts named `bootstrapRHadoop.sh`. After the file is created, you should save the file in the S3 storage. You can then specify `custom action` in **Bootstrap Action** with `bootstrapRHadoop.sh` as the Bootstrap script. Lastly, you can click on `Create cluster` and wait until the cluster is ready. Once the cluster is ready, one can see the master public DNS and can use the EC2 key-pair to access the terminal of the master node.

Beware! Terminate the running instance if you do not want to continue using the EMR service. Otherwise, you will be charged per instance for every hour you use.

See also

- Google also provides its own cloud solution, the Google compute engine. For those who would like to know more, please refer to `https://cloud.google.com/compute/`.

Index